D0099606

WINE TRAILS

PLAN 52 PERFECT WEEKENDS IN WINE COUNTRY

We've all experienced it on our travels - whether watching a sunset in Italy with a glass of chilled Prosecco or at a barbeque in Australia with a beefy Shiraz - when a local wine could not be more perfectly suited to the moment.

Tasting wine in the place it was made can be a revelation. This book plots a course through 52 of the world's greatest wine regions, with weekend-long itineraries in each. We encounter California's cutting-edge wine scene, and the idiosyncratic wines of France's Jura mountains, and we venture into Spain's extraordinary wineries and along Portugal's beautiful Douro River. And we even reach the cultural frontiers of winemaking in Lebanon and Georgia. In each, our expert writers, including wine buyers and sommeliers, review the most rewarding wineries to visit and the most memorable wines to taste.

This is a book for casual quaffers; there's no impenetrable language about malolactic fermentation or scoring systems. Instead, we meet some of the world's most enthusiastic and knowledgeable winemakers and learn about each region's wines in their own words. It is this personal introduction to wine, in its home, that is at the heart of wine-touring's appeal.

CONTENTS

01

Courtesy of Bodega Salentein

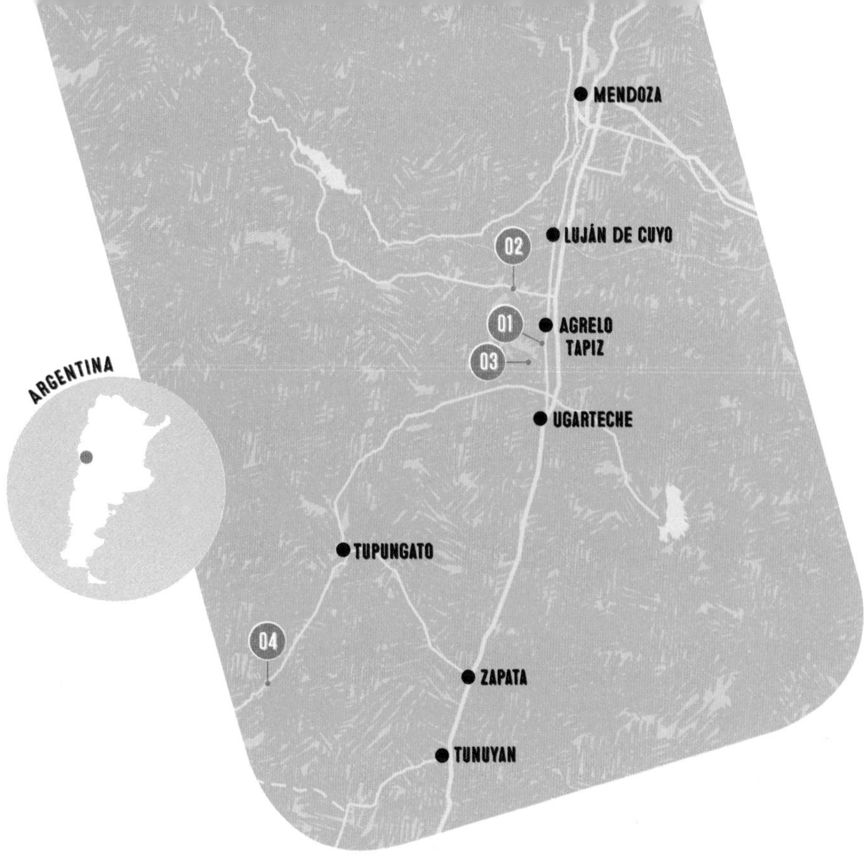

[Argentina]

MENDOZA

Saddle up for some adventurous tasting in the mountainous capital of Argentina's thriving wine scene, where old-world expertise meets new-world innovation.

Maybe you can't distinguish between Italian wine regions on a map, or explain the difference between French and American oak barrels. But unless you've been living under a rock, chances are you've noticed that right now Argentina is hot on the international wine scene. Think about it: you can't glance at a wine list without seeing the word 'Malbec', or turn on the radio without hearing a chef talk about the best-value Argentinian bottles for your summer barbecue.

If the runaway popularity of Argentinian wine strikes you as sudden, you're not alone. Even Argentinian people didn't realise how fantastic their wine could be until fairly recently, though it's safe to say they were always fully aware of the natural beauty of Mendoza. The nation's wine-producing capital occupies a spectacular stretch of sun-drenched landscape at the foot of the snowcapped Andes. Even if there weren't any vineyards around, it would still be a popular travel destination, thanks to its gorgeous weather and picture-perfect opportunities for hiking, horseback riding, skiing, fishing, whitewater rafting or cycling. Luckily for travellers there is indeed a glass, or several, waiting for you at the end of that bike ride.

The wine produced in Mendoza, whether in the longer-established region of Luján de Cuyo or the up-and-coming Uco Valley, isn't just the product of the natural landscape. It's the result of a new generation of winemakers that knows the rules of French or Italian winemaking – and knows how to break them. It's a South American playground for innovation, the meeting point between tradition and new technology. Raise your glass: here in Mendoza, it's a brave new world.

GET THERE
Mendoza El Plumerillo is the nearest major airport, 8km from Mendoza. Car hire is available.

Courtesy of Casa de Uco

01 TAPIZ

You'll know you've arrived at Tapiz when you spot the llamas. Dozens graze in the fields around the vineyards, controlling weeds, producing fertiliser and providing wool that local artisans use to make traditional blankets and ponchos, on sale to visitors in the winery's boutique.

The picturesque llama family is a pleasingly old-fashioned counterpoint to the state-of-the-art (and sustainable) winemaking technology Tapiz employs inside. The two signature wines are Malbec and Torrontés, made with grapes harvested here, in Agrelo, as well as in the Uco Valley and further afield in Argentina's northernmost wine region of Cafayate in Salta. They're presided over, in part, by the world-renowned French winemaker Jean-Claude Berrouet, who works as a consultant with the brand. For a particularly memorable experience, book a tour of the vineyard by horse-drawn carriage, followed by tasting wines straight from the barrels.

www.bodega-tapiz.com.ar; tel +54 261-490 0202; Ruta Provincial (RP) 15, km 32; 9.30am-4.30pm Mon-Fri, to 12.30pm Sat & holidays

'We have found this place where I think we can make the best wines in the world because of the climate and soil combination...'

–Laura Catena, President of Bodega Catena Zapata

02 RUCA MALÉN

According to the cofounder of Bodega Ruca Malén, you don't need to hear descriptions of his wines: you need to taste them yourself. 'As is the case with any work of art,' Jean Pierre Thibaud has said, 'pleasure can only derive from personal discovery'.

Perhaps the best way to discover this particular wine experience is through a leisurely meal at the restaurant. The five-course lunch with wine pairings, served in a sun-filled dining space overlooking the surrounding vineyards, is considered one of the finest in Mendoza. A word to the wise: after indulging in a feast like this one, you might not have any room left for tasting more wine until the following day. Although the winery takes its name from an old Mapuche legend, the wine tastings and blending classes at Ruca Malén are all about

01 The vineyards of Bodega Salentein

02 Plan a lakeside getaway at Casa de Uco

03 Malbec wine grapes in Mendoza

04 Bodega Catena Zapata

05 Explore the vineyards of Casa de Uco in style

06 Bodega Salentein's underground cellar

07 Grapes in the vineyards of Salentein

08 Casa de Uco's restaurant is top class

Yadid Levy © Alamy

Courtesy of Catena Zapata

Courtesy of Casa de Uco

modern winemaking techniques. *www.bodegarucamalen.com; tel +54 261-15 4540974; RN 7, km 1059, Agrelo; tastings 10am, 11am & 3.30pm Mon-Fri, 10am & 11am Sat*

03 CATENA ZAPATA

Like Mendoza itself, Catena Zapata represents an appealing balance between old traditions and contemporary winemaking. The vineyard was founded by Nicola Catena, an Italian immigrant to Argentina who planted his first Malbec vines in 1902. It later became the experimental playground for Nicolás Catena – arguably the most celebrated winemaker in Argentina – and his daughter, Laura, current president of Bodega Catena Zapata and author of the talked-about 2010 book *Vino Argentino: An Insider's Guide to the Wines and Wine Country of Argentina*. Her energetic and unpretentious approach is revolutionising the face of Argentinian wines.

Look for Luca, Laura's line of small-quantity, artisanal-quality wine made from Argentina's old vines; taste the winery's classic Malbecs straight from the barrels or the fermentation tanks on one of several tour and tasting options for visitors.
www.catenawines.com; tel +54 261-413 1100; Cobos s/n, Agrelo; 9am-6pm Mon-Fri

04 SALENTEIN

Located in the Uco Valley, the Dutch-owned Bodega Salentein is as much an architectural landmark as a destination for wine enthusiasts. The main building was designed in the shape of a cross. Each of the four wings serve as a small winery with two levels – stainless steel tanks and French wooden vats on one floor, and an underground cellar for aging wine in oak casks on the other. The central chamber, or the crux of the cross, functions as a state-of-the-art amphitheatre modelled after the look and feel of a classical temple.

Check the calendar ahead of time: in addition to regular tastings, Salentein hosts a line-up of musical performances and art exhibitions in its barrel room and gallery. Where better to sample the brand's famous Pinot Noir from the 2009 harvest? Make a weekend of it and check into the 16-room Posada Salentein. Don't miss the fantastic Sunday *asado criollo*, a traditional Argentinian

barbecue with a gourmet twist – the feast lasts for several hours.
www.bodegasalentein.com; tel +54 026-2242 9500; RP 89, Los Árboles, Tunuyán; 9am-5pm Mon-Sat

Courtesy of Bodega Salentein

ESSENTIAL INFORMATION

WHERE TO STAY

HUENTALA HOTEL
Complete with a wine cellar, this elegant 81-room hotel is located near one of Mendoza's main squares – a good choice if you'd like to stay in town. *www.huentala.com; tel +54 261-420 0766; Primitivo de la Reta 1007, Mendoza*

CASA DE UCO VINEYARD & WINE RESORT
This sleek, sustainably built lakeside getaway, featuring a stylish restaurant and complimentary horseback riding on its large property, is located within easy reach of many of the best wineries in the Uco Valley. *www.casadeucoresort.com; tel +54 9261-476 9831; RP 94, km 14.5, Tunuyán*

WHERE TO EAT

BODEGA MELIPAL
The lavish lunch with wine pairings in Luján de Cuyo, overlooking vineyards nearly as far as the eye can see, is a wine-country classic. *www.bodegamelipal.com; tel +54 261-479 0202; Ruta 7, km 1056, Agrelo*

1884 RESTAURANTE
Located in a romantic old house and courtyard garden, 1884 is a landmark restaurant by pioneering Argentinian chef and winemaker Francis Mallmann. *www.1884restaurante.com.ar; tel +54 261-424 3336; Belgrano 1188, Mendoza*

WHAT TO DO

Arrange a hike, a horse-riding excursion, a rafting adventure, or even a side trip to Aconcagua — the highest point in the southern hemisphere — with one of the many outdoor outfitters in town. For an active excursion closer to the city centre, rent a bicycle, either independently or as part of an organised winery tour. Back in town, stop by the Vines of Mendoza tasting room to sample wine from the surrounding region. *www.vinesofmendoza.com; tel +54 261-438 1031; Belgrano 1194, Mendoza*

CELEBRATIONS

The event of the year in Mendoza is the Fiesta de la Vendimia, or the annual harvest festival, taking over the city for 10 days at the beginning of March. Although the celebration honours all of the region's fruits, the grape, of course, takes centre stage. Highlights include traditional foods, folkloric concerts and a colourful parade and pageant to crown the queen of the festival. Be sure to book ahead: Vendimia draws huge crowds, both from Argentina and abroad. *www.vendimia.mendoza.gov.ar*

Courtesy of Casa de Uco

01
HHW

Courtesy of Hahndorf Hill

LOBETHAL
02
01
03
WOODSIDE
OAKBANK
BALHANNAH
04
05
HAHNDORF
AUSTRALIA

[Australia]

ADELAIDE HILLS

The hills are alive with the sound of kookaburras! South Australia's most accessible wine region will welcome you with a range of cool-climate wines.

Think of all the tourist-board images of Australia: endless, red-rocked deserts, surfers on a cresting wave, perhaps a didgeridoo playing in the background. Now recalibrate – and welcome to a side of Australia that's not often presented to the rest of the world. From the jacaranda-lined streets of Adelaide's CBD, the M1 freeway climbs southeastward and the trees get thicker, the road quieter. You'll probably pass a few cyclists out for a spin, and apple or cherry orchards. Just half an hour later you'll be in the heart of the Adelaide Hills.

This part of South Australia was settled in the 19th century by Germans and Lutherans fleeing persecution and there's a certain European feel to the pretty winding roads that link twee towns like Hahndorf. These days it's a popular weekending destination for residents of the South Australian state capital, intent on trying and buying some up-and-coming wines from the Hills' small-scale producers. This is a true cool-climate region; as other grape-growing regions in Australia wonder about rising temperatures, the Adelaide Hills enjoys ideal growing conditions for Sauvignon Blanc and a fresher form of Shiraz. There's not much of a Germanic connection in the vineyards (Australia's best Riesling is still found in Clare Valley, see p17) but some have had success with Grüner Veltliner. The Hills is a young, compact wine region but it's growing up fast; only a few years ago, there were no signposts to the wineries on the roads – but that's changing.

Adelaide itself is a city for gourmands, with one of Australia's best food markets and a thriving farm-to-fork local produce scene. The only time the city gets busy is during the Adelaide Festival in March. The rest of the year, this sedate little city makes a great base.

GET THERE
Adelaide has the closest airport with car rental. Tours from the city are also available.

01 GOLDING WINES

Although Golding Wines' first vintage was in 2002, the winery has close connections to the fruit-growing heritage of the Adelaide Hills; Darren Golding's father was a local apple and pear merchant. Together they designed and built the cellar door with an Aussie aesthetic: a tin roof, bare wood, brick and stone.

They started with parcels of Pinot Noir and Sauvignon Blanc but quickly became more adventurous, including planting what they thought was Albariño (see p250). 'The plants were given to Australia by the Spanish government,' says Darren. 'It was only a few years later that we were alerted that the Albariño was in fact Savignan, a grape from the Jura in France, where it makes *vin jaune* (see p86). Michael Sykes, Golding's winemaker, uses it to make Lil' Late (Harvest), a sweet wine with tropical flavours.

But the staples of the winery are the Handcart Shiraz, which shows the fruity spicy side of Shiraz, and a Burgundy-style Pinot Noir. 'The cool nights in the Adelaide Hills preserve the acidity,' explains Darren, 'leading to vibrant, elegant wines, red or white.' The Hills, reckons Darren, have a huge future. So where else would he recommend in the region? 'Head up to Mt Lofty Ranges,' suggests Darren. 'The wines are good and if you go out the back you can look over Piccadilly Valley.'
www.goldingwines.com.au; tel +61 08 8389 5120; 52 Western Branch Rd, Lobethal; 11am-5pm daily

02 MT LOFTY RANGES

'All I want is to produce wines representative of this place,' says owner Garry Sweeney, whose wife, Sharon, decided on the location for Mt Lofty Ranges. She chose well because the cellar door's location is enviable, with views down into a small, verdant valley from its perch at 550m.

Growing grapes gives entry into a close-knit community. 'Everyone lends a hand,' he says. 'If your tractor breaks down, someone will come round. In my first year I didn't know how to prune and other winemakers came over to show me.' Their lessons were learned: Mt Lofty Ranges' Pinot Noir, Riesling and Chardonnay are delicious.

The tasting room features reclaimed materials, an open fireplace and a terraced decking that leads down to the vines. If you arrive any time from mid-March to early April you may catch Garry and the team among the vines, hand-picking the year's harvest.
www.mtloftyrangesvineyard.com.au; tel +61 08 8389 8339; 166 Harris Road, Lenswood; 11am-6pm Fri-Sun, 11am-5pm Thu & Mon

03 BIRD IN HAND

Set back from the road, the first impression of Bird in Hand winery is of the pair of ancient shutters that owner Andrew Nugent and his wife Susie brought back from France and which now hang on the cellar door. The entire venue has a French feel, thanks to a shady terrace. In the vineyard the winery hosts live music occasionally.

There's plenty happening with the wine too, with three levels to taste: the Two in the Bush entry-level wines, the premium Bird in Hand range (which includes Shiraz, a Merlot

Cabernet and a Montepulciano), and in certain years, the Nest Egg series for cellaring. The Shiraz, in particular, is an exemplary cool-climate red, fruity and spice without being overblown. *www.birdinhand.com.au; tel +61 08 8389 9488; Bird In Hand Rd & Pfeiffer Rd, Woodside; 10am-5pm Mon-Fri, 11am-5pm Sat & Sun*

04 SHAW + SMITH

Shaw + Smith is one of the larger cellar doors in the Hills. The focus is on four wines: a Sauvignon Blanc, a Chardonnay, a Pinot Noir and a Shiraz. For $15 you taste all four with a platter of cheese; the Sauvignon Blanc is the most successful, lying someway between a fruity Marlborough, New-Zealand style and a spartan Sancerre from France. *www.shawandsmith.com; tel +61 08 8398 0500; 136 Jones Road, Balhannah daily 11am-5pm*

05 HAHNDORF HILL

At Hahndorf Hill, which is pioneering several Austrian grape varieties, you'll not only be testing your tastebuds with interesting wines but also some tongue-twisting names. The warm days and cool nights of the Hills suit Grüner Veltliner, which owners Larry Jacobs and Marc Dobson first planted in 2006; South Australia's first Grüner Veltliner vintage was released in 2010. Blaufrankisch, the red version of the grape, has been grown at Hahndorf for more than 20 years – both benefit from the high mineral content of the blue slate, quartz and ironstone soil. The pair also make a pear-scented Pinot Grigio, and a great cool-climate Shiraz to try while enjoying the views over the vines and gum trees. *www.hahndorfhillwinery.com.au; tel +61 08 8388 7512; 38 Pains Rd, Hahndorf; 11am-5pm daily*

01 Hahndorf Hill cellar door

02 Darren Golding of Golding Wines

03 Bird in Hand

04 Shaw + Smith

ESSENTIAL INFORMATION

WHERE TO STAY

AMBLE AT HAHNDORF

At Amble's country-luxe base in Hahndorf there's the Fern studio, the Wren cottage and an apartment (Amble Over). Wren features a spa bathroom and private deck; Fern a private courtyard with a barbecue. *www.amble-at-hahndorf.com.au; tel +61 (0)408 105 610; 10 Hereford Avenue, Hahndorf*

FRANKLIN BOUTIQUE HOTEL

The Franklin is the hip, new option in Adelaide, a much-needed meeting of demand for twee-free accommodation. The basic ('deluxe') rooms are small but so stylish that you won't mind; pay more for bigger bathrooms and more inventive lighting in the premium and superior rooms. *www.thefranklinhotel.com.au; tel +61 08 8410 0036; 92 Franklin Street*

WHERE TO EAT

CHIANTI

With local growers as suppliers, the chefs at Chianti, Adelaide's long-standing and much-loved Italian restaurant, are spoiled for choice. And they could probably tell you where the crispy pig's ear in the *risoni con frattaglie* or the garfish fillets in the *pesce al cartoccio* came from. *www.chianti.net.au; tel +61 08 8232 7955; 160 Hutt Street, Adelaide*

WHAT TO DO

Kangaroo Island is a popular excursion from Adelaide. It's not only inhabited by kangaroos but lots of amazing marsupials, and, in the ocean, dolphins and seals. *www.tourkangarooisland.com.au*

CELEBRATIONS

The Adelaide area has not one but two annual festivals. In the summer, the Crush festival takes over more than 30 wineries for three days in January. It's not just tastings; there's food, music and an Alice in Wonderland-themed ball to finish the weekend. In winter, July's Winter Reds Weekend has become a regular fixture, again with around 30 local wineries participating and plenty of log fires crackling. *www.crushfestival.com.au*

Courtesy of Skillogalee

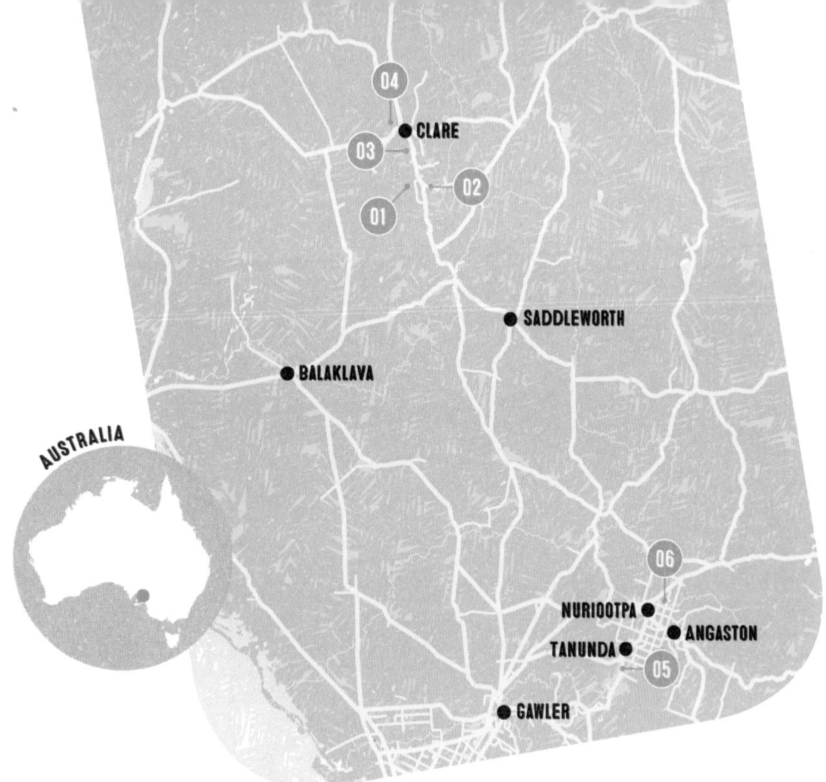

[Australia]

CLARE VALLEY

Take the Riesling Trail through sleepy Clare Valley to meet friendly winemakers and sample some of Australia's most food-friendly wines.

Follow a back-road south out of a town called Clare – a left, a right, and a left under a canopy of blue-green gum trees – and a few minutes later you could be sipping from a glass of chilled Riesling on the porch of Skillogalee. Skillogalee is one of around 40, mainly family-run wineries in South Australia's Clare Valley, an Edenic plateau (not a valley) about two hours' drive north of Adelaide. Most of the wineries have cellar doors offering tastings and often platters of locally sourced produce, and the welcome at each is as warm as the Australian sun.

Clare, says Skillogalee owner Dave Palmer, is a well-kept secret. This is one reason why it makes the Wine Trails cut; unlike Barossa, the cellar doors don't have parking spaces for coaches. Another reason is that it's extremely pretty, with secluded wineries hiding down shady lanes. And the final reason is what those wineries make – some of the best Riesling in the world.

Riesling is a distinctive white wine most often associated with northern Europe (see Alsace, p66, and the Mosel Valley, p118) but in Clare they've taken the grape, lost some of its sweetness and added a strong mineral edge. What ends up in your glass here is arguably the best possible companion for Asian food.

Most wine-tourers will be arriving from Adelaide – beyond Clare, the terrain gets increasingly rugged until you arrive in the Flinders Ranges and the start of the true Outback. Before you arrive in Clare you'll pass through the Barossa, now home to many of Australian wine's biggest names. We'd recommend bypassing it entirely if it wasn't for a couple of the more interesting wineries there that work with Australia's oldest vines. We've added them to the end of the itinerary but you can stop on your way up to Clare if that's easier.

GET THERE
Adelaide has the closest airport; Clare is a couple of hours' drive away, beyond Barossa Valley.

Courtesy of Skillogalee

01 SKILLOGALEE

'We were city kids but always had a yen to do something in the country,' says David Palmer. So Dave and Diane Palmer bought Skillogalee, a vineyard with a cottage little-changed since it was built by a Cornish miner in 1851. As Barossa was being settled by Germanic people, so British, Irish and Polish settlers ventured further up to Clare; the Cornish came out to work in the mines.

When the Palmers took over the winery in 1989 they knew nothing about winemaking, admits David. 'A local said "just watch when your neighbour gets his tractor out and take yours out then", so that's how we learned.'

Today, son Dan is the winemaker, producing some of Clare's best wines, and daughter Nicola is the chef at the cellar door's cosy restaurant. Skillogalee's basket-pressed Shiraz, with a minty, acid edge, is more food-friendly than reds from Barossa, which tend to have higher alcohol levels. His very best wines are bottled under the Trevarrick label. The family wanted the vineyard to become sustainable so they plant cover crops to protect the soil, and the skins, seeds and stalks are composted and returned to the earth.

In their out-of-the-way location down an eucalypt-lined lane, the Palmers are living the rural Australian idyll, with echidnas under the verandah, frogs in the pond and 'roos out back. 'At sunset,' says Dave, 'we take a bottle and some glasses up to the top of the hill and watch the sun set over the dry sheep and wheat country to the west.'

www.skillogalee.com.au; tel +61 08 8843 4311; Trevarrick Rd, Sevenhill; 10am-5pm daily

02 PAULETT WINES

It was the head winemaker at Penfolds who recommended Neil and Alison Paulett start a winery in Clare Valley. 'It's a reliable region,' says Alison Paulett, 'the elevation brings hot days and cool nights, which slow the ripening and lend the Riesling its austere style.' Winemaker Neil's Polish Hill River Riesling has waves of citrus and a strong mineral backbone, helping it to age for 10 years or more. Their single-vineyard Andreas Shiraz, named after the property's first Polish owner, comes from 80-year-old vines and then spends more than two years in French oak barrels. 'The most important thing,' laughs Alison, 'is getting people to know where Clare is.' Their wines are spreading the word.

www.paulettwines.com.au; tel +61 08 8843 4328; Polish Hill River Rd, Clare, 10am-5pm daily

'To make a product that gives people so much pleasure is a privilege.'

–David Palmer, Skillogalee

Courtesy of Tim Adams Wines, Jim Barry Wines

Courtesy of Paulett Wines

01 Skillogalee cellar door

02 Skillogalee vines

03 Skillogalee's David Palmer at work

04 Tim Adams wines

05 Tom and Sam Barry of Jim Barry Wines

06 The view from Paulett Wines

03 TIM ADAMS WINES

Brett Schutz, a winemaker at Tim Adams, in the heart of Clare Valley, believes European makers of Riesling are adopting the Australian style, with lower sugar levels. In return, the Clare Valley is adopting an European idea: 'The essence of *terroir* is important here. No two areas of Clare are the same; there are microclimates so you can blend minerality from Watervale with fruitier grapes from the warmer north end of Clare.' The result is a brisk, dry, crisp Riesling, thanks to a fast 14-day fermentation. 'All Tim asks us to do is express the fruit through the wine.'
www.timadamswines.com.au; tel +61 08 8842 2429; Warenda Rd, Clare; 10.30am-5pm Mon-Fri, 11am-5pm Sat & Sun

04 JIM BARRY WINES

For some of Clare's most exciting wines, from its highest and oldest vineyards, head up to the far side of town. First planted in the 1960s, the Armagh vineyard, named after the green hills of Irish settlers' home county, makes one of the world's finest Shiraz wines. The Florita vineyard in Watervale, one of the area's oldest, produces the monstrously good Lodge Hill Riesling.
www.jimbarry.com; tel +61 08 8842 2261; 33 Craig Hill Road, Clare; 9am-5pm Mon-Fri, 9am-4pm Sat & Sun

05 TURKEY FLAT

On your way back to Adelaide, stop in the Barossa Valley at Turkey Flat, where some of the world's oldest and gnarliest Shiraz vines grow. 'They're 170 years old,' says winemaker Mark Bulman, 'and it's a privilege to be working with them.' The reason why there are such ancient vines here is that the Barossa has long been free from the plant disease phylloxera that devastated French vineyards. The region is the source of many of Australia's most famous red wines but it's not as pretty a place to tour as Clare Valley. Turkey Flat is one of two wineries worth visiting and from February to the middle of March you'll find them in a whirlwind of juice-stained activity as the grapes are picked and fermented in batches. At the cellar door, a former butcher's shop, a bottle of the Butcher's Block red is astounding value for $20.
www.turkeyflat.com.au; tel +61 08 8563 2851; Bethany Rd, Tanunda; 11am-5pm daily

Courtesy of Turkey Flat

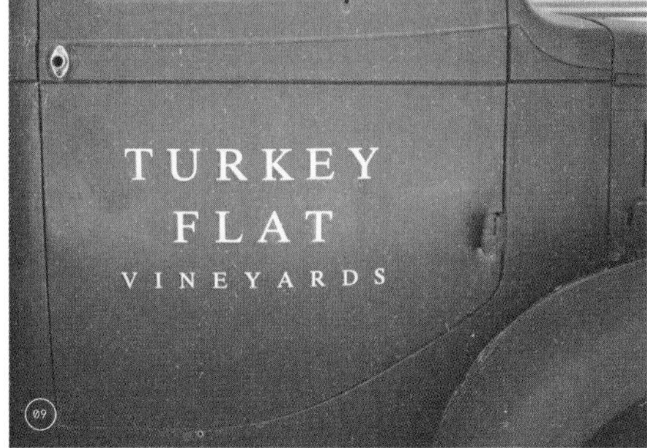

06 GIBSON WINES

To meet Rob Gibson, one of Barossa's mavericks (or at least taste his wines), you'll need to make a detour to the village of Light Pass on the north side of Barossa. Here his rammed-earth cellar door, with its rusty tin roof and bare-brick courtyard – complete with pétanque court and hopscotch, is a family-friendly space in which to get to grips with the former Penfolds winemaker's handiwork. Rob managed to acquire some of the oldest parcels of vines in the Barossa and his signature 'The Dirtman' Shiraz is one of the best introductions to Barossa out there. *www.gibsonwines.com.au; tel +61 08 8562 4224; Lot 190 Willows Rd, Light Pass; 11am-5pm daily*

07-09 Turkey Flat cellar door

ESSENTIAL INFORMATION

WHERE TO STAY

CLARE VALLEY MOTEL

The Clare Valley Motel is an affordable base for a weekend away among the vines. It has been renovated over recent years by owners Lee and Jan Stokes but retains the quaint vibe of a traditional country motel. *www.clarevalleymotel.com.au; tel +61 08 8842 2799; 74a Main North Road, Clare*

SKILLOGALEE

An overnight stay at Skillogalee's cottage, perhaps after a home-cooked meal in the restaurant, allows you to wake up to breakfast in the peace and quiet of the vineyard. That's a win-win. *www.skillogalee.com.au; tel +61 08 8843 4311; Trevarrick Rd, Sevenhill*

WHERE TO EAT

SEED

Newly germinated in Clare, Seed is an all-day eatery in an atmospheric old building. Fresh, healthy, regional cuisine is served, including platters for sharing. In the evening the wine bar is buzzing. *tel +61 08 8842 2323; 308 Main North Rd, Clare*

WHAT TO DO

Following the course of a disused railway line between Auburn and Clare, the fabulous Riesling Trail is 24km of traffic-free cycling trail. The gentle gradient means you can walk or push a pram along it easily. Take your time and explore the dozens of detours to cellar doors along the way. Bikes can be hired at either end of the route. *www.rieslingtrailbikehire.com.au*

Some three hours' drive beyond Clare, the Flinders Ranges National Park is a highlight of South Australia. Its saw-toothed ranges are home to native wildlife and, after rain, carpets of wild flowers. An 80-sq-km natural basin known as Wilpena Pound is the big-ticket drawcard. There's accommodation at the Wilpena Pound Resort.

CELEBRATIONS

Slurp previews of the latest wines from the local makers at the annual Clare Valley Gourmet Weekend in May. Around 20 wineries participate, with food and live music also on the menu. *www.clarevalley.com.au*

[Australia]

MARGARET RIVER

Margaret River is an oasis of amazing food and wine in vast Western Australia. A weekend here combines wine with Indian Ocean beaches and magical landscapes.

The sunsets off the Western Australian coast, whether you're sitting in a harbourside bar in Fremantle or on a deserted beach, are show-stoppers. Time seems to slow down and you find yourself pondering life's biggest questions, such as 'how many bubbles are released in a glass of champagne?'

The sun is definitely rising on the Margaret River wine region. It's never been a secret to Australians that much of the country's finest wine is made way out west, but with competitively priced flights to Perth, the region is opening up to the rest of the world. And what a treat it is! The region, which is 275km south of Perth, is bounded by the Indian Ocean to the west and extends about 90km north and south between Cape Naturaliste and Cape Leeuwin. Around Margaret River are some of the world's tallest trees, cave systems dating back 40,000 years, whales, wildflowers, and wild coastlines with world-class surfing. There's an eye-opening clarity to the light, and Western Australia's colours seem to be turned up to 11. Beyond the state's cities – Perth and near neighbour Fremantle, far-out Broome – the natural world rules in primary colours: red deserts, blue oceans and the yellow sun.

Except, that is, for the temperate oasis that is Margaret River. Quality not quantity is the watchword here: Margaret River produces 3% of Australia's wine, but a quarter of its premium wines. Which is perhaps another reason why wine critic Jancis Robinson said: 'Margaret River is the closest thing to paradise of any wine region I have visited in my extensive search for knowledge.'

Talking of knowledge: the answer to the champagne question is around 20 million...

GET THERE
The Western Australia capital of Perth has the closest airport. Margaret River is about 3hrs to the south by car.

Courtesy of Knee Deep Wines

01 CAPEL VALE

Start the trip at the most northerly winery, which is about an hour's drive from Margaret River. Capel Vale was founded by Perth-based Dr Peter Pratten in 1974, with a single vineyard beside the River Capel, making it one of Western Australia's pioneers. It's now a much larger producer, growing a huge range of grapes, including Sangiovese, Tempranillo and Nebbiolo as well as Margaret River's staple crop of Cabernet Sauvignon and Chardonnay in a variety of locations along the coast. Many of the wines are rated highly by James Halliday, Australia's most prominent critic.

But rather than the scores, the reason to visit Capel Vale is to get a lesson in matching food with wine, thanks to all the different wines made here. The restaurant matches its wines to a wide range of dishes from all over the world, inspired by Spanish tapas bars, Italian *enotecas* and Japanese sushi bars. Some of the tips will be familiar: steak with Shiraz, lobster with Chardonnay - just don't try chocolate with Cabernet.
www.capelvalecom.au; tel +61 08 9727 1986; 118 Mallokup Rd, Capel; 10am-4.30pm daily

02 KNEE DEEP WINES

At Knee Deep, owned by the family of another Perth doctor, Philip Childs, the emphasis is on Margaret River's classic varieties: Chardonnay, Sauvignon Blanc and Cabernet Sauvignon. 'Margaret River provides consistently ideal growing conditions for these grapes,' says winemaker Bruce Dukes. 'The long and gentle growing season is moderated by the Indian Ocean, which provides plentiful rain during winter and a cooling influence. The hot, dry summers create perfect ripening conditions.'

The warm climate is matched by the warm welcome at the cellar door, and when Philip Childs isn't skippering his 50ft racing yacht, you might find him behind the counter.

If you need to refuel, lunches are available at the Knee Deep restaurant, using very artfully arranged organic ingredients for Asian-inspired dishes, such as local lobster with udon, smoked dashi and kizami nori. 'Margaret River is a food and wine lover's paradise with exceptional quality local produce,' says Bruce.
www.kneedeepwines.com.au; tel +61 08 9755 6776; 160 Johnson Rd, Wilyabrup; open 10am-5p, daily

03 CULLEN WINES

There's magic happening at Cullen Wines and it might be because of the moonlight.

Cullen was founded in 1971, when Margaret River pioneers Kevin and Diana Cullen planted a plot of Cabernet Sauvignon and Riesling.

01 Sunset at Leeuwin Naturaliste National Park

02 Knee Deep vineyard

03 Bruce Dukes of Knee Deep Wines

04 Knee Deep cellar door

05 Cullen Wines' restaurant

The winery has a habit of being in the forefront of a movement: it was one of the earliest to become organic and it was the first vineyard in Australia to be carbon neutral.

Now led by daughter Vanya, who has gained experience in Burgundy and California before becoming chief winemaker in 1989, Cullen Wines became a fully biodynamic winery in 2004, which is where the moon plays its part. Biodynamic lore says that key processes such as planting and harvesting should be done in tandem with the cosmic rhythms of the planets; for example, planting should be done when the moon and Saturn are in opposition. There's much more to biodynamics than the moon's movement, such as cow horns filled with manure, but the core of the ethos is about working in harmony with nature so that chemicals are eschewed and nothing extra is added to the wines. A spiral

Andrew Watson © Getty Images

Courtesy of Leeuwin Estate, Vasse Felix

Andrew Watson © Getty Images

garden has been planted at Cullen to explain biodynamics and it's a fascinating experience.

Vanya's wines are essentially natural wines, expressing the land on which they're grown, which is an old, granite and gravelly loam. Red or white, the results in the bottle are unerringly sublime wines that wow critics the world over.
www.cullenwines.com.au; tel +61 08 9755 5277; 4323 Caves Rd, Wilyabrup; open 10am-4.30pm daily

04 VASSE FELIX

Luck is at the heart of Vasse Felix. The winery takes its name from French seaman, Thomas Vasse, who was swept overboard when his ship was surveying the Australian coast in 1801. Founder Dr Tom Cullity added Felix – lucky - to the lost sailor's name when he established Margaret River's first winery in 1967. But he didn't get any at the outset: the crop for the winery's first vintage in 1971 was mostly eaten by birds. A peregrine falcon was brought in to scare off the pests, but promptly disappeared into the distant trees; a falcon motif was added to the logo.

Things soon looked up, and under the present winemaker, Virginia Willcock, the wines, especially the Premier Chardonnay, have become classic examples of what Margaret River does best. To understand what that is, take the two-hour tutored tasting at the cellar door. The restaurant, reputed to be the best in the region, is open daily for lunch.
www.vassefelix.com.au; tel +61 08 9756 5000; cnr Tom Cullity Dr/Caves Rd, Cowaramup; open 10am-5pm daily, tutored tastings 10.30am Mon-Fri

05 VOYAGER ESTATE

Continuing south, homing in on the town of Margaret River, you should choose between Voyager or Leeuwin, both among Margaret's grandest estates. If you want to check out elegantly understated Cape Dutch architecture, manicured gardens and Australia's second largest flagpole, Voyager's the one. The walled gardens, designed by South African landscape designer Deon Bronkhorst, are a beautiful place to wander when the rose bushes are flowering.

Voyager was established in 1978, but under winemaker Steve James it retains a spirit of adventure, using wild yeasts for the white wines, and experimenting with its project wines. There'll always be something interesting to sip.
www.voyagerestate.com.au; tel +61 08 9757 6354; 1 Stevens Rd, Margaret River; 10am-5pm daily

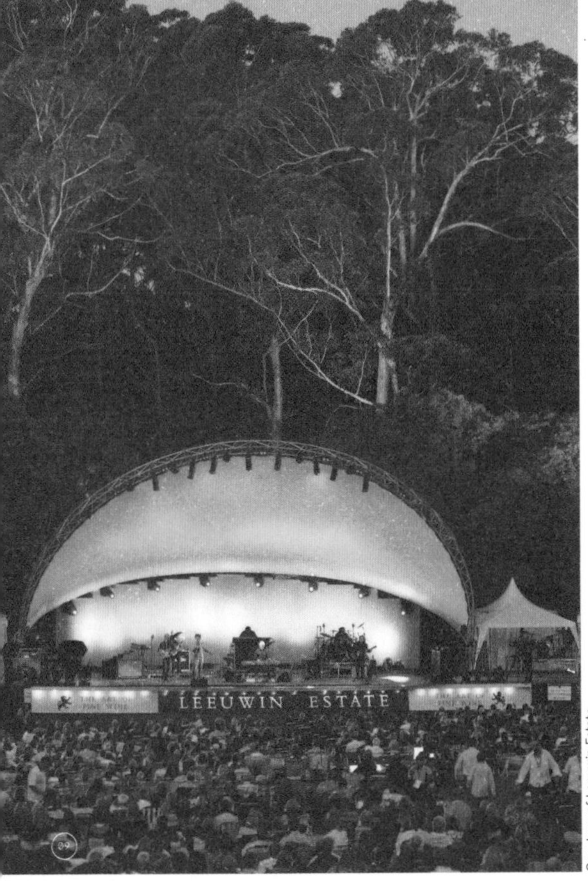

Courtesy of Leeuwin Estate

06 LEEUWIN ESTATE

Superlative wines await at this family-owned winery, another of the estates in Margaret River dating from the 1970s. The Art Series Chardonnay is regarded as one of Australia's finest, alongside the Cabernet Sauvignon and Shiraz. The ethos at Leeuwin is to always reflect the land and the weather in the wine, as winemaker Tim Lovett says: 'Every vintage is different. It's about showcasing a sense of place.' All Margaret River's finest ingredients - the maritime climate, the ancient Australian soils, the skilled and thoughtful winemakers, such as Paul Atwood and Tim Lovett - come together at Leeuwin.
www.leeuwinestate.com.au; tel +61 08 9759 0000; Stevens Rd, Margaret River; open 10am-5pm daily

06 Leeuwin Estate's Art Series

07 Voyager Estate

08 Vasse Felix's Barrel Hall

09 Live music at Leeuwin Estate

ESSENTIAL INFORMATION

WHERE TO STAY

BURNSIDE ORGANIC FARM
These rammed-earth and limestone bungalows have spacious decks and designer kitchens, and the surrounding farm hosts a menagerie of animals and organic avocado and macadamia orchards.
www.burnside-organicfarm.com.au; tel +61 08 9757 2139; 287 Burnside Rd, Margaret River

EDGE OF THE FOREST
Prepare to update your expectations of what a motel should be. This delightful spot is set in bird-filled gardens next to a State Forest, with walking trails from the front door.
www.edgeoftheforest.com.au; tel +61 08 9757 2351; 25 Bussell Hwy, Margaret River

WHERE TO EAT

BOOTLEG BREWERY
Take a break from the grape at Bootleg Brewery. Head brewer Michael Brookes can also recommend some local mountain-biking trails, if that floats your boat.
www.bootlegbrewery.com.au; tel +61 08 9755 6300; Puzey Rd, Wilyabrup

WHAT TO DO

Surfers will want to hit the powerful reef breaks of the beaches between Capes Naturaliste and Leeuwin. Around Dunsborough the better locations are between Eagle and Bunker Bays. The annual surfer competition is held around Margaret River Mouth and Southsides.

From June to September, humpback and southern right whales make a pitstop in Flinders Bay, off Augusta, south of Margaret River. And from September to December, whales, including the rare blue whale, frequent Geographe Bay to the north; there are whale-watching cruises available.
www.westernaustralia.com

CELEBRATIONS

The annual Margaret River Gourmet Escape showcases the region's world-class food and wine over a weekend in November. It draws guest chefs, such as Heston Blumental in 2014, and has plenty of open-air events.
www.gourmetescape.com.au

01

[Australia]

MORNINGTON PENINSULA

Hightail it out of Victoria's state capital for a weekend among the vines and lanes of this peninsula, and enjoy revitalising beach walks, great wines and local dining.

The Mornington Peninsula has long played an important role in Melbourne society. It's a place where wealthy wine enthusiasts – Melbourne's great and good – have sunk more than a few thousand dollars into their dream project, with the reasonable expectation of seeing the most pleasing results in the bottle rather than on the balance sheet.

Since the revival of the Peninsula's vineyards in the mid-1970s (grapes were first planted here in the 19th century) the 25-mile tendril of land has seen more than 50 cellar doors open, luring weekending cityfolk down the Nepean Highway. The Peninsula is relatively developed along the northwest coast but becomes wilder the further south you go, until you reach the Mornington Peninsula National Park. But along the central ridge around Red Hill, where many of the wineries are located, it is almost quaint in places, with twisty lanes, charming village corners and green valleys.

GET THERE
Melbourne is the closest city; the Mornington Peninsula is an easy 1hr drive south.

Pinot Noir's spiritual home might be Burgundy, but it has settled very happily here on the other side of the world. Australia's only wine-growing region with a truly maritime climate, the Mornington Peninsula's Pinot Noir grapes love the cool sea breezes that prolong its ripening cycle, increasing flavour. Characteristics of the Peninsula's Pinot include a transcendent scent – earthy, spicy yet, fruity – that seems to flick a pleasure switch deep within the brain, and a lighter body than Pinots from elsewhere in the New World. Few other grapes are as memorable. Chardonnay is just as distinctive a wine on the peninsula, with a delicacy not found elsewhere; only a few wineries have the know-how to get the best from this partnership. When you've tasted enough wines for the day, drive down to the east coast and watch the sun set from one of the forest-backed beaches.

Rachel Lewis © Getty Images

01 Cape Schank

02 Ten Minutes by Tractor

03 Aerial view of Stonier

04 Stonier's wines

05 Barrel testing at Stonier

Courtesy of Ten Minutes By Tractor, Stonier

01 TUCK'S RIDGE

If you could bring together all the elements that make the Mornington Peninsula special, you might end up with a place like Tuck's Ridge. Overlooking a patchwork of fields and hedgerows on both sides of a gently sloping valley, you could almost be in the English countryside, were it not for the regimented lines of vines. Tuck's Ridge, owned by stockbroker Peter Hollick, specialises in Pinot Noir and Chardonnay, producing highly-regarded, food-friendly wines. 'Pinot Noir is great with food, especially salmon, because it is "grippy"' says Verona Richmond at the cellar door.

To understand the region, you need to know that Mornington Peninsula vineyards are a bit higher, so a couple of degrees cooler than average, and there's no frost as it's close to the sea. The cooler the climate, the longer the grapes take to ripen; hot climates can produce heavier ('syrupy' is the unkind description) wines.

'Pinot Noir,' says Verona, 'is a thin-skinned, high-risk grape, so everybody gets nervous around picking time. It's a fickle grape and goes through peaks and troughs of flavour, so keeping it for five years doesn't necessarily make it a better wine, just different.' And according to Verona, the price of a wine isn't an indication of whether you'll like it. She adds: 'My philosophy is why wait? Open the bottle and make that the special occasion.'

www.tucksridge.com.au; tel +61 03 5989 8660; 37 Shoreham Rd, Red Hill South; 11am–5pm daily

02 MONTALTO

Montalto is one winery that succeeds in covering all the bases: world-class wines, great food, and paths that lure visitors deep into the vineyard. But what makes Montalto a must-visit cellar door is its Chardonnay. Once described by James Halliday as 'power and grace personified', it's as enjoyable an example of the grape as you'll ever find. Picked from Montalto's main north-facing vineyard and from the plot behind the cellar door, the wine, despite its scarcity, has earned accolades from all over the world.

Montalto is owned by the Mitchell family, and the vineyard dates back 20 years, although the modern cellar door only opened in 2001. 'While we see ourselves as a winery, our philosophy is to be a destination to draw people to the Mornington Peninsula,' says John Mitchell. 'No matter where people are in the world, when they drink our wines we want them to remember the whole experience.' To that end, the Mitchells have an olive grove with 1500 trees (you can taste the olive oil in the cellar door), four locations around the valley set aside for summer picnics, a restaurant supplied by herb and vegetable

Courtesy of Stonier

gardens, and an orchard. Afterwards, there are sculptures sprinkled around the vineyards to discover and a wetland walking trail. As John Mitchell says, the Mornington Peninsula offers more than wine, though, in Montalto's case, they're not doing too badly on that front either.
www.montalto.com.au; tel +61 03 5989 8412; 33 Shoreham Rd, Red Hill South; 11am–5pm daily

03 STONIER

Geraldine McFaul, winemaker at Stonier since 2003, has earned a reputation for producing some of the Mornington Peninsula's most expressive Pinot Noirs, wines with a rock-solid sense of place. Stonier is one of the first wave of vineyards on the peninsula, with its Chardonnay vines dating from 1978 and the Pinot Noir vines from 1982. But it is perhaps Geraldine McFaul's research trips to Burgundy that influence Stonier's Pinots the most. She produces just Chardonnay and Pinot Noir in three categories, ranging from blends from the younger vineyards to bottles from single vineyards, a dedication to *terroir* derived from Burgundy. Stonier's distinctive, airy cellar door, designed by Melbourne architect Daryl Jackson, is the perfect venue for these ambitious wines.

Bunches are counted in late December, when some may be pruned (fewer bunches means more flavour, as the vine's energies are concentrated). 'That's when our viticulturalist starts getting stressed about ordering barrels - at $1200 to $1500 each - and we all take bets on how much will be produced,' says cellar door manager Noella. Stonier is right on the east coast of the peninsula and the cool conditions suit Chardonnay too: 'Warmer areas produce bigger, buttery chards,' explains Noella. Look for a mineral edge instead in Stonier's Chardonnay, which is as refreshing as a walk on the beach across the road. 'But if you prefer Pinots,' adds Noella, 'go and try Nat White's at Main Ridge'.
www.stonier.com.au; tel +61 03 5989 8300; 2 Thompsons Lane, Merricks; 11am–5pm daily

04 MAIN RIDGE ESTATE

The rutted, pot-holed dirt track leading to Nat White's cellar door (as well as the tasting fee and signs warning off coach parties) seems designed to deter casual quaffers. It's an impression not dispelled by the tall, bespectacled figure of Nat White himself behind the countertop. Reserved and scholarly, the former engineer looks like there's nothing he'd rather do than close up the cellar door and get back to his grapes. But that's perfectly understandable, given that his vines were the first to be planted during the Peninsula's revival in

Courtesy of Main Ridge, Visions of Victoria

06 Nat White of Main Ridge Estate

07 Crushed grapes

the mid-1970s and produce some of the most fascinating wines from Red Hill's volcanic soils. 'We were the first winery on the Mornington Peninsula,' he says, over a tasting of his Half Acre Pinot Noir, 'so we planted several varieties to see what would take. We grow enough to produce 1200 cases of Pinot Noir and Chardonnay and we've kept on enough Merlot for a barrel a year and some Pinot Meunier.'

After a roadtrip through France in the 1970s, Nat and his wife Rosalie returned to Australia unable to forget about the Pinot Noirs of Burgundy. They planted the first vines at Main Ridge in 1975 and crushed their first grapes in 1980, aiming to replicate the lighter, fruitier Pinot Noirs of Burgundy. 'I find the Mornington Peninsula's cooler climate produces less tannic Pinots,' he explains. Nat produces two Pinots from the same sloping plot: the Half-Acre is picked from vines rooted in shallow soil, while the Acre comes from deeper soil. Treated identically in all other respects, including an 18-month sojourn in French oak barriques, the smaller berries from the Half-Acre make for a noticeably more intense mouthful. Lessons in wine-making don't come more comprehensible. It's no wonder that Nat White prefers to let his wine speak for itself.

www.mre.com.au; tel +61 03 5989 2686; 80 William Road, Red Hill; Mon–Fri 12–4, Sat–Sun 12–5

05 TEN MINUTES BY TRACTOR

With its jazz soundtrack and a modern, minimalist interior, Ten Minutes By Tractor is one of the most chic cellar doors on the Mornington Peninsula. Wine is produced from three vineyards, all, you guessed it, ten minutes from each other by tractor. Owner Martin Spedding, who has run TMBT since 2004 alongside mentor Richard McIntyre, believes the region is coming of age now since the first vines were planted in the 1970s: 'Of the 60 or 70 wine producers here, a great majority of them are producing fantastic wine.'

This includes TMBT, where top- of-the-range wines go for $60 a bottle. 'These are small-yielding vineyards and the wines are expensive as a result.'

With a deck overlooking a valley and a small plot of vines, the cellar door restaurant offers food tailored to the estate's wines. 'Pinot Noir is better with food than some of

Australia's heavier reds,' says Martin. 'The types of foods we're now eating in Australia – a fusion of Asian and Mediterranean flavours – is food with delicate layers of flavours. People are looking for wines that complement not dominate food.' *www. tenminutesbytractor.com. au; tel +61 03 5989 6080; 1333 Mornington–Flinders Rd, Main Ridge; 10am–5pm daily*

06 RED HILL ESTATE

Wooden crates are still scattered around the old sorting shed at Red Hill Estate, on the road back to Shoreham, but the space around them has evolved into the tasting room of this 20-year old vineyard. Out the back, Max's Restaurant has views over green countryside all the way down to the sea and Phillip Island. Chef Max Paganoni selects local produce – strawberries from Sunny Ridge, cheese from Red Hill's own artisan cheesery – for his Italian-influenced menus. On summer weekends you can expect at least one wedding to be taking place in the gardens.

Back in the cellar door, Red Hill's wines are no less enjoyable. Concentrating on Chardonnay and Pinot Noir, Red HIll winemakers used traditional techniques, including wild yeasts and smaller bunches of berries to up the skin-to-flesh ratio. The result is a complex, earthy Classic Release Pinot Noir and a Chardonnay that is similar to those of the Yarra Valley – less big and brassy than you may find elsewhere. Both are designed to cellar for a long time; up to 15 years in the case of the Pinot. *www.redhillestate.com.au; tel +61 03 5989 2838; 53 Shoreham Rd, Red Hill South; 11am–5pm daily*

ESSENTIAL INFORMATION

WHERE TO STAY

CAPE SCHANK RESORT

Although you can stay in Cape Schank's actual lighthouse (see below), this RACV resort has a bit more space. It overlooks wild Bass Strait. *www.racv.com.au; Trent Jones Drive, Cape Schanck*

WHERE TO EAT

RED HILL BREWERY

Red Hill's brewery grows its own hops, and brews enough European-inspired ales – from strong Belgian-style lagers and German pilsners to English stouts and bitters – to keep beer-curious wine-tourers refreshed. The English, Belgian and German theme continues with Ploughman's platters and *waterzooi*, the Belgian fish stew. *www.redhillbrewery.com. au; tel +61 03 5989 2959; 88 Shoreham Road, Red Hill South*

PORTSEA HOTEL

At the very tip of the peninsula, Portsea's hotel serves good pub grub, with views on the side. *www.portseahotel.com.au; tel +61 03 5984 2213; 3746 Point Nepean Rd, Portsea*

WHAT TO DO

Pack your hiking shoes for the one-hour bush walk to Bushranger's Bay, at the south-east tip of the peninsula. It's an untamed place, rich in wildlife, from the frogs croaking under the tea trees to the kangaroos bounding along the beach at sunset. Look south to see the Cape Schanck lightstation, which dates from 1859 and houses a small museum and self-catering accommodation. *www.parkweb.vic.gov.au; tel 03 5988 6184*

CELEBRATIONS

The main event is the biennial Pinot Noir Celebration (February), when winemakers from all over the world converge on the Mornington Peninsula to sniff each other's Pinots and swap pruning tips. Later in the year the Winter Wine Weekend (June) is an opportunity to meet the producers, attend seminars and taste wine; accommodation gets booked early up for both occasions. *www.mpva.com.au/events*

01

© Robin Barton

COROWA
WAHGUNYAH
RUTHERGLEN
HOWLONG
Murray River
Murray River
01
02
03
04
AUSTRALIA

[Australia]

RUTHERGLEN

Deep in northern Victoria, there's something sweet and unique happening. Some of Australia's oldest wineries make its most unusual wines in this rural region.

Rain in Rutherglen. The farmers are rejoicing. The cockatoos, washing-powder white against the greenery, seem happy. And the winemakers have that look of bewilderment that comes with unexpected good fortune. For Rutherglen, deep in northern Victoria, four hours from Canberra, seven from Sydney, can suffer from 40°C (104°F) summers, with grapes having to be harvested in a mad rush – even in the middle of the night – before they cook into a jam. But the rain cools things down and prolongs the ripening time of the region's unique Muscat and Tokay vines. And the longer on the vine, the better for Rutherglen's remarkable fortified Muscats and Tokays – butterscotch-flavoured, raisin-rich dessert wines.

Aside from the heat, Rutherglen has its own challenges: newer wine regions such as King Valley, closer to Melbourne, have siphoned off visitors. Then there's the wine itself: in the age of the calorie-conscious diner, who orders a sweet wine (a 'sticky' in Aussie lingo) any more? Who even orders dessert? But Rutherglen's Muscats and Tokays, like Banyuls of southern France, deserve their place at the table, for being heady, idiosyncratic and wantonly indulgent. Wines aside, another reason to tour Rutherglen is the region's history. Several of its key wineries, such as All Saints and Morris, started in the mid-19th century and their stories are entwined with that of Australia, featuring colonial pioneers and gold miners, all set to a backdrop of the broad Murray River.

GET THERE
You'll need a car to drive from Melbourne (3hrs) or Canberra. Base yourself in Rutherglen.

02

01 MORRIS WINES

Starting a 'stickies' winery is a 20-year investment, which is why Rutherglen is dominated by fourth- and fifth-generation family wineries and has few new openings. This winery's family roots reach back to George Francis Morris, from Lancashire, England, who founded it in 1859. Like many of his peers, he'd moved to Australia in his teens in search of opportunity, specifically gold. The adage that the people who make money in gold rushes are those selling the picks was true in Morris' case. But eventually he sold his share in a gold-mining outfitters and started planting vines with the proceeds. By 1885 Morris had more than 80 hectares (198 acres) of vines and was the largest producer in the southern hemisphere. Five generations later, the Morris family is still making award-winning wines; the silverware in the trophy room dates back to the 19th

Courtesy of Campbells Wines, All Saints

01 Rural Rutherglen

02 A tasting at Campbells Winery

03-05 All Saints winery

Courtesy of All Saints. © Robin Barton

century. They make a huge range of fortified wines, including tawny ports, and some full-bodied red wines, including a rustic Durif that has a cult following in Australia.
www.morriswines.com.au; tel +61 02 6026 7303 ; Mia Mia Rd, Browns Plains; 9am-5pm daily

02 ALL SAINTS

Don't be deceived by appearances: All Saints winery may look like a Scottish castle, complete with flag-topped turret (indeed, it's based on the Castle of Mey in Caithness, Scotland) but it's an all-Australian icon. Back in the 1860s, when it was founded, the winery had an earth floor and was built from red bricks fired on-site. The estate's history is tied to that of the Rutherglen region: its original owners, George Sutherland Smith and John Banks arrived from Scotland aged just 23 and 20 respectfully. Trained as engineers, they designed bridges and buildings throughout Victoria, including part of the jail in nearby Beechworth that accommodated the bushranger Ned Kelly. Then the friends started planting vines at the current site in 1869, winning the first gold medal for Australian wine in 1873 in London.

Today, under the guidance of (now former) winemaker Dan Crane, All Saints' wines have continued to win awards. 'A long autumn and cool nights, thanks to the cold air rolling off the Australian Alps, mean the grapes retain their acidity,' he explains. This gives the fruit's flavours a chance to catch up with its sugars. The Muscat and Tokay grapes are picked as late in the season as late May then pressed using their weight. But you'll have to wait at least eight years and up to 20 to taste the results in All Saints' fortified wines.
www.allsaintswine.com.au; tel +61 02 6035 2222; All Saints Rd; 9am-5.30pm Mon-Sat, 10am-5.30pm Sun

03 VALHALLA WINES

You can take a break from the history lessons when you reach Valhalla. Anton Therkildsen – half-Danish, half-Scottish – arrived in Rutherglen in 1997 when studying winemaking. Within two years he'd bought a plot of land and was married to a local GP, Antoinette. He planted Durif and Shiraz in the heavier soils, Grenache and Mourvedre in the loamy midweight soils and Marsanne and Viognier in the lightest soils. With the help of free cuttings from other vineyards, borrowed tractors, and the corner of a friend's winery, Anton's first vintage was on its way.

But he still needed a winery – and he wanted it to be sustainably built. They decided on a straw-bale design with 1m-thick walls. In 2007 the walls went up in three weeks, the double-insulated roof in another three weeks and the rendering in a final three week burst. In just over two months they

06

06-08 Campbells Wines

07

had a passive solar-powered winery that didn't require air conditioning – quite an achievement when temperatures in Rutherglen range from -4°C to 40°C (25°F to 104°F). And all the rainwater is captured.

'There's no recipe – I look at the fruit as it comes in and how it is best going to express itself.' *–Anton Therkildsen, Valhalla Wines*

Anton's sustainable approach extends to the vines, with free-range geese providing fertiliser, and wild flowers to attract predators and deter pests. 'I wanted to bring different energies to the vineyard, working with natural rhythms, which is something we've lost as a society,' he explains. 'It was important to us to farm naturally and sustainably and to return to traditional winemaking principles. Our ethos is to do the best we can and make it available to the average consumer. Make it well and with integrity.'

Valhalla also aims to spread the word about winemaking. Not only does Anton get his children to help at harvest, but he also offers winemaker-for-a-day workshops. 'I love it,' he says. 'It's a big part of vintage, showcasing how it's made. Big wineries can be dangerous places but I encourage people to get stuck in and have a taste' Dip a finger into a foaming and fermenting vat of just-pressed Durif and it'll taste of deep, sweet blackcurrants.

www.valhallawines.com.au; 163 All Saints Rd; tours & winemaking experiences by appointment

04 CAMPBELLS WINES

Campbells is a family-owned winery that is part of Australia's winemaking heritage. In the mid-19th century, John Campbell, a Scottish immigrant (yes, there's a pattern), arrived in Rutherglen to seek his fortune in northeast Victoria's gold rush. But he realised there was no gold. Instead, as he was told by one of the region's first winemakers, there was more gold in the top six inches of soil. Following suit, Campbell planted the family's first vines 140 years ago. He named his first wine Bobbie Burns, after a gold mine on a hill opposite the cellar.

Courtesy of Campbells Wines

Campbells retains a lot of history. The storehouse, reinforced to keep people out, was used until the 1920s. Under the beams in the original part of the winery are 1000L, 100-year-old barrels of Muscat and Tokay. Every three months the winemaker tastes each barrel and between vintages a catflap-like door in the front lets (small) people crawl inside to clean them.

All the grapes used are grown on the site and include Durif, a variety developed by French botanist Dr Durif in the 1880s, which is resistant to heat. Having a dark colour and high alcohol content, it is used for port and robust table wines. Campbells also does its own bottling so whatever time of year it is, there should be something going on. *www.campbellswines.com.au; tel +61 02 6033 6000; 4603 Murray Valley Hwy; 9am-5pm Mon-Sat, 10am-5pm Sun*

ESSENTIAL INFORMATION

WHERE TO STAY

TUILERIES

This luxurious place stands next to Jolimont Cellars. There's a tennis court, pool and an outstanding restaurant. No prizes for guessing what the self-contained King Vineyard units overlook. *www.tuileriesrutherglen.com.au; tel +61 02 6032 9033; 13 Drummond St, Rutherglen*

WHERE TO EAT

Most of the eating options in Rutherglen are strung along the handsome Main St, which gives a taste of rural Australian architecture.

TASTE

The top fine dining destination in Rutherglen is this multipurpose venue on the Main St. Cafe by day, swanky restaurant by night, serving a degustation menu with matching wines or à la carte. The bar has an interesting range of local Durif wines too. Open for breakfast, lunch and dinner (Wed-Sun). *www.taste-at-rutherglen.com; tel +61 02 60329765; 121b Main St, Rutherglen*

WHAT TO DO

If you've made it up to northeast Victoria, it makes sense to explore as much as possible of this fantastic part of Australia. Half an hour by car southeast of Rutherglen is Beechworth, arguably Australia's most appealing country town. It's based around a crossroads, with plenty of well preserved buildings along each road, many with stories attached, such as the jail. There's also an excellent brewery and several good pubs and restaurants. A couple of hours west of Rutherglen is Echuca, on the Murray, where riverboats ply their trade. *www.visitvictoria.com*

CELEBRATIONS

Rutherglen's annual Winery Walkabout takes place in June on the Queen's Birthday long weekend holiday in Victoria. There are tastings at around 20 wineries and plenty of activities for families to take part in; the Country Fair on the Sunday features a grape stomp and a barrel-rolling competition. *www.winemakers.com.au*

01

[Australia]

TAMAR VALLEY

Encounter devilishly delicious Pinot Noir and outstanding local produce in the north of Tasmania on a road trip along the Tamar River.

A wine made with Pinot Noir grapes seems to inspire rapture like no other can. People describe good Burgundy in almost mystical terms. In the cult wine film *Sideways* (is this the only cult wine film?), Miles attempts to explains his love of Pinot Noir: 'It's thin-skinned, temperamental, ripens early... needs constant care and attention... and it can only grow in these really specific, little, tucked-away corners of the world.' And one of those tucked-away places is the Tamar Valley (and the Piper River region next door) in northern Tasmania, which shares a similar climate to the famed Côte d'Or in Burgundy.

If you can tear yourself away from the other attractions of Tasmania – staggeringly beautiful beaches, multiday hikes through pristine wilderness, a one-of-a-kind art gallery – a weekend beside the Tamar River will introduce you to some of the world's finest Pinot Noirs and some deliciously more-ish local produce; northern Tasmania is Australia's orchard, with farmers markets a regular feature of weekend life. The island's food scene is the match of its wine – be sure to try fresh seafood with the Tamar's white wines and its lamb with the Pinot Noirs.

The origins of Tasmanian wine lie in a vineyard just east of Launceston once called La Provence and now known as Providence. It was planted with Pinot Noir and Chardonnay in 1956 by Jean Miguet, the son of a winemaking family. By the 1990s, wines from this part of northern Tasmania were winning international medals.

Starting the tour further up the Tamar River means that you finish close to the Southern Ocean, for a contemplative walk along a deserted beach. 'Haunting and brilliant and thrilling and subtle...' is how Miles describes Pinot Noir in *Sideways*; it's a description that also applies to Tasmania.

GET THERE
Launceston can be reached by plane from most Australian cities and by ferry from Melbourne.

Courtesy of Josef Chromy

01 JOSEF CHROMY

This landmark winery is led by one of Australian wine's more remarkable characters. Having survived 11 years of Nazi and Soviet occupation, a penniless 19-year-old left his Czech village and made his way to Australia. Over the next 40 years he built up a fortune in the butchery trade and poured the proceeds of his company's stock market float into the nascent Tasmanian wine industry, establishing Tamar Ridge in 1994 and investing in what is now Bay of Fires. Now in his 80s, Josef Chromy has hardly slowed down but it's winemaker Jeremy Dineen who has the task of creating Chromy's eponymous wines. 'My winemaking is mostly influenced by the site,' says Jeremy. 'Just as a person displays their heritage by accent, great wines should reveal their origins by the unique characteristics of their vineyard.' He's got a geographic advantage in nurturing Chromy's Pinot Noir vines: 'Our southerly latitude gives us the cool climate and long ripening season required by Pinot Noir. Being an island, the ocean has a huge moderating effect on Tasmania's climate so we don't get extremes of heat or cold.'

Jeremy Dineen has seen Tasmanian wine evolve over recent years. Not only is there more first-class fruit being grown, but a new generation of younger winemakers has the determination to produce distinctive, expressive wines. So, what inspires Jeremy's own winemaking? 'Some of the amazing single vineyards of the Mosel [see p116]. And Tom Waits.'

www.josefchromy.com.au; tel +61 03 6335 8700; 370 Relbia Rd, Relbia; 10am-5pm daily

02 VELO WINES

Cycling and wine have long been bedfellows. Indeed, in the earliest days of the Tour de France, riders would raid cafes and bars at the foot of mountains, carrying out bottles with which to fortify themselves for the tough climb ahead.

Sadly, by the time that Australian Olympic cyclist Michael Wilson had turned professional that practice had stopped. However, as the founder – and qualified viticulturist – of boutique-sized Velo Wines, he gets to enjoy wine whenever he likes. Michael makes the reds, including a Pinot Noir and a Cabernet Sauvignon, from some of the island's oldest vines, planted in 1966 by Graham Wiltshire, a pioneer of Tasmanian wine. And he still gets to race his bike, and even hosts sportives such as the Rapha

01 The Tamar River

02 Josef Chromy cellar door

03 Cheese and wine at Tamar Ridge

04 Josef Chromy vineyard

05 Vines at Velo Wines

Courtesy of Tamar Ridge, Velo Wines

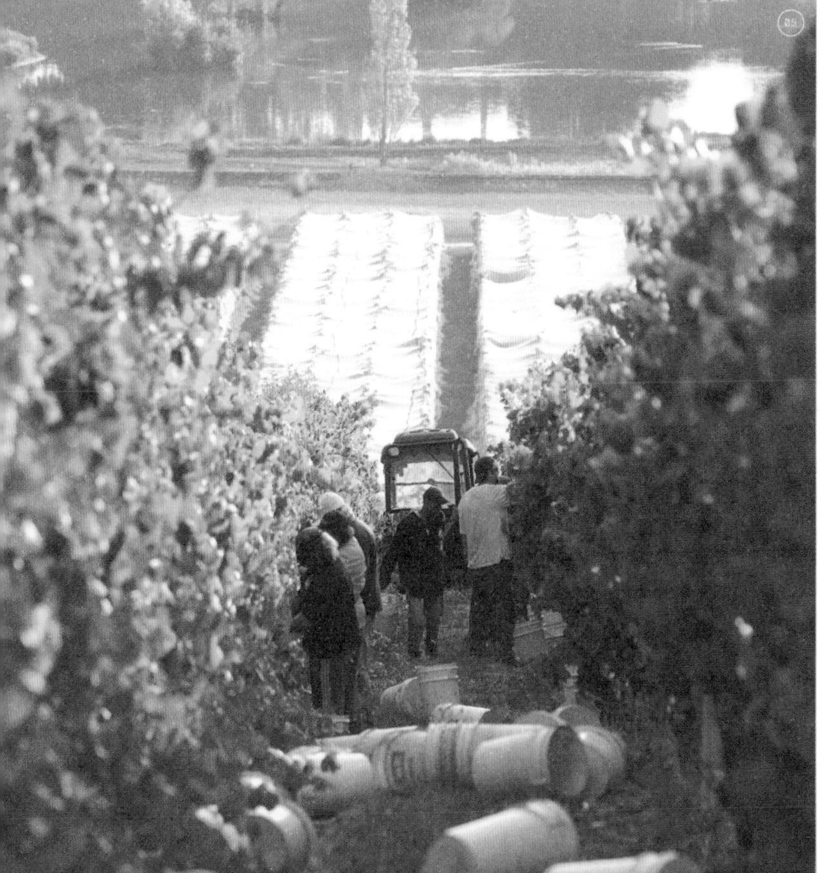

Prestige Launceston – but these days the riders usually have just a coffee.
www.velowines.com.au; tel +61 03 6330 3677; 755 West Tamar Hwy, Legana; 10am-5pm Wed-Sun; Barrel Room restaurant open for lunch & dinner at weekends.

03 TAMAR RIDGE

Follow the blue-and-yellow signs of the Tamar Valley Wine Route to Tamar Ridge, where you can take a break and unpack a picnic on a lawn overlooking the river as it broadens. This is one of the region's larger cellar doors and was purchased from Dr Andrew Pirie, the man behind Tasmania's most successful wine brands, by the big business Brown Brothers. In 1994, Pirie entered a Tasmanian Chardonnay in the blind-tasting International Wine Challenge –

Courtesy of Bay of Fires

and came away with the Best White Wine trophy. Pirie is still involved with Brown Brothers and produces a range of excellent sparkling wines, but his legacy at Tamar Ridge are white wines, including a straw-coloured, botrytis-affected Riesling dessert wine and a peachy Chardonnay.
www.brownbrothers.com.au; tel +61 03 6330 0300; 1a Waldhorn Drive, Rosevears; 10am-5pm daily

04 STONEY RISE

The sporting connections continue at Stoney Rise, where former cricketer Joe Holyman now presides over this small winery, just a 20-minute walk from the Tamar's shore. Since hanging up his wicket-keeping gloves, Joe has worked in wineries in Portugal and France before returning home to restore Stoney Rise. He makes two tiers of wine, the entry-level Stoney Rise label and also Pinot Noir under the Holyman label, made from grapes from a single parcel of vines. The Holyman Pinot Noir is aged in oak barriques, which makes for a wine with plenty of depth and fruit. Try it in the cellar door, which overlooks the Tamar as it nears the ocean.
www.stoneyrise.com; tel +61 03 6394 3678; 96 Hendersons Lane, Gravelly Beach; 11am-5pm Thu-Mon; closed Jul-Sep

05 IRON POT BAY

Tucked away down a sideroad, Iron Pot Bay backs right onto the Tamar River in what is a magical setting. The winery is in a clapboard cottage, crammed with curios, but is being renovated by new owner Julieanne Mani. That hasn't stopped her from winning awards with Iron Pot Bay's HOBO sparkling wine; the winery specialises in grapes such as Chardonnay and Pinot Meunier, with which they create their unwooded white wines. After sampling them, take a stroll down to the river or set up a picnic under some of the shady trees in the garden.
www.ironpotbayvineyard.com.au 703 Rowella Rd, Rowella

06 BAY OF FIRES

For the final stop, depart the Tamar Valley and compare notes with the neighbouring – and slightly cooler - Pipers River region just a few kilometres east. Bay of Fires is named after an incredibly beautiful stretch of Tasmania's east coast, itself christened by Captain Tobias Furneaux in 1773 when he noticed a number of fires along the coast,

06 Penny Jones at Bay of Fires

07 Bay of Fires cellar door

08 Tamar's wine-touring route

08

© Robin Barton

evidence of Aboriginal communities. At the winery, Tasmanian-born Penny Jones, who has experience of winemaking in several Australian wine regions and has travelled widely in Europe and the USA in pursuit of winemaking know-how, crafts exceptionally successful Pinot Noirs, which layer black cherry, oak and tannin to superb effect. She has helped Bay of Fires become one of Tasmania's headline wineries, but she's not done it alone. Bay of Fires has a sister brand, House of Arras, which is dedicated to traditional Champagne-style sparkling wine and helmed by Ed Carr. This too is one of the best examples of Australian sparkling wine.
www.bayoffireswines.com.au; tel +61 03 6382 7622, 40 Baxters Rd, Pipers River; 10am-5pm daily

ESSENTIAL INFORMATION

WHERE TO STAY

RED FEATHER INN

At the ocean-end of the Tamar Valley, on the east side of the river, Red Feather Inn is one of Tasmania's best boutique hotels and also offers dinner and even cookery classes. The accommodation is in a series of historic sandstone buildings.
www.redfeatherinn.com.au; tel +61 03 6393 6506 42 Main St, Hadspen

WHERE TO EAT

STILLWATER

Stillwater is set in a stylishly renovated 1840s flour mill beside the Tamar in Launceston. It serves laid-back breakfasts, relaxed lunches – and then puts on the ritz for dinner, with delectable seafood, meat and vegetarian dishes.
www.stillwater.net.au; tel +61 03 6331 4153; 2 Bridge Rd, Ritchie's Flour Mill, Launceston

WHAT TO DO

The Tamar Valley is on the doorstep of some of the most impressive and pristine natural scenery in the world. Tasmania's east coast is scooped with white-sand beaches and bays, backed by ancient forests. To the west is Cradle Mountain, a national park offering outstanding hiking among Tasmania's highest peaks and some of the local wildlife, including wombats and wallabies. But no trip to Tasmania would be complete without a stay in Hobart and a visit to the Museum of Old and New Art (MONA), an idiosyncratic and awe-inspiring venue with its own on-site winery (Moorilla). Tasmania is a small island: the drive from Launceston to Hobart takes two hours.
www.parks.tas.gov.au; www.mona.net.au

CELEBRATIONS

In Launceston, Festivale is an annual summer party celebrating Tasmanian food, wine, beer and music, taking over the historic City Park for three days on the second weekend of February. It's a chance to try some of food-obsessed Tasmania's local produce.

In the state capital Hobart, MONA hosts two annual extravaganzas, FOMO and MOFO, that share the museum's avant-garde take on art and culture.
www.festivale.com.au

01

Courtesy of Visions of Victoria

[Australia]

YARRA VALLEY

Fabulous wineries, attractive towns, innovative art galleries, roaming 'roos: the Yarra Valley easily tempts as a perfect weekend retreat, moments from Melbourne.

Many good things came out of the 1960s. One of the best was the idea by such pioneers as Guill de Pury of Yeringberg winery to plant vines in the Yarra Valley again. Grapes had been planted around the gentle slopes of the Yarra Ranges since the first settlers arrived in the 1830s but winemaking had petered out until Guill's group of hobbyist winemakers picked up the reins again. Starting with just 2 hectares (5 acres) at Yeringberg, Guill now farms more than 20 hectares (50 acres). That expansion has been mirrored across the valley, with about 100 wineries and more than 50 cellar doors, large and small, now sprinkled around the country towns of Yarra Glen and Healesville.

Described by wine writer and resident James Halliday as 'a place of extreme beauty', the Yarra Valley is just an hour from Melbourne. But the large numbers of visitors from the big city – especially at weekends – seem to be effortlessly absorbed into this Arcadian retreat. There are more than enough wineries and beauty spots to find some space of your own. The Yarra river, marked by a line of River Red gum trees, runs straight through the middle of the valley, north of the Maroondah Highway. On a hot day the temptation to find a shady swimming spot and chill a bottle of Chardonnay in the river is irresistible. With all the daytrippers, the valley can sustain a stellar supporting cast of swanky restaurants (often in the wineries), foodie shops, such as the Yarra Valley Dairy and numerous delicatessens in Healesville, plus boutique B&Bs. This makes the Yarra Valley Victoria's leading wine-touring destination, and perhaps Australia's. But remember that you're more likely to meet actual winemakers like Guill de Pury at the smaller cellar doors – and that's the joy of wine touring.

GET THERE
The closest airport is Melbourne's, about an hour away by car.

01 MANDALA WINES

Although Mandala's cellar door, with its cantilevered roof, looks contemporary, the vines, primarily Pinot Noir and Chardonnay, have been around for almost 20 years. Picks of the bunch are the single-site wines – The Rock, The Prophet, The Matriarch and The Butterfly, which are available for tasting on selected weekends. Single-vineyard wines in Australia are an attempt to introduce the idea of Old World *terroir*, where a wine is imbued with the characteristics of a specific plot of land. Taste the two Pinot Noirs, 'The Matriarch' and 'The Prophet', each from separate vineyards and make up your own mind. Another highlight at Mandala is the restaurant, which serves Mediterranean-influenced food.
www.mandalawines.com.au; tel +61 03 5965 2016; 1568 Melba Hwy, Dixons Creek; 11am-4pm Mon-Fri, 10am-5pm Sat-Sun

02 TARRAWARRA ESTATE

No other winery in the Yarra Valley has quite the same visual effect as Marc and Eva Besen's remarkable creation. Shadows cast by concrete columns sweep across a courtyard framed by rammed-earth walls and the arcing glass of the TarraWarra Museum of Art. The complex rests atop a ridge between Healesville and Yarra Glen and is the work of Melbourne architect Allan Powell, who seems to have been inspired by the Yarra's light and its earth.

With a carpark often filled with sportscars, an entrance that curls between high-sided walls before opening out to views over vines and landscaped grounds to the north, visiting this winery is certainly an event. Luckily Clare Halloran's wines stand up to the build-up: her Chardonnay, typically aged 10 months in oak, is a well-defined example of the grape. The other big draw here is the TarraWarra Museum of Art, which hosts exhibitions of modern (post-1950) Australian art from the Besens' own collection.
www.tarrawarra.com.au; www.twma.com.au; tel +61 03 5962 3311; 311 Healesville-Yarra Glen Road, Yarra Glen; 11am-5pm daily

03 YERINGBERG

It was the gold diggers who first followed the Yarra Track up to Victoria's goldfields in the 1850s, because the Yarra River couldn't be crossed in flood. The track became a road, and as people settled in the valley, vines started to flower and the first wine boom swept the Yarra in the 1880s.

The second wave of pioneers, such as Guill de Pury, arrived in the 1960s and his Yeringberg winery stands on the site of an original 150-year-old vineyard and many

01 The Yarra Valley

02 Yeringberg

03 TarraWarra Estate

04 Harvest at Mandala Wines

05 Food at TarraWarra Estate

Courtesy of Visions of Victoria, Mandala, Yeringberg

of its features date from that era. Another connection with the past is Yeringberg's Marsanne Roussane white wine, which uses the grape varieties originally planted in the Yarra and happens to age beautifully. ***www.yeringberg.com; 810 Maroondah Hwy, Coldstream; visits by appointment***

04 WARRAMATE

They've got a few 'roos loose in the top paddock at Warramate. But they won't take offence if you point this out. 'Oh yes, they're always up in the top field during the day, but as the sun sets they come down to the vines in front of the cellar door,' says owner June Church. 'We planted oats down each aisle. It makes the grass sweeter so the kangaroos prefer to eat that than munch on our vines.' Jack and June Church retired to Warramate, one of the oldest vineyards in the Yarra Valley, 30 years ago but son David does the winemaking now. Unlike many Yarra wineries, here they cultivate several grape varieties, including Cabernet Sauvignon, Pinot Noir, Riesling and the winery's signature Shiraz.

Warramate's wonderful location, with views east and west across the valley from the wooden verandah is very appealing. The wide-spaced vines are managed by a system of minimal intervention. They handpick all the grapes, do their own bottling and refuse to irrigate the vines. 'Jack saw how it worked in Europe 40 years ago with no power and no water,' explains June. 'You don't need water for good grapes, just deep roots. We strive for quality not quantity.' It's a pretension-free place where the wine is allowed to speak for itself. The results can be variable, but so is nature.

Courtesy of TarraWarra Estate

Courtesy of Visions of Victoria, Steven Morris © Getty Image

06 Giant Steps / Innocent Bystander in Healesville

07 Coldstream Hills

www.warramatewines.com.au; tel +61 03 5964 9219 27; Maddens Lane, Gruyere; 10am–6pm daily

05 COLDSTREAM HILLS

Is it inviting payback to start a winery when you're Australia's best-known wine critic? The question didn't stop James Halliday, who put his money where his mouth was and founded Coldstream Hills in 1985. After all, how hard can it be? With Andrew Fleming in charge of the winemaking, the wines, especially the Pinot Noir, have been widely praised. In part their success has been down to the setting of the closely planted vines around a natural, north-facing amphitheatre, much as they would be in Europe.
www.coldstreamhills.com.au; tel +61 03 5960 7000; 31 Maddens Lane, Gruyere, 10am–5pm daily

06 MORGAN VINEYARDS

It was a retired Welsh ex-Army captain, Roger Morgan, who planted this vineyard, now owned by Simon and Michele Gunther, who are renovating the cellar door. And if a Welsh man can complain about the weather, that says something about the climate of this corner of Australia: 'You get extremes of weather here – some years can be really hot and dry with winds from the north, but cold weather systems also roll in from the south.' That unpredictability continues in Roger's grape of choice: the enigmatic, frustrating Pinot Noir. Pinot Noir, he explained, likes cool, sunny places, such as Tasmania, New Zealand and the Yarra Valley. 'It's a thin-skinned, disease-prone grape, so I planted it on the east side of the north-facing vineyard where it gets the morning sun, which dries the canopy.' On the west side of the vineyard he planted Cabernet Sauvignon, a robust grape that can take the heat of the afternoon sun. At 30 years of age, the vines are in the prime of their life. The result is a tangy Pinot Noir and a food-friendly, mineral-rich Chardonnay.
www.morganvineyards.com.au; tel +61 03 5964 4807; 30 Davross Court, Seville; 11am–4pm Mon–Fri, 11am–5pm Sat–Sun

07 FIVE OAKS

Wally Zuk is the brains behind Five Oaks. Once Australia's leading nuclear physicist, the genial Canadian retired in 1999 to his hilltop vineyard just south of the Lilydale–Woori Yallock road and now applies science to getting the best possible wine from his rows of Cabernet Sauvignon. He picked his spot after careful research: 'The top soil at Five Oaks is 25m deep on a layer of coal, which gives us great drainage. We're in the lee of Mt Dandenong so we don't suffer from frost or hail.'

Five Oaks, named after the five oak trees between the cellar door and the Zuks' house, produces some of the best Cabernet Sauvignon in the Yarra Valley. While other wineries have taken on the challenges of Pinot Noir, Zuk has specialised in developing his favourite grape; a vertical tasting of his Cabernets reveal that they just get better and better. Exceptional years are bottled as SGS (Seriously Good Shit) reserves. 'The SGS is picked from the top 25 rows in the vineyard,' explains Wally. 'The south side gets the most sun but all three distinct areas have undergone separate crushings since 1997.'

Thanks to the vineyard's elevated position, Wally's grapes get a little more growing time than grapes down in the valley. 'From late January and February onwards vines put a huge effort into fruit,' he explains. 'The flavour goes into the skins and they don't need much more water, just warm weather and sunshine.' The later the harvest, the more sugar in the fruit. After pressing, the grape juice is aged in French oak barrels. But the spirit of scientific investigation continues at the Zuks' Hail-A-Cab tastings (tickets $55), when, after a tasting of his CabSavs since 1998, the guests get to mix their own blends.
www.fiveoaks.com.au; tel +61 03 5964 3704; 60 Aitken Road, Seville; 10am–5pm Sat–Sun, other times by appointment

ESSENTIAL INFORMATION

WHERE TO STAY

HEALESVILLE HOTEL
If creaky floorboards and antique plumbing don't put you off, the Healesville Hotel, approaching its centenary, is an atmospheric base for exploring the region.
www.healesvillehotel.com.au; tel +61 03 5962 1037; 256 Maroondah Hwy, Healesville

WHERE TO EAT

GIANT STEPS / INNOCENT BYSTANDER
While you're enjoying pizza straight from the wood-fired oven, you can watch the Giant Steps / Innocent Bystander winery at work from the split-level dining room. Founders Allison and Phil Sexton (the brewer who brought Little Creatures beer to the world, earning the everlasting gratitude of many drinkers) have added a cheese room, an artisan bakery and even house-roasted coffee to their cellar door.
www.innocentbystander.com.au; tel +61 03 5692 6111; 336 Maroondah Hwy, Healesville

YARRA VALLEY DAIRY
Pay homage to the fromage at the Yarra Valley Dairy, the best place to buy cheese in the area. Hard or soft, most cheeses are made on-site. An eating area behind the counter is where you can enjoy a platter of cheeses, crackers and olives.
www.yvd.com.au; tel +61 03 9739 0023; McMeikan's Rd, Yering

WHAT TO DO

Get up close to more than 200 species of Australian creatures, including Tasmanian devils, koalas and sleepy wombats at the Healesville Sanctuary.
www.zoo.org.au/healesville

Lift off at sunrise for an hour-long flight over the vineyards followed by breakfast at Yering Station.
www.gowildballooning.com.au

CELEBRATIONS

On the second weekend of October each year, the smaller wineries along the Warburton Hwy open their doors for ShedFest. It's an opportunity to meet the winemakers, try wines you'd otherwise miss, and enjoy great food and some live music.

01

[Canada]

NIAGARA

Experience the Niagara region's constantly improving wines and cheery, vacation-style lakeside atmosphere along well-orchestrated rural wine trails.

A young and exciting wine region, and Canada's largest, Niagara sits on the southern shores of Lake Ontario, two hours south of Toronto, and is home to more than just ice wine. The Niagara Escarpment, a long ridge formed by ancient erosion, is responsible not only for the mesmerising waterfall, but also for a singular *terroir* with a diversity of soil types. Add that to a latitude of 43°N (equivalent to Avignon in the Rhône) and big shifts between day and night temperatures, and there is a potential here for a panoply of different grapes, despite the fairly level vineyard lands. Unlike other youthful wine zones around the world, there's little pressure to wed Niagara's identity to any single one. Still whites, reds, even sparkling wines are made in Niagara with equal success, at wineries of varying size and scope.

It's hard to overstate the growth rate: by 1974 – long after Niagara's hybrid-grape-fuelled heyday at the turn of the 19th century – only six wineries remained in the Niagara region. Today, nearly 100 wineries are located here, working with over 32 different varietals, mostly *vinifera*. The feeling on the ground is like that of starting over. As a visitor, it's easy to be infected with that same giddy sense that anything is possible, especially after experiencing the hospitality of Niagara's many historic villages and its beautiful lakefront views.

GET THERE
Buffalo-Niagara is the nearest major airport, 61km from Inniskillin. Car hire is available.

Of course, long before a modern wine scene took root, Niagara was an international tourist mecca, thanks to the enduring attraction of the nearby falls, a cluster of Canada's prettiest towns and a bevy of natural hikes and getaways. A strong hospitality network has thrived here for decades, and the rapid growth of 'wine tourism' in Niagara is built on it. A warm and professional welcome awaits every guest, not only at the tasting rooms and vineyards, but also in the numerous cafes, bakeries, restaurants and shops.

Along with Prince Edward County, it will be exciting to see what the future will bring for this rising region.

Courtesy of Pearl Morissette

Courtesy of Ravine Vineyard Estate Winery

01 INNISKILLIN WINES

Inniskillin is a foundational estate for modern Niagara; when it received its winery licence in 1975, it was the first to have done so in decades, and it helped kick off the new growth we're witnessing today. Inniskillin was central in helping identify Niagara with sweet ice wine – and is still most famous for its ice wines of Riesling, Vidal and Cabernet Franc. However, it produces a very wide range of still wines, white and red, in multiple tiers of quality. It is obviously a larger producer with multiple interests, but a visit and tasting here is essential to understanding Niagara's past and present. Located just a few minutes off the Niagara River, up Line 3 Rd, enter the estate's stately white gates for a warm welcome; the grounds include a wine bar and a casual seasonal grill.

www.inniskillin.com; tel +1 905-468-2187; 1499 Line 3 Niagara Pkwy, Niagara-on-the-Lake; 10am-6pm summer, to 5pm winter

02 FROGPOND FARM

Opened in 2001, Frogpond Farm is proud of being 'Ontario's first organically certified winery'; since 2006, the facilities have been fully powered by 'green' electricity derived from wind and water. As such, it represents one of the many viable directions for the future of Niagara winemaking. Currently, its wines are fairly evenly divided between white and red, including two hybrid wines, from Vidal and Chambourcin. The dry, Alsatian-style Rieslings are of special note.

www.frogpondfarm.ca; tel +1 905-468-1079; 1385 Larkin Rd, Niagara-on-the-Lake; 11am-6pm summer, to 5pm winter

03 RAVINE VINEYARD ESTATE WINERY

Just a few blocks south of Frogpond Farm, this is a new estate (2008) located on an old farm (1867). Fifth-generation owner Norma Jane Harber and her husband Blair work with winemaker Martin Warner to produce a fairly wide range of well-known international varietals – Chardonnay, Riesling, Cabernet Sauvignon and Merlot. The Cabernet Franc, however, is probably their finest wine – and one of Ontario's best – thanks to the warmth of their sites. Make sure to taste their two bottlings in the cask room.

Here, you can participate in a range of themed visits, suited to your interests, such as a Historical Tour or a Winemaking Tour, or a private tasting. There is also an excellent farm-to-table restaurant, which might be the

01 Meet the locals at Pearl Morissette

02 Ravine Vineyard Estate Winery

03 Wine by Pearl Morissette

04 Inniskillin Winery

'[Niagara] is a very, very challenging area to grow grapes. Now it is changing – there is a new generation that is very much embracing the local movement.'

–François Morissette, winemaker of Pearl Morissette

Courtesy of Pearl Morissette

real star of the whole project. *www.ravinevineyard.com; tel +1 905-262-8463; 1366 York Rd, St Davids; themed tours multiple times daily*

04 PEARL MORISSETTE

Partner Mel Pearl and winemaker François Morissette represent one of the few, and finest, estates to ask 'which grape varietal expresses the best wine for Niagara?' and act on it. To discover the answer, they've spared little effort or expense. Burgundy-trained François works with over 12 hectares (30 acres) of Cabernet Franc, Chardonnay, Pinot Noir and Riesling from two separate vineyards (and appellations) of variable age. The cellar is one of the coolest in Canada: filled with a host of different ageing vessels, it speaks of a restless search for the finest wine. Pearl Morissette's high quality,

Wolfgang Kaehler © Getty Images

however, is mostly due to the vines' impeccable management – if you visit between spring and autumn, ask for a vineyard tour – and don't forget to ask about the swimming pool. Pearl Morissette is located just east of Tawse Vineyard, up Highway 81. *www.pearlmorissette.com; tel +1 905-562-4376; 3953 Jordan Rd, Jordan; Sat & Sun by appointment*

05 TAWSE WINERY

Tawse is one of Niagara's most recognised estates (garnering multiple awards), and one of the largest. Ten varietals are planted in six vineyards over a whopping 80 hectares (200 acres), and are bottled in a wide stylistic range: sparkling, white, rosé, red and dessert. The vineyard practices include a combination of organic and biodynamic methods. The property itself is both grandiose and intimate: a wide driveway leads past manicured lawns, a smart fountain and tree-lined meadows to an impeccably equipped tasting room with a wrap-around bar (where it's easy to mingle with other travellers), and a Euro-style barrel cellar. While here, don't forget to check out the aromatic, tropical Quarry Road Gewürztraminer and the plush Estate Gamay Noir. *www.tawsewinery.ca; tel +1 905-562-9500; 3955 Cherry Ave, Vineland; 10am-5pm Mon-Fri, 10am-6pm Sat & Sun*

Courtesy of Vineland Estates

05-06 Vineland Estates Winery and its restaurant

07 Ravine Vineyard's restaurant

ESSENTIAL INFORMATION

WHERE TO STAY

INN ON THE TWENTY

This fairly luxe 'hospitality wing' of Cave Spring Vineyards – the tasting room of which is across the street – offers nearly every amenity, including a spa, and a restaurant with long experience of pairing Ontario wines with local food (the dinner menu includes recommended pairings – from Cave Springs, of course). The wine list also showcases a respectable selection of Niagara wines from other producers. *www.innonthetwenty.com; tel +1 905-562-5336; 3845 Main St, Jordan Station*

PRINCE OF WALES

On a cool pedestrian-friendly street in the heart of one of the area's most charming cities, this historic landmark, fully restored in 1999, has been a hotel since 1864. Its proper Victorian exterior fronts tree-lined Simcoe Park, is down the street from the famed Shaw Festival, and is three blocks from the Niagara River. *www.vintage-hotels.com/princeofwales; tel +1 905-468-3246; 6 Picton St, Niagara-on-the-Lake*

WHERE TO EAT

RAVINE VINEYARD RESTAURANT

In addition to the winery, the folks at Ravine also run a terrific, award-winning farm-to-table restaurant, where they bake their own bread, raise their own pigs and serve their own organic produce. Yhe menus are seasonal. *www.ravinevineyard.com/restaurant; tel +1 905-262-8463; 1366 York Rd, St Davids; lunch 11am-3pm, dinner 5-9pm*

VINELAND ESTATES WINERY RESTAURANT

A couple of blocks south of Tawse Winery, this is a classy lunch destination. The restaurant is housed in a beautiful 19th-century farmhouse, above a wine cellar where vintages go back to 1983, and features classic Euro-Canadian dishes made with local ingredients. *www.vineland.com; tel +1 888-846-3526; 3620 Moyer Rd, Vineland*

WHAT TO DO

THE SHAW FESTIVAL THEATRE

This is one of the largest theatre festivals in North America, with year-round performances of Bernard Shaw classics scheduled alongside current plays. *www.shawfest.com; tel +1 905-468-2172; 10 Queen's Parade, Niagara-on-the-Lake*

LAKESIDE PARK BEACH

This popular lakefront destination on the north side of St Catharines is central to summer attractions, including Fishing Adventures and a Harbour Trail.

CELEBRATIONS

The last three weekends of January, the sprawling Niagara Icewine Festival celebrates Ontario's proudest product in multiple locations throughout the town of Niagara-on-the-Lake. At the New Vintage Festival in St Catharines, during the middle of June, visitors can taste fresh bottlings from nearly 30 regional wineries.

Courtesy of Ravine Vineyard Estate Winery

01

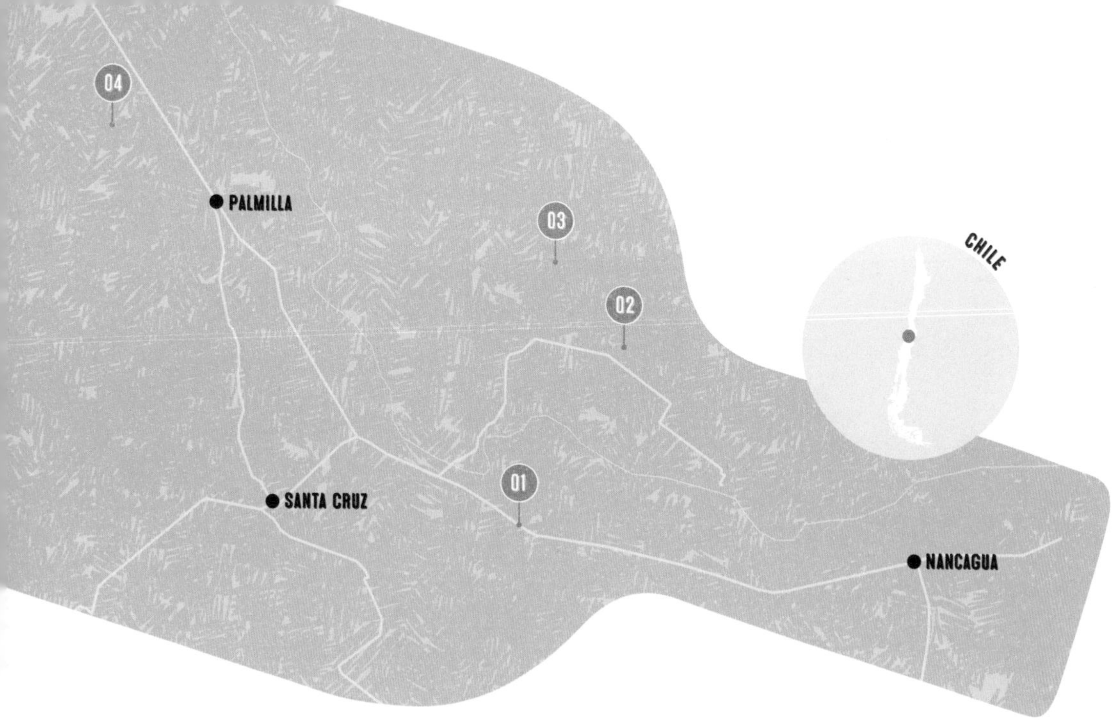

PALMILLA
SANTA CRUZ
NANCAGUA
CHILE
01
02
03
04

Courtesy of Vina Lapostolle

[Chile]

COLCHAGUA

Chilean wine is shaking up the wine world and the Colchagua Valley, a tranquil spot between the mountains and the Pacific Ocean, is where to surrender to its charms.

Wedged between the Andes and the Pacific Ocean, Chile has the perfect landscape and climate for growing grapes: ample sunshine, cool nights, rich soil and abundant water. Although memorable Carmenères and Sauvignon Blancs are produced in several regions, the Colchagua Valley, located just two hours' drive south of Santiago, is the country's largest and most well-known, and coming years will see continued expansion of the region into the hillsides and towards the sea.

Perhaps somewhat surprisingly, given the quantity and quality of wine made here, the Colchagua isn't overly developed for tourism. Santa Cruz, the town in the heart of the region, remains a relatively quiet place; local organisations such as Ruta del Vino, with a helpful office on the town's main square, assist visitors to make the most of their time. Transportation can be costly and difficult to arrange, so most travellers who intend to visit several wineries rent cars in Santiago and drive down.

The tranquillity, at any rate, is part of the Colchagua Valley charm. And just because it's quiet doesn't mean it's not cutting edge: many of the scene's pioneers are younger entrepreneurs and winemakers who've only set up their businesses in the last decade or two. The old vines are the secret: red wines produced here are world famous, consistently ranking among *Wine Enthusiast*'s lists of most exciting wines, and the region is widely considered one of the most important in all of South America. Indeed, thanks to these sophisticated wineries and the striking natural landscape, Colchagua often draws comparisons with Napa Valley. Taste the wine while looking at a map and considering a detour to the beach – you'll see that California and Chile have more in common than you expected.

GET THERE
Santiago is the nearest major airport, 172km from Santa Cruz. Car hire is available.

Courtesy of Vina Lapostolle, Viu Manent

01 VIU MANENT

This family-owned winery is a destination in itself: in 2015, as part of its Wine Tourism Awards, the UK's *Drinks International* magazine named Viu Manent's La Llavería the top winery visitor centre. That's because there's more to do than sip and swirl: in addition to tastings, the winery offers horse-drawn carriage rides through the vineyards, cooking classes, an equestrian centre, a fair-trade boutique, a cafe where you can balance out the wine with a strong cappuccino and free wi-fi so you can Instagram the whole thing.

How about the wine itself? Just flip through a copy of *Wine Spectator*: the single vineyard Cabernet Sauvignon and Malbec from 2011 both scored a high 90 points. The winery is steeped in tradition: the brand was founded in 1935 by a father-son team of Catalonian immigrants to Chile. ***www.viumanent.cl; tel +56 2-379 0020; Carretera del Vino km 37, Cunaco; 10.30am-5pm daily***

02 MONTES

This well-respected winery started out as the passion project of a man who didn't know much about the subject. 'My only contact with wine was Sunday lunch – and that was it,' says Aurelio Montes of his lifestyle before taking his first agronomy course at university. By 1987, he says, he was eager to challenge local winemaking standards. 'Chilean wineries were not going for quality,' said Montes. 'They were happy to make an average product to sell for an average price. I wanted to make high-quality wines.'

That he did: you can taste the brand's signature reds at his modern winery, set into the hillsides. Stay for lunch with wine pairings at Bistro Alfredo – the chef specialises in the seafood cuisine of Chilean Patagonia – and finish with a guided hike into the hills looking over the vines. ***www.monteswines.com; tel +56 72-281 7815; Camino a Milahue de Apalta s/n; 9am-6pm daily***

03 VIÑA LAPOSTOLLE / CLOS APALTA

Lapostolle is the most exclusive winery in the valley, and arguably in all of Chile, a level of prestige that can be explained in two words: Grand Marnier. The Marnier Lapostolle family founded and owns the brand of the world-famous liqueur, so it stands to reason that they're adept at making wine, too. Indeed, these Chilean wines, produced using French techniques, are considered some of the country's best – 'French in essence, Chilean by birth' is the brand's tagline.

But the family's ascent to the top was quick: they've only been making wine here since the mid-1990s. 'I couldn't imagine we could produce a wine like Clos Apalta quite that quickly,' cofounder Alexandra Marnier Lapostolle has said of her arrival on the Chilean wine scene in 1994. 'But from the very beginning I knew we had great *terroir* and vines which were between 60 and 80 years old,

01 The wine cellar at Lapostolle

02 Travel the old-fashioned way at Viu Manent

03 Grape harvesting at Lapostolle

and I knew we had the potential, providing we focused on quality.'

The winery is located in a traditional Chilean-style hacienda in the town of Cunaco, a short drive from Santa Cruz. A range of tasting and tour options are available, including a horseback-riding tour through the vineyards, and Lapostolle will provide complimentary transportation from Santa Cruz. *www.lapostolle.com; tel +56 72-2953 350; Ruta I-50, Camino San Fernando a Pichilemu, km 36, Cunaquito; 10.30am-5.30pm Mon-Sat, 10.30am tour Sun*

04 MONTGRAS

Not to worry if a horse-drawn carriage ride through the vineyards sounds too sedate for your taste: you can also zip-line over the beautiful scenery at MontGras. This friendly winery attracts adventurous types with activities from horseback riding and hiking to mountain biking.

Even the wine tasting can be a hands-on opportunity here if you sign up for one of the 'make your own wine' workshops. The pioneering winemakers are known for experimenting with new technology and for their role in establishing the Colchagua Valley Wine Route to bring more tourists to the region. *Wine Enthusiast* called their 2009 Quatro Red 'always one of Chile's best values; an overperformer year after year'. *www.montgras.cl; tel +56 72-2822 845; Camino a Isla de Yáquil s/n, Palmilla; open 10am-4.30pm*

ESSENTIAL INFORMATION

WHERE TO STAY

HOTEL SANTA CRUZ PLAZA

In the town of Santa Cruz, the Hotel Santa Cruz Plaza is elegant and central. The lovely swimming pool is the perfect place to relax. *www.hotelsantacruzplaza.cl; tel +56 72-2209 600; Plaza de Armas 286, Santa Cruz*

HOTEL TERRAVIÑA

Set among the vineyards of a long-running family winery, this cosy wine lodge is a travellers' favourite in the region. *www.terravina.cl; tel +56 72-2821 284; Camino Los Boldos s/n, Santa Cruz*

WHERE TO EAT

VINO BELLO

A gourmet Italian restaurant – the only one in town – with romantic al-fresco seating overlooking the vineyards. Vino Bello is in the same winery complex as Hotel TerraViña. *www.vino-bello.com; tel +56 72-2822 755; Barreales s/n, Santa Cruz*

PANPAN VINOVINO

A restored bakery that dates from 1830, this casual but classic Chilean eatery is 6km (4 miles) outside Santa Cruz on the Carretera del Vino. *panpanvinovino.cl; tel +56 9-5193 823; ; I-50, km 31, Cunaco*

WHAT TO DO

Santa Cruz is home to the largest private museum in Chile. The Museo de Colchagua includes pre-Columbian artefacts, weapons, Mapuche silver, vintage cars, and steam-driven machinery and winemaking equipment. Stop by for an hour; it will give you a helpful insight into the wine region's cultural context. *www.museocolchagua.cl; tel +56 72-2821 050; Errázuriz 145, Santa Cruz*

CELEBRATIONS

Colchagua's annual Fiesta de la Vendimia celebrates the autumn grape harvest at the start of March. Wine flows freely at the local wineries' stands in the Plaza de Armas; highlights include traditional food, singing, dancing and the crowning of a harvest queen. Book well ahead: the quiet town sees a huge influx of visitors. *www.vendimiadesantacruz.com*

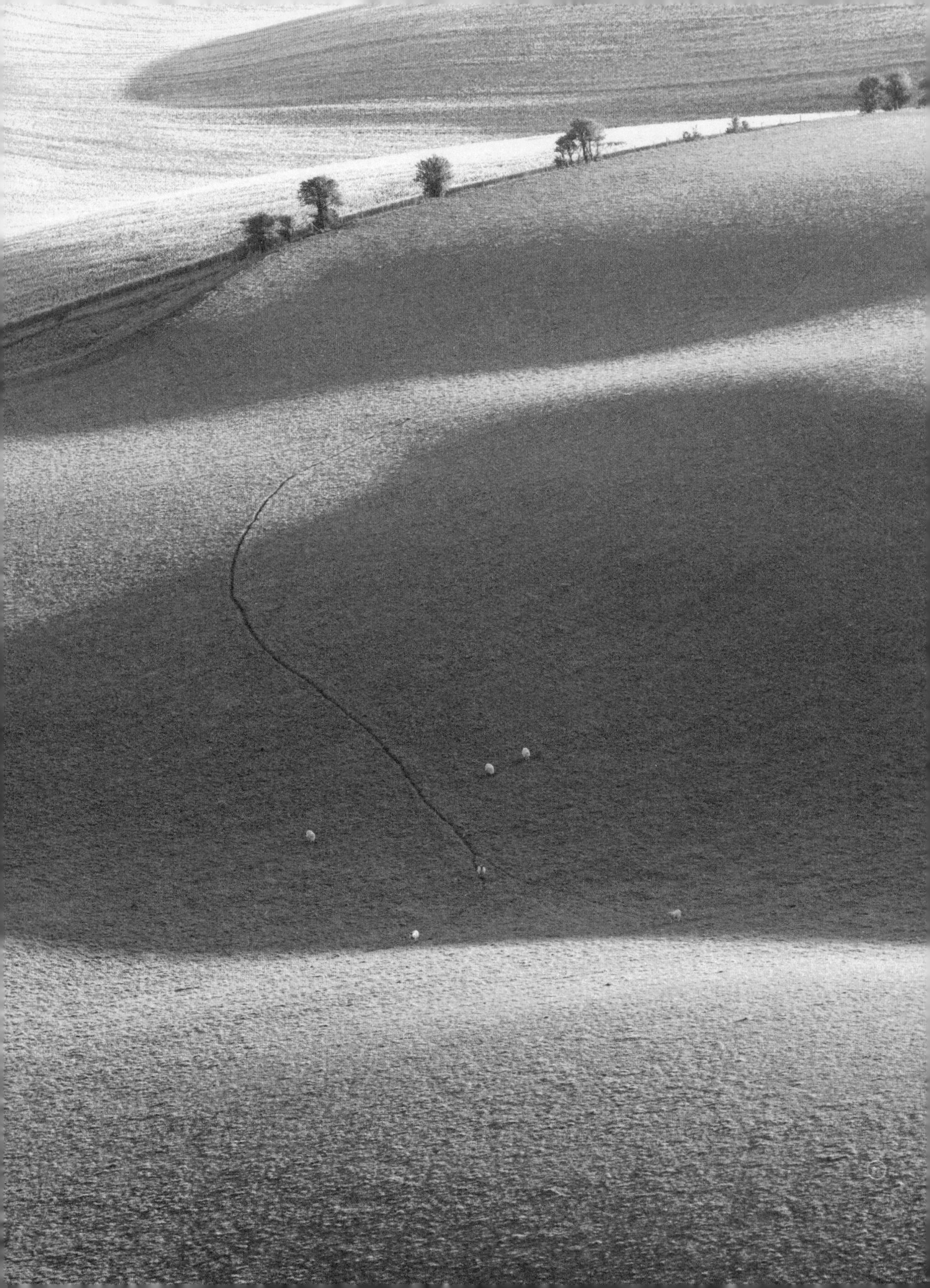

Slawek Staszczuk © Alamy

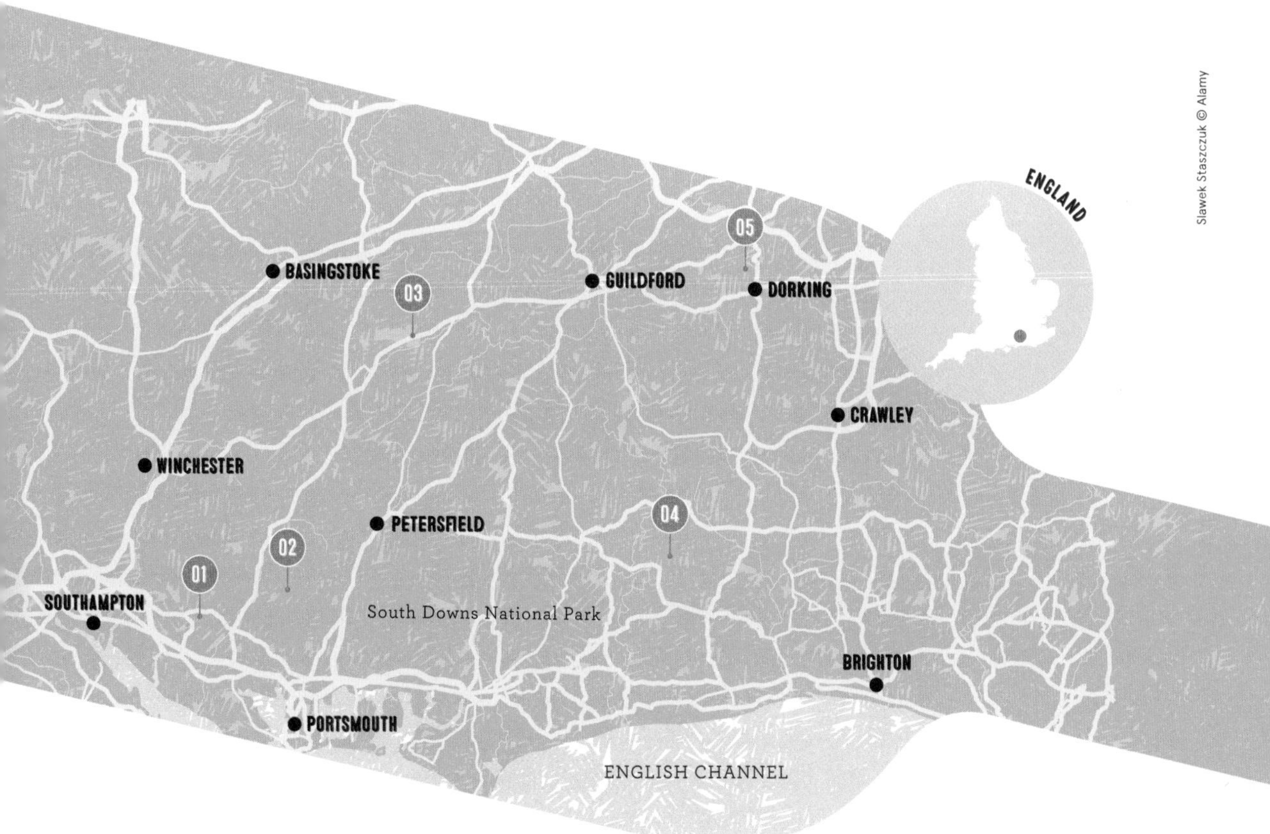

[England]

SOUTH DOWNS

It's fizzy, refined and winning awards: English white wine sparkles in the summer, the perfect time to take a tour of Southern England's vineyards.

Overhead a skylark sings in the blue sky. Green fields sweep down from a chalk ridge laced with white tracks. To the south lies the sea, to the north the counties of Hampshire and Sussex. These are England's South Downs in summer, a place of villages, hiking trails and, incredibly to some, vineyards. For the South Downs, now a National Park, are a narrow, 160km-long spine of chalk hills that run southeast all the way from Winchester, an ancient capital of England, to Eastbourne, and then the same seam of rock re-emerges on the other side of the Channel in Champagne country.

English wine was long a laughing stock, not least among the French, being too thin, too sour or over-sweetened. But in the last ten years, the South Downs region has been the source of some excellent Champagne-style sparkling wines. In truth, England's wineries are spread out over quite a distance, from Tenterden in Kent to others in Cornwall, and a tour taking in all of them would be impracticable. They don't all lie on the South Downs; many are further inland, and few are open to the public (so far - that will change). But there are a few concentrated in tranquil Hampshire to make a weekend exploring English wine and some of the county's other attractions enjoyable and, perhaps, something of a revelation.

GET THERE
Southampton and London Gatwick are the closest airports but the region is only an hour from London by train

Courtesy of Jenkyn Place

01 THREE CHOIRS

As the twisted vines testify, this vineyard in Wickham, on the south-west tip of the South Downs National Park, is one of the oldest in England. But English vine-growing goes much further back; at the time of the Norman Conquest in the 11th century grapes were being made into wine.

Currently, Three Choirs is better known for its restaurant, serving locally sourced produce.
www.three-choirs-vineyards.co.uk/hampshire; tel +44 (0)1329 834700; Botley Rd, Shedfield, Southampton; 2.30pm Wed-Sun cheese & wine tour (fee applies)

02 HAMBLEDON VINEYARD

It's been 10 years since Chardonnay vines were planted at Hambledon. 'The chalk on which we grow our vines was formed on the seabed of the Paris basin some 65 million years ago,' says managing director Ian Kellett. 'The same chalk is found in the best Chardonnay areas of the Côtes des Blancs in Champagne.' With winemakers Hérve Jestin of Champagne Duval Leroy, and Antoine Arnault, a graduate of Reims University, on board, Hambledon's French connection is strong.

A short drive north of Three Choirs, Hambledon Vineyard is set in the idyllic Hampshire village of the same name, a place of hills, fields, woods and little-used flint-strewn lanes.
www. hambledonvineyard.co.uk; tel +44 (0)2392 632358; Hambledon; visits by appointment

03 JENKYN PLACE

'We were at an event at Nyetimber in 2004,' recalls Simon Bladon, 'and the wine was very good. I asked them where it was from and they said "here". So I came back and planted a field of vines, as you do.' Jenkyn Place is on the northern edge of the chalk band, with the Downs about half an hour's drive south. This is a very pretty corner of Hampshire, close to Chawton where author Jane Austen lived. Jenkyn Place is open to the public for only a few days in July each year, as part of the Hampshire Fare food festival - but summer's the best time to visit anyway.
www.jenkynplace.com, www.hampshirefare.co.uk; Hole Lane, Bentley; open days in July

04 NUTBOURNE VINEYARD

Cross the border into West Sussex to visit Nutbourne Vineyard. Nearby Nyetimber may have been in the vanguard of the English sparkling wine revolution – but it's not open to the public. However, Nutbourne in Pulborough is open to all, and in 2015 its still white wine won a gold medal

Courtesy of Nutbourne Vineyards

at the International Wine and Spirit Competition, the first English still wine to win. The sparkling wines are also sensational.

The family-owned winery is based in a 19th-century windmill midway along the Downs. The Jazz in the Vines concerts take place in August. *www.nutbournevineyards.com; tel +44 (0)1798 815196; Gay St, Pulborough; 2pm-5 Tue-Fri May-Oct; 11am-5pm Sat & bank holidays*

05 DENBIES WINE ESTATE

From Pulborough, turn towards the North Downs for Denbies in Dorking, one of England's largest vineyards. It specialises in sparkling white wines; with the Demi-Sec displaying classic Champagne scents of brioche and pear. *www.denbies.co.uk; tel +44 (0)1306 876 616; London Rd, Dorking; 9.30am-5.30pm daily Apr-Oct; to 5pm Nov-Mar*

01 The South Downs National Park

02 Simon Bladon of Jenkyn Place

03 Nutbourne Vineyards

ESSENTIAL INFORMATION

WHERE TO STAY

HOTEL DU VIN

For city-centre accommodation and a well-crafted wine list, try the Hotel du Vin in Winchester, gateway city at the west end of the South Downs. Part of a chain that prides itself on its wine, there's another Hotel du Vin in Brighton at the opposite end of the South Downs. *www.hotelduvin.com; Winchester & Brighton*

THE FLINT BARNS

At the eastern end of the Downs, the Rathfinny Estate, a newly planted vineyard near the white cliffs of Beachy Head, offers accommodation in basic but modern and comfortable rooms. It's part of a redevelopment that also includes a tasting room - but you'll have to wait until 2017 to try the first sparkling wines. *www.rathfinnyestate.com; Alfriston, East Sussex*

WHERE TO EAT

HAWKLEY INN

Between Jenkyn Place and Nutbourne Vineyard, close to Hampshire's border with Sussex, this country pub does superb lunches, which can be enjoyed in the large garden if the weather permits. *www.hawkleyinn.co.uk; tel +44 (0)1730 827205; Hawkley*

JSW

Jake Watkins' inn-with-rooms has a Michelin-starred restaurant serving Modern British dishes. *jswrestaurant.com; tel +44 (0)1730 262030; 20 Dragon St, Petersfield*

WHAT TO DO

Now a national park, the South Downs have long attracted hikers, mountain bikers and horse riders. The South Downs Way trail runs, up and down, for 160km (100 miles) from Winchester to Eastbourne but is accessible at lots of points so you can stretch your legs a section at a time. *www.southdowns.gov.uk*

CELEBRATIONS

The annual Hampshire Food Festival in July is a month-long, county-wide celebration of local produce, from buffalo mozzarella near Stockbridge to gin from Winchester. The wine events, including pop-up suppers and tasting tours are always popular. *www.hampshirefare.co.uk*

01

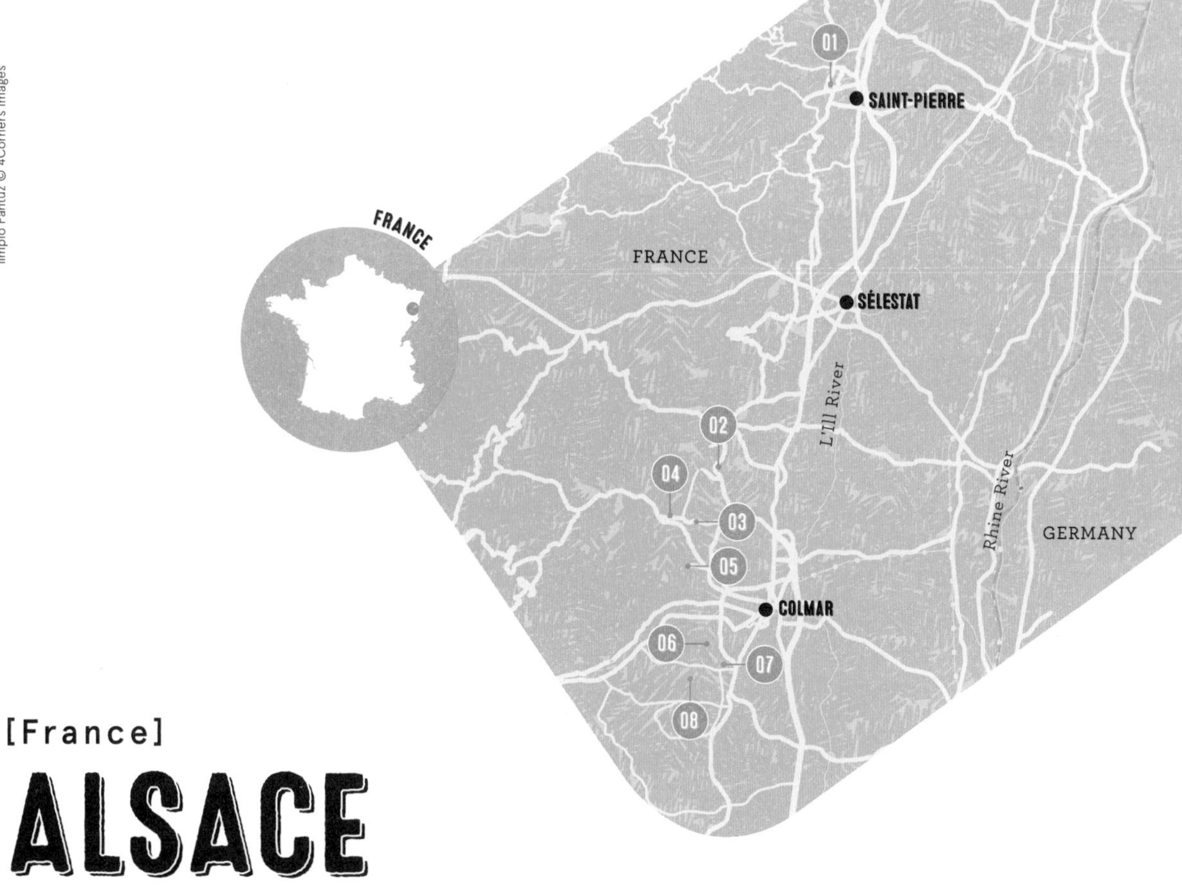

[France]

ALSACE

Take a trip through the picturesque villages of northeast France to sample distinctive white wines among traditional, timbered wineries.

Winemaking in Alsace has had its ups and downs throughout a long history that begins with the Romans planting the first grapes. In the Middle Ages, records show 160 villages growing vines, while by the 16th century, they were making some of the most prized wines in Europe. Then came 300 years of war, phylloxera and political ping-pong, with the territory passed back and forth between France and Germany. A renaissance has taken place over the last 50 years, seeing a significant increase in quality, and today Alsace is in the vanguard of the movement towards organic cultivation. The picture-perfect vine-clad hillsides here are the ultimate *terroir* for white wines, with Pinot Noir the only red among the seven official grape varieties. Each village, each winemaker, creates a complex patchwork of interpretations of Riesling, Gewürztraminer, Pinot Blanc and Gris, Muscat and Sylvaner.

Nowhere in France can compare when it comes to the welcome given to wine tourists. Alsace was the first region to organise its own Route du Vin, some 60 years ago, and today local *vignerons* are always coming up with new ideas to attract winelovers: bike tours and marathon races through the vines, food and wine fairs, a procession honouring Alsace's iconic Gewürztraminer past the fairy-tale half-timbered houses of Bergheim (a strong candidate for the most beautiful village in France) and night-time illuminations of medieval churches as bottles of bubbly Crémant are popped in celebration. And throughout Alsace there is a long tradition of winemakers opening up their rustic houses as welcoming *chambres d'hôte*, the French version of a B&B. Rather than a formal tasting, guests are often privileged to sit down with the winemaker after work in the evening for a relaxed session trying some of his favourite vintages, a long aperitif that often ends up continuing over dinner in the local bistro.

GET THERE
EuroAirport Basel Mulhouse Freiburg is the nearest major airport, 99km from Mittelbergheim. Car hire is available.

'Alsace produces the ultimate gastronomic wines, perfect to pair with everything from spicy Szechuan noodles to an Indian curry, sushi to Stilton.'

–Etienne Hugel, vigneron

01 DOMAINE ALBERT SELTZ

Mittelbergheim may be a member of France's exclusive 100 'Plus Beaux Villages', but it is totally unspoilt and rarely visited. Local *vigneron* Albert Seltz is a 16th-generation winemaker and a champion of the humble Sylvaner, which he describes as 'the grape no one wants to talk about and prefers to imagine does not exist'. Sylvaner is often overlooked compared to the likes of Riesling, and Seltz went on a crusade to make French officialdom recognise the Sylvaner vines around here as a Grand cru. Visitors can sit back as Albert takes them through a dozen of his sensational Sylvaner vintages, from the wonderfully drinkable Mittelbergheim Village through to a seductive 2001 Vieilles Vignes, which he poetically describes: 'Look at the colour, a dull gold that is autumn. Smell the nose; now imagine that with sautéed wild mushrooms'. Don't expect to see official certification on his bottles, though, as Albert exclaims, 'Me, pay for bureaucrats to control my wines? You've got to be joking! I'm not Bio, I'm not Biodynamique, I'm Albert Seltz!'
www.albert-seltz.fr; tel +33 3 88 08 91 77; 21 Rue Principale, Mittelbergheim

02 DOMAINE BECKER

This friendly, unpretentious winery is a typical example of how Alsace *vignerons* have grasped the potential of wine tourism, selling large amounts of their production directly to visitors arriving for a tasting. An old barn of the Beckers' rambling farm has been converted into a giant *wistub* (traditional Alsatian winebar), with an ambience more like a jolly pub than a sophisticated wine bar, and in addition to her own organic wines Martine Becker also promotes local specialities: snails, honey, jam, foie gras and distinctive Alsace pottery. Martine is a real character, always ready to jump in her battered Citroën Deux Chevaux for a bumpy ride in the vineyard, and is a mine of legendary village tales: 'Can you imagine that during the Second World War over 150 of the villagers used to sleep down in our cellar at night to avoid bombs – and Papa said they also

01 The village of Niedermorschwihr

02 The Alsace region brims with charm

03 In the gardens at Vignoble Klur

04 Maison Emile Beyer is in the village of Eguisheim

© John Brunton

drunk a lot of our stock to avoid the occupying German army getting it!' *www.vinsbecker.com; tel +33 3 89 47 90 16; 4 Route d'Ostheim, Zellenberg*

03 DOMAINE PAUL BLANCK ET FILS

Sitting in the rustic wood-panelled tasting room of Domaine Blanck's 16th-century cellar, surrounded by vast oak casks painted with traditional Alsatian scenes, it is quickly apparent that Philippe Blanck is expert at explaining the complex world of Alsace wines, from a simple Sylvaner to a Grand cru Pinot Gris, or the difference between the luscious Gewürztraminer late harvest, Vendange Tardive, and the opulent nectar of Grains Noble, created by *botyris cinerea* – noble rot. Pulling the cork from a bottle of rare Pinot Noir Grand cru, Philippe offers advice that is appropriate for all Alsace cellar visitors: 'Rather than just drop by in the hope of a tasting, people should understand that it is always worth calling first for an appointment, the genuine way of meeting and exchanging views with the winemaker. Visitors here should do three things: see our fabulous vineyard landscapes, try the wine with the winemaker himself, then ask him where to eat, as our wines are best when you taste Alsatian cuisine at the same time'. *www.blanck.com; tel +33 3 89 78 23 56 32; Grand'Rue, Kientzheim*

04 DOMAINE WEINBACH

The Route du Vin that runs into Kaysersberg, another idyllic Alsatian village, is marked by a long stone wall protecting an ancient vineyard, a small part of a 30-hectare (74-acre) estate where Catherine Faller and her son Theo make a sensational selection of wines. The grand mansion and winery behind the wall is an ancient Capuchin monastery where monks planted the surrounding 5-hectare (12-acre) Clos des Capucins in 1612 – documents note they also bred snails! The monks were evicted during the French revolution and Catherine's grandfather bought the property in 1898. Tasting vintages such as the complex, concentrated Pinot Gris Altenbourg 2012 or a luscious late-harvest Gewürztraminer, Catherine is full of suggestions for food pairings, and this is characteristic throughout Alsace, where the wines really seem perfect to accompany every dish. 'Can't you imagine this Muscat with fresh asparagus, the Pinot Blanc with a cheese souffle,' she enthuses, 'or our full-bodied Pinot Noir W Reserve alongside a succulent leg of lamb?' *www.domaineweinbach.com; tel +33 3 89 47 13 21; 25 Route du Vin, Kaysersberg; by appointment*

05 VIGNOBLE KLUR

Members of the Slow Food Movement, the Klur family have created a paradise getaway for eco winelovers. While Clement Klur produces an outstanding selection of biodynamic wines, he has also transformed his family mansion into a bohemian B&B, where guests take part in everything from wine courses and traditional Alsatian cooking classes to poetry readings. The grounds extend over vegetable gardens, ponds, a sauna and a solarium, and walking tours are organised through the stunning terraced vineyard looking out over Katzenthal – Valley of the Cats. There is also a casual bistro specialising in wine-pairing snacks, such as fresh goats' cheese with Riesling, a Pinot Gris and chestnut mousse. Klur is innovative in the cellar too, offering many vintages using screw-top – almost heretical in Alsace – and, from the younger vines, the affordable, drinkable Katz range for fans of cat labels. *www.klur.net; tel +33 3 89 80 94 29; 105 Rue des Trois Epis, Katzenthal*

06 DOMAINE BARMÈS-BUECHER

The tasting room in this impassioned winery is a cool contemporary salon of minimalist stone and wood, and Genevieve Barmes and her daughter Sophie begin by popping open a bottle of their popular bubbly, the delicately dry Brut Crémant Zero Dosage, made from a blend of four grapes. The *vigneron* here is 24-year-old Maxime, Sophie's brother. The whole family are ardent devotees of biodynamic winemaking, from the feng-shui type design of the vaulted cellar to the use of a horse to plough between the vines wherever

possible. Both Genevieve and her late husband, Francois, came from classic farming families – across the road from each other – and as far back as the 1980s they were determined to end chemical-dominated cultivation and go organic to produce higher-quality wines with their own individual personality. And it has certainly paid off, as apart from regular glowing tributes from the doyens of world wine criticism, the quality of the vintages speak for themselves. Try their signature Gewürztraminers, from the classic 2009 Rosenberg to the 2005 Grand cru Steingrubler, in which the taste of the fruit is quite simply explosive.
www.barmes-buecher.com; tel +33 3 89 80 62 92; 30 Rue Sainte Gertrude, Wettolsheim

07 MAISON EMILE BEYER

Visitors flock to enchanting Eguisheim, unchanged since the Middle Ages, gathering in the town square to stare up at the iconic storks' nests balancing atop the church steeple. One of the traditional brightly coloured half-timbered houses on the square has been the winemaking home of the Beyer family since 1580. Today they have a modern winery on the outskirts of town, but tastings are held here in the cobbled courtyard. As is the case all over Alsace, be prepared for a marathon session, as the Beyers produce some 30 different wines on their 16-hectare (40-acre) organic estate. Try a surprisingly dry Muscat or the full-bodied oak-aged Pinot Noir, though the stars of the show are their Grand cru Rieslings. While Maman Beyer holds court serving the wine, her son, Christian, a 14th-generation winegrower, notes, 'Records exist that grapes were first grown on these rolling hillsides by the Romans, and I believe when you are standing among the vines that produce our Riesling Grand cru Eichenberg – Hill of Oaks – you absorb this incredible history and heritage.'
www.emile-beyer.fr; tel +33 3 89 41 40 45; 7 Place du Château, Eguisheim

08 GERARD SCHUELLER

There is no sign outside the 500-year-old manor where the provocative Bruno Schueller makes his incredible wines. And no tasting room either, just a rickety table wobbling with a dozen half-opened bottles squeezed in between steel vats and barrels, and a workspace where labels are stuck – by hand – onto magnums of his highly original Bulle de Bild, a sparkling Gewürztraminer blended with 10% Riesling grape juice, which Bruno refuses to call a Cremant. It turns out that he often falls foul of the authorities with his unorthodox 'natural wines' failing to pass official tasting tests, but it doesn't seem to bother him, especially as he sells everything he produces, with the world's most famous restaurants, such as Noma and Can Roca, queuing up to serve his vintages. 'I like to leave my wines open when tasting just to see whether there is an effect of oxidisation. But I'm not scared, and they only seem to get better the longer they are open,' he explains. And this is borne out when the tasting begins, as he opens a young 2012 Riesling that is almost too young to appreciate, and then digs out a bottle opened two weeks ago of a wonderful lush, dark-amber 2008 Riesling Grand cru.
Tel 03 89 49 31 54; 1 Rue des 3 Châteaux, Husseren les Châteaux; call for visit

04

Hiroshi Higuchi © Getty Images

ESSENTIAL INFORMATION

WHERE TO STAY

CLOS FROEHN

Guests are pampered at Martine and Alphonse Aubrey's 17th-century cottage, which overlooks the vineyards. At breakfast, Alphonse (formerly the village baker) serves cakes and pastries. *www.clos-froehn.com; tel +33 3 89 47 95 68; 46 Rue du Schlossberg, Zellenberg*

SYLVIE FAHRER

While the rooms are simple in this reasonably priced B&B, breakfast is served in a grand half-timbered salon. Evening wine tastings are held in a converted barn filled with barrels and tractors. *www.fahrer-sylvie.com; tel +33 3 89 73 00 40; 24 Route du Vin, Saint Hippolyte*

WHERE TO EAT

WISTUB DU SOMMELIER

An Alsatian *wistub* is a cosy mix of winebar and pub, but this smart place complements gourmet cuisine with an extensive wine list, featuring all the village *vignerons*. *wistub-du-sommelier.com; tel +33 3 89 73 69 99; 51 Grand'Rue, Bergheim*

CAVEAU MORAKOPF

You won't see many tourists in this snug, welcoming bistro, but locals tuck into enormous portions of *jambonneau* (crispy pork knuckle) or delicious goose foie gras. *www.caveaumorakopf.fr; tel +33 3 89 27 05 10; 7 Rue des Trois Épis, Niedermorschwihr*

BRASSERIE L'AUBERGE

Colmar is the wine capital of Alsace, and this century-old Auberge is a temple to traditional cuisine, especially a steaming plate of tangy *choucroute* (sauerkraut dressed with sausages). *Tel +33 3 89 23 17 57; 7 Place de la Gare, Colmar*

WHAT TO DO

The Ballon des Vosges national park is a paradise for lovers of rambling, biking and canoeing.

CELEBRATIONS

Molsheim holds a memorable weekend festival in June including a half-marathon run through vineyards.

01

01 The medieval town of Semur en Auxois

02 Le Charlemagne in Pernand-Vergelesses

03 Château de Corton André, Burgundy

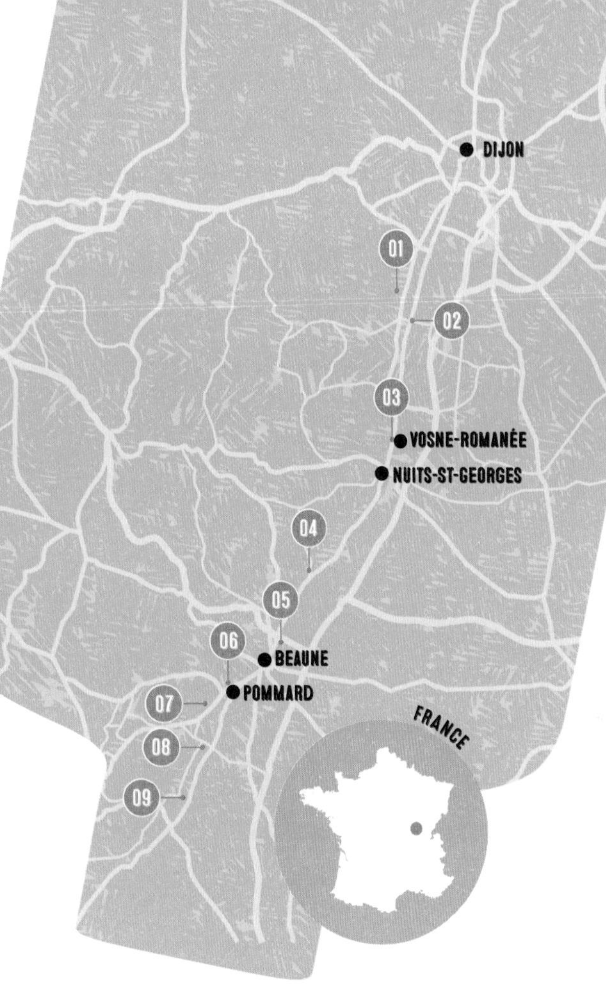

[France]

BURGUNDY

It's easy to feel daunted by Burgundy's reputation, but don't – the locals love to share the secrets of their legendary Pinot Noir with visitors.

Burgundy stretches as far as the vineyards of Chablis, Macon and the Côte Chalonnaise, but the quintessential heart of this historic winemaking region is the 50-mile stretch of road along the Côtes de Nuits and Côtes de Beaune, from Dijon down to Santenay. This is known as La Côte d'Or, the Gold Coast, and it is no exaggeration to state that the illustrious vineyards that line both sides produce what are probably the most famous wines in the world. This essentially monoculture *terroir* of perfectly manicured vines quite simply provides the perfect interpretation of Pinot Noir and Chardonnay, grapes that may be grown all over the rest of the world but which attain unassailable peaks here in Burgundy.

The taste, colour and aroma of a Burgundy Pinot Noir really does vary according to its village of origin (even according to each parcel of vines), but it is always marked by an evocative fruity flavour, balanced acidity and a signature touch of minerality. In fact, so perfect are wines from Burgundy that the name of the grape is never written on the label, just the vineyard, known as a *climat*, along with the official classification of appellation – beginning with 'Village', then the more important recognition as a 'Premier cru', and the ultimate accolade, a 'Grand cru'.

Despite producing some of the world's most famous and esteemed wines for over 2000 years, most Burgundy winemakers, whose families have often owned their vineyards for centuries, are down-to-earth and give an exceptional welcome to visitors. This friendly reception is important because tasting wines in Burgundy can be a little intimidating at first, both for the incredibly high quality and the incredibly high prices. But once you sit down with the cheerful, ruddy *vigneron*, gently swirling a glass of subtly coloured Pommard or the soft golden hue of a Montrachet at a rough wooden table in a rustic cellar, it is impossible not to succumb to the friendly Burgundy charm, a million miles from the glitzy world of a three-star Michelin restaurant where the same vintage is being delicately poured by a smartly dressed sommelier.

GET THERE
Geneva is the nearest major airport, 269km from Fixin. Car hire is available. The train from Paris to Dijon takes 1hr 33min.

© John Brunton, Olimpio Fantuz © 4Corners Images

01 DOMAINE JOLIET PÈRE ET FILS

Fixin, which locals will tell you is pronounced 'Fissin', is just outside Dijon at the beginning of Burgundy's Route des Grands Crus. But sleepy Fixin does not actually boast a Grand cru and is often bypassed, as enthusiasts speed on to the mythical vineyards of Gevrey-Chambertin, Chambolle and Vougeot. All this may change, though, if Benigne Joliet fulfills his ambition of having his jewel of a vineyard raised to the status of Grand cru. Regardless, he is making exceptional wines, and the domaine is an ideal place at which to grasp the immense weight of history behind Burgundy winemaking.

The massive manor and wine cellar stands alone, looking out like a watchguard over the village of Fixin. The manor has remained unchanged since the day it was built in 1142 by Benedictine monks from the nearby Abbey of Citeaux, and it is quite a mystical feeling to look out over the original 5-hectare (12-acre) vineyard, which was planted at the same time by the monks. Sitting in the immense vaulted wine cellar, complete with a medieval wooden press, Benigne explains how this magical place inspires him. 'Every morning when I come in to check the barrels I imagine the scene a thousand years ago: the monks dressed in their habits, going out to work in the vines, no phones, no computers. I feel privileged to make wine here, and I swear there is a certain magneticism.'

As Benigne owns the whole of the Clos, it is classed as an exclusive Monopole, and unlike most Burgundy vintners, who produce a panoply of wines from their various parcels, he offers only two: a red and a white. The red (90% of production) is wonderfully elegant and achieves his aim: 'When someone finishes a bottle of my wine, well, they feel that the next thing to do is open another.'

Tel +33 3 80 52 47 85; Fixin; by appointment

02 PIERRE BOURÉE FILS

A statue of a Cistercian monk stands at the entrance to the 11th-century château of Gevrey-Chambertin, paying homage to the religious order that laid the first seeds a thousand years ago of Burgundy's winemaking traditions. But in a sign of the times, the château and its 2.3 precious hectares (5½ acres) of vines have recently been sold to a businessman from China. Down below the vineyards on the busy road to Beaune, enterprising vintner Bernard Vallet has created La Table de Pierre, where wine lovers can choose the vintages they want to taste, paired

03

with a menu of typical local dishes. With its ancient brick walls and communal wooden tables, La Table de Pierre tastings are invariably a lively affair, where the sommelier pulls the corks of rare vintages, and guests tuck into a hearty plate of locally cured charcuterie. Lots of helpful hints on how best to taste the wine are offered, and afterwards everyone heads down to the cellars.

Bernard is the fourth generation of this respected estate, and a maze of ancient cellars are just across the road in his plush Maison de Vigneron. Although he buys in a significant amount of grapes to have an impressive list of more than 40 wines (from a superb white 2012 Pernand-Vergelesses to an opulent 2005 Clos de Vougeot Grand cru), the heart of the Domaine is the significant family-owned parcels here in Gevrey-Chambertin, including four Grands crus.

www.pierre-bouree-fils.com; tel +33 3 80 34 30 25; Route de Beaune 40

03 DOMAINE RION

Vosne-Romanée looks like just another tranquil Burgundy village surrounded by vineyards. But behind almost every anonymous gate lies some of the world's most famous domaines: Romanée-Conti, Liger-Belair and Gros. The vineyards – La Tache, Richebourg, Romanée – date back to at least the 11th century, and are, quite simply, priceless. Not surprisingly, few of these famous names are open for visits, but the Rion family can claim a long heritage as residents of Vosne-Romanée, even if today their cellars are on the busy road linking Beaune with Dijon. 'My father decided back in the 1950s that it was just not practical to be based in the village', explains fifth-generation *vigneronne*,

Courtesy of Maison Champy

04 The village of Pernand-Vergelesses

05 The atmospheric Château de Gilly

Armelle Rion. 'Small producers like us had to wash our barrels out on the pavement, and delivering the grapes during harvest was a nightmare. Here we have plenty of room to both make and age our wine, as well as receiving visitors.' Armelle uses mainly new wood for ageing her Vosne Romanée, Clos de Vougeot and Chambolle Musigny, insisting, 'The wines from the 90-year-old vines we cultivate here are complex enough to absorb the tannins.'
www.domainerion.fr; tel +33 3 80 61 05 31; 8 Route Nationale, Vosne-Romanée

04 DOMAINE CAPITAIN-GAGNEROT

One of the oddities of Burgundy is that with so many domaines owning small parcels, it is by no means assured that the best wines come from a cellar actually in the village that bears the name of a Grand cru. This is certainly the case for Aloxe-Corton, an utterly idyllic hamlet with a fairy-tale castle. Few tourists stop off in busy adjacent Ladoix, and the Maison Capitain-Gagnerot sits on the trunk road to Dijon. But visitors are warmly welcomed to try the quite exceptional selection of Corton Grands crus, including an outstanding white Corton-Charlemagne, as well as the less-renowned but complex Premier cru of Ladoix itself.

It is only recently that the sign outside the estate has read 'Domaine', indicating an independent winemaker, as this was previously a well-known *Maison* – that is, one of the *negociant* merchants who not only produce but also buy wine from other *vignerons*. After two centuries of buying *and* cultivating grapes, this modern-thinking family now concentrates solely on its own 16 hectares (39½ acres).
www.capitain-gagnerot.com; tel +33 3 80 26 41 36; Rue de Dijon 38, Ladoix-Serrigny

05 MAISON CHAMPY

The venerable Champy is the doyenne of Burgundy's wine merchants, the first-ever *negociant*, initiating back in 1720 the complex business of buying grapes and 'mout' (pressed and sometimes slightly fermented grape juice) from smallholder *vignerons*. Today Champy is eclipsed by such giant *maisons* as Drouin, Jadot and Bouchard (the latter alone produces over three million bottles), which are based in Beaune, Burgundy's wine capital, with centuries-old labyrinthine cellars and organised tour guides. But Champy is in a different class – old-fashioned and artisanal (it only buys in grapes for 350,000 bottles) while producing organic wines on its own vineyards in Volnay, Pommard and Pernand-Vergelesse. And a visit to the 15th-century cellar is memorable, passing cobwebbed alleys where you spy priceless treasures – dusty bottles labelled Romanee 1865, Richebourg 1875, Montrachet 1877.
www.champy.com; tel +33 3 80 25 09 99; 5 Rue du Grenier-à-Sel, Beaune; by appointment

06 THIERRY VIOLOT-GUILLEMARD

They say in the village of Pommard that Thierry Violot-Guillemard is more deeply rooted here than one of his vines. Certainly, a tasting in his tiny cellar, or even better, a couple of nights in the welcoming B&B run by his wife, Estelle, is the perfect introduction to the ingrained hospitality of a typical Burgundy vigneron. His 6-hectare (15-acre) organic estate spreads over Volnay, Beaune, Monthelie and Mersault, but Thierry is defined by his exceptional interpretation of Pinot Noir in Pommard. 'Our most important work is always in the vineyard, with as little intervention in the cellar as possible. And then, the wine must be left alone to age,' he philosophises, after delving into the murky depths of the cellar to pull out an ancient vintage.

'In Burgundy we don't talk about *terroir* but *climat*: location, soil, under soil, altitude, slope and 1000 years of work.'

–Youri Lebault, Burgundy wine guide and author

Vineyards in Burgundy are historically tiny, but Thierry reckons that one of his plots, the Clos de Derriere St Jean, could hold the record: at only a tenth of a hectare it looks smaller than a back garden.

www.violot-guillemard.fr; tel +33 3 80 22 49 98; 7 Rue Sainte-Marguerite, Pommard

07 DOMAINE GLANTENAY PIERRE ET FILS

With its commanding church and solemn war memorial, Volnay, which looks down on the Côte de Beaune, seems an austere village. But there is nothing austere about the elegant wines produced here. That is certainly the case for the vintages presented in the homely tasting room of the Glantenay family. Domaines in Burgundy can suffer when one generation passes on to another, often dividing up the estate. But Pierre Glantenay has handed the reins to his 23-year-old son Guillaume, who has taken the huge responsibility of building a dazzling modern cellar, perfect for making wine from the ancient vines encircling Volnay. 'I am committing myself to the domaine for a very long time with this kind of financial investment,' he says, smiling, 'but we have such a unique *terroir* that with the new cellar I really believe I can make even more exceptional wines than my father.'

www.domaineglantenay.com; tel +33 3 80 21 61 82; Rue de la Barre, Volnay

08 DOMAINE YVES BOYER MARTENOT

With its grand château-like town hall covered with coloured roof tiles, Mersault is one of Burgundy's iconic destinations. *Vignerons* here tend to be highly opinionated – especially if you raise the touchy subject of organic certification, which most dismiss with a wave of the hand. By contrast, Vincent Boyer, who produces a selection of distinctively mineral Premier crus from Mersault, immediately comes over as a humble, down-to-earth winemaker: 'Our vines are mostly very old, on average 50 to 60 years and many over 90 years, which means low yields but high quality. I have been moving towards organic for the last few years, all but eliminating the use of chemicals, but I won't yet sign up for the inflexibility of certification because when you can lose 50% or even 80% of your harvest through a hail storm, as has happened here and in Pommard in the last three years, you need to keep your options open or face financial ruin.'

www.boyer-martenot.com; tel +33 3 80 21 26 25; 17 Place de L'Europe, Mersault

09 DOMAINE JEAN CHARTRON

At the end of the Côte de Beaune is the most famous name in Burgundy for white wine: Montrachet. Here, five Grands crus are concentrated around the villages of Chassagne-Montrachet and Puligny-Montrachet. Don't expect to discover ancient subterranean cellars in Puligny – a geological anomaly makes it impossible to excavate. But a visit to the modern winery of Jean-Michel Chartron, who comes from a family of *vigneron*-coopers, is perfect for plunging into the history and mystery of Montrachet. Tasting with a 'pipette' from the barrel, Jean-Michel describes what it is like to make what is often known as the world's greatest wine: 'It can be difficult, because you are a "model", but nothing can take away the sheer happiness of working this unique soil. I don't feel that I own my vines, but rather that I am a guardian for the centuries of workers who have toiled the land before and the future generations. My name on the bottle is not important.'

After wandering through these historic vineyards, it feels like a privilege to just taste one of these wines in the actual village of Puligny-Montrachet, and most people can't resist buying at least one bottle. They are not cheap, but these are wines to save for that special occasion, and a 10-year-old bottle of Batard-Montrachet, say, with its intense aromas and flavours of apple, almonds and spices, is perfect to savour over a romantic meal at home, accompanying scallops or a lobster.

www.jeanchartron.com; Grand Rue, Puligny-Montrachet; tel +33 3 80 21 99 19

ESSENTIAL INFORMATION

WHERE TO STAY

CHÂTEAU DE GILLY
Fairy-tale castle by the iconic Clos de Vougeot and vineyards of Romanee-Conti. Four-poster beds and a 14th-century vaulted dining room awaits. *www.chateau-gilly.com; tel +33 3 80 62 89 98; Gilly-les-Citeaux, Vougeot*

CHAMBRE D'HOTE FOUQUERAND
The winemaking Fouquerand family run a simple cottage B&B in this idyllic village. Be sure to try the local bubbly, Cremant de Bourgogne. *www.domaine-denisfouquerand.com; tel +33 3 80 21 88 62; Rue de l'Orme, La Rochepot*

CHÂTEAU DE MELIN
Romantic château B&B with verdant park and lake. Each evening Arnaud Derats hosts in the medieval cellar a tasting of his wines that originate at small parcels from Mersault to Chambolle-Musigny. *www.chateaudemelin.com; tel +33 3 80 21 21 29; Hameau de Melin, Auxey-Duresses*

WHERE TO EAT

RESTAURANT LE CHARLEMAGNE
Encircled by vineyards, Le Charlemagne resembles a zen temple, and Michelin-starred chef Laurent Peugeot surprises with a fusion of *terroir* tastes with Japanese flavours. *www.lecharlemagne.fr; tel +33 3 80 21 51 45; Route de Vergelesses, Pernand-Vergelesses*

LA TABLE D'OLIVIER
Respected *vigneron* Olivier Leflaive has transformed Puligny-Montrachet with his hotel and restaurant, where the menu is tailored for wine pairings. *www.olivier-leflaive.com; tel +33 3 80 21 37 65; Place du Monument, Puligny-Montrachet*

LES ROCHES
Guillaume Crotet's cosy restaurant is perfect for classic Burgundy dishes like *oeufs en meurette*, poached eggs and smoky bacon in a red wine sauce. *www.les-roches.fr; tel +33 3 80 21 21 63; St Romain*

WHAT TO DO

Mix boating, cycling and wine tasting on a barge cruise along Burgundy's historic canal. *burgundy-canal.com*

CELEBRATIONS

Since 1851, on the third Sunday in November, the Hospices de Beaune holds its world-famous charity wine auction.

05

Courtesy of Château de Gilly

01

01 Champagne-Ardenne

02 Notre-Dame de Reims

[France]

CHAMPAGNE

Pop! The land that produces the king of sparkling wines is a treasure trove of rolling hills, ancient cellars and traditions just waiting to be opened.

Champagne is France's great enigma: the world's most famous bubbly and an undisputed icon of Gallic glamour, yet most French people have little idea of the complex, almost mystical, secrets that go into producing Champagne.

A trip into the magical land of Champagne is very much an emotional experience. Here you can witness perfectly cultivated vines hanging with clusters of grapes bursting with juice that will soon be harvested and begin the long, complex transformation into the one and only Champagne. Take a pilgrimage through the centuries-old maze of cellars beneath the likes of Ruinart or Pommery that resemble a holy subterranean cathedral, or savour the simple pleasure of a smallholder *vigneron* pouring a bubbly glass of his latest vintage. Accept the sly persuasion that he may sell most of his grapes to the famous producers, but keeps the best for his personal production sold directly from the independent winery.

The region's bucolic vineyards stretch across rolling hills and sleepy villages that begin just an hour's drive from Paris, although wine lovers often limit themselves to a trip to Reims. A regal city, Reims is home to the likes of Veuve Clicquot and Mumm, where incredible cellars, storing millions of bottles, are packed every day for tours. But Champagne is a complex mosaic of thousands of tiny *vignerons*, some making their own Champagne, others just supplying grapes to the luxury Champagne houses, an almost feudal relationship unchanged for centuries. So, after visiting Reims, head off into the countryside and meet these independent winemakers, who will explain the blending of Champagne's three grapes – Chardonnay, Pinot Noir and Pinot Meunier – the difference between 'millesime' vintage and an NV (the Anglicised Non Vintage), and insider secrets like the use of the 'liqueur de dosage' of cane sugar added in the final 'assemblage', which brings a special dimension to each Champagne.

GET THERE
Charles de Gaulle is the nearest airport, 130km from Reims. The train from Paris to Reims takes 50min. Car hire is available.

01 REIMS

The city of Reims is home to Champagne's own royalty, with curious visitors allowed into the hallowed cellars of the likes of Mumm and Pommery, Veuve Clicquot, Heidseck, Lanson and Taittinger. It is the perfect place to get an idea of the hidden secrets of the world's arguably favourite beverage, with gushing guides explaining the centuries-old alchemy that goes into its production. Each of the *Grandes Maisons* offers something different, but which one to choose? Lanson has just reopened its 150-year-old cellars after a €14 million renovation, including a quite incredible 'cuvage' with 101 giant steel vats holding the equivalent of five million bottles. Lanson is well known for its range of Pinot Noir Champagnes and has been served at the royal court since the time of Queen Victoria. Taittinger stands out as being one of the rare family-owned houses, and its two-level 13th-century cellars are primarily reserved for ageing the signature vintage Comtes de Champagne, a remarkable cuvée. The neo-gothic castle towers of Pommery resemble a kitsch Disneyland, but this is the one must-see cellar. Madame Pommery, 140 years ago, conceived dry Brut Champagne as a counterpoint to sweet bubbly, and her 18km of cellars are like none other. This is where you will discover 'les crayères', some 120 awesome chalk holes dug in Gallo-Roman times to construct the city of Reims, which Madame Pommery decided were perfect ventilation for the maze of tunnels she constructed for her cellar that today holds some 20 million bottles.
lansonchampagne.com; taittinger.com; vrankenpommery.com

02 CHAMPAGNE GARDET

Over two thirds of all Champagne, including 90% exported around the world, is produced by the 290 *Negociants Manipulants*, the *Grandes Maisons* who own hardly any vines but purchase grapes at harvest. Not all are multinationals, though, and a visit to the venerable Gardet, founded in 1895 and still supplying Britain's House of Commons, is a much more personal experience than being taken round by a company wine guide of the likes of Moet & Chandon or Pommery. Gardet has remained a relatively small maison, owning a mere 5 hectares (12 acres) of vineyards, but produces a million bottles a year using grapes from another 100 hectares (247 acres) they buy in. To begin with, they are out in the countryside, in a sleepy village surrounded by vineyards. To organise a visit, you need to call or email in advance. Gardet replies with advice on accommodation and eating out, and then visitors are received at the headquarters in an ornate art-nouveau glass verandah filled with tropical plants. The visit to the 'cuverie', where the wine is made, and then to the labyrinth of cellars, takes over an hour and gives a good explanation of all the stages of Champagne's complex production.
www.champagne-gardet.com; tel +33 3 26 03 42 03; 13 Rue Georges Legros, Chigny-les-Roses

03 CHAMPAGNE E BARNAUT

The bustling village of Bouzy is unique, since many winegrowers here exercise their right to make the non-bubbly Bouzy Rouge, a Pinot Noir that is expensive because, as one grizzled *vigneron* moaned, 'we could be making a lot more money by selling the grapes for Champagne!' Philippe Barnaut is a fifth-generation winemaker with strong ideas: 'People used to talk always about Le Champagne as a homogenous product, but what interests me is the diversity of Champagne. I vinify each parcel of each *terroir* separately before moving on to the crucial assemblage. Twenty years ago I was treated as a heretic, but now everyone is following this like a new fashion.' Philippe has taken the daring step, for a Champagne producer, of opening an Aladdin's-cave store for wine tourists in an ancient house that sits above four floors of cellars. Apart from offering tastings of his outstanding range of Champagne, the rustic wooden-fronted boutique stocks delicious regional foodie specialities – wild-boar pâté, lentils, mustard from Reims – and a kaleidoscope of wine gadgets.
www.champagne-barnaut.com; tel +33 3 26 57 01 54; 2 Rue Gambetta, Bouzy

04 CHAMPAGNE MERCIER

While most of Champagne's famous names may be based in Reims, it is lively Épernay that is the genuine wine capital, with a host of fun wine bars, gourmet restaurants and bistros. In terms of cellar visits, the mammoth 27km 'cave' of Moet & Chandon is closed for renovations till the end of 2015, while Perrier-Jouet and Pol Roger are closed to the public. But over 100,000 visitors arrive each year at Mercier, still probably the most popular Champagne in France itself. The founder, Eugene Mercier, was the publicity-seeking Richard Branson of his time, taking clients up in hot-air balloons and building an immense wooden barrel holding 250,000 bottles of Champagne that

was transported by oxen to Paris in 1900 to rival the Eiffel Tower as the star show of the Exposition Universelle. Today it dominates the entrance of Mercier's outstanding cellar, where a lift plunges visitors into an eerie maze of tunnels. A small electric train wends its way through a small part, and you realise how deep underground the cellar workers are. *www.champagnemercier.fr; tel +33 3 26 51 22 22; 68 Ave de Champagne, Épernay*

05 CHAMPAGNE TRIBAUT

Before arriving for a tasting at the friendly Tribaut family winery, where the sunny terrace overlooks a panorama of vineyards, be sure to take a tour of the idyllic village of Hautvilliers, known as the birthplace of Champagne. There is a Rue Dom Perignon, named after the Benedictine monk who, 300 years ago, is said to have invented the process of double fermentation that creates Champagne's unique bubbles. While their children run the estate, Ghislain and Marie-José Tribaut spurn retirement to welcome wine tourists. 'I am a typical "*Recoltant Manipulant*",' explains Ghislain, 'the term in Champagne for someone who cultivates and harvests their grapes, selling the large majority to a *Negociant Manipulant – Grandes Maisons* like Krug and Taittinger – but I save enough to produce 150,000 bottles myself.' After tasting Marie-José's delicious *gougères*, light puff pastry filled with Gruyère, paired with a dry Rose Brut, many visitors end up coming back here to help out during the grape harvest. *www.champagne.g.tribaut.com; tel +33 3 26 59 40 57; 88 Rue d'Eguisheim, Hautvillers*

06 CHAMPAGNE ASPASIE

Paul-Vincent Ariston describes himself as an 'artisan *vigneron*' and a visit to his 400-year-old stone farmhouse is a step back in time. Rather than just stopping for a tasting, it is worth taking a room in his comfy B&B, as then there is time for a full tour of the cellar with Paul-Vincent, who bubbles with as much enthusiasm as his Champagne. He proudly shows a huge wooden grape press, ancient but functioning, explains the 'degorgement', when sediment is frozen in the neck of the bottle and spectacularly popped out before final bottling, and then insists that 'rather than using the electric *giropalette*, that turns 500 bottles automatically during fermentation, I prefer the old-fashioned *remuage* of each one by hand.' He has some fascinating special cuvées, such as the totally unique Brut Cepages d'Antan, which has none of the usual Champagne grapes but, rather, three rare varieties – Le Petit Meslier, L'Arbanne and Pinot Blanc – that were grown here centuries before Champagne was popularised. *www.champagneaspasie.com; tel +33 3 26 97 43 46; 4 Grande Rue, Brouillet*

07 CHAMPAGNE PANNIER

Pannier is one of Champagne's better-known cooperative winemakers, a *Recoltant Cooperateur* to use the official title, with a growing reputation for high quality. Based near Château-Thierry, more well-known to Parisians for its safari park than vineyards, this is where much of the Pinot Meunier grape is grown. Pannier boasts a breathtaking labyrinth of cellars – stretching 30m beneath the earth – which date back to the 12th century when they were excavated for stone to build churches in the region. Today, you still feel you are exploring primitive caves rather than a wine cellar. Pannier was a well-known family producing Champagne, dating back to 1899, and when there were no more descendants in 1974, a group of 11 *vignerons* formed a cooperative to take over. Today this has mushroomed into a vast winery representing 400 growers. Although they produce millions of bottles a year, the cooperative keeps Pannier separate as their prestige brand, blending the local Pinot Meunier with Chardonnay and Pinot Noir from vineyards from the faraway Côte des Blancs and Montagne de Reims. *www.champagnepannier.com; tel +33 3 23 69 51 30; 23 Rue Roger Catillon, Château-Thierry*

'The relationship between the *Grandes Maisons* and the *Recoltants* is complex, but we depend on each other to make this unique product.'

-Emmanuel Mercier, great-grandson of the founder of Champagne Mercier.

08 CHAMPAGNE FALLET DART

Just an hour's drive from Paris, this part of the agricultural Marne

valley was only incorporated into the exclusive members-only club of the Champagne appellation in 1937, though the sign outside this ancient estate proudly announces that the family have been *vignerons* since 1610. Paul Dart is a dynamic young winemaker, followed everywhere by his massive St Bernard dog, Elios. Both of them make visitors feel very much at home. Tastings are free, and for those who call in advance, Paul takes the time to conduct a winery tour. Although the estate is medium-sized, stretching over 18 hectares (44 acres), it still has something like one million bottles ageing in its cellar. Be sure to taste the Clos du Mont, a blend of vintages from a vineyard dating from the 7th century. And as traditionalist winemakers, the winery is also proud of its Ratafia, a luscious aperitif, and an elegant Fine de Champagne, aged in barrels like a Cognac.
www.champagne-fallet-dart.fr; tel +33 3 23 82 01 73; 2 Rue des Clos du Mont, Drachy, Charly sur Marne

01 Food and Champagne pairing at Au 36, Hautvilliers

© John Brunton

ESSENTIAL INFORMATION

WHERE TO STAY

DOMAINES LES CRAYERES
For the full Champagne experience, reserve at this grand château built by the family of Madame Pommery. It's sumptuously furnished, with a two-star Michelin restaurant.
www.lescrayeres.com; tel +33 3 26 24 90 00; 64 Blvd Henry Vasnier, Reims

PARVA DOMUS
Claude and Ginette Rimaire pamper guests in their cosy home on Ave de Champagne, which Churchill named 'the world's most drinkable address'. Hearty breakfast, and glass of Champagne on arrival included.
www.parvadomusrimaire.com; tel +33 3 26 32 40 74; 27 Ave de Champagne, Épernay

WHERE TO EAT

LA GRILLADE GOURMANDE
Favourite Épernay address where *vignerons* rub shoulders with owners of the *Grandes Maisons*. Try the hearth-grilled meat or delicate dishes like pigeon stuffed with foie gras.
lagrilladegourmande.com; tel +33 3 26 55 44 22; 16 Rue de Reims, Épernay

AU 36
A perfect address for food and Champagne pairing, this designer bar serves a plate of local specialities – creamy Chaource cheese, Reims ham, smoky lentils and pink macarons – with three different Champagnes.
www.au36.net; tel +33 3 26 51 58 37; 38 Rue Dom Pérignon, Hautvillers

BISTROT LA MADELON
Far from Champagne's many gourmet dining rooms, this old-fashioned village bistro serves a generous *plat du jour* such as slow-cooked veal.
www.bistrot-madelon.com; tel +33 3 26 53 14 18; 7 Grande Rue, Mancy

WHAT TO DO

Notre-Dame de Reims is a must-see 800-year-old Gothic cathedral, the historic venue for the coronation of the kings of France.

CELEBRATIONS

Épernay celebrates Habits de Lumière for three days in mid-December, when Champagne flows amid fireworks, flamboyant light shows and street theatre.

01

Pearl Bucknall © Alamy

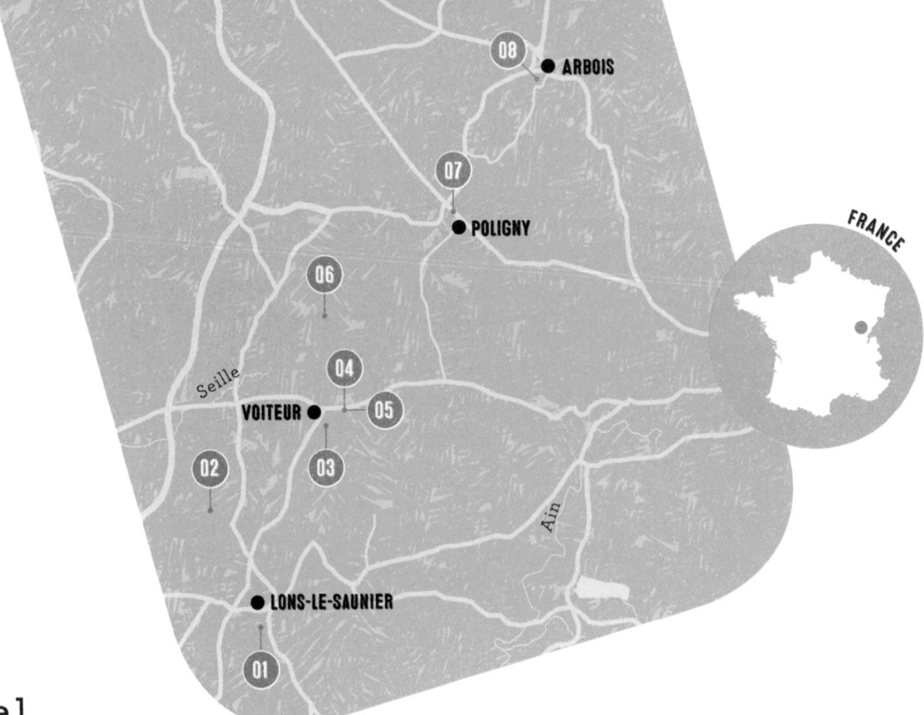

[France]

THE JURA

This oft-overlooked region tucked away on the Swiss border, quietly making wine for centuries, holds some quirky surprises for even experienced wine-tourers.

Wine has been made in the mountainous Jura for well over a thousand years. But it is only recently that this corner of France, right on the Swiss border, has begun to make a name for itself in the world of wine. The region has a rich biodiversity of lush valleys and thick forests, with vineyards adjacent to agricultural and grazing land. The majority of grapes cultivated are little-known indigenous varieties, from delicate light reds – Trousseau, Poulsard – to the remarkable Savagnin, which makes a white wine perfect for long ageing. A new generation of *vignerons* are making their mark here, using modern winemaking techniques alongside the Jura's traditional method.

And nothing quite prepares you for a tasting of the extraordinary Vin Jaune. No one is left undecided about Vin Jaune, so be prepared to love it or hate it. While the distinctive aroma immediately seems different from other wines – a mix of walnuts, hazelnut and exotic spices – the taste is altogether something else, incredibly dry yet somehow fruity and nutty at the same time. The wine is a brilliant cooking ingredient, with all Jura households stocking a bottle in the kitchen, where it's added to dishes like chicken with a creamy sauce of morel mushrooms. It's also an ideal pairing with the Jura's tart Comté cheese. Made purely from Savagnin grapes, Vin Jaune is barrel-aged for six years, but with a pocket of air left open; its oxidising effect is limited as the maturing wine is covered by a natural *voile*, a film of yeast, in almost exactly the same way Spanish sherry is produced in Jerez.

Visitors to the Jura have to be aware that wine tourism is still in its early days here, but that makes for an even more refreshing welcome when travellers turn up for a wine-tasting in a little-known backwoods domaine. Not many of these young Jura *vignerons* have opened up their homes as a B&B, but that will come with time. For now, they are concentrating all their efforts and finance on winemaking, though many are already making plans to convert parts of their rambling stone farms into holiday homes.

GET THERE
Geneva is the nearest major airport, 143km from Montaigu. Car hire is available.

❶ DOMAINE PIGNIER

A tasting at this historic domaine is the perfect introduction to the Jura. Ask Marie-Florence Pignier, a seventh-generation *vigneronne*, to take you down for a tour of the astonishing 13th-century cellar. The vast, high, vaulted barrel-chamber resembles a cathedral, so it is not surprising to learn that this was originally a monastery founded in 1250 by *vigneron*-monks who planted the original vineyard. At one time there were 200 hectares (494 acres) of vines around Montaigu, although the Pigniers' 15 hectares (37 acres) are all that remain.

The wines produced today are organic and highly contemporary. Pignier was the first Jura winery to complete biodynamic certification, and now certain cuvées are 'naturel', with no sulphite added, allowing for an explosion of fruit flavour from the Trousseau and Poulsard red grapes. Don't miss the Vin Jaune either, which Marie-Florence proudly claims 'is the ultimate wine for ageing, even if you want to wait a century!'
www.domaine-pignier.com; tel +33 3 84 24 24 30; 11 Place Rouget de Lisle, Montaigu

❷ DOMAINE VANDELLE

Etoile sits in a bucolic valley encircled by a series of rolling hills covered with vineyards and woods. 'Pretty much each hill and its vines is owned by a different village *vigneron*,' recounts Philippe Vandelle, 'and each of us make wines with a different personality due to the variations of soil and exposure to the sun.

This used to be the land of '*vache et vin*', where families made both wine and Comté cheese. But in the last century, with the effects of phylloxera wiping out vineyards and much of the male workforce disappearing during the World Wars,

David Brabiner © Alamy

it is only in the last 30 years that families like mine can concentrate uniquely on wine.' The Vandelles came to the Jura over two centuries ago from Belgium, and Philippe's cousin still owns the grand Château de l'Etoile.

Philippe has converted a stone labourer's cottage into a snug tasting room, and it is a surprise to learn that 30% of his production is devoted to Crémant du Jura, made following the classic Champenoise method.
www.vinsphilippevandelle.com; tel +33 3 84 86 49 57; 186 Rue Bouillod 39570 L'Etoile

03 FRUITIÈRE DE VOITEUR

As you drive out of Voiteur, you can't miss the massive and spectacular limestone outcrop with Château-Chalon balancing on its summit to the left of the road, while opposite is an imposing modern winery. 'A Jura *fruitière* has nothing to do with fruits,' explains Bertrand Delannay, the director here, 'but is rather an agricultural cooperative devoted to one of the region's two specialities – wine or cheese.' Like most things in the Jura, the Fruitière is not an impersonal industrial-scale enterprise, but a family-style co-op with just 50 associates spreading over 75 hectares (185 acres). There is a challenging 19 wines to taste, with eminently affordable prices and a lot of variety. 'Many Jura *vignerons* specialise only in barrel-aged wines as that is the tradition here, but we try to offer some easier-to-drink alternatives too, such as a young floral Chardonnay aged in steel vats.' Indirectly, the *fruitière* is another reason why young *vignerons* come to the Jura to get started, as many *associes* (cooperative members) lease their vines on the almost feudal system of *metayage*, where winemakers who cannot get financial backing 'pay' one quarter of their harvest to the owner in lieu of rent.
www.fruitiere-vinicole-voiteur.fr; tel +33 3 84 85 21 29; 60 Rue de Nevy, Voiteur

04 DOMAINE SALVADORI

Medieval Château-Chalon, classified as one of France's most beautiful villages, looks down on a criss-cross patchwork of vineyards, including 5 hectares (12 acres) cultivated by jovial *vigneron*, Jean-Pierre Salvadori. His rustic cellar-cum-museum is right on the main street. It is always open for visits, if you call first; Jean-Pierre's wife prepares home-baked patisseries, the perfect pairing for his exquisite Vin Jaune. He is adamant that Château-Chalon vintages are unique, explaining, 'Vin Jaune produced around our village has its own appellation, with slightly different methods of production compared to other Vin Jaune you will taste. And if we feel the quality of the late harvest of the Savagnin grape is not high enough, then we simply don't make a cuvée that year.' The unique 'clavelin' bottle for Vin Jaune holds just a precious 62 centilitres – which tradition recounts is the amount left from one litre after the wine's compulsory wood-ageing of six years and three months.
tel +33 3 84 44 62 86; 10 Rue des Chevres, Château-Chalon

05 DOMAINE CREDOZ

The winery of Jean-Claude Credoz is just down the road from Domaine Salvadori, a winery rooted in tradition. Credoz is a modern viticulteur, cultivating 9 hectares (22 acres) solely around Château-Chalon, 'so I'm just five minutes from my vines'. Jean-Claude is a humble winemaker: he doesn't attend wine fairs and doesn't have a website; instead his reputation has grown and solidified by word-of-mouth. His excellent sparkling Crémant is sold-out a year in advance, while enthusiasts come just to taste his Macvin, the unique Jura aperitif that he makes from the must (juice) of Savagnin grapes and a distilled marc (pulped skins) aged for four years in oak. While initially a luscious fruity taste, Macvin surprises with the

Bon Appetit © Alamy

alcoholic kick of its aromatic marc. Working essentially old vines, some over 80 years, and ageing from three to seven years in ancient barrels that pass on barely any oaky tannins, his white wines – Chardonnay, Savagnin and Vin Jaune – are elegant and subtle on initial tasting, but with all the grape's delicate expression coming out in what Jean-Claude lovingly describes as the 'longueur' of the after-taste. *Tel +33 6 80 43 17 44; Rue des Chèvres, Château-Chalon; by appointment*

06 LES DOLOMIES

Don't expect to sample Vin Jaune at Celine Gormally's garage cellar, as it needs six years to age and she only founded her Domaine in 2010. 'There is a great feeling of solidarity here,' she explains. 'I immediately sought organic certification and was helped by a like-minded group of Jura viticulteurs called Le Nez dans le Vert. And when I first started, I was able to rent parcels of wonderful 70-year-old vines at a fair-trade price from an agricultural association.' To further lessen the financial burden, Celine has started her own private club, Location de Cep, where members order wine for the forthcoming vintage but pay a year in advance, with many coming as unpaid help during the harvest. Her whites are bottled by individual parcels of vines, and the Pinot Noir is surprisingly full bodied for the Jura. And ask to try the Chat Pet, a naturally fermented bubbly. *www.les-dolomies.com; tel +33 6 87 03 39 98; 40 Rue de l'Asile, Passenans; by appointment*

07 DOMAINE BADOZ

The Badoz family trace their winemaking tradition back 10 generations to 1659, and Bernard Badoz launched the Percee du Vin Jaune festival in 1977, where every *vigneron* in the Jura presents their wines, which launched this little-known region onto the world wine map. Bernard is officially retired, having handed the reins to his ambitious son, Benoit, who has already doubled the size of the estate – 'though you can never keep Papa out, because as soon as he leaves the cellar he climbs back in through the window,' laughs Benoit. Visitors today come to their modern boutique in the bustling centre of Poligny, where you can taste Comté cheeses from a cousin's farm, organic honey and such regional artisan charcuterie as

smoky Morteau sausage. Benoit has created a new range of special cuvées that are really worth trying. 'Edouard', named after his son, is Chardonnay aged in barrels made especially from wood in the forest above Poligny, while 'Arrogance', which he modestly named for himself, sees a crisp, acidic Savagnin aged normally rather than oxidised with the traditional *voile* of yeast used for Vin Jaune.
www.domaine-badoz.fr; tel +33 3 84 37 18 00; 3 Ave de la Gare, Poligny

08 DOMAINE RIJCKAERT

Arbois is the lively winemaking capital of the Jura, but you need to take the back lanes to find the cellar of dynamic *vigneron* Florent Rouve. The signs at the entrance to the idyllic hamlet of Les Planches offer trout fishing, goats cheese and a forest ramble to an enchanting waterfall. But Florent doesn't have a sign, nor a tasting room; instead he hosts visitors in the local *gîte*. No one goes away disappointed, however, after tasting his sensational artisan wines. Florent is a white-wine fanatic, working exclusively with Chardonnay and Savagnin, so there are no reds, Macvin or Vin de Paille to taste, and no Vin Jaune either, as this perfectionist has no intention of producing one until he is good and ready. His barrels are stacked in two 17th-century cellars that are mouldy, cold and humid, perfect conditions, according to Florent, to age using the traditional *voile* method. 'I press the juice, bring it down into the barrels and begin ageing on the lie. Then wait. It really isn't complicated to make good wine, you just need patience,' he says with a wry smile.
www.rijckaert.fr; Arbois; tel +33 6 21 01 27 41, call for visit

01 The picturesque village of Château-Chalon

02 Vineyards of Château-Chalon

03 Wine route in the Jura

ESSENTIAL INFORMATION

WHERE TO STAY

LE RELAIS DE LA PERLE
Nathalie Estavoyer welcomes travellers to her beautifully restored *maison de vigneron*, organising wine tastings and even a hot-air balloon trip over the vineyards.
www.lerelaisdelaperle.fr; tel +33 3 84 25 95 52; 184 Route de Voiteur, Le Vernois

GOTHIQUE CAFE CHAMBRES D'HOTES
The magnificent Romanesque abbey of Baume-les-Messieurs is already one of the Jura's most spectacular sights. Stay in one of its private apartments, transformed into a magical B&B.
chambresdhotesbaume.free.fr; tel +33 6 42 19 56 01; L'Abbaye, Baume-les-Messieurs

WHERE TO EAT

BISTROT CHEZ JANINE
Madame Andre keeps raucous *vignerons* quiet with her hearty *Planche Comtoise* heaped with cheeses, saucisson, smoked ham and home-pickled gherkins.
tel +33 3 84 44 62 43; Route de la Vallee, Nevy-sur-Seille

LA FINETTE TAVERNE D'ARBOIS
Rustic wooden chalet in Jura's winemaking capital; feast off such regional specialities as succulent chicken slow-cooked in Vin Jaune.
www.finette.fr; tel +33 3 84 66 08 78; 22 Ave Louis Pasteur, Arbois

BISTROT DE PORT LESNEY
With its red-checked tablecloths and zinc bar, the Pontarlier oozes Gallic charm, and chef Arnaud Collet prepares such traditional dishes as frogs' legs in a garlicky parsley sauce.
www.bistrotdeportlesney.com; tel +33 3 84 37 83 27; Port-Lesney

WHAT TO DO

Visit the subterranean world of the Salins-les-Bains Unesco World Heritage salt mines.

CELEBRATIONS

Each year on the first weekend of February, a different village hosts La Percee du Vin Jaune, where 40,000 wine lovers arrive to toast the new vintage.

[France]

THE LANGUEDOC

Craggy cliffs and wooded valleys greet visitors to this dynamic wine region, fast becoming one of France's most exciting.

01 The medieval town of Carcassonne

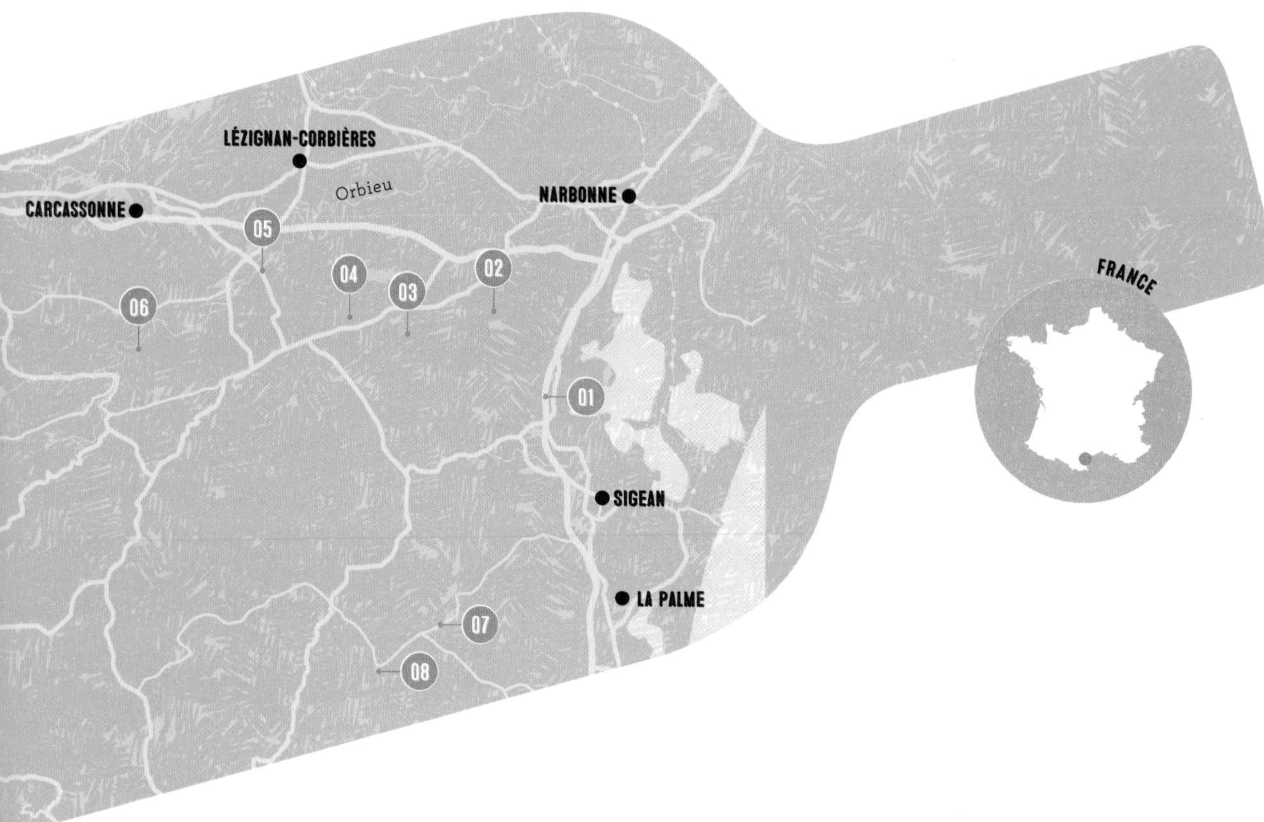

Some of the most exciting and innovative wines emerging in France are coming from the vast Languedoc-Roussillon region, which covers much of the south, from the Spanish border up to the vineyards of Provence and the Côte d'Azur. A third of France's wine is produced here, but for years the region suffered from over-production and poor quality. Not any more. The winery scene has changed dramatically, with a flood of new appellations, the huge popularity of Vin de Pays wines and advances in both the vineyard and cellar. Dynamic young *vignerons* are drawn here, not to contribute to the old system of the winemaking cooperative, but to set up their own small vineyards, often organic and biodynamic. There are the new stars of the region: intense reds from Pic St-Loup and La Clape, bubbly Blanquette de Limoux, and the crisp white Picpoul de Pinet, perfect with local oysters. And one corner, the Corbières, wedged between Montpellier and Perpignan, remains under the radar, waiting to be discovered.

GET THERE
Toulouse is the nearest major airport. The train from Paris to Narbonne takes 4hrs. Car hire is available.

The sheer variety of the landscapes here is spectacular, with vineyards pressing up against the Mediterranean along the flamingo-filled lagoons of Peyriac-de-Mer, through dramatic limestone hills and valleys where travellers can stay in affordable *chambres d'hôtes* hidden away in isolated medieval hamlets, right up to the wild mountain castles built by the Cathar tribes in the 12th century in the towering foothills of the Pyrenees. Finding a restaurant in this rugged corner is not always easy, but when you do, the Grenache, Syrah and Carignan reds from Corbières are sturdy, spicy and robust, high in alcohol and a perfect complement to the equally hearty cuisine of the region – dishes such as a duck confit and white-bean cassoulet, cuttlefish slow-cooked with spicy chorizo and blood sausage, and lamb roasted with wild rosemary.

01 DOMAINE FABRE-CORDON

Amandine Fabre-Cordon is typical of the numerous passionate young women earning respect as independent *vigneronnes* in the Corbières today. Her father, Henri, started off as a vineyard labourer, renting parcels of vines under France's *'fermage'* leasing system, and now owns his own small estate of 12 hectares (30 acres). Amandine took over in 2011, after learning her craft in New Zealand and California, and has firm plans for the domaine. The *terroir* here is known as *Corbières Méditerannée*, as the sea is just 3km away at the picturesque fishing village of Peyriac. The domaine has an especially strong selection of white and rosé wines – Grenache Blanc, Viognier and Vermentino. Since 2013, the vineyard is certified organic, and visitors are always welcome for a tasting, and there's a *gîte* (holiday home) for rent too.

Other dynamic women winemakers to check out nearby are Cecile Bonnafous (www.domaine-esperou.fr) and Fanny Tisseyre (www.graindefanny.com). ***www.chateaufabrecordon.fr; tel +33 4 68 42 00 31; L'Oustal Nau, Peyriac-de-Mer***

02 ABBAYE DE FONTFROIDE

This magnificent medieval abbey is the perfect place to get a feel for the history and winemaking heritage of the Corbières. Located just outside Narbonne, the ancient capital of the region, Fontfroide was founded in 1093 by monks, who immediately planted vines to provide wine for religious services. At its peak, these Cistercians controlled thousands of hectares. Abandoned at the end of the 19th century, the abbey was bought by the Fayet family in 1908, and today it is run by their granddaughter Laure and her husband, Nicolas de Chernon Villette. He describes himself as an artisan winemaker, cultivating 36 hectares (89 acres). Although Nicolas still sells 60% of his production to the local cooperative, he is beginning to make some fine wines in their nearby modern cellar, especially a dry Muscat and Cuvée 1093, a very surprising Syrah. The tour round the abbey and its wonderful gardens followed by a tasting is simply unforgettable. ***www.fontfroide.com; tel +33 4 68 45 11 08; Route Departemantale 613, Narbonne***

03 DOMAINE CALVEL

Ghislain and Pascale Calvet have big plans to transform their rambling family farmhouse into a wine-tasting cellar, with cultural events and a *gîte* to welcome visitors. But for the moment, enthusiasts interested in discovering their exceptional wines must call for an appointment and directions to an industrial warehouse on the edge of the village. This is authentic garage winemaking – no sign outside and pretty chaotic when you enter, with cement vats, oak casks, and boxes stacked everywhere. But an impromptu tasting around a barrel becomes a memorable affair once Ghislain starts opening up some of their older vintages, such as the complex 2006 Cru Boutenac, which really needs a few years of ageing to be properly appreciated. Their vineyard of mainly centenary Carignan vines lies along the rolling foothills of Les Causses mountains, and was started by Pascale in 1996 when she inherited 8 hectares (20 acres), selling her grapes direct to the winemaking cooperative. By 2002, they had 15 hectares (37 acres), and had constructed this makeshift cellar to make their first vintage. Today, working with their son, the estate is up to 22 hectares (54 acres). ***Tel +33 6 88 76 88 10; 16 Rue de la Rivière, Saint-André-de-Roquelongue***

04 CHÂTEAU LES OLLIEUX ROMANIS

As its name implies, this vast estate in the heart of the Boutenac Cru (a tiny but high-quality appellation within Corbières) has roots going back to Roman times, and today with 150 hectares (370 acres) of vines the château is one of the largest private domaines in the Corbières. But there is a very warm, human welcome provided to visitors by the enthusiastic team of *vignerons* that surround the owner, Pierre Bories, once a high-powered Parisian financier. There is still a feeling that this is an old-fashioned farm, with donkeys wandering about, sheep and goats grazing, and chickens running around everywhere, while Pierre is always accompanied by his faithful shaggy dog, Nounours (Teddy Bear). Pierre's ancestors bought the property in 1896 and built the imposing winery and cellar that stand today atop a hill with stones from the estate quarry. His parents made the crucial decision not to pull up and plant new vines in the 1980s, meaning he inherited a tremendous selection of vines, some 120 years old, growing in a mix of red clay and sandstone. Although not certified organic, they use no herbicides and pesticides. ***www.chateaulesollieux.com; tel +33 4 68 43 35 20; Route Départementale 613, Montséret***

05 DOMAINE LEDOGAR

The Ledogar family have been making wine in Ferrals for numerous generations, closely associated with the local winemaking cooperative until the arrival of the uncompromising brothers, Xavier and Mathieu. They are what could be termed 'natural wine' fundamentalists, and since 1997 have created a sprawling 22-hectare (54-acre) vineyard, essentially around the esteemed *terroir* of the Boutenac Cru, producing wines that are 100% organic, working the vine around a lunar calendar, with no sulphur and a hand-picked harvest. Over a dozen different grape varieties are cultivated – not just classic Carignan and Grenache but Mourvedre, Maccabeu and Merselan too – which are vinified separately in small parcels before assemblage. They have a small tasting room in the centre of Ferrals, and discussions can get passionate - perhaps providing a good moment to adjourn to a brilliant new bistro across the road, Chez Bembe, run by a giant of a rugby man, the other great passion around here.

Tel +33 6 81 06 14 51; Place de la Republique, Ferrals-les-Corbières; by appointment

06 DOMAINE LES CASCADES

Laurent and Sylvie Bachevillier are typical of the new generation of young *vignerons* choosing the Corbières as the ideal place to set up a winery. They are also very much aware of the potential of wine tourism, and have opened a charming three-room B&B and eco-*gîte* adjacent to their cellar. The domaine revolves around the concept of biodiversity, producing not only organic wine from the small 6-hectare (15-acre) vineyard, but vegetables, saffron, truffles and olive oil too. Instead of using chemical insecticides, Laurent takes out their two donkeys and three fearsome Hungarian sheep to graze among the vines. Their wines will take you by surprise. Cuvée S, named after Sylvie, is a natural wine, 100% Grenache with no sulphite added; while Cuvée L is a concentrated, extremely low-yield Syrah. There are several cellars in this village, and it is also worth checking out Domaine Rouire Segur, a more traditional Corbières producer, located just across the road.

www.domainelescascades.fr; tel +33 6 88 21 84 99; 4 Ave des Corbières, Ribaute

'The moment I saw these fabulous 100-year-old bush vines planted in the limestone hills of the Corbières, I knew this was the perfect place for me to make wine.' *–Jon Bowen, English winemaker*

07 DOMAINE SAINTE-CROIX

The landscape changes as you start climbing into the dramatic jagged mountains of Haut Corbières. There is very little agriculture, villages are few and far between, and ancient vines grow in a patchwork of small parcels on a variety of different soils – limestone, clay, schist, volcanic. It was this diversity that attracted adventurous English winemaker Jon Bowen and his wife, Elizabeth, to settle here 10 years ago. 'The climate is also fascinating,' says Bowen, speaking French with a marked Languedoc accent, 'as we have both the influence of the mountains and the sea, which is only 15km away.' In the cellar, he has strong ideas, preferring cement vats to steel, and sparingly using old barrels to age, 'just to give an idea of the wood, nothing more'. These organic wines immediately have a strong identity, be it the surprisingly full-bodied, mineral white, La Serre, an *assemblage* of Grenache Blanc with the lesser-known Grenache Gris, or the robust Magneric red, where he blends little known local grapes – Morrastel and Alicante – with old-vine Carignan and Grenache. This is very much an anarchic, garage winery, set in a wild, isolated village, so when visitors arrive, Jon just sets up bottles and glasses on an old wooden barrel, which serves as the impromptu tasting table.

www.saintecroixvins.com; tel +33 6 85 67 63 88; 7 Ave des Corbières, Fraisse-des-Corbières; by appointment

08 EMBRES CASTELMAURE

It is quite an expedition to discover this historic winemaking cooperative. It dominates an isolated hamlet of 150 souls, which is lost in the wild, windswept Cathar mountains, and which locals say 'is perched at the end of the world'. But it is worth the effort for the fantastic welcome, the buzzing ambience in the surprisingly modern tasting room and, above all, the extraordinary wines. You can't escape the culture of the winemaking cooperative in the Corbières, a system that historically has given *vignerons* financial security but has hardly garnered a reputation for quality wines. Not here in Castelmaure, though. Founded in 1921, there are 69 participants in the cooperative, all characters, but none more so than Patrick Marien, president for 29 years. With the cooperative's 400 hectares (988 acres) of ancient Carignan and Grenache bush vines, Marien and expert winemaker Berhard Puiyo (locally they're known as Fidel and Ché) constantly experiment – ageing in the bottle rather than barrels, using the old method of cement vats, low dosages of sulphite and devising creative labels that would be the envy of New York ad agencies. Each wine is a surprise, from the uncomplicated La Buvette, 'what we call our vin de soif' (easy to drink when you're thirsty), to the voluptuous barrel-aged N°3 Corbières.
www.castelmaure.com; tel +33 4 68 45 91 83; 4 Route des Canelles, Embres-et-Castelmaure

ESSENTIAL INFORMATION

WHERE TO STAY

CHÂTEAU DE L'HORTE
A winemaker B&B set in a grandiose 18th-century château with the four bedrooms located over the vast *chai* (barrel room). Pool and garden terrace for barbecue.
www.chateaudelhorte.fr; tel +33 4 68 43 91 70; Rue d'Escales, Montbrun-des-Corbières

CHÂTEAU DE LASTOURS
Lastours combines a state-of-the-art winery, giant outdoor contemporary sculptures, a restaurant and 10 B&B rooms in discrete cottages.
www.chateaudelastours.com; tel +33 4 68 48 64 74; Portel-des-Corbières

WHERE TO EAT

O VIEUX TONNEAUX
Peyriac is famous for its wetland lagoons and flamingos, and for this cosy bistro. Cristelle Bernabeu cooks a delicious *bourride d'anguille* (eel stew).
www.ovieuxtonneaux.com; tel +33 4 68 48 39 54; 3 Place de la Mairie, Peyriac-de-Mer

BISTROT PLACE DU MARCHÉ
Rub shoulders with *vignerons* in this lively gourmet bistro where Eric Delalande serves tasty dishes such as duck magret grilled with wild garrigue herbs.
tel +33 4 68 70 09 13; 8 Ave de la Mairie, Villeséque des Corbières

RESTAURANT LA LUCIOLE
This tiny winemaking village used to have a dozen bistros, but they all closed over time. Parisians Gilles and Helene Fliant reopened La Luciole; locals flock here for cuisine such as potato cakes stuffed with pig's trotters.
www.restaurantlaluciole.fr; tel +33 4 68 40 87 74; 3 Place de la Republique, Luc-sur-Orbieu

WHAT TO DO

The Corbières mountains are marked by awesome clifftop Cathar castles, dating back to a 12th-century religious war. Follow the route of the châteaux; don't miss the death-defying Château de Peyrepertuse.
www.payscathare.org

CELEBRATIONS

The small town Conhilac gets taken over for a month-long international jazz festival each November.

COSNE-COURS-SUR-LOIRE
LA VERRERIE
FRANCE
Loire River
05
06
04
03
02
01
07

[France]

THE LOIRE

Take your time and explore the crisp white wines and fairy-tale châteaux of the languid Loire River in central France by boat, bicycle or car.

The Loire is the longest river in France, and along its banks grow some of the nation's most famous and varied wines: the sharp white Muscadet and Anjou, sparkling Vouvray, and the fresh tannins expressed in the Cabernet Franc grape of Chinon and Saumur. And just 200km from Paris are the iconic vineyards of Sancerre, from which distinctive Sauvignon has become one of the world's best-loved wines. The grand medieval town of Sancerre sits majestically atop a vine-clad hill overlooking the dozen villages that cover the appellation. The first reference to wines from Sancerre date back to 583 AD when Gregory of Tours made reference to the vintages here. Up until the phylloxera epidemic of 1886, the majority of production was actually red wine – Pinot Noir – and it was only when the vines were replanted that the decision was made to change to the now famous Sauvignon Blanc.

Few people who today tour the state-of-the-art cellars of wealthy winemakers realise that just one generation ago there was a great deal of poverty here, with *vignerons* struggling to sell a little-known and little-respected wine, their families only surviving thanks to the financial contribution of their wives, who raised goats to make Crottin de Chevignol cheeses. Sancerre owes its present fame and success to two factors: the young generation of vintners who took their wines up to Paris after the end of WWII, opening wine bars and convincing the capital that Sancerre was a fashionable wine; and becoming early exponents of wine tourism by encouraging the same Parisians to visit Sancerre, see the vineyards and buy direct from the winemaker. This is still the case today, as wine tourists still get a very special welcome. And now the whole of the world seems to have fallen in love with Sancerre.

GET THERE
Paris Charles de Gaulle is the nearest major airport, 226km from Sancerre. Car hire is available.

01 DOMAINE ALPHONSE MELLOT

The perfect introduction to the wines of Sancerre is a tasting right in the heart of the town with Alphonse Mellot – either the irrepressible patriarch himself, who is a larger-than-life character, the unofficial king of Sancerre, who has almost single-handedly promoted the wine around the world; or his son, Alphonse Jr, who continued the work of his father by transforming the domaine in both the vineyards and cellar. For 19 generations, as far back as 1513, the Mellot family has been making wines here. Among their number was a certain Cesar Mellot who held the distinguished title of *Conseilleur de Vin* for the Sun King, Louis XIV.

This incredible history is apparent as you wander through the 15th-century cellars beneath the streets of Sancerre. Tasting the wines, though, alerts you to the advances of modern winemaking. Alphonse Jr has made this 50-hectare (123-acre) vineyard biodynamic, limiting each vine to just four to six bunches of grapes at harvest, and sending quality soaring. The cornerstone, La Moussière, is a classic flinty Sancerre, while the barrel-aged Cuvée Edmund has a richness of flavour and subtle aroma that is rare for a Sauvignon. And Generation XIX is a spectacular Pinot Noir, meriting comparison with great Burgundy vintages rather than Sancerre Rouge.

www.mellot.com; tel +33 2 48 54 07 41; Rue Porte César, Sancerre

02 DOMAINE ANDRE DEZAT & FILS

The *vignerons* of Sancerre have always made sure that visitors are warmly welcomed and few regions of France sell so much of their wine directly to the public through estate visits. The Dezat family were one of the pioneers of this philosophy, typified by the genial patriarch, Andre Dezat (universally known as Le P'tit De), who took over the domaine after WWII. Succeeded by his two sons, Louis and Simon, who are now aided by their two sons, Arnaud and Firmin, the family has a well-deserved reputation for producing outstanding, well-thought-out wines, perhaps fine-tuning each year but never following fads. Their signature Sauvignon Blanc is always aged in steel vats, while the excellent Pinot Noir matures in three- to five-year-old barrels, with a Cuvée Speciale from 50-year-old vines in new oak, perfect if you are patient enough to lay down the wine for a few years. Whatever time of day you pass by for a tasting, it is like dropping in on a party of old friends, with a mix, say, of Dutch tourists who have been buying for 20 years, Parisians up to restock their 'cave', and either the local priest or gendarme.

www.dezat-sancerre.com; tel +33 2 48 79 38 82; Rue des Tonneliers, Chaudoux, Verdigny

02

03 DOMAINE PAUL CHERRIER

Stephane Cherrier is a young *vigneron* with a lot of respect for the past. A proud portrait of his grandfather in WWI uniform hangs in the tasting room, and Stephane recounts how, 'My grandmother, like most villagers here, used to raise goats to make cheese, which often saved families from poverty when there was a bad harvest or before Sancerre became such a popular wine. In fact, until 10 years ago, we used to sell our wine in bulk to middlemen.' Stephane worked in vineyards in Chile, New Zealand and Australia before coming back to run the domaine. He has made rapid progress, cutting back the use of chemicals in the vineyard and experimenting in the cellar.

Part of his vines grow on the flat in argilo-calcaire soil, while those on the slope are marked by the more distinctive *terre blanche*, and it is these two soil types that really mark the wines of Sancerre. While his sharp, acidic Sauvignon is aged in steel vats, he is also working to develop the complex Cuvée Philippa in wooden barrels. There is no formal tasting room: Stephane takes visitors

BODY Philippe © Getty Images

on an enthusiastic tour of the cellar itself, not just opening bottles but plunging a glass pipette straight into the barrel to test for ageing before he decides it is time for bottling.
tel +33 2 48 79 37 28; Chemin Matifat, Chaudoux, Verdigny; by appointment

04 DOMAINE VINCENT GAUDRY

Vincent Gaudry is an artisan winemaker with strong ideas on winemaking. Sancerre is only slowly embracing the organic wine revolution, but since 2002, this domaine has been officially certified organic (what the French call *bio*). His ancient cellar may be in the village of Chambre, but the 11-hectare (27-acre) vineyard is spread out in parcels across the communes of Sury-en-Vaux, Saint-Satur, Verdigny and Sancerre, 'because I want grapes growing on the key different soils in the region,' explains Vincent, 'flinty silex, caillotte and argilo-calcaire'. Ageing the wine in small old barrels, he refuses to use air-conditioning in his cellar, preferring the natural temperature that changes with seasons: 'This was built in the 18th century and was fine for making wine then, so why change now?' His wines are explosive, especially Constellation du Scorpion, a Sauvignon made from a parcel of 100% Silex. 'I want to continue the unique characteristics we have with our wine,' he says, 'to respect our elders who have made Sancerre famous all over the world, and not change for change's sake.'
www.vincent-gaudry.com; tel +33 2 48 79 49 25; Petite Chambre, Sury-en-Vaux; by appointment

05 DOMAINE MARTIN

Of all the villages in the region surrounding Sancerre, Chavignol is the most picturesque, its ancient medieval houses tightly enclosed by two steep hillsides crisscrossed

03 Riccardo Spila © 4Corners Images

DUCEPT Pascal © Getty Images

with vineyards. The quality of the wines produced here can reach exceptional levels, with the village's name alongside the Sancerre appellation. The slopes, however, are incredibly difficult to work, both for tending the vines and precariously hand-picking during the harvest.

'The winemakers of Sancerre have always had a tradition of welcoming wine lovers who make the effort to come and visit us here.'

–Alphonse Mellot, winemaker

After working in different wine regions around France, Pierre Martin came back 10 years ago to help his father, Yves, with their 17-hectare (42-acre) estate. Together, they are moving with the times: the vineyards are being converted to organic, and Pierre and his wife plan to open a proper tasting room and B&B in the village. Pierrot does not need much persuasion to take visitors up to the top of his two prize vineyards: Les Culs de Beaujeu and Les Monts Damnes (the cursed mountains). You'll need a head for heights, though, as the vineyard drops off like the edge of a cliff, with perilous narrow steps linking each terrace. Back in the cellar, the wines are perfectly paired with the famous Crottin de Chavignol goats cheese. *Tel +33 2 48 54 24 57; Le Bourg, Chavignol; by appointment*

06 DOMAINE PASCAL ET NICOLAS REVERDY

You have to follow the narrowest winding road through picture-perfect vineyards to arrive in the tiny hamlet of Maimbray, whose 40 inhabitants include 10 winemaking families. Pascal Reverdy took over the 14-hectare (34-acre) domaine in 1992 and stopped selling grapes to the cooperative to concentrate on making his own wines. Today, Pascal is helped by his 14-year-old and 17-year-old sons, both committed to becoming *vignerons*. Don't be surprised if he begins a *degustation* by pouring his fresh, fruity Pinot Noir: 'I feel the Sancerre Blanc is too aromatic to taste first, as afterwards the rosé and red may appear bland.' This used to be a working farm, and the wine cellar resembles a museum, filled with ancient farming tools, while the cosy tasting room looks like the family dining room, with a long wooden table, kitchen and wood-fired stove. Just don't ask Pascal about the domaine's website. 'You've got to be joking!' he exclaims. 'We are in Maimbray, you know. We don't have a shop, bar or restaurant here. People just concentrate on making the best wine possible. A website is something I will let my kids sort out.' *Tel +33 2 48 79 37 31; Maimbray, Sury-en-Vaux*

07 DOMAINE HENRI PELLE

The sprawling 40-hectare (99-acre) property of the Pelle family spreads across Sancerre's appellation into the adjoining appellation of Menetou-Salon. There are many reasons this is a must-visit winery. It provides the perfect opportunity to judge the Sauvignon Blanc and Pinot Noir from Menetou-Salon, so long the poor cousin to Sancerre, but now the rising star whose quality threatens one day to eclipse Sancerre itself. And 28-year-old Paul-Henry Pelle himself is one of the stars of the newest generation of winemakers around here. He welcomes visitors to the state-of-the-art cellar, a labyrinth of vast Tronconic vats, used to limit the woody effect as wines age, and at the drop of a hat will whisk you off in his battered old army jeep for a tour of the surrounding vineyards. Be prepared to taste a lot of wines too, as Paul-Henry vinifies each *clos* of vines separately and often bottles them as individual cuvées, showing how the soil can completely change a wine. 'Yes, I have a lot of different cuvées,' he says, 'but that is what is exciting about making wines – otherwise I would just get fed up.' *www.domainepelle.com; tel +33 2 48 64 42 48; Morogues*

01 The gardens at Château de Villandry

02 Grape harvesting in the Bourgueil vineyard

03 Blois town on the Loire river

04 The castle of Saumur and its vineyard

ESSENTIAL INFORMATION

WHERE TO STAY

MOULIN DES VRILLERES
Winemaker B&Bs are rare in the Sancerre region, but visitors get a warm welcome from Christian and Karine Lauverjat, who include a full tour of their cellar as well as a tasting. *www.sancerre-online.com; tel +332 48 79 38 28; Sury-en-Vaux*

LA CÔTE DES MONT DAMNÉS
Jean-Marc Bourgeois is the son of one of the most famous Sancerre winemakers, but chose to become a chef before coming home to renovate an old hotel. Today, guests can relax in designer rooms and dine in his gourmet restaurant. *www.montsdamnes.com; tel +33 2 48 54 01 72; Place de l'Orme, Chavignol*

WHERE TO EAT

RESTAURANT LA TOUR
This Michelin-starred restaurant features the talents of chef Baptiste Fournier. Don't miss the *pigeonneau de St Quentin* (pigeon with grapes and wild mushrooms). *www.latoursancerre.fr; tel +33 2 48 54 00 81; 31 Nouvelle Place, Sancerre*

AU PETIT GOUTER
Brilliant village bistro with wines from over 50 local Sancerre producers, the perfect pairing with both the famous Crottin de Chavignol cheese, made by the owner's son, and another local speciality, a 'friture' of tiny deep-fried fish caught in the Loire. *tel +33 2 48 54 01 66; Le Bourg, Chavignol*

WHAT TO DO

Sancerre overlooks the mighty Loire River, and for a healthy break from wine tasting, go rambling or cycling along its banks, hire a canoe or, at the sand flats of the village of Saint-Satur, sunbathe at the water's edge and have a dip, though beware of currents.

CELEBRATIONS

Nothing goes better with a crisp, chilled Sancerre than a juicy oyster, and on the last weekend of October there is the Fetes des Huitres, a huge wine and oyster festival in the immense Caves de la Mignonne (www.caves-de-la-mignonne.com), an underground quarry dating back to the 14th century.

01 Chamonix Valley

02 Château de Glerolles & Lake Geneva

03 Ardèche canyon

Justin Foulkes © 4Corners Images

[France]

THE RHÔNE

From a phenomenal region of France, with snowy mountains in its north and broad, hot valleys to the south, come blockbuster red wines that will dazzle your palate.

The wine region of the Rhône Valley stretches from just below Lyon, past Avignon and right down through the south, where the mighty river meets the Mediterranean. Grapes have been grown here for more than 2000 years and there is a tremendous variety of wines to discover as you travel down the valley.

The Northern Rhône, from Vienne down to Valence, boasts spectacular scenery, with the river's steep banks covered by terraced vineyards, producing some of France's most famous wines: the intense Syrah of Côte-Rôtie, Cornas and Hermitage; and the elegant Condrieu made from the complex Viognier grape. Below Valence the landscapes become more Provençal, and Syrah is grown alongside Grenache, Mourvèdre and Carignan. These grapes are often blended, which can produce the potent and celebrated Châteauneuf-du-Pape; up-and-coming appellations such as Gigondas, Vacqueyras and Rasteau; or Côtes du Rhône, the classic wine you will find served in every French bistro. Travellers will quickly discover that winemakers in the northern Rhône tend to be more traditional. But once the road heads south of Valence – where plots of vines are much cheaper – a new generation of younger *vignerons* is moving in, eager to experiment, especially with natural wines, which are sweeping the fashionable wine bars of most European cities.

Wine tourism has become a well-organised art in the Rhône, with the traveller offered tempting places to stay on many domaines, while restaurants have woken up to the wonderful opportunities of wine pairings – a sharp white Crozes-Hermitage with local cheeses such as a creamy Saint-Félicien and tangy Picodon; the flinty Saint-Péray accompanying salt-baked line-fished seabass; and a robust Cornas perfect with a lean fillet of wild deer and forest berries.

GET THERE
Lyon is the nearest major airport, 49km from Chavanay. The train from Paris to Lyon takes 2hr 20min. Car hire is available.

Imagebroker © Alamy

01 DOMAINE DU MONTEILLET

Stephane Montez is one of those classic larger-than-life French winemakers. His new state-of-the-art cellar, perched high above the vineyards of Condrieu, is a lively rendezvous where local winemakers, wine merchants, chefs and curious tourists bustle in and out all day to taste his splendid wines. Walking out of the minimalist contemporary cellar with a glass of Condrieu in hand, visitors can gaze out over vineyards that stretch as far as the banks of the Rhône. Families can relax here too, as there is a kids' corner with games, something all winemakers in the Rhône Valley are encouraged to set up. Be sure to go to the back of the tasting room, as a glass wall lets you peek into a barrel cellar that is carved into the rockface.

'I am a 10th-generation winemaker,' Stephane proudly states, 'and we have just found a purchase act dated 1732 for a parcel of vines that I still own today.' Stephane has vines in the two most prestigious Rhône appellations, the red Côte Rôtie and white Condrieu, made from the Viognier grape, considered by some experts to be the greatest French white wine. He explains how, till the early 1980s, 'Condrieu was just known as "Viognier", as this was our own native grape, for centuries grown only here. Today, the whole world seems to be planting Viognier, from Australia to California and Chile, but it only becomes a great wine here because of the perfect combination of poor soil and a median climate, not too hot, not too cold.'

www.montez.fr; tel +33 4 74 87 24 57; 6 Le Montelier, Chavanay

02 FAYOLLE FILS ET FILLE

There are five winemakers in the pretty village of Gervans, and three are called Fayolle. But you have to drive through a maze of backstreets to reach the edge of a vineyard and the homely cellar of the Fayolle siblings, Laurent and Céline. Their family was the first to stop selling grapes to the cooperative and start bottling Crozes-Hermitage, the largest appellation in the Northern Rhône, stretching over 1600 hectares (3953 acres). Their 10-hectare

(24-acre) estate spreads from flat plains by the bank of the Rhône, where Laurent still ploughs with a horse, up to rolling hills where the soil changes to dense granite, and each traditional *gobelet* bush vine is attached to a long palisade stick to prevent breaking and bending. This is typical of Rhône cultivation, where up in Côte Rôtie the vine needs three palisades to protect it from fierce winds. Pontaix White, made from Marsanne vines over 60 years old, is predominantly aged in steel vats, which yield a delicate honeyish flavour.
www.fayolle-filsetfille.fr; tel +33 4 75 03 33 74; 9 Rue du Ruisseau, Gervans

03 CAVE DE TAIN

All along the vine-clad slopes of the Rhône you will see distinctive Hollywood-style signs of the famed *Maisons* that have long dominated the wine trade here. Chapoutier, Jaboulet and Guigal each boast their own domaines, but also act as *négoces* (traders), producing millions of bottles of wines from grapes they buy rather than grow. There is another big player, which does not go in for signs, but has a reputation for quality that sees critics nominate it as France's top winemaking cooperative. Founded in 1933, the Cave de Tain has 300 *associes vignerons*, covering 1000 hectares (2471 acres) of vines. Although it produce a staggering five million bottles a year, membership is restricted to winemakers within a radius of roughly 15km, and Tain is one of the rare cooperatives to own its own domaine. These precious vines include highly prized parcels that make it the second-largest owner of Hermitage, which is the name not only of the appellation, but also of the hill that looms over their cellar. A visit here also includes the newly opened cellars, a €10-million investment that ranges from a barrel room of 2000 barriques (wine barrels made of new oak) to the modern technology of cement 'hippos' for single-parcel vinification.
www.cavedetain.com; tel +33 4 75 08 20 87; 22 Route de Larnage, Tain-l'Hermitage

04 DOMAINE COURBIS

Driving into medieval Châteaubourg, you can't miss a huge mural advertising the St Joseph and Cornas wines of the Courbis brothers, Laurent and Dominique. The brothers can trace their family roots here back to the 16th century, though their modern cellar makes use of all the latest technology. It lies just at the bottom of a slope of vines so steep you can hurt your neck trying to see up to the summit, typical of the Cornas appellation, which rivals Côte-Rôtie with its vertiginous layered terraces. The vineyards of St Joseph stretch for 50km along the Rhône, and both the red and white vintages produced at Courbis are reasonably priced and need little further ageing to be enjoyed when opened. The Syrah is peppery and rich, while the white Marsanne is incredibly mineral, which is no surprise if you drive up to the Les Royes vineyard and see the barren rocky limestone the vines shoot up from.
www.vins-courbis-rhone.com; tel +33 4 75 81 81 60; Route de Saint-Romain, Châteaubourg

05 DOMAINE ALAIN VOGE

Alain Voge is a highly respected figure in the recent history of Cornas, which has metamorphosed from a little-known wine into a genuine contender for the title of the top Rhône wine, with steep prices to match. Monsieur Voge lives next door to his cellar, and although officially retired, he pops in most days to give his opinion. The estate is now run by Alberic Mazoyer, formerly from Chapoutier. In 10 years, Alberic has moved the estate to virtually 100% organic and biodynamic winemaking, a rare achievement in this part of the Rhône Valley. 'Just drive up to the walled terraces of the Cornas vineyard,' he suggests, 'and you will see that our work is just as much that of a builder, spending months each year restoring and repairing the walls that keep the vineyard together. These walls date back to Roman times and we often dig up artefacts and fossils. This is why the wine is relatively expensive, because we have to invest so much financially, and even more if we are to strictly follow organic cultivation.'

'People claim Syrah originally came from Greece, Sicily or even faraway Persia, but now we have official DNA proof that it was born on the slopes of the Rhône Valley.'

–Xavier Gomart, Director Cave de Tain

You have to negotiate the narrow backstreets of Cornas to discover the domaine's cellar, tucked away in a courtyard. The tasting room is decorated with distinctive modern paintings and sculptures, and visitors sit down around a big wooden table while Alberic or one of his assistants begins opening bottles. Usually only the latest vintages are available for tasting – which is problematic as Cornas needs to mature for a few years before it can be properly appreciated – unless Monsieur Voges himself makes an appearance and decides to let guests try a dusty, older bottle from his private collection.
www.alain-voge.com; tel +33 4 75 40 32 04; 4 Impasse de l'Equerre, Cornas

06 DOMAINE DU TUNNEL

Sitting in the comfy leather armchairs of his tasting boutique on Saint-Péray's high street, affable *vigneron*, Stéphane Robert, admits that he doesn't have a website, but asks if many winemakers can claim their cellar is housed in genuine 19th-century train tunnel. Stéphane began making wine in his parents' garage, and when he bought his first parcels of vines 20 years ago, he fiercely bargained for the town hall to sell him an abandoned tunnel too. Until now, he has concentrated on producing individual, high-calibre wines of little-known white Saint-Péray (including a terrific 100% Roussanne cuvée) and intense Cornas vintages, some from vines over 100 years old, which need many, many years of ageing before they reach perfect maturity. And now his tunnel is finally ready for inauguration. It accommodates a spectacular 150m-long cellar carved into the hillside, where he will vinify, store barrels for ageing, and receive guests for tasting.
tel +33 4 75 80 04 66; 20 Rue de la République, Saint-Péray

07 LE MAZEL

This corner of the southern Rhône is something of a Holy Land for crusaders of the natural wine movement, with a band of New Age *vignerons* making zero-sulphite wines that may sometimes be unstable, slightly oxidised or a little fizzy, but when perfectly made, will surprise even the most expert taster. Gérald and Jocelyne Oustric inherited a 30-hectare (74-acre) estate whose grapes used to go straight to the village cooperative. Gérald, however, was intent on making and bottling his own wine. He caught the natural-wine bug early and eliminated sulphur in 1997. Today he farms only 18 hectares (44 acres), renting out more than half of the area to two young similar-minded *vignerons*: Frenchman Sylvain Bock and an eccentric Czech, Andrea Calek, considered by some locals to be from another planet, but whose natural wines are lauded by critics and exported as far afield as Japan and the USA.

The place to go for a quiet tasting to really understand these unusual vintages is Gérald Oustric's cellar, an ancient stone cottage in the heart of the picturesque village of Valvignères. Behind a huge wooden door, you will discover the all-but-abandoned Portan grape in his C'est Im-Portant Cuvée, while Cuvée Charbonnières is a distinctive interpretation of Chardonnay, aged for one year in steel vats followed by two years in old wooden barrels. While Gérald works in his cellar, Jocelyne runs the tastings, explaining the characteristics that make their natural wines taste so unique. At the end, most visitors adjourn for a *plat du jour* at La Tour Cassée, the friendly bistro over the road, which has a brilliant wine list.
tel +33 4 75 52 51 02; Valvignères

08 MAS DE LIBIAN

As the Rhône heads south below Valence and Montélimar, the vineyards may not have famous names, but the winemakers are young, unconventional and pushing boundaries. In the dreamy Provençal village of Saint-Marcel d'Ardèche, the two major estates are both run by feisty clans of women. The bubbly Saladin sisters, Elisabeth and Marie-Laurence (www.domaine-saladin.com), make audacious vintages such as Tralala!, a fruity Grenache rosé, and Fan de Lune, a potent blend of Mourvèdre and Grenache Noir. Almost next door is the Mas de Libian, a matriarchial family of *vigneronnes* whose estate of venerable bush vines dates back to 1670. Hélène Thibon, together with her *maman* and sisters, has transformed Libian into an estate producing certified organic and biodynamic wines, and has returned to ploughing the soil with Nestor, a noble workhorse. Their most popular cuvée is Vin de Pétanque, a blend of Grenache and Syrah eminently drinkable on a steamy summer evening, while the fuller-bodied Khayyam is barrel-aged Grenache Noir, which the ladies named after the Persian poet 'because of his texts honouring wine and women'.
www.masdelibian.com; tel +33 4 75 04 66 22; Quartier Libian, Saint-Marcel d'Ardeche

Photoprofi30 © Getty Images

ESSENTIAL INFORMATION

WHERE TO STAY

LA GERINE
Perched high above the Rhône, this comfortable B&B is surrounded by the vineyards of Côte-Rôtie. Relaxing pool and spectacular views. *www.lagerine.com; tel +33 4 74 56 03 46; 2 Côte de la Gerine, Ampuis*

HOTEL MICHEL CHABRAN
Old-fashioned but charming inn on the mythical Route Nationale 7, which travels down to the south of France. Run by a Michelin-starred chef. *www.chabran.com; tel +33 4 75 84 60 09; 29 Ave du 45 ème Parallèle, Pont de l'Isère*

DOMAINE NOTRE DAME DE COUSIGNAC
Winemaker Raphael Pommier and his American wife, Rachel, welcome guests to a rustic farmhouse, where tastings of their organic wines are held every evening. *www.ndcousignac villegiature.fr; tel +33 6 27 30 69 92; Quartier Cousignac, Bourg Saint-Andéol*

WHERE TO EAT

AUBERGE MONNET
Romantic restaurant on an island in the Rhône serving regional specialities such as frogs' legs, stuffed pig trotter and tasty cheeses and charcuterie. Eric, the welcoming owner, has a brilliant selection of wines sold by the glass. *www.aubergemonnet.com; tel +33 4 75 84 57 80; 3 Place du Petit Puits, La-Roche-de-Glun*

LA TOUR CASSÉE
Cosy village bistro that mixes traditional Ardèche favourites (hearty cabbage soup) with exotic recipes, such as a tagine of duck confit with dates and quince. Excellent list of natural wines. *www.restaurant-tour-cassee.fr; tel +33 4 75 52 45 32; Valvignères*

LA FARIGOULE
Overlooking a vineyard, this old-fashioned auberge is perfect for a chilled Côte du Rhône rosé accompanied by a tasty caillette, the local take on meatloaf. *www.auberge-lafarigoule.com; tel +33 4 75 04 02 60; Bidon*

WHAT TO DO

From Vallon Pont d'Arc, head off for the day on a guided canoe trip along the Ardèche River, where you weave through spectacular gorges.

CELEBRATIONS

Two wonderful festivals at different ends of the Rhône, Jazz à Vienne (www.jazzavienne.com) for two weeks from 26 June, and Avignon's Theatrical Festival (www.festival-avignon.com) running through the month of July.

01

[Georgia]

KAKHETI

In this ancient, mountainous land, a youthful spirit and world-class traditional wines reward grape-loving travellers with a taste for the unknown.

The Georgian wine experience is like no other. The story of wine here is so old, so real, that it can make what we know of ancient Greece and Rome seem like recent history.

Georgia is widely recognised as the land where man first learned to tame the wild grapevine, around 6000BC. In most of the country, winemaking technology has changed little since then. Grapes are still harvested by hand, and foot-pressed in the hollowed-out trunks of ancient trees. The juice flows into underground clay amphoras, known as *qvevri*, where it ferments and matures without additives or manipulation. When the sealed *qvevri* is opened in the spring of the following year, its wine is clear, bright and uniquely pure. Of course, not all Georgian wines are made in this ancestral way – there are a host of industrial wineries working with tractors and steel – but enough natural artisans remain to keep the traditions alive.

In terms of production, the most important Georgian wine region is Kakheti, in the eastern hills. Nearly two thirds of the country's wine originates here; most of the wines are derived from white grapes, and many are kept in contact with their skins for an extended time. 'Kakhetian', in fact, is a stylistic adjective across Georgia, meaning a wine of exceptional weight and tannin. Yet even a brief visit reveals that Kakheti is not homogeneous, but an area of diverse microclimates, soil types and varietals. Most of the highest-altitude vineyards are here; in an average year, it's drier and warmer than elsewhere in Georgia.

The Gombori mountain range defines Kakheti, dividing it into 'Inner' and 'Outer' zones. Precariously perched on a wing of that range, the small city of Sighnaghi is Kakheti's cultural capital, and it's the natural gateway to any wider visit. Framed against the tall, snowcapped Caucasus, its image is iconic to both Kakheti and Georgia as a whole. As you're touring from here, prepare yourself for the fact that Kakheti's greatest wines tend not to be found in the open, but in villagers' backyards, buried underground, awaiting release.

GET THERE
Tbilisi International is the nearest major airport, 100km from Sighnaghi. Car hire is available.

01 NIKI ANTADZE

For Niki, winemaking is the latest in a series of careers. Starting in 2006, he elaborated his wines each year at a number of friends' spaces, some of which didn't even classify as 'cellars'. Today, he has about a dozen *qvevris* buried underground in the west-Kakhetian village of Manavi, beside a small apartment. Manavi has been recognised for many generations as a Grand cru site for its sunny, south-facing exposition, which allows the grapes an extra degree of ripeness. This is one of the best *terroirs* in the country for the white Mtsvane varietal.

There's no tasting room or retail shop; currently, Niki's finishing his *marani* (winery) with thinly plastered walls, insulated by hay bales and a high roof through which ambient air can flow. Bottom line: there's not much to see here. But if you can make it happen, this is one of the most crucial visits you can make in Georgia as a whole, precisely because Niki's in a period of transition.

Until the 2014 vintage, he basically bottled two wines, a Rkatsiteli and a Mtsvane. Now, in addition to the *marani* changes, he's deciding to bottle both single-vineyard and single-*qvevri* wines for the first time, along with other exciting experimentations, which include one of the finest red Saperavis in Kakheti. (Just keep in mind that he's not always available, and the quantities are very small.)

Take the S5 highway east from Tbilisi, then left and north, direction Manavi. For Niki's availability & further directions, check in at Gvino Underground Wine Bar (Tbilisi, tel +995 322 30 96 10); by appointment

02 PHEASANT'S TEARS

If you had to nominate the estate that has had the greatest effect on the global perception of Georgian wine, it would be Pheasant's Tears. Partners John Wurdeman (international spokesperson, painter, American expat) and Gela Patalishvili (multi-generation Georgian winegrower, consummate toastmaster) are as committed to ancestral methods of *qvevri* production with local varietals as they are to their promulgation – not only within Georgia, but also abroad. Pheasant's Tears has been immeasurably important in inspiring local growers to continue the work of centuries; at the same time, the team's energy in exporting multiple products is boundless.

A few of the white varietals they grow and bottle include Rkatsiteli, Kisi, Mtsvane, and Chinuri. Then

01 Harvesting grapes in Kakheti

02 The Rioni River Valley

03 Georgian wine fermented in *qvevri*

04 Alaverdi Cathedral

'Georgian traditional wine is family wine where it is made with special care and the expectation that anyone who drinks it will be filled with joy.'

–Archil Natsvishvili, Kakheti

there's the reds: Saperavi, Shavkapito and Tavkveri, along with one of the country's finest, oak-aged *chachas* (brandies). Each bears the stamp of long tradition and ethical production methods. A visit here will assure you of Kakheti's vital relevance to the wine world at large. In addition, they are completing construction in 2015 of what will be the largest and most comprehensive winemaking and ageing cellars in the country. Not to be missed.
tel +995 355 23 15 56; 18 Baratashvili St, Sighnaghi; by appointment

03 KEROVANI WINE CELLAR

This is one of the newest and most exciting projects happening in Kakheti today. After a flurry of work burying *qvevri* underneath his home, 41-year-old Archil Natsvlishvili bottled the first vintage of his family's wines – Rkatsiteli and Saperavi – in 2013 and is currently building a tasting/tourist welcome room that starts at his basement door. The wines are additive-free and have the potential to stand as benchmarks for the region. The 'tasting room' is at the base of the six-*qvevri* cellar and is as casual as you could wish – pure authenticity. The new bottle-ageing room is just above – don't forget to ask for a brief tour.
tel +995 599 40 84 14; 18 Aghameshenebili St, Sighnaghi; by appointment; tasting room opening autumn 2015

04 OKRO'S WINE

Engaging and charismatic, John Okruashvili heads this forward-thinking winery, which specialises in Rkatsiteli, and aims for as little sulphur additions as possible

Andrew Montgomery © Lonely Planet Images

05 Banqueting, Georgian-style

06 Pheasant's Tears Wine Merchant

to achieve optimum purity. He bottles a range of wines, at several approachable price levels, and affords the visitor a terrific overview of Kakheti's full potential.
tel +995 516 22 22 28; 7 Chavchavadze St, Sighnaghi; by appointment

05 SOLIKO TSAISHVILI

Niki Antadze has referred to Soliko as his *sensei*, a sentiment with which many other growers would certainly agree, if only for his pioneering influence. An academic and translator, Soliko started making wine as a side-project decades ago, and began to bottle wine in 2003 with four wine-loving friends. Soliko's wine is labelled 'Our Wine', which has a double meaning: this wine is not only 'ours' in terms of his group of friends, but also 'our' in terms of Georgian natural wine, as opposed to a Soviet industrial product.

Soliko's wines are exclusively *qvevri*. He employs some biodynamic methods and loves to experiment – he'll sometimes craft certain *qvevri* in a sherry style, change his blends and shift his thoughts on the use of stems. His unmanipulated, vineyard-specific Rkatsiteli and Saperavi bottlings are radical examples of Kakheti's unfettered taste profile. Again, he's essentially a home winemaker, so don't expect a fancy tasting room, but instead an evening of lengthy, detailed sampling in an intimate backyard setting, with birdsong in your ears and the maturing wine under your chair. And if you're there on a good night, when his talented wife is cooking, you'll get a view of how these wines pair with Kakheti's unique, piquant cuisine.
tel +995 599 11 77 27; Bakurtsikhe (20-min drive north from Sighnaghi on Hwy 5); tours by appointment

06 TWINS WINE CELLAR

This visit is vital not just for the wine; twins Gia and Gela Gamtkitsulashvili have also built guestrooms (see overleaf) and a veritable museum devoted to the art of the *qvevri*. A real working installation, this is a walk-through experience, complete with illustrations and full-sized models to help the visitor fully understand the importance of the ageing vessel to the taste of the finished wine; nearly 110 *qvevris* here are currently in use. A restaurant is also attached to the project – one can help bake bread, harvest grapes, participate in *qvevri* cleaning and maturation and observe distillation.
tel +995 551 74 74 74; Napareuli

07 KAKHA BERISHVILI

Kakha's Saperavi is a standard bearer for the varietal. A visit here to taste a short vertical of it transports you to a 1960s America that Pynchon might dream about, when cats like Timothy Leary, Dean Moriarty and Allen Ginsberg roamed the earth. The 'estate' is basically a hippy commune for agriculturalists with global taste, laid along the beautiful blue Didkhevi River, north of Sighnaghi, near Telavi. It's all too easy to hang out here all day, sip wine under the trees, discuss vintages, snack on amazing local produce and generally get smarter. The grapes are treated with bio preparations, and are transported 1km (0.5 miles) to the winery by horse carriage. The *chacha* brandy – if he has any – is transformative.
tel +995 551 60 76 08; Artana Village

ESSENTIAL INFORMATION

WHERE TO STAY

GUESTHOUSING

Although there are a number of hotels in Kakheti, staying with a local family, or 'guesthousing', can be the best way to go. Not only is it a great opportunity to make new friends, but your hosts will often provide homecooked meals, volunteer driver services for a small fee, and recommend visits to local landmarks. Check out www.hostelworld.com/sighnaghi for a short list of what's available.

TWINS WINE CELLAR

Eight standard and four luxury rooms are conveniently perched just above the Twins Wine cellar in Napareuli village, in northern Kakheti, which affords memorable views of the Caucasus mountains and the vineyards. If you're finishing your day with a wine tasting at Twins, this is the ideal place to sleep it off before moving on next morning.
tel +995 322 42 40 42; Napareuli

HOTEL PIROSMANI

Sure, the decor's a little wonky and the dining room is a bit too white, but the rooms are cosy, the balconies are great and the price is right. Above all, the location can't be beaten. It's right in the heart of the city, only minutes from everything – and right down the street from Kerovani Winery.
tel +995 355 24 30 30; 6 Agmashenebeli St, Sighnaghi

06

Sean Caffrey © Getty Images

WHERE TO EAT

PHEASANT'S TEARS

Chef Gia Rokashvili and his team do incredible work here; with wine pairings in mind, they craft fresh, innovative dishes deeply informed by tradition and supplied by the local market. In summer, the large private outdoor patio, equally suited to intimate diners and large groups, provides spectacular views and, often, spontaneous and joyful live music.
tel +995 355 23 15 56; Baratashvili St, Sighnaghi

WHAT TO DO

MONASTERY OF ST NINO AT BODBE

Just a few minutes' drive from Sighnaghi, this is one of the most sacred churches in the country. First built in the ninth century AD, it currently houses a convent and the tomb and relics of St Nino, who famously brought Christianity to Georgia, holding a cross of grapevines tied with her own hair.

The icons here are of consummate artistry; a mere walk over the grounds, pitched above the valley and surrounded by cypress trees, is a deeply moving experience.

LIVING ROOTS RANCH

Thanks to the hospitable team at Living Roots Ranch, just outside Sighnaghi, you can explore Kakheti's hilly, forested countryside as it should be seen: on horseback. No matter your skill level, there will be a horse and guide suited to you. Children are welcome. There are also plans into 2016 to establish guestrooms and even an artisanal brewery on site.

CELEBRATIONS

In May each year, the capital city of Tbilisi (about an hour's drive west of Sighnaghi) celebrates the New Wine Festival, supported by the Georgian Wine Club. Here, industrial companies show their wine alongside natural growers, village farmers and mid-sized wineries. It's one of the best places to witness the full spectrum of Georgian wine production. In autumn, close to harvest, the northern Kakhetian city of Telavi will often host a Kakheti-centric wine festival in Nadikvari Park.

01

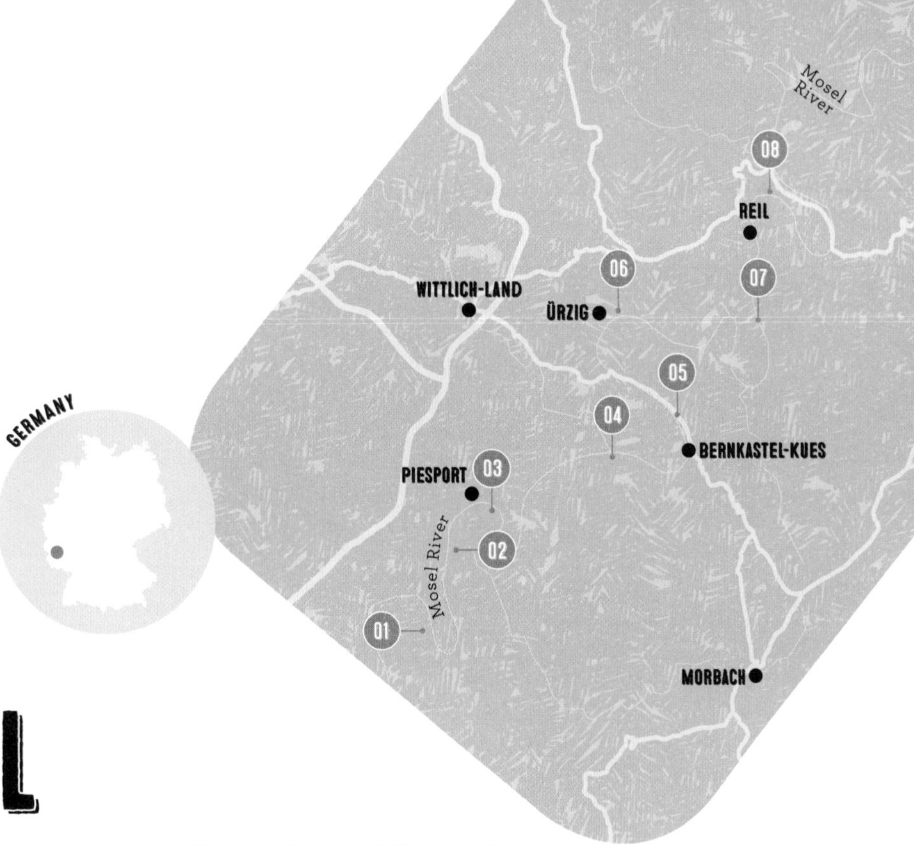

[Germany]

MOSEL

The Mosel's steep slopes provide the noblest setting in the world; tasting Riesling here in baroque homes and among the vines stirs the soul.

The serpentine journey along the Mosel valley, from Trier north to Koblenz, is perhaps the most breathtaking in the world of wine. Lining the Mosel River's edge, pristine medieval villages exude a timeless charm under the half-light of a sky where clouds form and vanish. Beside worn Roman wine vats, aromas of sun-baked slate and tender flowers steam from the earth. New vistas unfold by the minute and at every turn: mile after mile, dense vineyards rise at Expressionist angles, an amphitheatre broken up only by ancient stone sundials and vineyard names in high white Hollywood lettering. In summer and autumn, a kaleidoscope of blue, grey and scarlet-red stone blazes and winks out from beneath a bright green tapestry of leaves. History is in the air.

Riesling is the noble varietal here, and thanks to a nearly infinite number of *terroir* differences, it shows a remarkable diversity of expression, from bone-dry to ticklingly sparkling, half-sweet to unctuous. Gauging a Mosel wine is a three-dimensional experience, requiring several considerations at once: vineyard, grower and parcel. The single vineyard sites have been rated for quality by various standards over time. As in Burgundy, each of these vineyards tend to be farmed by several growers, and each grower has their own methods of production. (For some of the larger vineyards, the number of owners can number in the hundreds.) In addition, within each recognised single vineyard, there are smaller parcels with higher pedigrees. Navigating this interplay to discover which wines truly represent the region's extraordinary potential and speak to your palate can become a lifelong adventure.

Thankfully, touring the Mosel, by car or bicycle, is very easy; it's possible to visit up to four wineries per day – thanks, in part, to the wines' freshness and relatively low alcohol. Guesthouses, beer halls, parks and delightful cuisine are in plentiful display along the way. And your companion throughout is the mighty Mosel itself, from whose point of view very little has changed since the time of Ausonius and before.

GET THERE
Frankfurt is the nearest major airport, 160km from Leiwen. Car hire is available.

Courtesy of Batterieberg

01 CARL LOEWEN

Carl bottles Rieslings that are both immediately approachable and intensely mineralic. He's known for his interest in old, ungrafted vines, which provide a unique and delectable palate-feel. 'Don't miss' wines include his Schmitt-Wagner Spätlese Maximin Herrenberg, and the glorious Loewen Auslese Ritch.
www.weingut-loewen.de; tel +49 65 07 30 94; Matthiasstrasse 30, Leiwen; by appointment

02 A J ADAM

Andreas Adam is rightly considered one of the very finest winegrowers of the Mosel's 'new generation'. His wines are gaining something of a cult status, due to their stellar quality and tiny quantity; his holdings amount to less than 4 hectares (10 acres). In a land of challenging grades, this sub-region of the Dhron tributary is particularly steep and difficult to work – he's one of the few who continue to craft wines with a close eye to geology and to ferment with ambient yeasts without further additives. All of his wines are worthy of consideration, but especially the Feinherb Goldtropfchen and the Spätlese Hofberg.
tel +49 65 07 21 15; Bruckenstrasse 51, Neumagen-Dhron; by appointment

03 REUSCHER-HAART

Mario Schwang assumed the reins of this historic estate (it dates back to 1337) in 2006. His youthful energy has brought a fresh appeal to the wines, which were always among the finest of Piesport; they show an appealing fruitiness alongside creamy malt. The location is particularly charming, directly fronting the Mosel and a gorgeous spanning bridge.
www.weingut-reuscher-haart.de; tel +49 65 07 24 92; St Michaelstrasse 20, Piesport; by appointment

04 MAX FERD RICHTER

A full tasting at Richter can provide an unforgettable experience of the Mosel's complexity, and Riesling's versatility: not only does the estate bottle from no fewer than eight vineyards, each with a unique expression, but the current scion, Dirk Richter, possesses an encyclopaedic knowledge of the Mosel's history and potential. Expect these bottlings to be straightforward, clean and definitive of their origins.
www.facebook.com/MaxFerdRichter; tel +49 65 34 93 30 03; Hauptstrasse 85, Mülheim; by appointment

05 WILLI SCHAEFER

In the entire valley, it would be difficult to name a more beloved or sought-after set of wines than those from Willi Schaefer. The quantity is tiny, fewer than 3000 cases a year, and there are only two sites, but they're two of the Mosel's very finest: Himmelreich and Domprobst. Schaefer's wines convey a 'come-hither' sense of bonhomie, along with a hauntingly detailed sense of place. Pay special attention to the 'numbered' series of Ausleses from the Domprobst – among the most memorable you'll taste.
www.weingut-willi-schaefer.de; tel +49 65 31 80 41; Hauptstrasse 130, Bernkastel-Graach; by appointment

06 MONCHHOF/CHRISTOFFEL

The Gothic tasting room at Monchhof, all lacquered old wood and layered glass, provides a perfect counterpoint to their set of exuberant single-vineyard Rieslings. Rather uniquely for the valley, here you can experience a set of wines from different slate types – blue, red, and grey – side by side, and begin to come to grips with

what sets them apart. (Don't miss a taste of their stately bottling from the historic Prälat site.)
www.moenchhof.de; tel +49 65 32 93 164; Monchhof 54539, Ürzig; by appointment

07 IMMICH-BATTERIEBERG

Centred on the charming village of Enkirch, Immich-Batterieberg has one of the oldest histories in the Mosel: part of its holdings were first mentioned in a Royal deed dated 908, and from 1425 the estate was family-owned for over 500 years. Today, current winemaker Gernot Kollmann crafts glorious wines from four sites: Batterieberg, Steffensberg, Ellergrub and Zeppwingert. The rambling house and tasting rooms were built up over successive generations, and stand as a visual testament to the region's vital past.
www.batterieberg.com; tel +49 65 41 81 59 07; Im Alten Tal 2, Enkirch; by appointment

08 CLEMENS-BUSCH

Since they began making wine in the 1980s, Clemens and Rita Busch have become well-known for making 'natural' elaboration wines, which stand today among the purest in the valley. Clemens and Rita are down-to-earth and urbane – visitors are loath to leave their lovely timbered home.

Veins of blue and red slate underlie their mostly grey-slate sites, and the Buschs have been widely influential in re-identifying these once-recognised 'micro-*terroirs*', and bottling them separately. Of their wines, most of the Rieslings are dry; they also bottle small amounts of Pinot Noir, sparkling wine and distillate spirits.
www.clemens-busch.de; tel +49 65 42 22 180; Kirchstrasse 37, Pünderich; by appointment

01 Riesling vines above the Mosel

02 Batterieberg vineyard

ESSENTIAL INFORMATION

WHERE TO STAY

ZELTINGER HOF
A few kilometres north of Bernkastel, this classy small hotel offers a set of cosy rooms where pristine whitewash is set off by exposed old dark beams. The wine cellar here is absolutely fantastic.
www.zeltinger-hof.de; tel +49 65 32 93 820; Kurfürstenstrasse 76, Zeltingen-Rachtig

WEINGÜTER MÖNCHHOF VINOTHEK UND GÄSTEHAUS
This winery and guesthouse rises like a Gothic beacon from the base of the Urziger Würzgarten vineyard and offers spacious, colourful rooms. *www.moenchhof.de; tel +49 65 32 93 164; Moselufer D-54539, Ürzig*

WHERE TO EAT

ZUR TRAUBE, HOTEL RESTAURANT
This is no-frills traditional Mosel cuisine, exquisitely prepared. Make sure to grab a seat on the charming terrace, it affords one of the most tranquil views of the river.
www.zurtraubeuerzig.de; tel +49 65 32 93 08 30; Moselufer D-54539, Ürzig

DIE GRAIFEN: WEINE, LEBEN, ESSEN
Inside and out, the restaurant at Die Graifen exudes ambience and hospitality. Seasonal menus cater for both casual diners, with its tapas-style plates, and dinner guests looking for more substantial dishes.
www.graifen.de; tel +49 65 41 81 10 75; Wolfer Weg 11, Traben-Trarbach

WHAT TO DO

After your tour of the Mosel, kick your feet up and enjoy a beer from the leisurely perspective of a boat ride from Koblenz to Rudesheim.

From the centre of Rudesheim, the cable-car also offers stellar views of the Rhine River and its surrounding vineyards.

CELEBRATIONS

Year-round, there are dozens of festivals along the Mosel. In the first week of September, Bernkastel's four-day Wine Festival of the Middle Moselle is an absolute must. In early July, the town of Kröv hosts a Wine and Folklore Festival with international music and, famously, a floating stage on the river.

01

Courtesy of Thymiopoulos

[Greece]

Nature's bounty is the first and lasting impression of this verdant Greek mountainside region, its wild landscapes mirrored in her captivating wines.

Naoussa enjoys a gorgeous position, tucked into the forested slopes of the Vermio Mountains in the north-east highlands of Greece. The city itself is historically significant, and the region – full of ancient caves and supplied with abundant water – holds a special place in the Greek psyche. It is also home to the noble red wine grape widely seen as the finest in the country, Xinomavro.

Xinomavro means 'black and bitter' (a reference to its rich colour and strong tannin), yet the grape tends most often to the aromatic and perfumed. It's often compared to Nebbiolo for its powerful tannin, firm acidity and ageworthiness; in the best hands, it also shows a graceful, giving structure, reminiscent of Pinot Noir. Most importantly, what it shares with these two varietals is a reluctance to travel, a magic synergy with place. As Nebbiolo is to Piedmont, and Pinot Noir is to Burgundy, so Xinomavro is to Naoussa. Plantings of Xinomavro exist elsewhere, but its full, elegant, stately potential is only realised here. In fact, in 1971, Naoussa was the first modern winegrowing area in Greece to be recognised for top-quality wine – specifically for Xinomavro – thus setting a standard for subsequent regulations across the country. In terms of character, what distinguishes Xinomavro and makes it truly Greek is an irreducible herbal fragrance of fresh thyme and sage, and a piquant palate, redolent of sun-dried tomato, saffron and liquorice. It's an absolutely gorgeous accompaniment to dark olives, peppery vegetables and juicy lamb.

The best way to approach Naoussa is from Thessaloniki. As you're driving west across the flat plain of Emathia (it takes about an hour), the Vermio Mountains slowly rise to form a high, green crescent against the sky. Once in the mountains, the contrast you experience between their narrow, twisty roads and the wide expanse of the valley is delightful. When you reach the city itself, gaze east and south to the mainland of Attica: it's easy to see why this was an ancient crossroads and a lookout point from which to defend Greek culture. The hush of time past is perceptible here – take a moment to breathe it in before exploring the numerous family winegrowers whose homes dot the hills, and the famous estates that helped define modern Greek wine.

GET THERE
Thessaloniki is the nearest major airport, 93km from Naoussa. Car hire is available.

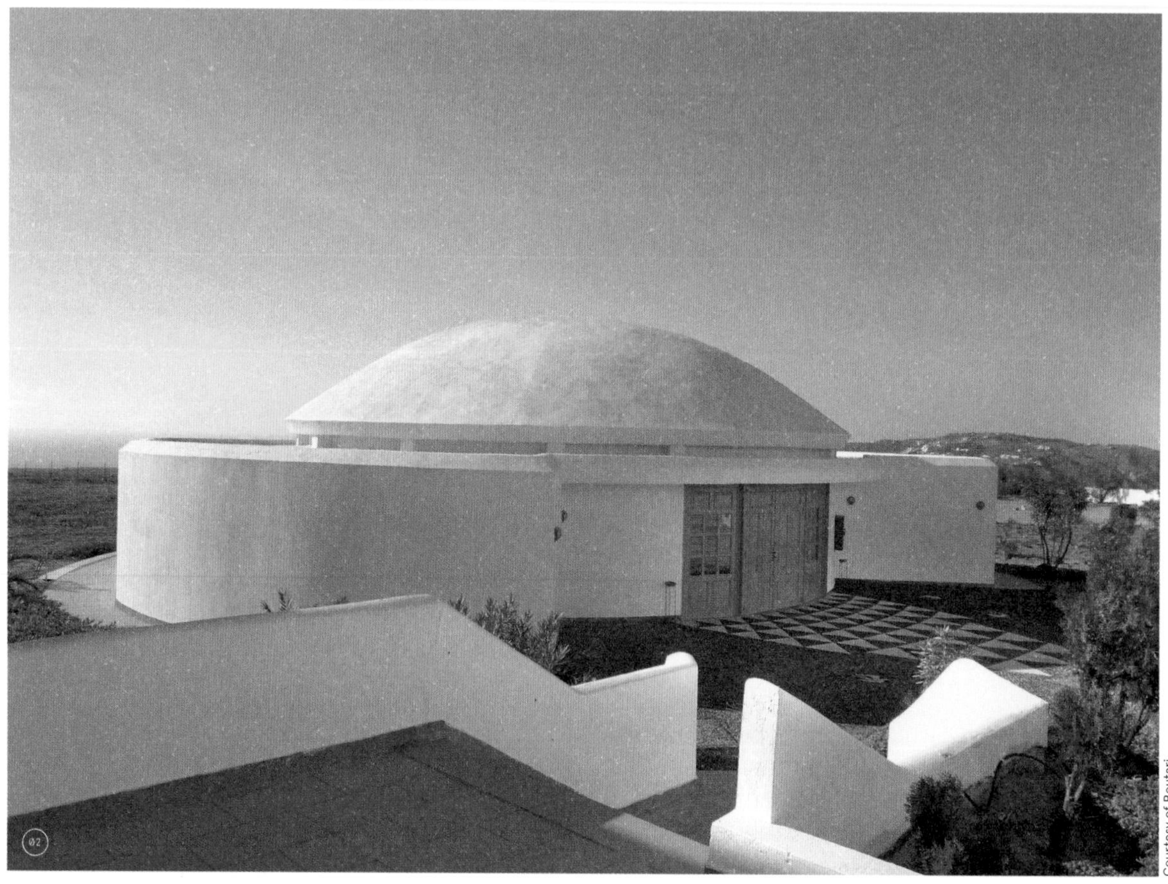
Ø2

Courtesy of Boutari

01 THYMIOPOULOS

Only in his mid-30s, Apostolos Thymiopoulos is one of the youngest and most talked about winemakers from the Naoussa region. In 2004, he began to bottle and sell the wine his family had grown for generations. He works with biodynamic principles and as little intervention as possible to show Xinomavro's fresher, more approachable profile. His Young Vines bottling captures that ambition – here, Xinomavro's piquant spice and garden-fresh vegetal notes are wed to a pure core of delectable fruit. He also produces a top-tier wine called Uranos, drier and more profound, intended for long maturation.

Upon visiting, Apostolos greets you with a wide smile and hearty handshake – his passion for Naoussa and its potential is infectious. In a part of the world where much of the younger generation has migrated to the cities, it's a refreshing encounter. Make sure to have him take you through the vineyards – the vines themselves are beautifully vigorous and strong, and directly speak to the character of the wines.

Tel +30 69320 64161; PO Box 62, Trilofos, Imathia; by appointment

02 BOUTARI WINERY

The first commercial Greek wine was a Xinomavro from Naoussa, bottled by the Boutari family in 1879. Over the last century, the Boutari company has grown exponentially to include estates countrywide, becoming nearly synonymous with Greek wine at large, yet its cradle, its heart and soul, remains here. The Boutari Naoussa winery is home to one of the largest cellars in Greece, with an astonishing number of older vintages. This is, in equal parts, a functional winery, a landmark and a museum, and is the ideal location to begin to understand Naoussa's crucial place in the history of Greek wine. From a wide, marble-lined portico, you enter rooms lined with bottles and awards, and are treated to a multimedia display telling the story of Naoussa wine, given a tour of the facilities, and an intimate tasting of the wines paired with local food.

In the face of population swings, vineyard diseases and the introduction of international varietals, Xinomavro's survival has not always been certain – it's often come close to extinction. This family's efforts have been key to keeping the grape alive and vital. *www.boutari.gr; tel +30 23320 41666; 59200 Stemimachos, Naoussa; 8am-3pm Mon-Fri, and by appointment*

03 TSANTALI

Another storied Greek estate, with roots running back to 1890, Tsantali bears a relation to Boutari, with multiple holdings throughout the country, a huge array of wines and a stake in the continued vitality of the Xinomavro varietal in Naoussa. Tsantali not only owns vineyards here, but also has contracts with a host of local growers, helping to keep its traditional methods alive and viable. There are only two Xinomavro bottlings here, Naoussa and Naoussa Reserve, yet their delicate, floral character deserve a visit and tasting.

Here, it can feel like you're on a rooftop of the ancient world. At your feet, dark gnarled vines rise up to frame a dozen shades of blue. Beneath you, a ring of old hilltops roll toward the distance in a series of waves before merging with the sky. *www.tsantali.com; tel +30 23320 41461; 59200 Naoussa (railway station); by appointment*

04 DALAMARA WINERY

Located on the eastern foothills of Mt Vermio, just outside the town of Naoussa, this historic, organic fifth-generation estate is currently run by Yiannis and Katerina Dalamara, with the help of a winemaker and consultant. Upon arrival, the guest is greeted with a delicious, rustic homemade Tsipouro paired with a dish of local olives. Make sure to spend some time on the outdoor patio savouring views of the vineyards and the falling shoulders of the facing hills. After, the Dalamaras will be happy to walk you through the winery for a tasting in their cosy stone-lined tasting room, and offer a tour of their modest winemaking facilities.

They make two white Malagouzia-led blends, oaked and un-oaked, and a red Xinomavro/Merlot blend called Aghechoros. But beside their addictive Tsipouro, the star wine here is the oak-aged Paliokalias Naoussa Xinomavro, which balances a rich body with a light, feminine perfume. Beyond the wines above, of special interest here are the 'cellar offerings', or 'confidential cuvées': experiments with new blends, clones and single vineyards only offered at the winery. *www.dalamarawinery.gr; tel +30 23320 28321; 59200 Naoussa; by appointment*

'There's been a palpable buzz building around Xinomavro lately... [it] has a grace, complexity, sophistication and allure people don't typically associate with the wines of Greece.'

–Ted Diamantis, Greek wine importer (Diamond Importers)

01 Harvesting Xinomavro grapes at Thymiopoulos

02 The Boutari winery

03 Cellars at Boutari winery

Courtesy of Boutari

Courtesy of Thymiopoulos

04 Biodynamic wine by Thymiopoulos

05 The dining room at Palea Poli

05 KARYDAS

By all accounts, Karydas is a 'boutique' winery. Only one Xinomavro wine is made, the property is tiny, the production is miniscule, and it always sells out. Upon visiting, however, you realise that there's nothing boutique about the estate – in fact, it doesn't feel like an estate at all, but instead, the house of a loving relative who just happens to make extraordinary wine. The Karydas family receives guests into their family home with an unforgettable warmth. Young, shy, 30-something Petros Karydas currently runs the day-to-day winemaking. Their Xinomavro vines grow in the backyard, in a perfectly exposed 2-hectare (5-acre) plot established in 1980. The 'winery' dates from 1994, and consists of cement-lined tanks and a few oak casks in the basement. The methods are utterly simple. The vines are tended by hand with the utmost care, and the grapes are harvested and fermented without fuss. The wine itself is absolutely pure; delicious in its youth, it also improves with age. (Do try Petros' mother's delicious 'wine cookies', made from the must left over from fermentation!) ***tel +30 23320 28638; 59200 Ano Gastra, Naoussa; by appointment***

06 KIR-YIANNI

'Kir-Yianni' means 'Sir John'; in Greek, the greeting connotes a special warmth and cordiality. The 'John' in question here is Yiannis (John) Boutari, of the famous Boutari winemaking family. Yiannis is a very important man in this part of Greece – his interests also include politics and wildlife preservation. In 1996, he left the larger family estates to his brother, Konstantinos, to start his own domaine after acquiring the Naoussa vineyards of Yianakohori and Amyndeo. The project has proven to be very successful. On the international level, there are few Naoussa labels so prevalent, or so quickly identified with the region. There are a dizzying number of wine products here, including not only Xinomavro, but also international varietals, and a host of different styles, from white to red to rosé to sparkling. A visit here makes for an educational counterpoint to a stop with Petros Karydas. The winery itself, in Yianakohori, is located at one of the highest altitudes in Naoussa. The tasting-room experience here can be lengthy, yet is terrifically enjoyable and intimate. And don't miss the sublime views of the vineyards, an occasional stone fortress, and distant mountain peaks.
www.kiryianni.gr; tel +30 23320 51100; 59200 Yianakohori, Naoussa; by appointment

ESSENTIAL INFORMATION

WHERE TO STAY

PALEA POLI

Located in the heart of Naoussa's 'Old City', Palea Poli's stone mansion (built 1900) houses eight rooms and one luxury 'executive suite' across three floors. They're all very affordable (prices around $100 per night), and terribly cosy, with elegant decor, exposed brick, a backyard, indoor fireplace, and one of the best breakfasts in the region.
www.paleapoli.gr; tel +30 23320 52520; Vassileos Konstantinou 32, Naoussa

GUESTHOUSE NIAOUSTA

This convenient and secluded guesthouse, 3 km (2 miles) behind Naoussa toward Mt Vermio, is a 'don't miss'. Beautiful local architecture, modernised rooms, a spacious surrounding lawn and patio affording long, regionwide views... this place has it all, and at a very low price. Add to that free wi-fi, on-site horseriding and a well-stocked bar, and you might find it hard to leave.
www.niaousta.gr; tel +30 23320 22374; Militsa, 59200, Naoussa

WHERE TO EAT

12 GRADA

A short drive south of Naoussa, this charming wine bar/restaurant stands as one of the region's finest watering holes. The food ranges from the simple to the fancy, but it's always great, and the room is often packed with friendly locals out for a bite and an ouzo or two.
tel +30 23311 00112; Sofou 11, Veroia

MARGARET'S ISLAND HOTEL RESTAURANT

The food here is classic Greek mountain fare, extremely well-prepared, but the location is the real draw. Nestled in the hills above Naoussa, the huge streamside patio is surrounded by trees and has the feel of a forest retreat.
tel +30 23 32 05 26 00; Agios Nikolaos, Naoussa

WHAT TO DO

THE TOMBS OF THE KINGS OF MACEDONIA

Drive several kilometres southeast of Naoussa to the village of Vergina to view a recent excavation (1977–8), which revealed the wealth of the ancient Macedonian kings. The tomb of Alexander's father, Philip II (382–336 BC), is here. Of most interest, perhaps, are artefact displays comparing the lives of ordinary citizens of the times with those of the aristocracy and royalty.

RIVER ARAPITSA

Just a few minutes' drive from Naoussa, you can take a walk along the storied Arapitsa, the ancient natural border between the plains of Emathia and the Vermio Mountains. In summer, green forests and waterfalls provide a backdrop for meditation on historical forces that have shaped this region.

SELI SKI RESORT

From December to March this resort offers some of the best skiing in Greece. Only 20km (12.5 miles) from Naoussa, it holds 18 sites, six lifts and, at the base, a number of restaurants and cafes.

CELEBRATIONS

From September to November, the city of Naoussa hosts a wide-ranging series of 'happenings' known as Wine and Culture Events, organised to educate visitors on the integral symbiosis between winemaking, culture, art and society in the region at large. In the spring, during Carnival Time, Naoussa also hosts a 12-day set of festivities centred on Ash Monday, during which Xinomavro flows with exceptional freedom.

Courtesy of Palea Poli

[Hungary & Slovakia]

TOKAJI-TOKAJ

Take a trip back in time, with vivacious and friendly companions, on a journey through Hungary and Slovakia to taste the mystical and ancient Tokaj wines.

Zsolt Szentirmai / tokajwineregion.com

HUNGARY & SLOVAKIA
SLOVAKIA
SÁTORALJAÚJHELY
HUNGARY
SÁROSPATAK
Bodrog River
Tisza River
TOKAJ
01 02 03 04 05 06 07 08

Picture a chilly autumn dawn. Along the low slopes of a forgotten range of celery-green hills in north-eastern Hungary and south-eastern Slovakia, through beguiling ancient villages, a lazy river winds. The moist air sends up mists that kiss the vineyards of this undulating, Unesco-protected landscape. For many grapes growing here, botrytisation has begun – perhaps the most peculiar process in winemaking. The fruit, already deliberately overripened, starts rotting, but this rot is a welcome one: drastically sweetening and acidifying grapes to form the singular taste of the legendary Tokaj Aszú wine.

Aszú (Vyber in Slovakia) was never short on admirers. Austro-Hungarian Empress Maria Theresa and Napoleon sang its praises. Louis XIV dubbed it 'wine of kings, king of wines'. Amber-hued, sweeter and more intense than any other wine in the world, the ultimate maverick of top-quality vintages is every bit as surprising to first-timers today. And although Aszú is the internationally recognised hallmark of the region, it's only the kick-off for the oenophile's odyssey. Because despite a pedigree going back to at least the 16th century, a half-century of communist practices dented Tokaj's prestige – and obliged the industry almost to reinvent itself post-1989. First it happened out on the terraces and in the century-old cellars: winemakers discovered an improbably diverse range of dry whites could flourish in Tokaj too, and these proved a hit with connoisseurs. Then it happened in the villages: other entrepreneurs realised Tokaj could tout more than just wineries, opening wine bars, wine spas, wine hotels, wine hikes… even wine-jam makers.

So Tokaj is still playing catch-up. But this means it has an undiscovered, utterly unpretentious feel. Winemakers happily chat to visitors. Just a couple of signs indicate Tokaj's existence from regional highways. And – as this is a region large on character, small on production and with little presence in international markets – a trip here guarantees a sip into uncharted territory.

GET THERE
Budapest Ferenc Liszt is the nearest major airport, 225km from Mád. Car hire is available.

01 SZEPSY PINCE

No two ways about it: István Szepsy is Tokaj's most important winemaker, and by radical yield control managed to revolutionise how the world perceived the region's wine in the 1990s. Even today, he is happy to significantly sacrifice a vine's output by cutting to maximise taste. And Szepsy himself, with his eccentricities and immense viticultural knowledge, is the main reason to stop by this Mád winery.

To truly *get* him, though, you need to visit his vineyards – which he has acquired in an extraordinary variety of locations, boldly going where Tokaj wine is very likely to follow. As Szepsy concedes, there is no knowing just how Tokaj could develop – testing out winegrowing in different terroirs is how he hopes to discover more about the area's potential. Stay tuned. And in the meantime, try one of his greatest successes thus far, a fragrant 2011 Furmint from his Úrágya vineyard.

www.szepsy.hu; tel +36 47-348 349; 3909 Mád, Batthyány utca 59; by appointment

02 HOLDVÖLGY

No-one's saying the quality of the wine at Holdvölgy is in doubt, but the 2km (1.2-mile) labyrinth of cellars are the highlight here, and make this a great family choice. Plum in the midst of the twisting streets of central Mád, this place only opened to the public in 2013.

Before your cellar descent, you're furnished with a map of the passages and then you're on your own. The challenge is to find where the wine is stashed, treasure-hunt style, and return to the surface – if you can!

www.holdvolgy.com; tel +36 20-806 6811; 3909 Mád, Batthyány utca 69; by appointment

03 DISZNÓKŐ

Even the tractor garage at photogenic Disznókő is a work of art (the design is based on a yurt and a volcano, apparently). The region's prettiest winery seems to excel at everything. It hosts a monthly Sunday produce market that's a networking event for winemakers; it has a highly-regarded restaurant and a wine shop, and it operates as a wedding venue. Visitors are also encouraged to take a turn around the estate (the 19th-century belvedere has some cracking views).

But where the wine is concerned, they're focused. One of the bigger Tokaj winemaking enterprises, they have the power to concentrate exclusively on producing the highly

expensive, time-consuming Aszú wines. In this respect, Disznókő are groundbreaking, and the vintages they turned out in 1993 represented the first of the striking new, post-communist Aszú. Gone was the old-school heaviness, and in its place citrusy freshness, along with a swing towards top-notch five- and six-*puttonyos* wines. Disznókő remains the most active innovator in the Tokaj business.

www.disznoko.hu; tel +36 47-569 410; 3931 Mezőzombor; by appointment

04 GRÓF DEGENFELD

Kudos to Gróf Degenfeld for being one of the few eco-wineries. The majesty of their lush landscaped grounds, elegant hotel and character-rich winery is enormously augmented by pesticide-free vineyards that lend a timeless pastoral feel to the estate. Every second row is planted with wild flowers to attract the bugs that kill harmful pests. They even have their own forest higher up the slopes to grow the wood for their barrels.

The Degenfelds are one of Hungary's old families, and the 200-year-old cellars, cutting back deep into the hill, still retain their 19th-century charm, including the original Degenfeld coat of arms on the creaking oak doors.

Look out on their varied wine list for their signature wine: a late-harvest partially botrysised Furmint. A good wine shop is also onsite.

www.grofdegenfeld.hu; tel +36 47-380 173; Terézia kurt 9, Tarcal; by appointment

05 TOKAJ KIKELET PINCE

As with many things wine-related, the French played a part with Hungarian Tokaj's brand reinvention post-1989. Stephanie Berecz, hailing from the Loire, exemplifies this trait. One of the best-regarded small producers, she refined her trade overseeing operations at nearby Disznókő, and the dinky winery she and her husband now run is the antithesis of the corporate experience: extremely personal and, at her own admission, utterly unpredictable.

'Every year the wine is different,' she says. 'Generalisations can never be made. A priority for us is being authentic: always faithful to the soil and the climate and their conditions. This belief is why we have developed our own yeasts, which are to do with being natural, and wanting to make the wines most representative of the area.'

Surprise tastings aside, tours include a hike above their vineyards

Zsolt Szentirmai / tokajwineregion.com

Zsolt Szentirmai / tokajwineregion.com

to a lake in a former quarry – good for a swim, but also to get an idea of the region's rock types (showcased here) that can influence the taste of a wine.
www.tokajkikelet.hu; tel +36 47-636 9046; 3915 Tarcal, Könyves Kálmán utca; by appointment

06 ZOLTÁN DEMETER PINCÉSZET

Unfortunately for the wine region's namesake town, Tokaj itself has few top-notch wineries – but Zoltán Demeter compensates for all that. As with Szepsy, his former colleague during their days at Gróf Degenfeld, this one-man, 7-hectare (17-acre) operation appeals most because of the idiosyncrasies of the owner. Wines here, for instance, mature to the sound of Mozart. The output is mostly dry whites.
www.facebook.com/demeterzoltantokaj; tel +36 20-806 0000; 3910 Tokaj, Vasvári Pál utca; by appointment

07 PATRICIUS

Grand-cru (first-class) vineyards don't guarantee first-class wines but having an entire estate of them certainly helps. Patricius are a major Tokaj player, but their pearl-white winery feels anything but frenetic, ensconced as it is in the middle of the vineyards. The remains of a castle crown the hill above. Beneath the buildings, a living wine museum in a plot laid out the old-fashioned way (as opposed to machine-friendly rows of vines) exhibits grape varieties present and past, including several the phylloxera epidemic eradicated.

But the winery is far more modern, with a state-of-the-art tasting-room-cum-gallery. With prior notice, degustations can feature pairings of Patricius wines with chocolates tailor-made by a local confectioner.
patricius.hu; tel +36 47-396 001; 3917 Bodrogkisfalud, Várhegy-dűlő 3357 hrsz; open 8am-4pm Mon-Fri, 10am-6pm Sat & Sun

08 TOKAJ MACIK

Your sojourn in the Slovak swathe of the wine region commences in the most atmospheric manner imaginable. In Malá Trňa village (with its main streets named 'Tokaj' and 'In-between Cellars' to give you an inkling of the dominant occupation hereabouts), Tokaj Macik winery guides you underground into a medieval maze of passageways befitting *Game of Thrones*. This lamp-lit, 13th-century cellar system was originally constructed as a defence

against Turkish invaders.

With cellar humidity levels reaching 95%, walls are coated in rare black mould called cladosporium cellare: Tokaj depends on this to achieve its special pungent taste. Down here, you receive an explanation of the coloured history of the wine, along with the six-flight degustation. In Slovakia, Vyber (the Slovak word for Aszú, remember) is what tastings mostly focus on. Tastings build up to the potent nectar-like six-*putňa* knock-out (darker and more aromatic than most Hungarian Tokaj).

Nearby, and half-hidden by grass, other cellars are used by small-scale Tokaj winemakers who offer even more personalised underground degustations.
www.tokajmacik.sk; tel +421 56-679 3466; Medzipivničná 174, Malá Trňa, Slovakia; by appointment.

01 View from the Öreg Király (Old King) vineyard, Mád, Hungary

02 Jazz in a vineyard, Hungary

03 A rare, hairy and Hungarian Mangalica pig

04 Picnic at the Great Tokaj Wine Auction, Sárospatak, Hungary

05 Temple of the Muses, Sárospatak, Hungary

06 Picking Aszú grapes at the Disznókő Estate

07 Harvest at the Disznókő Estate

ESSENTIAL INFORMATION

WHERE TO STAY

BARTA PINCE WINERY
A graceful guesthouse with huge rooms in a 16th-century farmhouse. The winery, with steep-sloping vineyards gaining maximum flavour from the elements, already has a reputation.
tel +36 30-324 2521; www.bartapince.com, 3909 Mád, Rákóczi utca 81

GRÓF DEGENFELD CASTLE HOTEL
This delightful terracotta-roofed mansion sits within landscaped grounds at the foot of the namesake winery. The style is Hungarian Empire heyday; tennis courts and a pool are alongside.
tel +36 47-580 400; hotelgrofdegenfeld.hu; Terézia kurt 9, Tarcal

WHERE TO EAT

ELSŐ MÁDI BORHÁZ
Vineyard-facing bistro showcasing every wine in the Mád Circle (Mád winemakers association) with a cutting-edge wine dispenser. They'll pack you picnics to take to the vineyards.
tel +36 47-348 007; www.mad.info.hu/elso-madi-borhaz; Hunyadi utca 2, Mád

GUSTEAU
Refined high-end dining in a tucked-away courtyard restaurant focusing on serving food to match the area's phenomenal wines.
tel +36 47-348 297; www.gusteaumuhely.com; 3909 Mád, Batthyány utca 51, Hungary

WHAT TO DO

Ease off the booze awhile with a jaunt to jam-makers Ízes Őrőmest in Tokaj. In this husband-and-wife outfit, he mans the winery and she makes the wine-inspired preserves.
At Andrassy Residence in Tarcal the VinoSense Spa offers Aszú facials and body wraps.
www.facebook.com/izesoromest; andrassyrezidencia.hu

CELEBRATIONS

For a weekend in June, cellars and restaurants in Mád stay open all night for feasting, music and frivolity. In late May, the ancient cellars around Malá Trňa, Vel'ka Trňa and Viničky participate in Urban open cellar day.
tokajwineregion.com; www.tokajregnum.sk

Zsolt Szentirmai / tokajwineregion.com

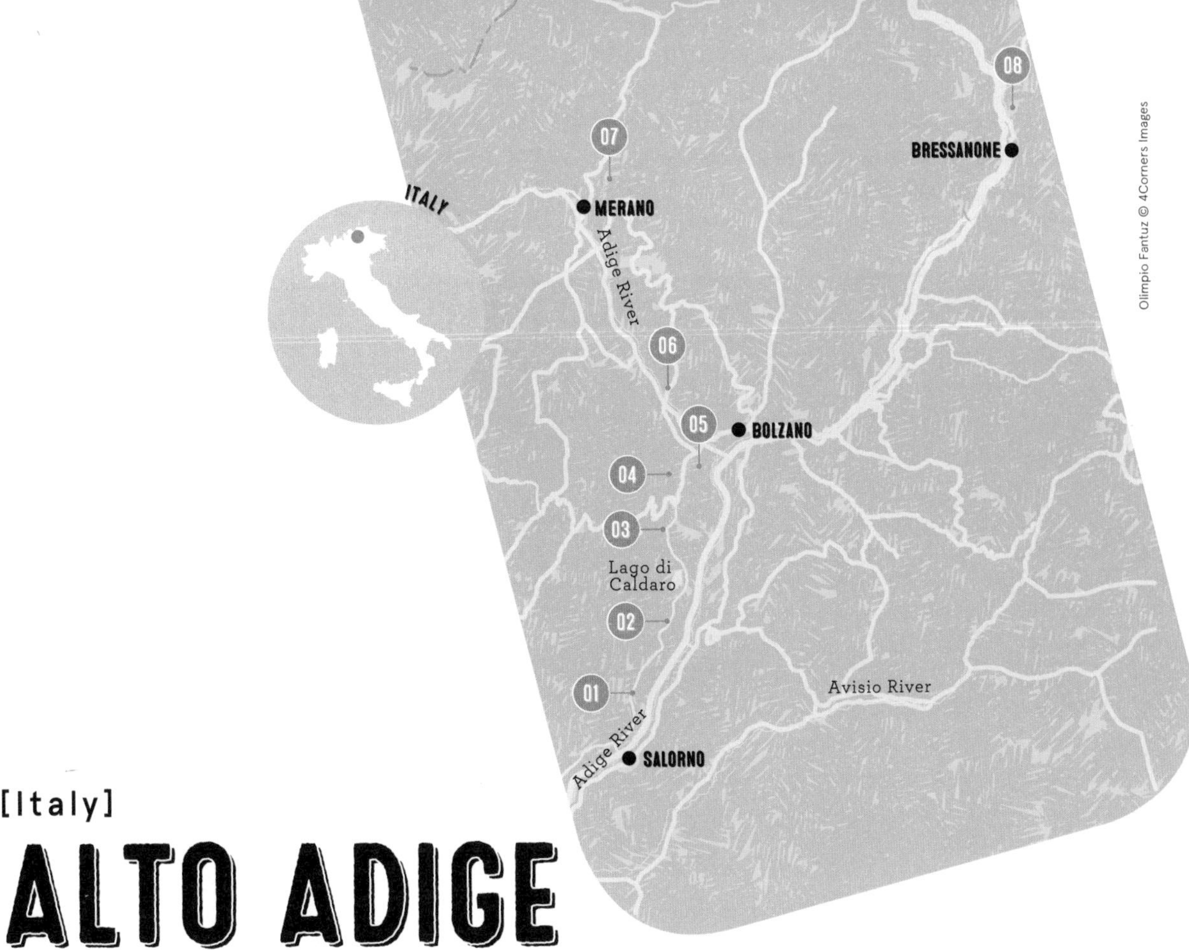

Olimpio Fantuz © 4Corners Images

[Italy]

ALTO ADIGE

With jaw-dropping scenery and terroirs *that range from Alpine to Mediterranean, this pocket-sized wine region packs a punch in sensational wines.*

The Italian Tyrol state of Alto Adige stretches up as far as the Alpine frontier with Austria, holding a unique semi-autonomous status. Village names are expressed in both Italian and German – from Bolzano (Bozen) in the south up to Bressanone (Brixen) in the north. Even though the region begins roughly just an hour up the *autostrada* from Verona, locals here will greet you with a cheery *Grüss Gott* instead of *ciao*, and rather than pasta and tiramisu, the favourite dishes are *canederli* bread dumplings and apple strudel.

The native Rhaetian tribes of Alto Adige were making wine and storing it in barrels long before the Romans arrived but, until recently, cooperative cantinas opted for low-quality, bulk production. Not today, though. You will find some of Italy's finest whites here: Pinot Bianco, Pinot Grigio, Chardonnay, Sauvignon and Gewürztraminer. Two indigenous reds deserve to be better known: the light, drinkable Vernatsch and intense Lagrein, and some cuvées of Pinot Nero Riserva can rival even those of Burgundy.

The scenery on Alto Adige's historic wine trail (*Strada del Vino*) is outrageously beautiful. It passes through the base of steep glacial valleys planted with thousands of fruit trees, while both sides are covered by a geometric maze of crisscrossing vineyards. This is one of the oldest wine trails in Italy, started back in 1964, and comprehensively covers the whole of the region. No matter how lost wine enthusiasts may get, there is always the distinctive sign of the *Strada del Vino* pointing them in the right direction. Throughout the year, the association organises walking, biking and horseriding trips through the vineyards, as well as foodie celebrations in winemaker villages.

GET THERE
Venice Marco Polo is the nearest major airport, 250km from Magrè. Car hire is available.

⓿1 ALOIS LAGEDER

Driving into Alto Adige from the neighbouring Trentino region, the first obligatory stop-off is the cantina of Alois Lageder, a pioneer winemaker. Since 1823, five generations of the Lageder family have dominated Alto Adige winemaking, always pushing the barrier with new innovations. Alois resembles an urbane, gentleman farmer from another epoch, but his ideas for the future are visionary. Way back in 1995 he created a revolutionary cantina, powered by solar energy. Today, the family's own 50 hectares (125 acres) are both organic and biodynamic, while over 30% of the 100 smallholders they buy grapes from have converted too.

While the numbers are vast – vineyards covering some 150 hectares (370 acres), producing 1.5 million bottles – the feeling here is still very down-to-earth, especially at Paradeis, the rambling 15th-century manor where tastings are held, with a small restaurant serving mainly vegetarian organic cuisine. The 35 different wines are clearly divided into the biodynamic Tenuta Lageder range and the classic Alois Lageder label from the smallholder vineyards, while the high-end selection from specific *masi* farmsteads features an outstanding Lowengang Chardonnay and Krafuss, an elegant but surprisingly fruity, full-bodied Pinot Nero.

www.aloislageder.eu; tel +39 0471-809580; Piazza S Geltrude 10, Magrè; open 10am-6pm Mon-Sat Mar-Oct, shorter hours Nov-Feb

⓿2 CANTINA TRAMIN

The sign at the entrance to the enchanting village of Tramin proudly states that this is 'home' of the world's Gewürztraminers, the aromatic grape that has been grown here for a thousand years and is now found all over the world. Tramin is also home to two of Alto Adige's most important historic winemakers, Elena Walch, whose cantina boasts giant wooden barrels over 150 years old, and the innovative Hofstatter family.

But at the outskirts of town right on the *Strada del Vino*, the dramatic avant-garde winery of the cantina *sociale* (cooperative association), resembling a maze-like green cube with a panoramic glass tasting room, dominates the landscape. The cantina sold most of its wine *sfuso* (in bulk)

01 Vineyards near Santa Maddalena, Bolzano

02 Tramin's avant-garde cantina

03 Alto Adige scenery

04 Cantina Terlano

05 The rustic Pfefferlechner

until Willi Sturtz was appointed winemaker in 1992. He began to raise the quality in the vineyards and cut yields. The cantina now produces 1.8 million bottles of high-quality wines annually. While both the Pinot Grigio and Muller-Thurgau are surprising, the special Gewürztraminer Nussbaumer cru is simply exceptional.
www.cantinatramin.it; tel +39 0471-096633; Strada del Vino, 144, Termeno; open 9am-7pm Mon-Fri, to 5pm Sat

03 KLOSTERHOF

Guests arriving at the *weingut* (estate) winery of Oskar Andergassen can be sure of a warm welcome from this jolly *vignaiolo* (winegrower). He is one of the new generation of small producers who have stopped selling grapes, choosing instead to make his own vintages from a perfectly positioned 4-hectare (10-acre) vineyard high above Lake Caldaro.

It can come as a pleasant surprise to be presented with only three wines to taste compared to the 25 or 30 that await visitors at the cantina *sociale*. Oskar concentrates on Pinot Bianco, Vernatsch and Pinot Nero, all very distinctive. The Pinot Bianco is aged in acacia-wood barrels, while the Vernatsch Riserva comes from ancient vines cultivated in the traditional Pergola system.

Oskar's son, Hannes, has just qualified as an oenologist and installed a distillery in the cellar, making rare Moscato Giallo and apricot grappa. Klosterhof is not just a cantina but a comfortable Tyrolean hotel too, with a vineyard pool and a cosy *weinstube* (wine bar) perfect to try home-cured speck, ham, and delicious mountain cheeses.
www.klosterhof.it; tel +39 0471-961046; Prey-Klavenz 40, Kaltern; open daily

04 CANTINA COLTERENZIO

Wherever you are in Alto Adige it is impossible to miss the distinctive black tower that marks the wines of the Colterenzio's cantina *sociale*. At any time of the day there is a steady stream of wine enthusiasts filling the tasting room of their contemporary winery, which has a range of wines that stretches from an affordable sharp Chardonnay and Pinot Grigio through to vintages such as Cornelius, a tremendous Merlot Cabernet blend

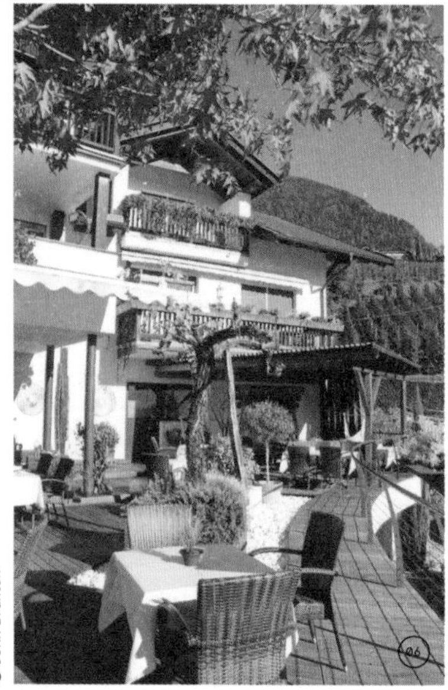

© John Brunton

06 The luxury Der Weinmesser hotel

that regularly picks up the coveted Tre Bicchieri, Italy's top wine award.

The winemaker here, Martin Lemayr, is something of a star, a local boy who was an influential oenologist for both Elena Walch and Hofstatter, and he is also a *socio* (member) with his own 1-hectare (2.5-acre) parcel of vines. The *cooperativa* was founded in 1960 by just 28 small vintners, while today there are 300 *soci* producing 1.8 million bottles.

www.colterenzio.it; tel +39 0471-664246; Strada del Vino 8, Cornaiano; 9am-12.30pm & 2.30-6.30pm Mon Fri, 9am-12.30pm Sat

05 STROBLHOF

The date 1664 is carved into the entrance of Stroblhof, and *vignaiolo* Andreas Nicolussi explains, 'Wine has always been produced at our *maso*, to go with the meat produce of the farm. In fact, we say here that a plate of speck is not complete without a glass of Vernatsch – this is what everyday life is all about here.'

Today guests staying at Stroblhof have a much more luxurious time, spoilt by a chef and pampered with a wellness spa and freshwater lake pool. The setting is quite something, with the *gasthaus* (inn) and its vineyard literally in the shadow of the towering Mandola mountain. The soil here is a mix of volcanic and chalk, producing a sharply acidic, mineral Pinot Bianco, which Andreas ages in large barrels, and a tannic Pinot Nero that stays 18 months in small barriques.

Although the estate runs to 5.5 hectares (16 acres), Andreas limits yields and only actually produces 40,000 high-quality bottles. He has replanted much of the vineyard, abandoning the Pergola for Guyot, and built a modern cantina below the hotel.

www.stroblhof.it; tel +39 0471-662250; Via Pigano 25, Appiano; daily by appointment

06 CANTINA TERLANO

Terlano is the story of a far-sighted winemaker, Sebastian Stocker, who transformed this relatively small, conservative *cooperativa*, founded back in 1893, into quite possibly the leading cantina in Alto Adige.

Stocker was convinced that Terlan's microclimate – hot days, cool nights – combined with the porphyr volcanic soil was perfect for ageing white wines. For many years the *soci* would have none of this, preferring to sell the wine young. So every year, beginning back in 1955, Stocker stashed a couple of hundred bottles of each wine in the cellar's hidden nooks and crannies. When he finally revealed all, the *soci* were furious, until they tasted how wonderfully the wines had aged.

Today, they have an unparalleled collection of 20,000 vintages and release a Rarity cuvée each year of the finest white grape that will age for 10 years before being released. Be sure to call for a visit to the futuristic cellar.

www.cantina-terlano.com; tel +39 0471-257135; Via Silberleiten, Terlano; 8am-6pm Mon-Fri, to noon Sat

07 INNERLEITER

The narrow lane up to Innerleiter zigzags through a series of hair-raising bends until you finally emerge at an altitude of almost 500m (1640ft). The reward is not just a romantic Alpine *gasthaus* hotel with breathtaking views across the snowcapped peaks of the Alps, but the chance to sample wines from probably the smallest independent vineyard in Alto Adige.

Karl Pichler cultivates just 1.7 hectares (4 acres) of vines that encircle the hotel. He has built a modern cantina and works alone without a wine consultant, making some bold decisions, such as to totally abandon cork in favour of screw-top. 'Many hotels here have vineyards like us,' he says, 'but they are always separate, and I wanted to bring the cantina and hotel together. So you can sit down in our tasting

room, try the chef's pairing snacks with each glass, and see the barrel-room through a glass wall.' His wines, aged only in stainless steel – Pinot Bianco and Sauvignon – are especially mineral and aromatic.
www.innerleiterhof.it; tel +39 0473-946000; Leiterweg 8, Scena; daily by appointment

08 ABBAZIA DI NOVACELLA

Even if they did not make some of the finest wines in Alto Adige, it would still be worth the detour to discover this magnificent Augustinian monastery, with its baroque chapels and ornate library. It has been cultivating vines since its foundation in 1142.

Today, these buildings and gardens remain a functioning monastery, the abbot in person holding ultimate responsibility for wine production. Fortunately they employ another of the region's expert winemakers, Dr Urban von Klebelsberg, to create the critical reputation of Novacella.

The Abbazia lies just outside Bressanone, and its white-wine vineyards rise up to almost 1000m (3280ft). Red wines come from another monastery near Bolzano, but in the Abbazia be sure to taste fruity, mineral Sylvaner, Muller-Thurgau, Veltliner, the full-bodied Kerner, a curious cross of Riesling and Vernatsch. And don't miss the aromatic Moscato Rose, which could easily be called rose-petal wine.
www.abbazianovacella.it; tel +39 0472-836189; Via Abbazia 1, Varna; 10am-7pm Mon-Sat

ESSENTIAL INFORMATION

WHERE TO STAY

GASTHAUS KRAIDLHOF
This tiny farmhouse surrounded by orchards and vines has a pool disguised as a freshwater pond in a Zen garden.
www.kraidlhof.com; tel +39 0471-880258; Hofstatt 2, Kurtatsch

DER WEINMESSER
Cristian Kohlgruber is a wine fanatic and sommelier. His luxurious hotel revolves around wine, from trips to the vineyard to tastings in the cellar and vinotherapy in the spa.
www.weinmesser.com; tel +39 0473-945660; Via Scena 41, Scena

GASTHOF HALLER
At the edge of bustling Bressanone, this Alpine chalet is a haven of peace where you can almost touch the owner's vineyard from your window. Food is served in a snug wood-panelled *weinstube*.
www.gasthof-haller.com; tel +39 0472-834601; Via dei Vigneti 68, Bressanone

WHERE TO EAT

PFEFFERLECHNER
Unique cantina featues a dining room that looks directly into a stable with horses and cows. There's a beer garden, a microbrewery and a copper alambic to distil grappa.
www.pfefferlechner.com; tel +39 0473-562521; St Martinsweg 4, Lana

HOPFEN & CO
In the heart of medieval Bolzano this 150-year-old *osteria* serves classic Tyrolean dishes like roast pig's knuckle and sauerkraut.
www.boznerbier.it; tel +39 0471-300788; Piazza Erbe 17, Bolzano

WHAT TO DO

Spend a day at Merano's historic Thermal Baths (Terme Merano) with its pools, sauna and spa.
www.termemerano.it; tel +39 0473-252000; Piazza Terme 9, Merano

CELEBRATIONS

Merano's wine and food festival is held in February; Egna hosts Pinot Nero Days in May, and in April/May the asparagus season is celebrated with wine pairings in Terlan. Torggele season in cantinas begins at the end of October, when you can taste partly fermented grape juice with roasted chestnuts.

01

Simeone Huber © Getty Images

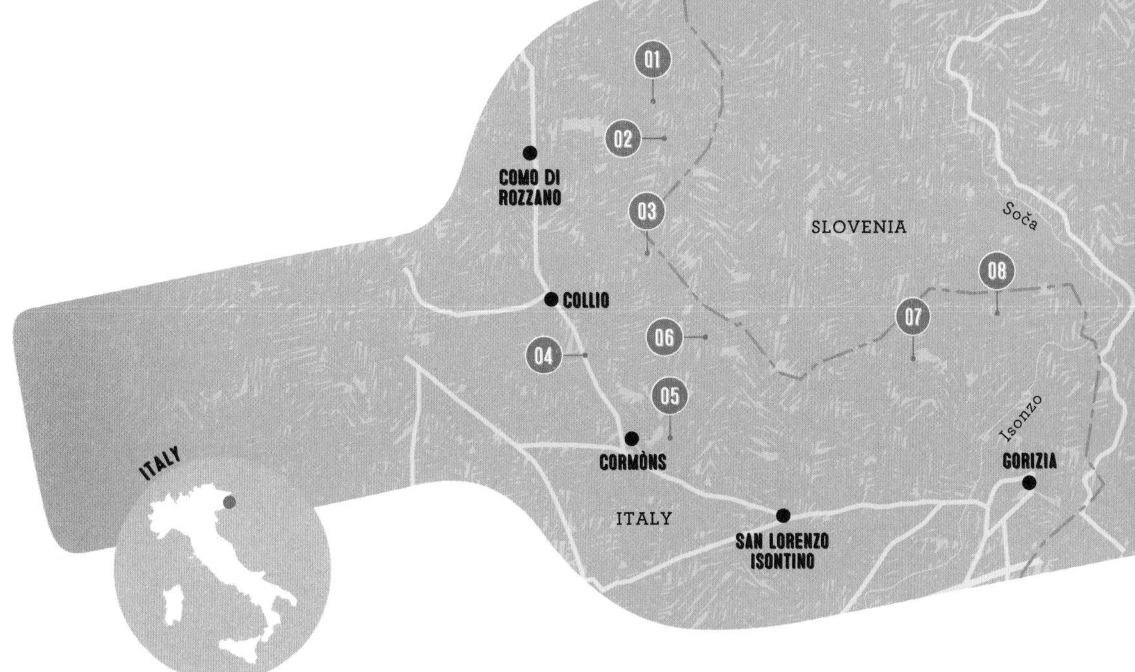

[Italy]

FRIULI

In undiscovered northeast Italy, snowy mountains and fertile plains are reflected in the variety of wines, from intense reds to fragrantly sweet whites.

The rugged Friuli region stretches from the shores of the Adriatic up to the Alps, forming a wedge between Italy's border with Eastern and Central Europe. Vineyards spread along the flat plains of the Piave, Italy's 'sacred river', where rough Raboso wine was a great favourite of Ernest Hemingway, to the Carso, a rocky peninsula running up towards Trieste, where cantinas are often hewn into underground caves.

Inland, the Collio Orientale – the eastern hills around the ancient town of Cividale – are famous for fascinating reds with such intense local grapes as Refosco and Pignolo, but the jewel in Friuli's crown is the Collio, a 50km necklace of hills. The clay and sandstone soil here produce some of the finest white wines in Italy: fruity indigenous grapes like Ribolla Gialla; the unique Picolit, late-harvested for a luscious dessert wine rivalling Sauternes; and the local favourite, Friulano, still referred to here as Tokai, even though this name can now only used by Hungary's famed sweet wine.

Many Collio winegrowers have opened up their estates as B&Bs, often inviting guests to whizz around the vineyards on signature bright-yellow Collio Vespas, and as Friuli is still very much undiscovered, you are sure of a warm welcome. The same is true of eating out; all over the countryside there are rustic *agriturismi* (farmstays) that open at the weekend and offer traditional Friulan fare, which is more influenced by Central European cuisine than Italian. Plump gnocchi stuffed with susina plums are perfect with a sharp Friulano, and the more characteristic Ribolla Gialla goes well with juicy baby squid sautéed with slightly bitter red radicchio. A favourite with everyone is Friuli's rich goulash stew; it's worth opening a bottle of one of the region's stellar reds, Livio Felluga's Sosso, a potent combination of Merlot and Refosco, to go with it.

GET THERE
Trieste-Friuli Venezia Giulia is the nearest major airport, 30km from Dolegna del Collio. Car hire is available.

02

01 VENICA & VENICA

Just before you drive into the sleepy village of Dolegna, a small sign on the right directs you down a narrow route to one of the Collio's most important wineries. Venica & Venica refers to two brothers, Gianni and Giorgio, who have turned the small vineyard founded by their grandfather 80 years ago into a slick, modern estate spanning 37 hectares (90 acres). They have made a name for their innovative, award-winning wines, but are also pioneers of oenotourism. They opened a luxurious B&B with a pool and a tennis court way back in 1985, and while the cellar is always open for tastings (apart from Sunday), you can call in advance to reserve a full two-hour tour with a detailed explanation on how their wines are made. There is a nominal charge of €10 for the tour and a tasting of five wines, which is unusual in Italy, but in practice, for those who buy wine – and most people do – the fee is waived. The one wine not to miss here is Ronco Bernizza, a surprising, steely Chardonnay perfect with *spaghetti alle vongole* (spaghetti with baby clams).
www.venica.it; tel: +39 0481-61264; località Cerò 8, Dolegna del Collio, 9am-6pm Mon-Fri, 10am-5pm Sat

02 RONCHI RO DELLE FRAGOLE

It takes some determination to drive up through the woods that cling to the hillside above Dolegna – don't count on the GPS working – but the reward at Ronchi Ro is to discover a small, new *azienda* (enterprise) where the *vignaiolo*, Romeo Rossi, is brimming with enthusiasm for the wine he is making, while his companion, Carolina, has created an idyllic B&B in their ancient stone farmhouse.

Romeo comes from a winemaking family and worked for many years for leading estates in the Collio. In 2005 he leapt at the chance to buy 3 hectares (7.5 acres) here, and devote himself to the cultivation of a single grape – Sauvignon. Romeo's approach is very technical, and when his wine ages, it is true that he achieves something similar to

the mineral 'Fumé' quality that so marks Sauvignon from Pouilly and Sancerre in the Loire. But Romeo is also a Friulan traditionalist, and after discovering a parcel of 50-year-old vines of the local Friulano grape, he also set about making a cuvée that, for him, does justice to this iconic wine.
www.ronchiro.com; tel +39 338-5270908; località Cime di Dolegna, Dolegna del Collio; by appointment

03 CRASTIN

Marked by the tall belltower of a medieval church, Ruttars sits right on the border with Slovenia and is the highest point of the Collio. The road quickly descends into Crastin, the tiniest hamlet imaginable with just a single ancient farmhouse where Sergio Collarig cultivates a small 7-hectare (17-acre) property.

He is a rough-and-ready *contadino*, what might romantically be termed a peasant farmer, who lives and works in the house he was born in, aided by his sister Vilma. Together they have progressed from producing *vino sfuso* (wine sold in bulk) to creating a small garage cellar producing 30,000 bottles of surprising wines. And it's not just the Friulano and Ribolla Gialla whites that Collio is so famous for, but also full-bodied Merlot and Cabernet Franc aged in oak barrels. Each weekend there are crowds of visitors as they open up as an *agriturismo*, with Vilma preparing generous plates of ham, sausages and cheeses while Sergio opens bottles for the tastings.
www.vinicrastin.it; tel +39 0481-630310; località Crastin, Ruttars; Mar–Jun & Sep–Dec by appointment

04 LIVIO FELLUGA

Presided over by the 100-year-old patriarch Livio Felluga, this is the family winery that has set the benchmark for excellence in both the Collio and adjoining Collio Orientale vineyards, where the vast estate stretches over a total of 160 hectares (395 acres).

'There were many doubters when I started clearing forest land and planting vines here 60 years ago,' recalls Signor Livio, 'but history told me that wine had been produced here for centuries and I was sure that this was the perfect place for white grapes like Friulano, Sauvignon and Pinot Grigio and our indigenous red Rofosco.'

The cantina is located just outside Cormons, where visitors are welcomed by appointment in a minimalist designer tasting room. But just across the road, you can savour Felluga's wines in Terra & Vini, a bustling *osteria* opened by Livio's bubbly daughter, Elda, where *viticoltori* noisily gossip at the long bar and food lovers feast on traditional Friulan *frico* (melted cheese with creamy polenta) accompanied by Felluga's signature Terre Alte, the perfect blend of Friulano, Pinot Bianco and Sauvignon.
www.liviofelluga.it; tel +39 0481-60203; via Risorgimento 1, Brazzano di Cormons; by appointment

05 PAOLO CACCESE

The hamlet of Pradis stretches over a series of rolling vine-clad hills overlooking Cormons, the winemaking capital of Collio. The only inhabitants are a dozen *viticoltori*, who all make exceptional wines.

Paolo Caccese's cantina sits atop the highest hill, an ancient stone house alongside three tall cypress trees, surrounded by his 6-hectare (15-acre) vineyard. Paolo is a genuine eccentric, dressed like a country gentleman, and resembling more the lawyer that he trained to be than a producer of a dozen elegant wines. His classic Friulano and Malvasia are delicious, but ask to try such oddities as the fruity Muller-Thurgau, aromatic Traminer and a luscious late-harvest Verduzzo. He defiantly ignores trends and fashions, still uses old-fashioned cement vats, and explains, 'I grow wonderful grapes here on a rich soil in an incredible position on the hillside, so I just do the minimal fine tuning in my cantina so as not to spoil the grapes and let them make their own magic.'
www.paolocaccese.it; tel +39 4387-979 773; località Pradis 6, Cormons; by appointment

06 RENATO KEBER

The meandering road out of Cormons towards San Floriano is marked on both sides by the Collio's distinctive winemaker signs, and at Zegla, a narrow lane leads you to Renato Keber, a one-of-kind *vignaiolo*. A quiet unassuming man, Renato has built a swanky tasting room with panoramic views over his vineyards, where he loves surprising visitors with his spectacular wines. 'I am only interested in ageing,' he states, 'as that is how you make great wines, rather than putting them on sale early when they are too young.'

The *terroir* around Zegla is marl and sandstone, and the harvest of these low-yield vines is hand-picked. Renato then waits seven years before bringing out each Merlot and

Cabernet vintage, but also follows the same philosophy with his whites, so it is quite a shock when he opens, say, a 2008 Pinot Grigio or a 2007 Sauvignon. 'My wines are marathon wines,' he jokes, 'and it is best to wait at least until you get to the 20km mark!'
www.renatokeber.com; tel +39 0481-639742; località Zegla 15, Cormons; by appointment

07 AZIENDA AGRICOLA FRANCO TERPIN

Franco Terpin is an anti-establishment artisan winemaker, the guru of a small group of natural, no-sulphite, wine producers. Certified organic, and favouring long maceration, natural yeast and absolutely no chemicals, Franco's wine spends a year in the barrel, another in steel vats, then three years ageing in the bottle. He produces 90% white wines on the small estate, which includes vines across the border in Slovenia. They have a quite incredible orange colour, known here as *vini arancioni*.

Call in advance for a tasting and be prepared for an unforgettable experience, as Franco will tell you, 'My wines are natural, and quite frankly, they are the only kind of wines I drink now – I can't stand a Chardonnay that has a banana aroma or the classic cat's pee of Sauvignon – these are chemically induced. With my wines you can drink a few bottles, party till 3am, and have absolutely no hangover the next morning.'
www.francoterpin.com; tel +39 0481-884215; località Valerisce 6/a, San Floriano del Colli; by appointment

08 PRIMOSIC

Friuli's Collio region runs out by the border with Slovenia in the village of Oslavia, where at the end of Main St stands the old Frontier Post between two countries divided at the end of World War II.

Back in the 19th century, the Primosic family supplied wine to be sold in Vienna, capital of the Austro-Hungarian Empire, which then included tiny Oslavia, but today Sylvester Primosic and his two sons

01 Friuli's landscape produces some of Italy's finest wines

02 Eat and drink at Enoteca Cormòns

03 Friulian grapevines

Boris and Marko have created a modern, dynamic winery very much in tune with modern Europe. They are at the forefront of a movement to recognise the potential of the long-neglected indigenous Ribolla Gialla grape, so be sure to try the sparkling Ribollanoir, where 10% of tannic Pinot Nero is added to the mineral Ribolla.

A few houses down the road is the cantina of one of Collio's most original winemakers, the reclusive Josko Gravener (www.gravener.it). Although he rarely opens his door to visitors, you can try Gravener's wines in Oslavia's Osteria Korsic (www.korsic.it), as they are something very special, fermented in vast terracotta amphoras buried in his cellar.
www.primosic.com; tel +39 0481-535153; località Madonnina d'Oslavia 3, Oslavia

ESSENTIAL INFORMATION

WHERE TO STAY

BORGO SAN DANIELE
Mauro and Alessandra Mauri make outstanding wines and have created a designer B&B with a pool adjacent to their cantina.
www.borgosandaniele.it; tel +39 0481-60552; via San Daniele 16, Cormòns

GALLO ROSSO
Join the friendly Buzzinelli family in their rustic *agriturismo*. Marzia cooks up a breakfast with freshly laid eggs, and in the evening taste their wines with Maurizio in the cellar.
www.buzzinelli.it; tel +39 0481-60902; località Pradis 20/1, Cormòns

WHERE TO EAT

LA SUBIDA
This once-rustic *osteria* has been transformed by the Sirk family into an elegant Michelin-starred restaurant with dishes like wild deer carpaccio with fresh horseradish.
www.lasubida.it; tel +39 0481-60531; via Subida 52, Cormons

AGRITURISMO STEKAR
A working farm and vineyard that Sonia Stekar opens as a restaurant each weekend lunchtime serving up goulash, plum gnocchi and to-die-for apple strudel.
tel +39 0481-391929; località Giasbana 24, San Floriano del Collio

ENOTECA REGIONALE DI CORMÒNS
This pulsating wine bar is a chance to mingle with local *vignerons*, sample some of the 100 wines available by the glass and gnaw on generous plates of meats and cheeses.
www.enotecacormons.it; tel +39 0481-63071; Piazza XXIV Maggio 21, Cormons

WHAT TO DO

The Abbazia di Rosazzo is a magnificent frescoed abbey, surrounded by vineyards where monks began making wine a thousand years ago.
www.abbaziadirosazzo.it; tel +39 0432-759091; Plazza Abbazia 5, Manzano

CELEBRATIONS

Gorizia celebrates Gusti di Frontiera, a food and wine festival in September, while the Jazz & Wine festival at the end of October sees a roster of musicians performing in cellars around Cormòns.

01

Massimo Ripani © 4Corners Images

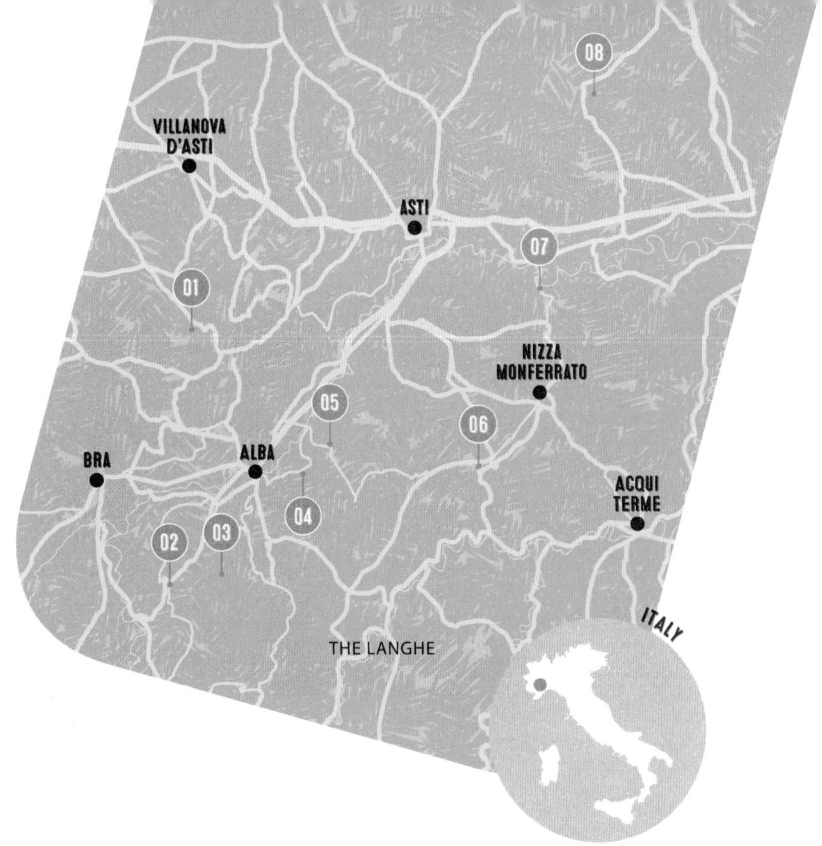

[Italy]

PIEDMONT

Dive into deep, delicious Barolo and Barbaresco red wines in this famously food-loving quarter of northern Italy, before checking out the local truffles.

No region in Italy quite compares to Piedmont's combination of fine wines, gastronomy and beautiful countryside, lying at the foot of the Alps. It would be quite easy to spend a whole trip just wandering through the picture-postcard vineyards and celebrated cantinas of the Langhe, whose hills produce some of the world's greatest, most structured red wines, Barolo and Barbaresco, as well as Nebbiolo, Barbera and Dolcetto. The vineyard landscape is unique and so perfect, that in 2014 it achieved the ultimate honour of being added to the exclusive list of Unesco World Heritage sites.

But it's worth exploring further to discover the surprising Grignolino and Freisa of the Monferrato region, which are made from native grapes, as well as the delicately sweet Moscato and bubbly Spumante produced around Asti and Canelli.

Meanwhile a new generation of young *viticoltori* (winemakers) are bringing to life the rural countryside of the Roero, just across the river from the Langhe, with Arneis and Favorita – both fresh, aromatic whites. Stay in a rustic *agriturismo* where food lovers can splash out on the ultimate gourmet extravagance: aromatic white truffles, or enjoy simple handmade pasta known as *plin*, which is stuffed and pinched together.

This is one of the most developed parts of Italy for wine tourism, with numerous winemaker B&Bs and splendid regional *enoteche* (wine shops), where dozens of different wineries are presented in a single tasting. However, the visitor will quickly realise that the Piedmontese are reserved people, very proud of their own culture and language. They may not fall over at first to ingratiate themselves with tourists, but you'll soon discover just how hospitable and friendly they are.

GET THERE
Turin-Caselle is the nearest major airport, 73km from Montà. Car hire is available.

01 MICHELE TALIANO

The Tanaro River divides the Barolo and Barbaresco vineyards of the Langhe from Roero, a more biodiverse landscape encompassing farm and woodlands too.

Red wines made in the Roero may never achieve the greatness of the best vintages from Barolo and Barbaresco in the Langhe, though today a new generation of Roero *viticoltori* are pushing new boundaries and producing some exceptional Barbera and Nebbiolo wines. It's when it comes to white wines that the Roero *terroir* comes into its own, making a serious reputation for the crisp, acidic Arneis and more fragrant Favorita.

Although the Taliano family have a small parcel of vines in Barbaresco, it is two other wines that really impress at a tasting in their modern winery. Their robust Roero Nebbiolo is perfect to accompany a plate of salami and prosciutto, while the more full-bodied 2009 Roero Riserva is best opened a while before and should be paired with a rich *brasato* of braised beef or wild boar. They are part of a new breed of winemakers turning back to old-fashioned cement vats instead of steel. Accompany Azio Taliani on a tour of the vineyard and you embark on an adventure safari on rutted tracks through dense forest before coming out at a breathtaking vista of graphic crisscrossing vines. Be sure to ask Azio to open a bottle of their intensely aromatic sparkling Birbet, made from Brachetto del Roero, a native grape that is fast disappearing.

www.talianomichele.com; tel +39 0173-976100; Corso Manzoni 24, Montà; by appointment

Massimo Ripani © 4Corners Images

02 CANTINA MASCARELLO BARTOLO

Maria Teresa Mascarello may not have a website or even a mobile phone, but visitors are certainly made to feel welcome at her tiny cantina in the heart of the medieval wine town of Barolo.

The winemakers around here are divided into modernists, who favour single vineyard cuvées, aged in small French barrique barrels, and traditionalists who insist on blending different parcels of vines and using huge Slavonian oak casks. Maria Teresa, following in the steps of her father Bartolo, a pioneer figure in Barolo winemaking, is definitely a traditionalist. She's a fierce defender of Barolo's historic identity, making wines of intense purity and finesse. And for the moment, the pendulum of popularity is swinging back in the direction of these kinds of wines.

Working a small 5-hectare (12-acre) estate of prime Nebbiolo vines, Maria Teresa does not resemble the typical red-faced Piemontese *viticoltore*, but rather a delicate pixie who looks miniscule as she walks past the towering wooden vats in her cantina.
Tel +39 0173-56125; Via Roma 15, Barolo; by appointment

03 PAOLO MANZONE

Serralunga is a spectacular amphitheatre of vineyards, and Paolo Manzone's *cascina* (farmhouse and cellar) is hidden away down a zigzag dirt track. A lengthy tasting session with Paolo is the perfect opportunity to understand the complex world of Barolo. He is an innovative *viticoltore*, forever experimenting but never abandoning the traditions surrounding Barolo's unique grape, Nebbiolo. It has been grown here for seven centuries, and takes its name from the mist that often descends on the vineyards in autumn.

He describes his crisp, fresh Dolcetto d'Alba as 'a wine I make for my father – not elegant but rustic, drinkable, like the wine he sold in demijohns'. Meanwhile the round, robust Nebbiolo d'Alba is 'my Burgundy because I think the Nebbiolo grape can stand on its own in the same way Pinot Noir does in France'.

He makes two very different Barolo, the traditional Serralunga, aged in large, old oak barrels, and the more modern Meriame, using smaller, new French barrels. And he has just built a Fort Knox–like strong room where he aims to stock 10 years of successive vintages to see how they develop.
www.barolomeriame.com; tel +39 0173-613113; Cascina Meriame, Serralunga d'Alba; open 10am-noon & 2-6pm Mon-Sat, 10am-noon Sun

04 CA DEL BAIO

Three generations work together in this idyllic winery nestling in a valley of vineyards. This is classic Barbaresco country, a wine that historically has been the 'little brother' of Barolo, but when you taste this family's vintages, you'll discover it can reach equally great heights.

The winemaking is in the hands of three dynamic sisters, Paola, Valentina and Federica, who recount 'when our great-grandfather bought the land in 1900, everyone thought he was mad, that it was just worthless woodlands. But he always believed in the potential of the soil and began planting vines, firstly selling demijohns in the post-war industrial boom of Torino, then bottling the wine himself and concentrating on quality'.

Their Treiso cru from around the winery is surprisingly supple, while the cru from vineyards in Barbaresco itself is far more complex and really needs to be aged. Don't miss the eminently drinkable Dolcetto – 'great with a pizza,' says Paola with a grin. There's also a wonderful Moscato d'Asti, just 5% alcohol but bursting with fruit, like a fizzy grape juice.
www.cadelbaio.com; tel +39 0173-638219; Via Ferrere Sottano 33, Treiso; by appointment

03

© Susan Wright

05 CANTINA DEL GLICINE

This unique cantina is a must-visit for Barbaresco lovers, stepping back in time when wine was made in a slower, more instinctive way, rather than depending on modern technology.

Adriana Marzi and Roberto Bruni are an eccentric couple but very serious about the wine they produce from their small 6-hectare (15-acre) estate. Before the tasting, Adriana takes you through a forbidding blood-red door that leads down to the cantina, what the Piemontese call 'Il Cutin', a natural grotto that is then hollowed out and extended into a maze of damp, cool cellars. This one dates back to 1582, and is like walking into a scene from *Lord of the Rings*, with mushrooms growing over the damp walls, greedily gobbled up by snails, dark corners stacked with ancient wooden barrels, and alcoves filled with dusty bottles laid down to age.

The younger Barbaresco vintages are not easy for tasting, as they really need a good few years more to fully mature, while even the supposedly less-complex Barbera and Nebbiolo are seriously intense. And beware that Adriana always insists visitors try her famous grappa.

www.cantinadelglicine.it; tel +39 0173-67215; Via Giulio Cesare 1, Neive; by appointment

06 GANCIA

The words Asti and Spumante have been famous throughout the world for more than 150 years as the symbol of Italian sparkling wine. Although today more attention is turned to bubbly Prosecco and the refined *metodo classico* of Franciacorta, the story of Spumante began in Piedmont, specifically at the house of Gancia, whose castle still dominates the medieval town of Canelli.

Inspired by a long stay in Champagne where he learnt the alchemy of producing *méthode champenoise*, Carlo Gancia returned in 1850 to Canelli, most famous for the aromatic, fruity Moscato grape, and planted Chardonnay and Pinot Noir to create the first Italian Spumante.

Like all the famous Champagne houses, Gancia has become a huge multinational, controlling 2000 hectares (5000 acres) of vines, which produce some 25 million bottles a year, and although the original Gancia family are still present, a Russian vodka company has a controlling interest. But a tour of the historic cantina in Canelli remains an unforgettable experience, not just for the maze of subterranean cathedral-like cellars, but for the family's unparalleled historic collection of advertising memorabilia that for a century promoted a unique Italian lifestyle. It's only open one Sunday per month, so call ahead for information.

www.gancia.com; tel +39 0141-8301; Corso Liberta 66, Canelli; by appointment

07 BRAIDA

Braida is forever associated with the name of the late Giacamo Bologna, another of the mythical figures of Piedmont wine, along with Angelo Gaja and Bartolo Mascarello. Planting the then humble grape of Barbera in the unsung region between Asti and Alessandria back in the 1960s, Bologna proved that Piedmont's great wines did not have to be restricted to the Nebbiolo-based Barolo and Barbaresco.

Using 100% Barbera and ageing for long periods in small French oak barrels to compensate for the lack of natural tannin, he produced stunning vintages of the full-bodied Bricco dell'Uccelone and the intense, late-harvest Ai Suma. In contrast, the wonderfully drinkable La Monella ('The Tomboy') is refreshing, *frizzante* and named after Giacomo's daughter Raffaella.

Today, this dynamic winery is run by Giacomo's children, Raffaella and Giuseppe, who have expanded the estate to over 50 hectares (125 acres), but continue to make wine following their father's principles. After a visit to the state-of-the-art cantina, don't miss lunch at their family Trattoria I Bologna.
www.braida.it; tel +39 0141-644113; Via Roma 94, Rocchetta Tanaro; open 9am-noon & 2-6pm Mon-Sat, also Sun Sep-Nov

08 IL MONGETTO

North of the Langhe, the wilder region of Monferrato may be less renowned for its wine than its neighbour, but being under-the-radar means wine travellers get a great welcome, and *viticoltori* here are cultivating a selection of indigenous grapes.

The brothers Carlo and Roberto Santopietro have converted an 18th-century *palazzetto* (frescoed mansion) into a guesthouse where guests stay the night, wines are tasted, and at the weekend a cosy dining room serves local specialities.

Carlo, a bearded giant of man, is the winemaker. He produces not just a robust Barbera aged in small oak barrels, but surprising reds such as the fruity but tannic Grignolino, a *vivace* (lively) Cortese, the slightly *amabile* (fruity and easy-to-drink) Freisa, which records show has been grown here since the 15th century, and Malvasia di Casorzo – sweet, fizzy and only 5% alcohol. Roberto meanwhile travels all over the world promoting Piedmont specialities like *bagna cauda* (hot dip) and *mostarda d'uva* (grape mustard).
www.mongetto.it; tel +39 0142-933442; Via Piave 2, Vignale Monferrato; open daily by appointment

01 The Langhe region of Piedmont

02 The Asti region of Piedmont

03 Truffle hunting pair in Piedmont

ESSENTIAL INFORMATION

WHERE TO STAY

CASA SCAPARONE
The wonderfully eccentric Battista Cornaglia ensures guests enjoy a memorable stay at his organic farm. There are cosy guestrooms and a raucous *osteria* (simple restaurant) where Battista often takes to the floor with local musicians.
www.casascaparone.it; tel +39 0173-33946; località Scaparone 8, Alba

CASTELLO DI SINIO
This 800-year-old castle dominates the hamlet of Sinio, surrounded by vineyards producing the greatest Barolo wine. Sumptuous rooms and a great welcome by owner Denise Pardini.
www.hotelcastellodisinio.com; tel +39 0173-263889; Vicolo del Castello, 1 Sinio

LE CASE DELLA SARACCA
A unique address where six medieval houses have been transformed into a labyrinth of grottoes, suspended glass walkways, swirling metallic staircases and bedrooms with floating bed or bathroom carved out of the rock.
www.saracca.com; tel +39 0173-789222; Via Cavour 5, Monforte d'Alba

WHERE TO EAT

OSTERIA DA GEMMA
Taste Signora Gemma's legendary Piemontese *cucina casalinga* (home cooking), in her *osteria*, with portions razor-thin *tajarin* pasta showered with pungent white-truffle shavings.
Tel +39 0173-794252; Via Marconi 6, Roddino

PIAZZA DUOMO
Chef Enrico Crippa has won a coveted three Michelin stars in this futuristic temple of gastronomy in Alba. Sublime cuisine.
www.piazzaduomoalba.it; tel +39 0173-366167; Piazza Risorgimento 4, Alba

WHAT TO DO

Turin was the first capital of modern Italy, with ornate baroque palaces, an amazing Egyptian Museum, the Museo Egizio di Torino, and historical cafes that have made an art of the evening *aperitivo*.
www.museoegizio.it

CELEBRATIONS

Every weekend from mid-October to mid-November, Alba hosts its famous white-truffle festival.

01

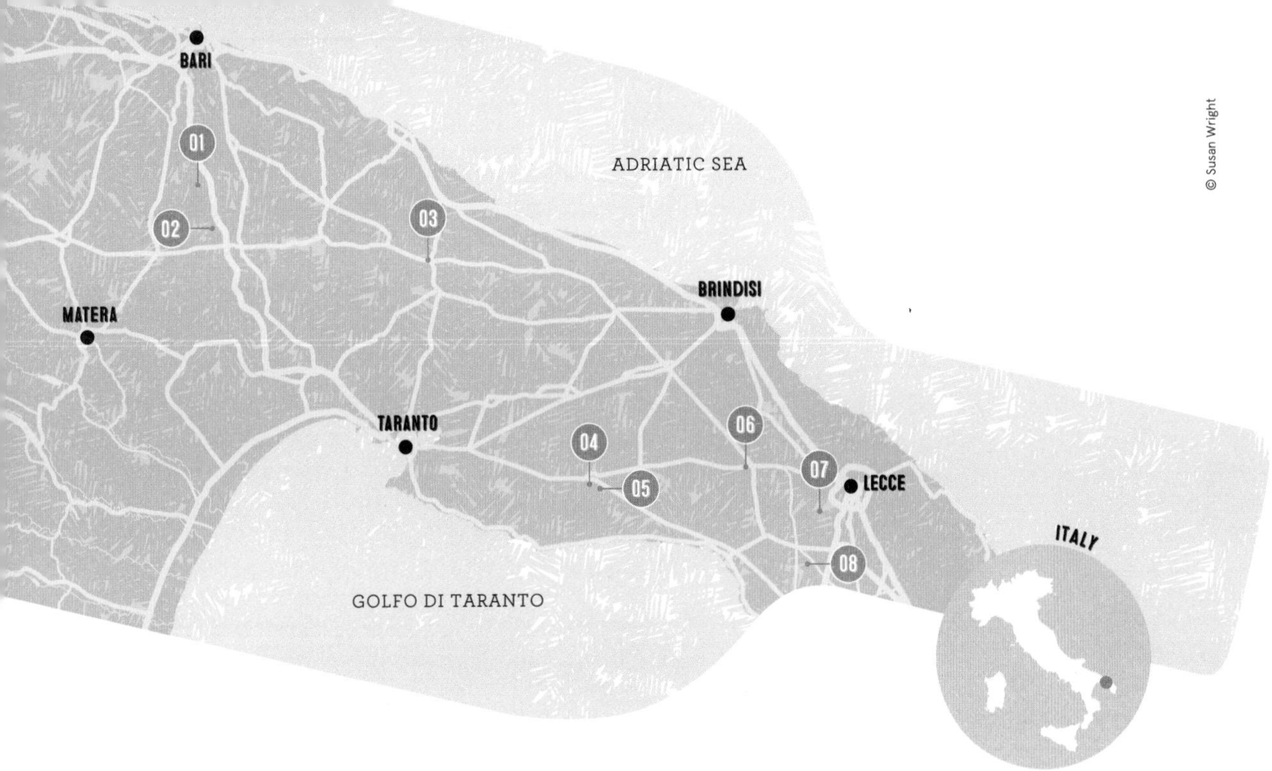

BARI
01
02
03
ADRIATIC SEA
MATERA
BRINDISI
TARANTO
04
05
06
07
LECCE
08
ITALY
GOLFO DI TARANTO

[Italy]

PUGLIA

Follow the sun down through the heel of Italy to olive groves and trulli *– and a range of rustic, resurgent wines that accompany the local cuisine perfectly.*

Puglia is the largest wine producer in Italy, a quintessentially rural region where cultivating grapes and olives is ingrained in the daily life of the *contadino* (farm worker). But for a long time it has been known for all the wrong reasons, historically supplying wine in bulk to Italy and much of Europe.

Things have changed, though, and today the world has woken up to the wine revolution taking place here. Forget so-called international grapes like Chardonnay, Cabernet and Merlot, and discover unique indigenous grapes – elegant Negroamaro, full-bodied Primitivo, cousin of California's Zinfandel, fruity Minutolo and Malvasia Nera.

The prime vineyards begin just north of Bari stretching down Italy's heel to Brindisi, Taranto, Lecce, Manduria and the Salice Salentino. The climate here is hot but tempered by breezes from the Adriatic and Ionian seas, meaning the wines are intense and strong in alcohol but by no means overpowering. And today the region's small independent estates produce wines of exceptional quality, making use of modern cellar techniques and taking care in the vineyard to limit yield and to cultivate old *albarelli* (bush vines).

Don't expect too much picturesque scenery of hills covered with vines, of the type you'd find in Tuscany or Piedmont. In Puglia, running down through to the base of the heel of Italy, landscapes are dominated by miles and miles of flat plains planted with hundreds of thousands of giant, gnarled olive trees, some more than three millennia old. Olive groves and vineyards alike are marked by the unique *trulli* white stone huts, some of which are still home to agricultural workers, although others are being converted into seductive B&Bs.

GET THERE

Bari is the nearest major airport, 40km (25 miles) from Acquaviva delle Fonti. Car hire is available.

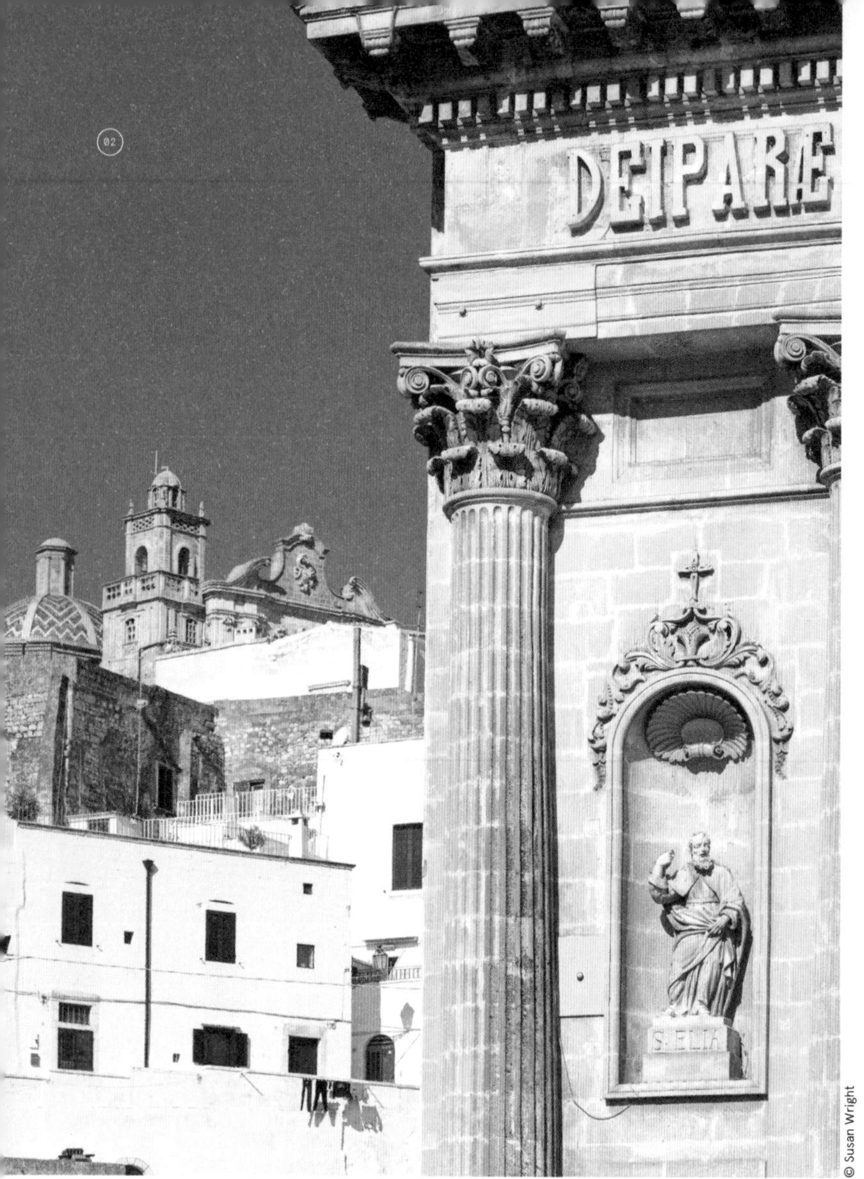

© Susan Wright

01 TENUTE CHIAROMONTE

Located just south of Bari, Acquaviva is a medieval town with a long history of winemaking. 'We like to say that this is a mini Rheims,' explains owner and winemaker Nicola Chiaromonte, 'as over 500 houses have their own cellar where wine has always been made.'

Nicola started the estate in 1993 with 2 hectares (5 acres) of ancient *albarelli*, which today has grown to 33 hectares (82 acres). His Primitivo Riserva is made from 80-year-old *albarelli*, including several centenary vines that predate the Phylloxera epidemic. He is firmly against the trend to lower the alcohol volume of Primitivo to sell to a wider market. 'If you drink a Primitivo that is 13% you will never understand what the wine is about – the grape needs to develop, to mature, and for the Riserva I even favour a partial *apassimento* [dessicating the grape on the vine].'
www.tenutechiaromonte.com; tel +39 080-3050432; Via Suriani 27, Acquaviva delle Fonti; by appointment

02 POLVANERA

Polvanera refers to the distinctive deep red soil that surrounds the ancient manor house of innovative *vignaiolo* (winegrower) Filippo Cassano. It takes an impassioned wine enthusiast to find Polvanera, hidden in the wild countryside outside of Gioa del Colle, beyond even a GPS.

'I come from a family of winemakers who for generations produced bulk wine, without the financial means to bottle their own vintages,' Filippo recounts. 'So I am determined to prove that this part of Val d'Itria can make the finest Primitivo as well as great wines from other native Puglia grapes.' He organically cultivates a vineyard of 30 hectares (75 acres), with a big proportion of bush vines, many 60 to 80 years old, and has excavated a quite incredible cellar hewn out of limestone 8m (26ft) underground. This is where he ages for long periods – but there is not a barrel in sight. Filippo rocks the usual trend, refusing to use any wood, preferring to leave the wine in the bottle. The results are spectacular, especially the Polvanero 17, Primitivo in *purezzo*, a dizzy 17% alcohol but still fresh and fruity.
www.cantinepolvanera.it; tel +39 080-758900; Strada le Lamie Marchesana 601, Gioa del Colle; open 9am-1.30pm & 3-5.30pm Mon-Sat, Sun by appointment

03 I PASTINI

While Puglia is making its name right now with Primitivo and Negroamaro red wines, there are also some highly original native white grapes too. No estate quite compares with that of the Carparelli family, whose vineyards stretch around the historic city of Locorotonda through Val d'Itria, also known as the Trulli Valley, after the distinctive whitewashed, conical stone houses here. A tasting includes a visit to the family's 17th-century *masseria* (traditional Puglian farmhouse), together with perfectly preserved *trulli* still used during the *vendemmia* (harvest).

White wine is their speciality, and the Carparellis are credited with rediscovering the unique indigenous Minutolo grape from the Muscat family, wrongly named for decades as a Fiano from Campania. They vinify and age their wines only in steel vats – the Minutolo is mineral, fresh and brimming with fruit – and they also produce Verdeca, the little-known Bianco d'Alessio and a luscious late-harvest Minutolo, the grapes of which are *passito* (dried in crates for 30 days).
www.ipastini.it; tel +39 080-4313309; Strada Rampone, Locorotondo; by appointment

04 MORELLA VINI

For the moment, Gaetano Morella and Lisa Gilbee are making genuine garage wines in an industrial warehouse on the drab outskirts of Manduria. But these garage vintages are also winning Italy's top wine awards.

Finding the cantina is a problem, as there is not even a sign, but a tasting is fascinating, as Melbourne-native Lisa explains the experiments she is making: old and new barrels, Nomblot cement eggs and strangely shaped cement vats called 'hippo'.

But this couple's real passion is Primitivo bush vines. 'Gaetano is from the north of Puglia and I was working as a flying winemaker all over Italy,' says Lisa. 'But we came to Manduria specifically for the ancient *albarelli* vines. So many have already been dug up or abandoned, and we are just trying to save as many as possible because, quite simply, they produce incredible wines.' A tour of their biodynamic vineyards is memorable, especially if you have tasted the elegant single-vineyard cuvée, La Signora and the highly concentrated Old Vines.
www.morellavini.com; tel +39 099-9791482; Via per Uggiano 147, Manduria; by appointment

05 CONSORZIO PRODUTTORI VINI

The role of the cooperative cantina in Puglia's wine history has not exactly been glorious. Many have rarely concentrated on quality, and still today prefer the economic security of supplying cheap wine in bulk. A notable exception is the venerable Consorzio of Producers of Manduria, the oldest cooperative in Puglia, formed in 1932. Regardless of size – 1000 hectares (2500 acres) owned by 400 *soci* (members) – it has maintained a reputation for innovation and excellent, affordable wines.

Visiting the immense cantina is the perfect introduction to the wines of Puglia. A tasting spans not just the iconic Primitivo di Manduria, the historic 'home' of Primitivo, but Negroamaro, white and rose varietals and a Fiano Spumante. Locals still pop in to fill up their demijohn with *sfuso* (bulk wine) from the pump. Beneath the cantina is a labyrinth of cement cisterns, brilliantly transformed into a museum documenting the history of wine and rural life here.
www.cpvini.com; tel +39 099-9735332; Via Fabio Massimo 19, Manduria; open 8am-1pm & 3.30-6.30pm Mon-Fri, 9am-1pm Sat

06 FEUDI DI GUAGNANO

Guagnano is a lively winemaker's village in the heart of the Salento region, serious Negroamaro land. While the main cantina is out of town, Feudi has a cosy wine shop and barrel room for tastings, presenting a range of potent, long-aged Negroamaro made from old bush vines, often including a 30-day *apassimento* after harvest in wooden crates.

Gianvito Rizzo is the winemaker, the *enologo*, and founding member of Feudi, a small informal group of wine enthusiasts. He remembers how they started 12 years ago, 'when a few friends realised that our parents, *contadini* (peasant) farmers, were selling off the family plots of traditional *albarelli* vines as they retired, and that a whole rural way of life was set to disappear. So we decided to hang on to our heritage, buy any other plots that were being abandoned, and today we have 15 hectares (37 acres), all tiny diverse parcels of vines.'

After a wine tasting, be sure to stop off at Guagnano's favourite *vignaiolo* haunt for lunch, L'Orecchietta, a pasta laboratory serving handmade orecchiette in a rich tomato sauce with *polpette* (meatballs).
www.feudiguagnano.it; tel +39 0832-705422; Via Provinciale 37, Guagnano; open 9am-12.30pm & 3-6.30pm Mon-Fri, 9am-12.30pm Sat

07 APOLLONIO

Marcello and Massemiliano Apollonia run a huge modern winery, the vineyards of which span the prime Negroamaro and Primitivo regions of Salento and Copertino. Running several different labels, they produce well over a million bottles a year,

'Today, winemakers have succeeded in transforming Puglia into one of the most exciting wine regions, distinguished by our exceptional indigenous grapes.' *–Piero Tamburrino, sommelier*

03

but the signature boutique Apollonia range is something completely different. The family comes from four generations of winemakers renowned for ageing Pugliese wines in barrels, and the oenologist of the family, Massemiliano, could well be described as the Wood King.

Touring the cantina, there is not a steel vat in sight, while even the cement cisterns are covered with oak inside. Again using primarily *albarelli* vines, Massemiliano experiments with different woods for different cuvées – French, American, Slavic, Hungarian and Austrian. He even visits the coopers to order the wood three years before the barrel is made when it is still a tree. Then the bottles are stored underground in a maze of former cisterns. His philosophy? 'Wood is fundamental for me, not just for the *profumo* (scent), but for the colour and stability of the wine, to age to immortality if possible.' ***www.apolloniovini.it; tel +39 0832-327182; Via San Pietro in Lama 7, Monteroni di Lecce; open 8.30am-4.30pm Mon-Fri, by appointment Sat & Sun***

⓪⑧ CANTINA SEVERINO GAROFANO

If any master winemaker is responsible for raising Negroamaro to the heights it has reached today, it is Severino Garofano. For 50 years he held the reins at the respected Copertinum cooperative – still very much worth a visit – moving the conservative *soci* from bulk to quality bottled wine. Not content with this alone, at the same time he acted as consultant to some of the most important Puglia estates, was the founding father of ground-breaking modern interpretations of Negroamaro, and still found the time to set up his own winery.

Today, he still watches over the family's 50-hectare (125-acre) vineyard, which is in the safe hands of his son, Stefano. The *azienda* (company) is housed in a wonderfully retro 1950s cantina, and the vinification is similarly traditional, still using the giant underground cement cisterns. But the wines are absolutely modern, especially the mellow Negroamaro Le Braci, aged for at least seven years, where a short *apassimento* on the vine means alcohol levels rise to almost 15% without affecting the elegance of the vintage. *garofano.aziendamonaci.com; tel +39 0832-947512; località Tenuta Monaci, Copertino; by appointment*

01 Traditional Puglian *trulli* hut

02 Classical architecture in Ostuni

03 Harvesting grapes in the Puglia region

Marco Pavan © 4Corners Images

ESSENTIAL INFORMATION

WHERE TO STAY

CANNE BIANCHE
Right at the edge of the beach, a fashionably chic resort with spa, cooking courses and even boat trips with local fishermen to catch *octopi*. *www.cannebianche.com; tel +39 080-4829839; Via Appia 32, Torre Canne di Fasano*

MASSERIA LE FABRICHE
Five minutes from the sandy beaches of the Ionian Sea, this perfectly restored, 18th-century *masseria* is surrounded by vineyards. Guests stay down below in a secluded olive grove in modern, minimalist junior suites. *www.lefabriche.it; tel +39 099-9871852; Contrada da la Fabriche, SP130, Maruggio*

WHERE TO EAT

OSTERIA DEI MERCANTI, MANDURIA
Hidden away in the historic centre of Manduria, this rustic *osteria's* menu changes each day and offers authentic Pugliese specialities such as *ciceri e tria* (chickpeas and fried pasta). *Tel +39 099-9713673; Via Lacaita 7, Manduria*

OSTERIA DEL POETA
Alberobella is home to Puglia's unique *trulli* stone cottages, a must-see. The perfect place for lunch is chef Leonardo Marco's gourmet *osteria*. *www.osteriadelpoeta.it; tel +39 080-4321917; Via Indipendenza 23, Alberobella*

LA SOMMITA
Ostuni looks out over a sea of olive trees, some dating back a thousand years. This restaurant features a reinterpretation of local cuisine by young chef Sebastiano Lombardi, *www.lasommita.it; tel +39 0831-305925; Via Scipione Petrarolo 7, Ostuni*

WHAT TO DO

Don't miss the baroque architecture of Lecce; its lanes form a maze of ornate churches and grand *palazzi* (palaces).

CELEBRATIONS

Stretching both before and after the Lent carnival period (February/March), the Carnevale di Putignano is both a sacred and profane celebration, combining religious rites with political satire. *carnevalediputignano.it*

01

[Italy]

SARDINIA

Discover the secrets of this Mediterranean isle's punchy wines before hitting the sensational beaches.

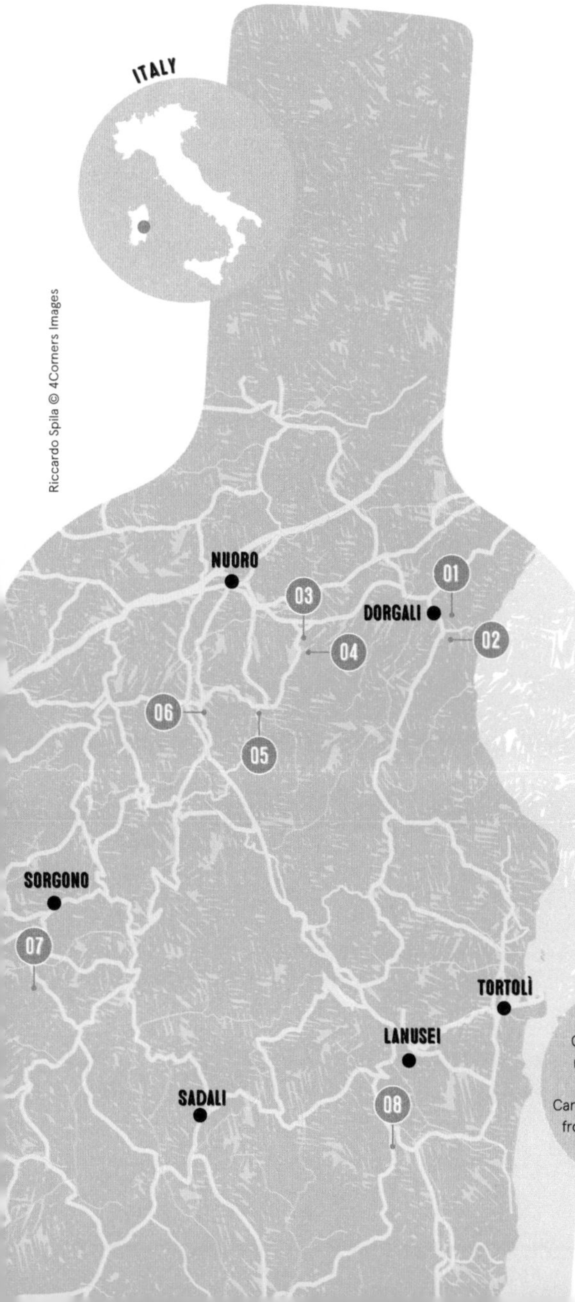

Sardinia is an autonomous region of Italy that sometimes seems to be an independent country all of its own. The stunning sea-and-mountain landscapes contrast Mediterranean beaches with a wild interior of peaks and bare lowlands.

For white wine lovers, the island produces aromatic Vermentino, Moscato and Vernaccia, but Sardinia is essentially red-wine country and that red wine is Cannonau – explosive, potent and not for the faint-hearted. Locals claim Cannonau, known elsewhere as Grenache, has grown here for 3200 years, making it the oldest grape in the Mediterranean.

Most of the vineyards, and the highest-quality wines, are produced in a triangle in Sardinia's centre that stretches along an idyllic coastline from Orosei to Barisada, and then into the mountainous Barbagia region. Patches of vineyards are dotted around what is essentially a pastoral landscape dominated by sheep. This is because there is a centuries-old tradition here of pretty much everyone owning small plots of vines and making wine at home. Things changed in the 1950s with the appearance of the cantina *sociale* (cooperative association) grouping several hundred winemakers, and now a new generation of independent winemakers is emerging, creating larger vineyards and concentrating on making quality Cannonau.

Outside the big cooperative cantinas, wine tourism is still in its early days, and it is almost always necessary to call first to arrange an estate visit. But once at the cantina, be prepared for a very special welcome from the Sardinian *viticoltori* who make guests that stop by for a tasting immediately feel like one of the family. Follow their recommendations for a local trattoria and discover a cuisine that is just out of this world: the best cheeses you will taste in Italy, home-cured prosciutto and salami, succulent roast lamb and the unforgettable *porcheddu*, spit-roasted suckling pig – perfect, of course, with an aged Cannonau Riserva.

ITALY
NUORO
DORGALI
SORGONO
TORTOLÌ
LANUSEI
SADALI
01
02
03
04
05
06
07
08

GET THERE

Cagliari is the nearest major airport, 215km from Dorgali. Car hire is available. Ferries from mainland Italy dock in Cagliari port.

02

01 CANTINA SOCIALE DORGALI

The cooperative winery of Dorgali, just by the seaside resort of Cala Gonone, was founded some 60 years ago, and is the ideal example of how a big cantina *sociale* can put hundreds of *viticoltori* under the same umbrella, produce 1.5 million bottles a year, yet succeed in making an excellent selection of wines.

The unpretentious cantina has something for all wine lovers, from the holidaymaker who comes in to pick up a bag-in-box of the eminently drinkable *vino da tavola* (table wine) to enthusiasts sitting down for a serious *degustazione* (tasting) of higher-end wines. These include the Cannonau Viniola Riserva and Hortos, a daring blend of indigenous grapes and Syrah, that have both won Italy's coveted Tre Bicchieri award.

www.cantinadorgali.com; tel +39 0784-96143; Via Piemonte 11, Dorgali; 8.30am-1pm & 3-5.30pm Mon-Fri

02 PODERI ATHA RUJA

Pietro Pittalis does not resemble a typical rustic Sardinian *vignaiolo* (winegrower). Immaculately attired, he proudly shows visitors round his tiny vineyard that is as close to perfection as you can imagine. The setting is magnificent, with the lines of manicured vines set against a backdrop of the magical Supramonte mountains separating these wild interiors from the sea.

Pietro is very clear on how to produce a great Cannonau. 'I cultivate a limited number of vines, only 20,000, and each one is cut back throughout the year to grow only five bunches of perfect grapes, which will be made into 20,000 bottles – one for each vine.' In the midst of the vineyards, he has turned a colourful stone cottage into a tasting centre, but this rich, intense Cannonau, aged two years in small oak barrels, really needs another four to five years before reaching maturity. So the best idea is to accompany Pietro back to the coast at Dorgali to taste some older vintages at the gourmet restaurant of his plush beach hotel.

www.atharuja.com; tel +39 347-5387127; Via Emilia 45, Dorgali; open 4-8pm May-Sep, by appointment Oct-Apr

> **'Like most villagers, I sold the grapes from my small plot to a cooperative, but now we want to take responsibility and make a truly great wine ourselves.'**
>
> *–Graziano Vederle, member Cantina di Orgosolo*

03 GOSTOLAI

Oliena is a buzzing winemakers' village, the unofficial capital of Cannonau country, but you need to head into the industrial outskirts to discover the modern cantina of Tonino Arcada.

If Tonino looks a little academic, almost more interested in talking history and poetry, it is no surprise to learn he was a school teacher before devoting himself to his vines. 'Lots of people in Sardinia want to drink young wines,' he says. 'Well, I don't. I like to age my wines to see how they develop and I am not in a hurry. You'll find my wines are a challenge – closed, intense, tannic.' The vintages are certainly out of the ordinary, especially a sensational 2006 Riserva D'Annunzio, named after the legendary Italian adventurer, Gabriele d'Annunzio, who visited Oliena as a 19-year-old reporter and immediately became a lifelong aficionado of Cannonau.

www.gostolai.net; tel +39 0784-288417; Via Friuli Venezia Giulia 24, Oliena; daily by appointment

04 AZIENDA AGRICOLA FRATELLI PUDDU

Located in the shadow of the granite cliffs of the Massico del Corrasi mountain, a visit to Nenneddu Puddu offers the opportunity to see the biodiversity of a Sardinian *azienda agricola* (agricultural business).

The estate spreads over 50 hectares (125 acres), 30 covered with vines and 15 planted with olive groves. They even have an extensive curing operation producing an irresistible range of Sardinian charcuterie. The star of Puddu's wine range is their Pro Vois, a Cannonau Nepente Riserva, using grapes from their oldest vines. They also have two oddities worth trying, Papalope, a declassified *vino da tavola* whose late-harvested Cannonau grapes are left to dry in the *passito* tradition, and Papalope Bianco, a complex, intense white wine, using the rare Grenache Blanc.

www.aziendapuddu.it; tel +39 0784-288457; Località Orbuddai, Oliena; open 8.30am-1pm & 2.30-5.30pm Mon-Fri

Johanna Huber © 4Corners Images

05 CANTINE DI ORGOSOLO

The wild mountain town of Orgosolo is a symbol of the inherent independence that Sardinian people claim as their right, marked by the *murales*, over 200 huge political frescoes covering the walls of most of the houses.

Orgosolo is also home to a genuine garage winery producing some of the most original Cannonau on the island. Six years ago, 19 diverse smallholders – including a tobacconist, electrician, hospital worker and shepherd – each owning around 1 hectare (2.5 acres) of vines, grouped together to make an artisan Cannonau. Vines range from five to 70 years old, some are at 250m (820ft) above sea level, others as high as 1000m (3280ft). And although they get occasional advice from a top oenologist, this merry band prefers to spend hours in a rented garage around their hodge-podge of steel vats and oak barrels discussing vinification and ageing.

'We make one wine that has stayed in the barrel for only three months, easy to drink straight away, and a Riserva that ages for three years,' says one *viticoltori*. 'And if we don't sell them, then we'll just drink them ourselves!'

www.cantinediorgosolo.it; tel +39 0784-403096; Via Ilole, Orgosolo; by appointment

06 AZIENDA GIUSEPPE SEDILESU

Giuseppe Sedilesu bought a small plot of Cannonau vines 35 years ago and has overseen his three children extend it to 17 hectares (42 acres) of bush vines, which produce a stunning range of Cannonau that today are among the award-winning stars of the Sardinian wine scene.

The estate is an intriguing mix of modern and traditional, from recently planted to gnarled 100-year-old vines. The family is moving with the times by producing organic and biodynamic wines, but still use oxen to plough the soil and harvest the grapes by hand.

The family oenologist, Francesco Sedilesu, says, 'We concentrate almost exclusively on red wines, which are intense and complex, sometimes rising to 16% alcohol, but never disturbing the natural expression of the grape, which for us is the soul of Cannonau.' The only surprise is that during the tasting, instead of the usual cheese and salami, there is a plate of bitter chocolate, a perfect complement to these powerful vintages.

www.giuseppesedilesu.com; tel +39 0784-56791; Via Vittorio Emanuele 64, Mamoiada; open 9am-1pm & 3-6pm Mon-Fri

07 LE VIGNE DI FULGHESU

While Cannonau is not that well known outside Sardinia, the obscure Mandrolisai denomination ranks as an even rarer discovery. Winemakers around the villages of Atzara and Meana have the opportunity to make Mandrolisai, a unique blend of Cannonau and two local grape varieties, Muristellu and Monica.

Stop off in Atzara at the *enoteca* (wine shop) of the excellent Fradiles winery, but then trek out to the cantina of Peppe Fulghesu, who makes unforgettable wines, many of them natural, producing an incredible explosion of the fruit of the grape. Peppe's vineyard lies at the end of a rutted track, but the reward is a terrific welcome and a tasting accompanied by his home-cured salami and freshly made ricotta cheese. And it doesn't need much to encourage Peppe to take visitors for a hike up the hill to see a rare *nuraghe*, one of Sardinia's famed prehistoric stone huts dating back to 1000 BC. *tel +39 0784-64320; Via Su Frigili Cerebinu, Meana Sardo; by appointment*

08 ANTICHI PODERI DI JERZU

The Jerzu region, located between the sandy beaches of the Bay of Ogliastra and the Gennargentu mountains, has a long tradition of wine production, and has the right to produce its own Cannonau denomination.

Founded in 1950, this dynamic cantina *sociale*, with its 450 *soci*, is very active in Jerzu's social life, especially each August when it organises the Sagra del Vino, a weeklong music and wine festival.

The huge winery dominates Jerzu and is marked by a tower that has been converted into a tasting room with panoramic views. And there is a lot to taste because, as is the case with each cantina *sociale*, there is a huge choice on display – including Sardinian speciality, Mirto, a lethal liqueur made from myrtle berries. *www.jerzuantichipoderi.it; tel +39 0782-70028; Via Umberto 1, Jerzu; open 8.30am-1pm & 3-7pm Mon-Sat*

01 Su Portu beach in Torre Chia

02 Carignano grapevine

03 View towards the town of Bosa

ESSENTIAL INFORMATION

WHERE TO STAY

SU GOLOGONE
Unique luxury resort lost in the countryside with a restaurant, pool and spa and a museum-standard collection of traditional arts and crafts. *www.sugologone.it; tel +39 0784-287512; località Su Gologone, Oliena*

AGRITURISMO CANALES
Rustic mountain hideaway overlooking an emerald-green lake. Fresh cheeses are delivered each morning, and wine comes from its own vineyard. *www.canales.it; tel +39 0784-96760; località Canales, Dorgali*

DOMUS DE JANAS SUL MARE
Simple family hotel with a stunning location by a bay with an ancient watchtower that protected the village from marauding pirates in medieval times. *www.domusdejanas.com; tel +39 0782-28081; Via della Torre, Bari Sardo*

WHERE TO EAT

RISTORANTINO MASILOGHI
Favourite hangout of Oliena winemakers, Gianfranco Maccareno's romantic trattoria features the best *porcheddu* you will ever taste. *www.masiloghi.it; tel +39 0784-285696; Via Galjani 68, Oliena*

CIKAPPA
The cuisine here is simple, but uses rare produce such as mountain ferns, wild boar and, for fans of nose-to-tail eating, lamb sweetbreads, brain and *coratella* (lungs, heart and liver). *www.cikappa.com; tel +39 0784-288024; Corso Martin Luther King 2, Oliena*

WHAT TO DO

From the Cala Gonone seaside resort, hire a boat to sail into the mysterious Bue Marino cave filled with stalactites and stalagmites, then sunbathe on idyllic Cala Luna beach.

CELEBRATIONS

The hamlet of Mamoiada hosts an extraordinary animist carnival just before Lent. Villagers are transformed into wild *mamuthones*, fearful-looking creatures clad in masks and thick sheepskin fleeces draped in heavy cowbells. Bonfires are lit and a large quantity of wine is drunk.

01

GREVE IN CHIANTI
08
07
06
VOLPAIA
05
RADDA IN CHIANTI
CASTELLINA IN CHIANTI
04
01
03
02
ITALY
SIENA

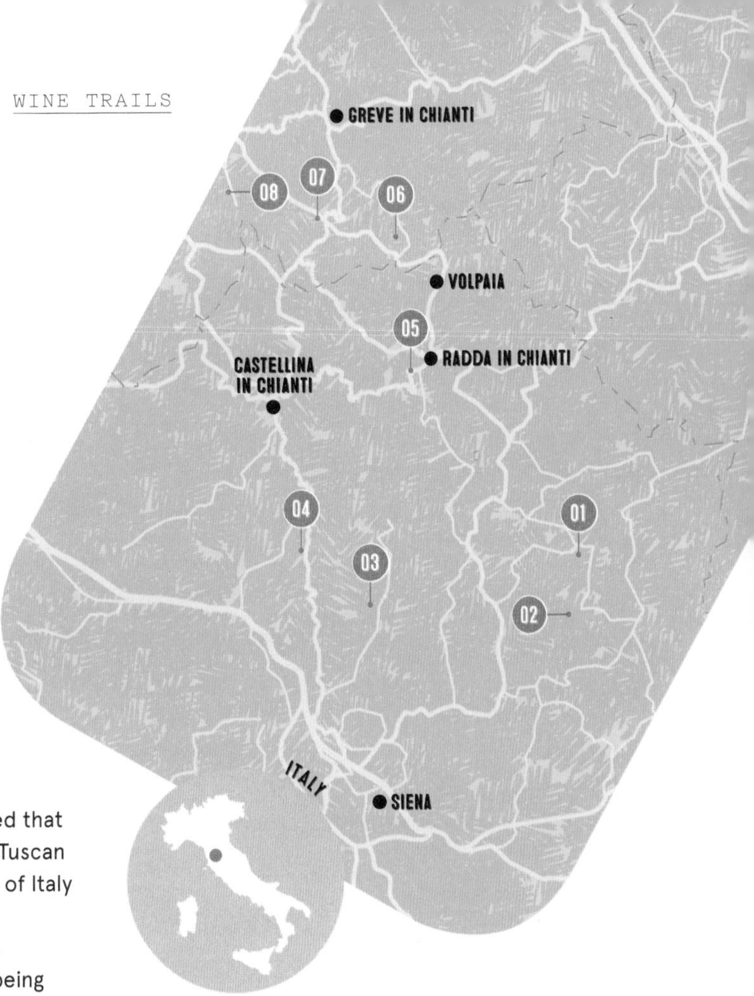

[Italy]

TUSCANY

With its swaying cypresses, hilltop villages and exceptional red wines, Tuscany exudes an old-fashioned romance that's hard to resist.

Wine and Tuscany are so closely associated that for many, the vintages produced in the Tuscan hills symbolise all the glamour and style of Italy in the same way that Champagne evokes France.

It was the Etruscans who first made wine here, using huge terracotta *amphorae* that are today being rediscovered by certain natural winemakers. As early as the 5th century BC, Tuscan wines were exported to France and Greece, and Florence founded its own Wine Merchants Guild as early as 1282. So Tuscany has always been the ambassador of Italian wine, from ancient times through to the days when the eponymous straw-covered flask of Chianti became the house wine of every pizzeria in the world. And today, Tuscany's wine has moved on to the wine lists of the world's finest restaurants, with the top Tuscan producers appearing alongside those of Bordeaux and Burgundy.

Tuscany is the perfect location for producing outstanding red wine with the native Sangiovese grape, but centuries of tradition have come under threat as winemakers have started blending it with 'international' varietals like Cabernet Sauvignon and Merlot. These are the so-called Super Tuscans, wines produced outside the ancient regulations that offer immediate, accessible quality that is easier to sell internationally. While some Super Tuscans, primarily in the Maremma, have made their mark and are here to stay, every mode has its day, and today the mood is returning to traditional winemaking based purely on the potential of Sangiovese. That is definitely the case in the historic Chianti Classico region, where the story of Tuscan winemaking began.

It is difficult to know where to start when planning a wine journey here, where vineyards nestle in undulating hillsides and valleys from the outskirts of Florence all the way to the Mediterranean. Exclusive wines such as Sassicaia and Ornellaia are produced in the relatively new maritime vineyards of windswept Maremma. The medieval cities of Montalcino and Montepulciano continue to impose strict rules on the making and ageing of their venerable Brunello and Vino Nobile vintages, and in Chianti, the controversy created by the emergence of the Super Tuscans seems to be slowly disappearing.

GET THERE
Pisa is the nearest major airport, 120km from Gaiole di Chianti. Car hire is available.

01 CASTELLO DI BROLIO

The story of Chianti begins here at the enchanting Castello di Brolio. It may today have become something of a Disneyland castle, but it remains a must-see stop-off. From the car park it's a good 20-minute hike down the hill to the highly organised tours, wine shops and souvenirs.

While wine in Tuscany dates back to Etruscan times, it was Barone Bettino Ricasoli, former prime minister of Italy and enthusiastic winemaker, who is credited with creating the blend of grapes that produce the distinctive personality of Chianti Classico, in 1874. This perfect expression and interpretation of the San Giovese grape has survived until today.

The Ricasoli dynasty owned Brolio from 1141, along with half the countryside between Florence and Sienna. But the *castello* and the wine business went through a difficult period, and it was bought by the American liquor giant Seagrams in 1971. But in 1991, the family bought back the property, and the present descendant, Barone Francesco, has overseen the restoration of Brolio's reputation as a respected winemaker.

www.ricasoli.it; tel +39 0577-730220; Gaiole di Chianti; open 9am-7.30pm Mon-Fri, 10am-7pm Sat & Sun Mar-Oct

02 LE BONCIE

The tiny 5-hectare (12-acre) vineyard of Le Boncie sits right opposite Borgo San Felice, one of Chianti's biggest wineries, but they could be a million miles apart.

Giovanna Morganti, along with cult French winemaker, Nicolas Joly, was one of the founders of Vini Veri, which today has grown into the influential 'natural wine' movement.

01 Sangiovese vineyards in Castellina in Chianti

02 Dario Cecchini, master butcher

03 Dining al fresco at Dario Doc

She is an uncompromising *viticoltrice* (winegrower), planting her vineyard from scratch in 1990. These freestanding *alberelli* (bush vines) resemble immaculate bonsai trees surrounded by a jungle of wild plants and weeds. Her work in the cantina is exceptional, fermenting in open-topped tanks with regular *batonnage* (stirring of the lees).

Giovanna makes just one wine, a Chianti Classico like no other you will taste – intense, complex and concentrated. While 90% of the grapes are Sangiovese, she adds little-known local varietals such as Mammolo, Colorino and Fogliatondo, and is fiercely critical of fellow winemakers who have been influenced to add in so-called 'international grapes' Merlot and Cabernet Sauvignon.

www.leboncie.it; tel +39 0577-359383; località San Felice, Castelnuovo Berardenga; by appointment

03 FATTORIA DI CORSIGNANO

Sitting out on the sunny terrace of Corsignano's tasting room sipping a glass of chilled Chardonnay, you can spot the towers of Sienna like a medieval Manhattan, just 15km (9 miles) away. This old-fashioned farm has been thoroughly transformed by the enterprising Mario and Elena Gallo into a contemporary wine resort with elegant guest rooms, a pool, and a trattoria with cookery courses.

Mario Gallo came from a family of *viticoltori* who never managed to own vines themselves, and used to take wine down to the *osterie* (taverns) of Siena in traditional straw-covered *fiaschi* (flasks). Although Mario invested young to buy this *fattoria* (farm), he had to rent out the 7 hectares (17 acres) of vineyard for the first 10 years. Since then, he has totally replanted, cultivates organically, and although he has never studied oenology, draws on a mix of traditional advice from his *babbo* (father) and technical direction from a consultant. The result is a mix of wines that range from a light, drinkable *vino da tavola* (table wine), what Mario calls 'old-style Chianti', to a robust Classico and the more elegant Riserva. He's even trying his hand at producing a Super Tuscan, blending the local Sangiovese grape with Merlot and Cabernet Sauvignon, which will need quite a few years of ageing.

www.fattoriadicorsignano.it; tel +39 0577-322545; località Consignano, Castelnuovo Berardenga; by appointment

04 VILLA POMONA

Traditions die hard in Chianti country, as visitors will quickly understand when they meet the passionate, down-to-earth winemaker Monica Raspi in the charming *fattoria* where she makes wine and olive oil. Guests stay in an ancient olive mill converted into holiday apartments.

Monica explains, 'I was born here, but went off to Florence to study as a veterinarian. But as soon as my mamma said she was going to sell the villa and our vineyards I couldn't bear to lose our family heritage.' She abandoned her career, did a crash course in oenology, and has moved her family to the villa, making her own wines since 2007, 'and mamma looks after the bed and breakfast.'

While her tiny cantina is a cluttered mix of giant wooden *bottes* (barrels), steel and cement vats, she is moving the vineyard towards organic certification, and favours the traditional method of blending Sangiovese with native grapes such as Colorino.

www.fattoriapomona.it; tel +39 0577-740473; località Pomona 39, Castellina in Chianti; by appointment

05 VAL DELLE CORTI

A wine tasting with Roberto Bianchi often ends up with an impassioned discussion over several bottles of his outstanding wines accompanied by a plate of delicious Tuscan sausage and cheeses. This feisty artisan *vignaiolo* (winemaker) explains, 'My family came back to our home here from Milan in 1974. The wines we made then – traditional Chianti Classico with Sangiovese in *purezza* (using a single varietal) – were out of fashion as everyone was desperate for a high score by the likes of Robert Parker. But now things have gone full circle and our wines are back in demand.'

Don't expect too much choice: Roberto makes a supple *vino da tavola*, perfect for drinking young, a tannic but elegant Chianti Classico that bursts with fruity flavour, and a Riserva only when he feels the harvest merits it. His organic vineyard is small at only 6 hectares (15 acres), and in his chaotic garage cantina are only aged barrels, because according to him, 'there is already enough tannin in the Sangiovese grape.'

www.valdellecorti.it; tel +39 0577-738215; Val delle Corti 141, località La Croce, 53017 Radda in Chianti; by appointment.

06 FATTORIA DI LAMOLE

The road to Lamole weaves through thick forest before emerging at one of the most beautiful villages in the Chianti region, some 600m (2000ft) above sea level.

© Susan Wright

Paolo Socci is a fiercely traditionalist winemaker. His *alberello* bush vines are organic, the harvest hand-picked, and in the cantina he favours giant old wooden barrels: 'I want my wine tasting of Sangiovese tannin, not oak.' Paolo proudly tells visitors, 'We can trace records that show our family have been in Lamole since 1071, but since WWII this village has changed dramatically due to mass emigration, falling from a population of 700 to just 90. This left no people to tend the vines of our unique system of cultivation on *terrazza* [stone terraces].'

His 2008 Selezione is sensational, made solely with grapes grown in the micro-vineyard within the 7km (4 miles) of *terrazzi* that Paolo has painstakingly rebuilt. Apart from the crusade to restore these centuries-old terraces, he has also renovated a small medieval hamlet of cottages at the edge of Lamole into a comfy B&B for visitors. ***www.fattoriadilamole.it; tel +39 055-8547065; Lamole, Greve in Chianti; by appointment***

07 FONTODI

Down below Panzano lies a showpiece vineyard planted in a sunny amphitheatre known as La Conca d'Oro. It is the heart of the Fontodi estate that covers 80 hectares (200 acres) of vines and 33 hectares (82 acres) of olive groves. A 30-strong herd of Tuscany's iconic Chianina cows completes this far-sighted sustainable organic farm.

Unlike many of Chianti's big wineries, a visit here is a casual affair and free of charge. In fact, the amiable *viticoltore*, Giovanni Manetti, insists, 'Even if people stay two hours they don't have to feel they must buy a bottle.' The Manetti family bought Fontodi nearly 50 years ago, but have an association going back to 1600 with another Tuscan tradition, the production of terracotta pottery. Giovanni is even experimenting in the cantina with ageing a wine in an *orcio* (terracotta

amphora), a technique used by the Greeks and Romans. Their modern flagship wine, Flaccianello della Pieve, is 100% Sangiovese, but is outside of the Chianti DOC (*denominazione di origine controllata*), positioned as a so-called Super Tuscan. You will taste a surprising Pinot Nero, and the luscious Vin Santo, made from grapes straw-dried for five months and barrel-aged for five years.
www.fontodi.com; tel +39 055-852005; Panzano in Chianti; by appointment

08 RIGNANA

At one time or another a trip through Chianti will entail heading off into the unknown and driving down one of the *strada bianca*, the notorious dirt tracks that crisscross the Tuscan countryside, where you'll discover romantic villas, vineyards, farms and restaurants. One of these hidden jewels is Rignana, the magical winery of Cosimo Gercke, a rather dashing, aristocratic-looking character. His 18th-century villa, decorated with pastel frescoes, hosts sumptuous guest rooms, an olive mill converted into a trattoria, a pool at the edge of an olive grove and even a medieval chapel where you can get married.

Cosmo's Italian-German family bought the estate in the 1960s, and when he took over in 1999 he replanted the whole vineyard and today produces an absorbing mix of organic Chianti Classico, a tannic Merlot aged for two years in small oak barrels, and a fruity, light Rosato, most of which gets consumed for sunset aperitifs at the villa itself.
www.rignana.it; tel +39 055-852065; Via di Rignana 15, Greve in Chianti; by appointment

04 The Duomo in Florence

05 Sangiovese vineyards near Montalcino

ESSENTIAL INFORMATION

WHERE TO STAY

FATTORIA LA LOGGIA
Giulio Baruffaldo opened his medieval wine and olive-oil *fattoria* for guests back in 1986. There are spacious rooms, a to-die-for pool and sculptures and paintings everywhere from the artists-in-residence programme.
www.fattorialaloggia.com; tel +39 055-8244288; Via Collina 24, San Casciano in Val di Pesa

LE MICCINE
Canadian *vigneronne* (winegrower) Paula Papine Cook only arrived in Chianti a few years ago, but her wines are already winning top awards and this guest villa next to her cantina features an inviting infinity pool.
www.lemiccine.com; tel +39 0577-749526; località Le Miccine 44, Gaiole in Chianti

WHERE TO EAT

ANTICA MACELLERIA CECCHINI
Dario Cecchini is the unofficial King of Chianti, a dramatic master butcher famed for his *costata alla fiorentina* – T-bone. A cheap-and-cheerful trattoria, Dario Doc, is at the back of the butchers.
www.dariocecchini.com; tel +39 055-852020; Via XX Luglio 11, Panzano in Chianti

A CASA MIA
Village *osteria* serving huge portions of *cucina casalinga* (home cooking) such as tagliatelle with porcini, presented by the rock 'n' roll hosts, Cosimo and Maurizio.
www.acasamia.eu; tel +39 055-8244392; Via Santa Maria a Macerata 4, Montefiridolfi

BAR UCCI
Volpaia is a romantic medieval village high up in the hills of Chianti. Tuck into Tuscan specialities on Ucci's sunny terrace.
www.bar-ucci.it; tel +39 0577-738042; Piazza della Torre 9, Volpaia

WHAT TO DO

Take a break from wine tasting with a day exploring the Renaissance palaces, churches and museums of nearby Siena.

CELEBRATIONS

Both Greve in Chianti and Panzano host week-long wine festivals in September.

Massimo Ripani © 4Corners Images

05

01

[Italy]

VENETO

Its most famous export is Prosecco, party drink par excellence, but Veneto is also home to a multitude of quaffable reds, from light and fresh to hefty hitters.

Prosecco, made from the Glera grape, has become the world's favourite bubbly almost overnight. The picture-perfect vineyards that produce it stretch from the border with Friuli to Valdobbiadene. They're a paradise for wine travellers, with friendly winemaker B&Bs and rustic local *osterie*.

The Veneto has made its mark on Italy's wine map as one of the biggest wine-producing regions, featuring a diverse, high-quality range of both reds and whites. The volcanic hills around Padua, the Colli Euganei, are making a name for themselves with a variety of wines, from elegant barrel-aged Merlot and Cabernet Franc to the surprisingly fizzy Fior d'Arancio, whose unique orange-blossom aroma rivals a Moscato from Asti. Meanwhile producers such as Inama and Pieropan are taking the crisp, white Soave to new levels of excellence.

GET THERE
Venice Marco Polo is the nearest major airport, 64km from Premaor. Car hire is available.

Then from Verona to Lake Garda you enter Valpolicella country, where wine produce has shifted from the kind you would order in a pizzeria into some of Italy's finest red wines. Based around Corvina, a native grape, Valpolicella caters for every taste, from the Classico, young, fresh and easy to drink, to the Ripasso, where grape pomace has been macerated to add body. And then comes Amarone. This is quite simply a unique wine; the grapes are dried for three to four months – the *passito* process – before fermentation begins, then aged mainly in oak for a minimum of three years before going on sale. Tasting it is a serious business, as alcohol content can rise to a heady 17%. It is the perfect complement to traditional Veneto dishes such as slow-cooked wild-boar stew or, even better, used as an ingredient in a memorable risotto all'Amarone.

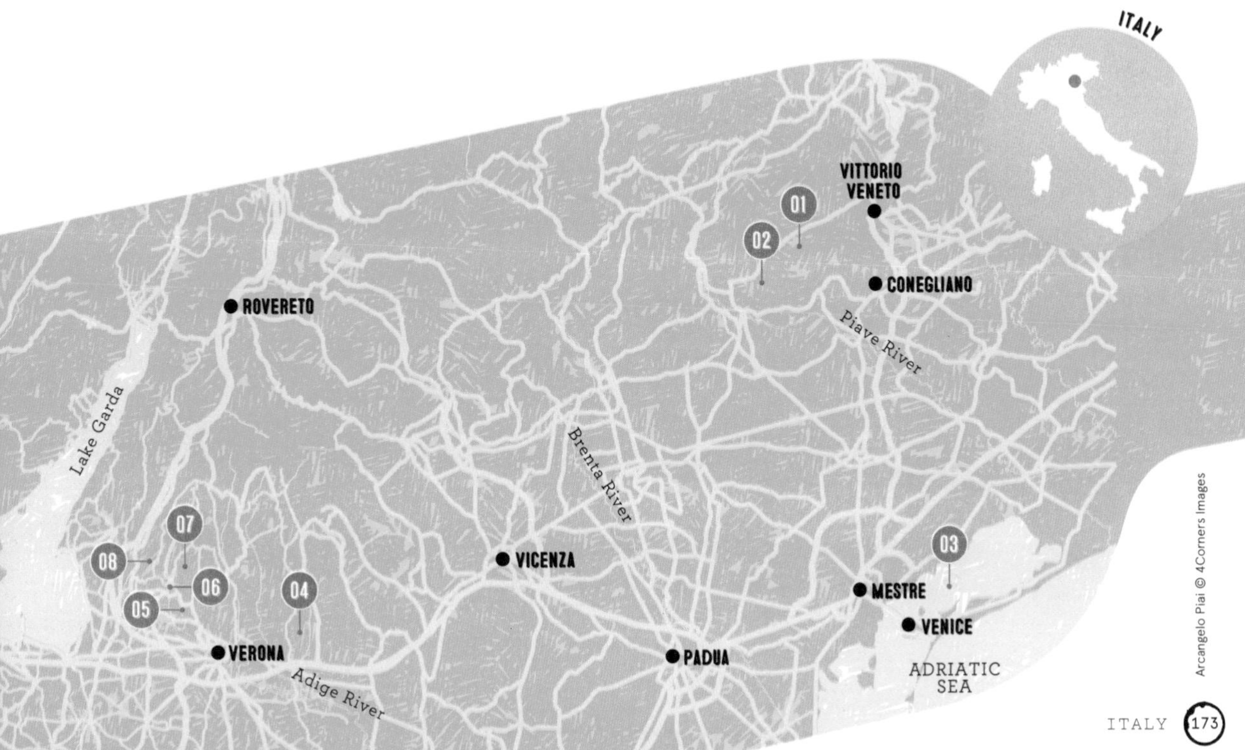

Arcangelo Piai © 4Corners Images

01 GREGOLETTO

The Prosecco vineyards that run along verdant valleys between Conegliano, Valdobbiadene are some of the most beautiful in Italy, and in the sleepy village of Premaor, the Gregoletto family have been cultivating vines since 1600. Their wines are the perfect mix of strict tradition, represented by the hands-on 83-year-old papa, Luigi, and the innovation of his two dynamic sons, Giovanni and Giuseppe.

A tasting here spans not just an excellent Brut Prosecco and their signature Frizzante, but also white wines from little-known indigenous grapes. You are bound to get caught in conversation with Giovanni Gregoletto, a wonderfully eccentric character, as happy discussing poetry, music and philosophy as wine. His lunchtime canteen is Trattoria al Castelletto, where slick executives from the nearby Benetton offices rub shoulders with Prosecco *viticoltori* (winegrowers).

www.gregoletto.it; tel +39 0438-970463; Via San Martino 81, Premaor; by appointment

02 CASE COSTE PIANE

While the Prosecco region is enormous today, selling even more bottles than Champagne, the jewel in the crown of this bubbly is a miniscule *terroir* just outside Valdobbiadene, unofficial capital of Prosecco-land. Here, around the village of Santo Stefano, winemakers battle to own a small parcel of the 107 hectares (265 acres) that constitute the elegant Cartizze, Prosecco's own Grand cru and one of the wine world's most expensive pieces of real estate, at around €1,000,000 per hectare (2.5 acres).

But in the same village, there is an artisan winemaker equally famous in his own way. You have to call Loris Follador in advance to get him out of the vineyards to meet in his rustic cellar for a tasting. Loris only makes 70,000 bottles a year of his wonderful Casa Coste Piane, but you'll find it stocked in Italy's top restaurants, given it's a firm favourite of devotees of Slow Food. This rustic Prosecco is naturally fermented in the bottle – *sur lie* or *col fondo* – meaning it is *frizzante* (crisp) rather than bubbly, slightly cloudy and best served decanted.

Tel +39 0423-900219; Via Coste Piane 2, Santo Stefano di Valdobbiadene; by appointment

01 The Prosecco Wine Road, Valdobbiadene

02 Prosecco vineyards in autumn

03 A tasting at Venissa

© John Brunton

03 VENISSA

You can't come to the Veneto and not visit Venice, and now there is a great reason to head here. Gianluca and Desiderio Bisol, one of Prosecco's leading producers, have heavily invested in replanting a micro-vineyard in the Venice lagoon, on the near-deserted island of Mazzorbo. They have chosen an all-but-forgotten native grape, Dorona, and while the yields are very small, the wine, named Venissa, is quite incredible, especially considering the vineyard is almost a 'non-*terroir*', with sandy, salty soil right at sea level.

The grapes are vinified in Tuscany, at Montalcino, but visitors here are treated to a tasting in the ancient wine *tenuta* (estate) and a tour of the vineyard. You can stay overnight in their small hotel, and dine in a Michelin-starred restaurant overlooking the vines.

Wine has been produced in Venice and its lagoon for centuries, and over on the island of Sant'Erasmo, French *vigneron* Michel Tholouze has also planted a vineyard, while Laguna nel Bicciere is an active association of Venetians bringing the vineyards of the Serenissima back to life.
www.venissa.it; tel +39 041-5272281; Fondamenta Santa Cristina 3, Isola di Mazzorbo, Venezia; by appointment

04 MASSIMAGO

While the historic Valpolicella vineyards stretch from Verona towards the shore of Lake Garda, many younger winemakers are making their mark in the other direction, towards the rolling hills of Soave. This is certainly the case for Camilla Rossi, who took over the family estate in 2003 when she was only 20.

This rambling 25-hectare (62-acre) *tenuta* is hidden away in the middle of thick woods and olive groves, and so far only 10 hectares (25 acres) are planted with vines. Guests can stop off for a tasting or stay over in their luxurious Wine Relais, complete with vineyard pool and spa. Camilla bubbles with enthusiasm, proclaiming, 'This is not a traditional winery. We're not interested in making wines like our *nonno* [grandad].'

Customers can create their own personalised label, and the winery regularly commissions classical music, downloadable from their site, to be enjoyed with particular wines.
www.massimago.com; tel +39 045-8880143; Via Giare 21, Mezzane di Sotto; 9am-5pm Mon-Fri

05 SANTA SOFIA

There are many grand *azienda* (enterprises) that have contributed to the long and famous history of Valpolicella – Bettrani, Allegrini, Masi, Bolla – but an historic cantina that operates on a more human scale is Santa Sofia, which has been making wines since 1881. Housed beneath a magnificent colonnaded Palladian villa and formal garden, which can also be visited, a maze of cellars, some dating back to the 14th century, store the giant Slavonian oak barrels and smaller French barriques that age their impressive range of reds. In a huge 18th-century grange, a much wider selection of Veneto wines mature in steel vats – Soave, Bardolino and Custoza.

Giancarlo Begnoni took over the estate in 1967, and has forged a serious reputation, not just for the explosive Amarone and luscious Recioto, but surprising blends outside the DOC (*denominazione di origine controllata*) such as the potent Arleo, which includes 15% Cabernet Sauvignon and Merlot, and needs at least 10 years' ageing.
www.santasofia.com; tel +39 045-7701074; Via Ca' Dede' 61, Pedemonte di Valpolicella; by appointment 9am-noon & 2.30-5pm Mon-Fri

06 VALENTINA CUBI

Valentina Cubi is a symbol of the new generation of innovative female winemakers in Valpolicella. Arriving at her state-of-the-art winery, be prepared for some surprises. Valentina, who looks like everyone's favourite auntie, bought this 10-hectare (25-acre) vineyard in 1970, but rented it out and only took

CONTINENTAL

04

control in 2000 when she retired as the village schoolteacher, with her first wines coming onto the market to great acclaim in 2005.

She immediately began a production that was certified organic, rare in Valpolicella, and is now moving towards incorporating biodynamic techniques in her winemaking, too. She has launched the surprising Sin Cero, a 'natural' Valpolicella without sulphites. Her wines are not complex, and really stand out as something different compared to classic intense Amarone vintages. They reflect her personal philosophy on the region's wines: 'Real Valpolicella doesn't have to have pretensions, and should be light and easy to drink, good with just a plate of salami as well as the traditional rich wild-boar stew'.

www.valentinacubi.it; tel +39 045-7701806; Casterna 60, Fumane; open 9am-12.30pm & 3-6pm Mon-Sat by appointment

07 LE BIGNELE

This small, family-run vineyard dates back to 1818, and visiting Luigi Aldrighetti's traditional winery is like stepping back into the past. Luigi gestures to the characteristic vines that surround the cantina, explaining that 'for Valpolicella, we use the classic Pergola Doppia system of high hanging grapes that grow off both the right and left of the main vine – like two outstretched arms'.

The 70-year-old Luigi says he now leaves everything to his two children, Nicolo and Silvia, but it is quickly evident once he starts opening bottles that he still keeps a pretty sharp eye on everything. Chattering away mainly in Venetian dialect, he brings out the Classico Superiore, Ripasso, Amarone and Recioto, excellent-value vintages dating back to 2003, and says with a glint in his eye that 'the secret of a great wine here is *uva sana*, a healthy grape, rather than complicating things too much in the cantina'.

www.lebignele.it; tel +39 388-4066545; Via Bignele 4, Frazione Valgatara, Marano di Valpolicella; open 8.30am-6.30pm

08 STEFANO ACCORDINI

A narrow route zigzags through the vineyards of the Alte Colline hills of Valpolicella, coming out at the modern cantina of the Accordini family. Looking out over a panorama of crisscrossing vines as far as the eye can see, this is the ideal spot for a tasting to begin to understand the history of the region.

Tiziano Accordini remembers, 'My ancestors started off, like most Valpolicella winemakers, as sharecroppers – *mezzadri* – delivering half their grapes to the landowner and keeping half themselves. We have a picture of our grandfather on a cart piled high with barrels, pulled by oxen that he would ride down to Verona to sell to the local *osterie*.' His parents slowly became landowners, and while the present-day estate covers 13 hectares (32 acres) of small parcels in a patchwork across the hills, Tiziano has invested in a futuristic eco-winery, where computer-operated controls look like something from a spaceship, and his wines reflect an intriguing mix of modern technology and *contadino* (rural) traditions, especially the rich, concentrated Recioto, perfect with chocolate.

www.accordinistefano.it; tel +39 045-7760138; Camparol 10, Frazione Cavalo, Fumane; open 9am-5.30pm Mon-Sat, by appointment Sun

04 The Venice lagoon, home to the Venissa microbrewery

05 Il Follo winery in Santo Stefano

ESSENTIAL INFORMATION

WHERE TO STAY

ALICE RELAIS NELLE VIGNE

Right at the beginning of the Prosecco road, the Cosmo brothers run a top winery, Bellenda, while their two wives, Cinzia and Marzia, have transformed a grand mansion into a B&B. *www.alice-relais.com; tel +39 0438-561173; Via Giardino 94, Carpesica di Vittorio Veneto*

AGRITURISMO SAN MATTIA

This biodiverse *agriturismo* (farmstay) produces award-winning wines and grows their own vegetables for their restaurant. *www.agriturismosanmattia.it; tel +39 045-913797; Via Santa Giuliana 2, Verona*

RELAIS ANTICA CORTE AL MOLINO

A farmhouse offering six spacious rooms. Guests can picnic in the gazebo surrounded by vines. *www.robertomazzi.it; tel +39 045-7502072; Via Crosetta 8, Sanperetto di Negar*

WHERE TO EAT

DA GIGETTO

A favourite restaurant of Prosecco winemakers. Try spaghetti topped with juicy *chiodini* mushrooms or grilled radicchio from Treviso. Amazing wine collection in the labyrinthine cellars. *www.ristorantedagigetto.it; tel +39 0438-960020; Via Andrea de Gasperi 5, Miane*

ENOTECA DELLA VALPOLICELLA

More than 100 Valpolicella estates are on the wine list of this elegant wine shop, and the chefs, Ada and Carlotto, pair them with classic recipes such as risotto all'Amarone and pumpkin gnocchi. *www.enotecadellavalpolicella.it; tel +39 045-6839146; Via Osan 45, Fumane*

WHAT TO DO

Two Palladian villas not to miss are Villa Pisani in Stra on the Riviera del Brenta and Villa Maser, outside Asolo, with fabulous frescoes by Veronese. *www.villapisani.beniculturali.it; www.villadimaser.it*

CELEBRATIONS

Verona is worth visiting anytime, but for a special occasion book tickets for an outdoor opera in the immense Roman Arena. *www.arena.it*

[Lebanon]

BATROUN VALLEY

Terraced vineyards and olive groves are scattered across the hills in this emerging wine region overlooking Lebanon's Mediterranean coast.

Most wine lovers have heard of the Bekaa Valley, but few outside Lebanon are familiar with that country's other major wine-growing area, the hilly hinterland behind the ancient port city of Batroun on the Mediterranean coast. Here, the terrain is scattered with stone, gnarled olive trees and drifts of wildflowers. Maronite monasteries are hidden among stands of oak trees, and village houses cluster around simple whitewashe d churches.

It's an ancient and spectacularly beautiful landscape where the copious sunlight, cooling sea breezes and well-drained soil (a mixture of clay, sand and limestone) provide perfect conditions for growing premium grapes. Over the past two decades, a number of boutique producers have established vineyards, built wineries and produced vintages that are becoming more complex and impressive by the year. Cabernet Sauvignon and Syrah grapes do particularly well, and most of the vineyards focus on red varietals, with secondary plantings of Chardonnay, Riesling and other white grapes. Almost all of the wineries have embraced organic growing methods and hand-harvest their grapes.

Only 56km (35 miles) from central Beirut, Batroun is easily accessed via the main coastal highway. Heading inland, it's possible to follow an itinerary locally known as La Route des Vins du Nord (the Northern Wine Route), which wends its way uphill from Batroun through this picture-postcard landscape, passing terraced vineyards and hidden hamlets aplenty. As well as the wineries mentioned, the Monastery of Kfifane, part of the Adyar cooperative (www.adyar.org.lb), welcomes visitors by appointment. Adyar, which was the first all-organic winery in Lebanon, grows grapes at eight Maronite monasteries across the country. Its best-regarded wines are the Monastère De Mar Moussa and Monastère De Annaya (look for the 2011 vintages of both).

GET THERE

Beirut-Rafic Hariri is the nearest major airport, 63km from Batroun. Car hire is available.

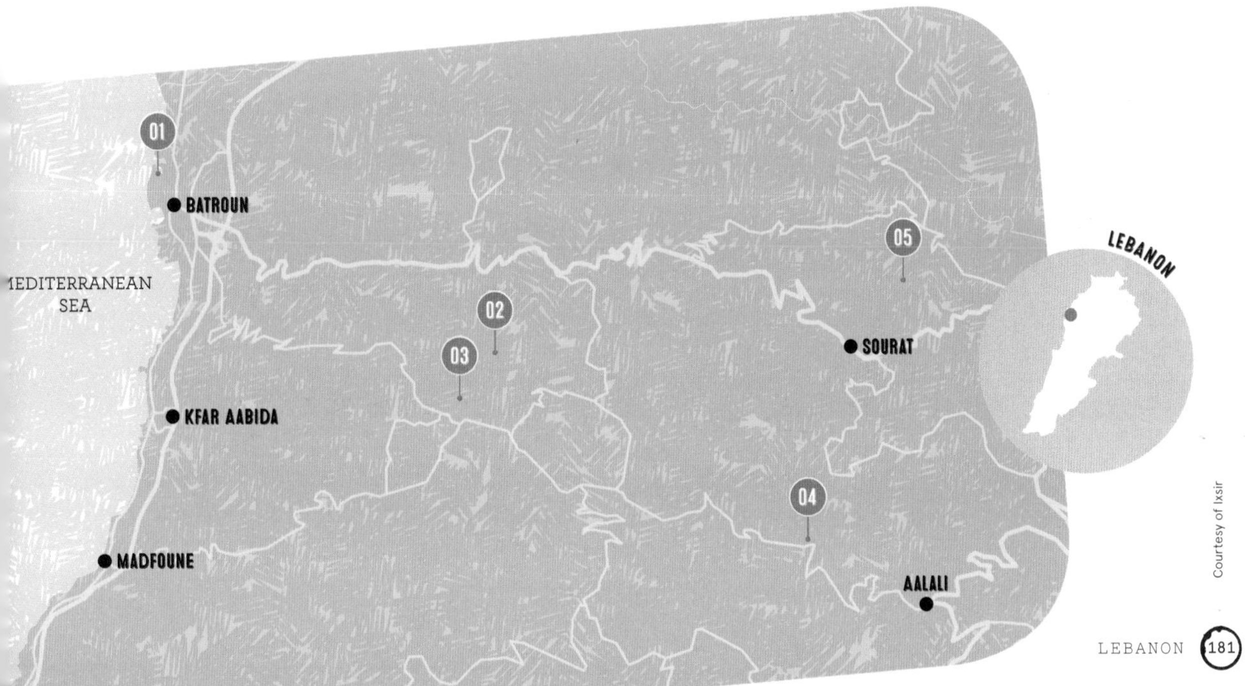

Courtesy of Ixsir

Courtesy of Batroun Mountains

01 BATROUN MOUNTAINS

'I believe that a quality bottle of wine is made in the vineyard and not in the winery,' says Assaad Hark, the winemaker and driving force behind this family-run business in Batroun. California-trained, Assaad sources his organically certified grapes from narrow terraced vineyards in six local villages overlooking the Mediterranean Sea. All were designed to maximise sun exposure and this, along with the dry, well-drained and stony local soil, contributes to fruit of intense colour and flavour, across the nine styles of wine Batroun Mountains produces.
www.batrounmountains.com; tel +961 3-928299; Rawabi Ave, Batroun; 10am-5pm by appointment

02 IXSIR

There's been a buzz around this company since its establishment in 2008, and a visit to its winery in Basbina certainly helps to explain why. Spanish-born, French-trained winemaker Gabriel Rivero is producing impressive wines here using grapes sourced from vineyards in six mountainous Lebanese regions, and the complimentary 45-minute tour and tasting is a great introduction to his art.

The focal point of the estate is a handsome 17th-century stone house that now plays host to a restaurant and shop. But most of the action occurs in the state-of-the-art underground winery, which was designed by Raëd Abillama Architects and has been recognised internationally for its sustainable design (in 2011, CNN dubbed it one of the world's greenest buildings). Over lunch, consider sampling the estate's highly regarded EL IXSIR Red – a blend of Cabernet Sauvignon, Syrah and Merlot. The grapes for this are sourced from a vineyard at an elevation of 1800m (5900ft), the highest in the northern hemisphere.
www.ixsir.com.lb; tel +961 71-631613; Basbina; 10am-4pm Tue-Sun winter, to 6pm summer by appointment

03 COTEAUX DE BOTRYS

Though the Lebanese have been making wine for millennia, most of the major producers are relatively new to the business. Not so Neila al-Bitar, whose family first settled in the wildflower-carpeted hills above Batroun in 1760 and started to distil arak almost immediately. This tradition turned into a business in 1992, when Neila's father, retired general Joseph al-Bitar, decided to produce the fiery aniseed spirit commercially. Wine production followed, with 5000 vines planted in 1998 and the first vintages appearing in 2002; the estate now has 50,000 vines and produces six styles of wine. Neila is particularly proud of the 2007

Château Syrah and 2008 Château Cabernet Sauvignon, but notes that the 2009 Château des Anges, a lively blend of Syrah, Mourvèdre and Grenache, is also highly regarded. *www.coteauxdebotrys.com; tel +961 6-721300; Main Rd, Eddé; Sat & Sun by appointment*

04 DOMAINE S.NAJM

Owned and operated by husband-and-wife team Salim and Hiba Najm, this small estate in the picturesque mountain village of Chabtine produces one wine (a blend of Cabernet Sauvignon, Grenache and Mourvèdre), an arak and a splendid cold-pressed extra-virgin olive oil produced from the fruit of 200-year-old trees. Salim's training as an agricultural engineer and Hiba's as an oenologist (she studied in Bordeaux) make them a formidable team. *www.domaine-snajm.com; tel +961 70-623023; Chabtine; by appointment*

05 AURORA VIN DE MONTAGNE

Spectacularly sited among a forest of oak and olive trees overlooking the Mediterranean, this small family-run vineyard is one of two recognisable landmarks in the village of Rachkidde – the other is the 19th-century Maronite Church of Saints Sergius and Bacchus. Owner and self-taught winemaker Dr Fady Geara produces four wines: a blend of Merlot and Cabernet Sauvignon, and single-grape vintages of Chardonnay, Sauvignon Blanc and Cabernet Franc. All can be tasted during the estate's weekend openings. *www.aurorawinery.com; tel +961 71-632620; Rachkidde; 10am-1.30pm & 5-7pm Sat & Sun by appointment*

01 The stone house at Ixsir

02 Winemaking at Batroun Mountains is a family affair

ESSENTIAL INFORMATION

WHERE TO STAY

L'AUBERGE DE LA MER

Tucked between two historic churches, this recently opened boutique hotel in a 19th-century stone building offers elegantly presented rooms, a rooftop Jacuzzi and wonderful sea views. *www.laubergedelamer.com; Harbour, Batroun*

BYBLOS SUR MER

Overlooking the harbour of the ancient town of Byblos, 17km (10 miles) south of Batroun, this classy hotel is a popular weekend getaway for romantically inclined Beirutis. Rooms are spacious, there's a seafront pool and the in-house restaurant features a glass floor floating above excavated ancient ruins. *www.byblossurmer.com; Rue du Port, Byblos*

WHERE TO EAT

CHEZ MAGUY

Head to this ramshackle fisherman's shack near Batroun's Phoenician sea wall to enjoy fish so fresh it's almost writhing. The sea-facing terrace is an idyllic setting on warm evenings. *Tel +961 3-439147; Batroun*

NICOLAS AUDI À LA MAISON D'IXSIR

Traditional Lebanese fare is given a modern twist by chef Nicolas Audi at IXSIR's stylish restaurant. Audi describes his cuisine as 'inspired by the Lebanese *terroirs*', and his seasonal creations are expertly paired with house wines. *www.ixsir.com.lb; tel +961 71-773770; Basbina*

WHAT TO DO

Once important trading ports, the ancient towns of Byblos and Batroun have retained significant traces of their Phoenician, Greek, Roman, Crusader and Ottoman heritage, and are well worth a visit to see their many sights.

CELEBRATIONS

The harvest season in Lebanon usually falls between August and October, so this is a great time to visit. Additional incentives are offered by the Byblos International Festival (usually held mid-July to mid-August) and the Batroun International Festival (August). Both attract big-name international musical acts. *www.byblosfestival.org; www.batrounfestival.org*

01

Courtesy of Dar Zerhoune

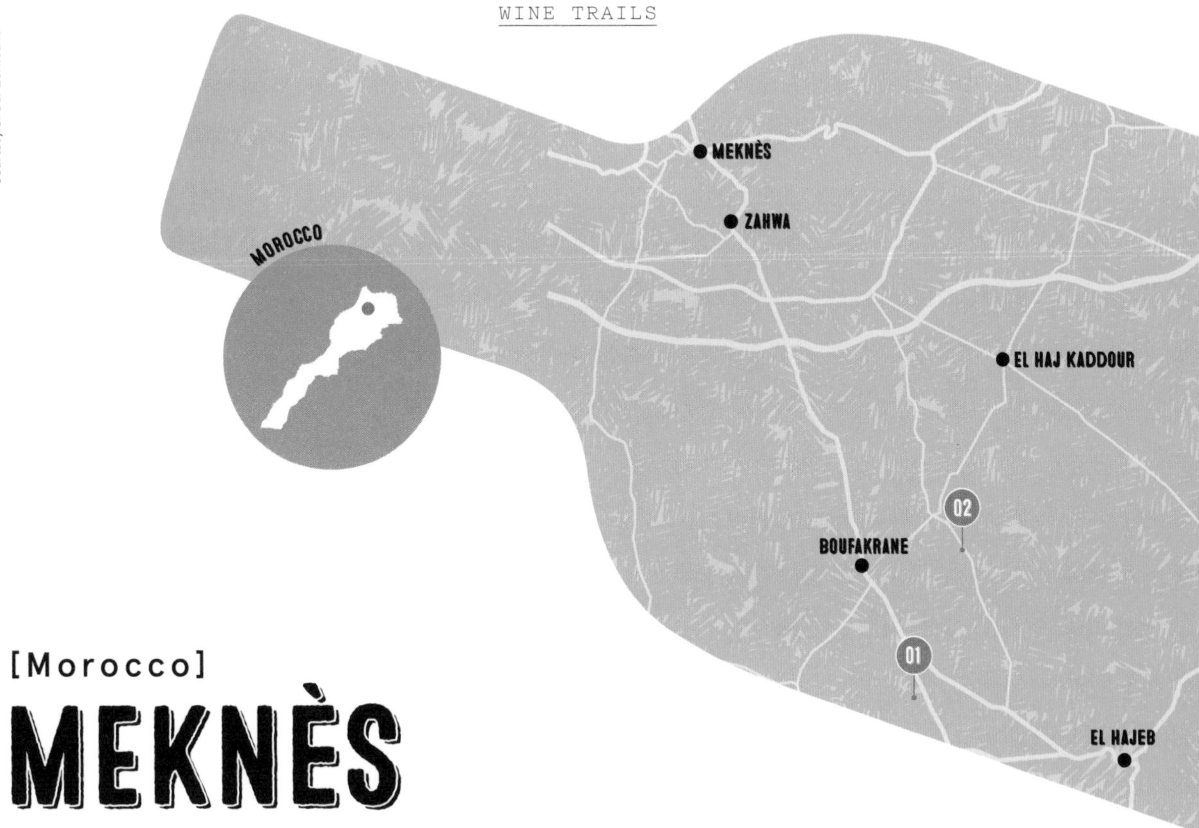

[Morocco]

MEKNÈS

Leave the medina behind and take a peek beyond the olive groves to discover the hidden world of Moroccan wine in the Atlas Mountains.

While the Phoenicians are credited with early wine production in Morocco, the Romans knew they were onto a good thing when they installed King Juba II at Volubilis to provide provisions for the Roman army. Volubilis and the nearby city of Meknès are surrounded by the foothills of the Middle Atlas Mountains of northern Morocco, studded with olive trees, orange groves, abundant vineyards and poppy-flecked wheatfields. The Meknès region, at an altitude of about 600m, is blessed with a temperate climate, moderate rainfall, generous amounts of sunshine and naturally rich soils.

During the Protectorate years (1912–56), the French made wines here to export home but the 'wine-lake', an oversupply of wine in Europe during the 1960s, put paid to that. After some years in the doldrums, the industry is now developing fast and about 95% of production is consumed within Morocco.

As drinking alcohol is not allowed in Islam, it's all very discreet: vineyards are hidden behind olive trees, there is no local marketing, only a handful of vineyards welcome visitors and there are no sales on site. Retail outlets are closed during Ramadan and around religious holidays, although there are no restrictions on non-Muslims drinking wine.

That said, recent years have seen an explosion of boutique wineries and a great improvement in the wines on offer. It is an exciting time, with the choice available doubling every year. There are a few *appellation d'origine contrôlée* (origin-certified; AOC) wines, but winemakers are enthusiastically experimenting with different grape varieties. Morocco's signature wine is the fruity, spicy Gris – pale pink and made from Cinsaut, Grenache, Caladoc or Marselan grapes. Meaty reds are usually blends of Cabernet Sauvignon, Mourvèdre, Cinsaut and Syrah, while white wines are made from Sauvignon Blanc, Semillon and Chardonnay. There is even a new Blanc de Blanc sparkling wine.

GET THERE
Rabat-Salé is the nearest major airport, 145km from Boufekrane. Car hire is available.

Jan Wlodarczyk © Alamy

In the tasting room after the farm tour, a full-bodied Chardonnay is followed by a crisp Gris that makes the perfect summer aperitif

01 DOMAINE DE LA ZOUINA

Touring the vineyards in a 4WD, winemakers Christophe Gribelin and Guillaume Constant show off their impressive *domaine* where top-rated Volubilia and Epicuria wines are made. Christophe tells the story of his Bordeaux-based winemaker father Gérard and friend Philippe Gervoson on a golfing holiday in Morocco in 2001: they were so struck by the richness of the Meknès *terroir* and the beauty of the area (*zouina* means beautiful in Moroccan Arabic) that they bought the farm and started planting immediately.

It is a glorious landscape with olive trees, carefully tended vines and stately cypress trees. Christophe and Guillaume have a passion for winemaking that shines through as they point out where each variety is planted. As they are not tied to the strict regulations of Bordeaux *appellation* controls, they are able to have a row or two of experimental varieties. The planting reflects the care needed to select varieties that withstand the soaring temperatures and cope with the *chergui*, a hot, dusty wind from the Sahara. Herbicides and pesticides are avoided, but the farm is not yet fully organic.

In the tasting room after the farm tour, a full-bodied Chardonnay is followed by a crisp Gris that makes the perfect summer aperitif. The Volubilia red is ripe with berries and has soft tannins. It is served with lunch that includes the estate's own olive oil, fresh goat's cheese from a nearby farm, salads and *kefta* (minced beef) kebabs grilled over the coals. In 2006, the Volubilia olive oil won the World's Best Extra-Virgin Olive Oil prize in Italy.

Moroccan wines are generally robust and complement very nicely the subtly spiced cuisine. Food writer Tara Stevens in Fez suggests that the oakiness of Moroccan Chardonnay melds perfectly with a classic chicken tagine cooked with salty pink olives and zesty preserved lemons. She finds the Volubilia Gris has a good freshness and is comparable with those produced in the Camargue region of France. The rosé would go down well with the herbiness of a lamb *mechoui*, a traditional dish of lamb roasted on a spit and served with salt and cumin. Save the more substantial reds for a rich beef tagine slow-cooked with apricots, almonds or prunes, and to complement spicy *merguez* sausage.

info@plan-it-morocco.com; tel +212 535-638708; Boufekrane, Meknes; by appointment

02 CHÂTEAU ROSLANE

Moroccan Farid Ouissa has been making wine here for two years, having grown up and trained in France. He appreciates the huge potential in Morocco and the encouraging amount of research and experimentation he can do. His current favourite grape is the Petit Verdot, a clone that adapts well to the climate and soil conditions and is used to add structure to Cabernet Sauvignon wines.

Château Roslane is the *grande dame* of the local industry, producing the vast majority of Moroccan wines at 35 million bottles per annum. It has the only AOC wine in the country, the flagship wine of the same name. Their Beauvallon red is made of Carignan grapes from 60-year-old vines that are not irrigated. While these two may be among the best wines in the country, this outfit is not resting on its prestigious laurels. The new Le Clos des Vignes and Solo ranges are exciting additions. Solo white is a very pleasant surprise, being much fresher and lighter than many Moroccan whites. Made of 100% Sauvignon, it is not oaked and is perfect with a seafood *pastilla* (pie). Solo Red is 100% Syrah and like Beaujolais, is good chilled in summer. But the biggest surprise is the rosé – a Cabernet Sauvignon harvested before it has fully ripened – it is strawberry pink with a pink label, a pink capsule and even a pink cork. Ouissa calls this a 'swimming-pool wine' and it's aimed entirely at the female market.

A 1½-hour wine tour at the château takes in the cellars and research unit and a tasting of five or six wines led by the knowledgeable Fadoua Aabibou. It's all beautifully set in landscaped gardens. A hotel and spa is due to open in the grounds in 2016. *www.lescelliersdemeknes.net/en; tel +212 535-638708; Boufekrane, Meknès; by appointment*

01 The town of Moulay Idriss in northern Morocco

02 The Roman ruins at Volubilis

ESSENTIAL INFORMATION

WHERE TO STAY

RYAD BAHIA

A traditional courtyard house in the Meknès medina with just seven rooms, a good restaurant and lots of local advice. *www.ryad-bahia.com; tel +212 535-554541; Tiberbarine, Meknès Medina*

DAR ZERHOUNE

This is a gem of a guesthouse. The terrace is perfect for lounging while admiring the view. Take a cooking class, or hire a bike to explore the area. *www.darzerhoune.com; tel +212 642-247793; 42 Derb Zouak, Tazga, Moulay Idriss Zerhoune*

WHERE TO EAT

SCORPION HOUSE

Perched atop Moulay Idriss, the exclusive Scorpion House serves a superb private lunch paired with local wines explained by an expert. It's open by appointment only. *www.scorpionhouse.com; tel +212 655-210172; 54 Drouj El Hafa, Moulay Idriss Zerhoune*

WHAT TO DO

Take to the hills with a picnic from Dar Zerhoune: the forested mountains above Moulay Idriss offer splendid walking amid magnificent vistas. Local olives, salads, vegetable *pastilla*, freshly baked bread and *chermoula*-spiced chicken are followed by freshly homemade cakes.
Or head to Dar Namir in nearby Fez for a hands-on cooking course with wine pairing at Dar Namir Gastronomic Retreats. Begin with an aperitif of Moroccan sparkling wine, followed by three different wines with a five-course meal. *www.darnamir.com; tel +212 677-848687; 24 Derb Chikh el-Fouki, Fez Medina*

CELEBRATIONS

Meknès celebrates one of the largest *moussems* or saint's days in Morocco on the eve of the Prophet's birthday – a moveable feast that falls 11 days earlier each year (in 2016, it will be on 11 December). Join the party at the Sidi Ben Aissa mausoleum just outside the medina for singing, dancing and a thrilling *fantasia* (musket-firing cavalry charge).

01

[New Zealand]

CENTRAL OTAGO

Deep in New Zealand's South Island, Central Otago is home to world-class Pinot Noir and rugged horizons that just beg for further exploration.

Central Otago is the pin-up of New Zealand tourism, famed for sublime alpine scenery and the energetic resort town of Queenstown. Vaunted for adrenalised pursuits such as skiing, hiking, mountain biking and skydiving, it's also the setting for some world-class winemaking.

Its wild landscapes make up the world's southernmost wine region and New Zealand's highest, ranging between 200m and 450m above sea level. Vineyards are spread throughout the deep valleys and basins of six sub-regions – Gibbston, Bannockburn, Cromwell Basin, Wanaka, Bendigo and Alexandra.

The industry is reasonably young, the few vines planted back in 1864 were an early forerunner of an industry that has only burgeoned since the mid-1990s. The scene remains largely in the hands of friendly boutique enterprises and winemakers still experimenting with *terroir* not yet fully understood.

GET THERE

Auckland is the nearest major airport. Flights go from Auckland to Queenstown airport, 9km out of town. Car hire is available.

Soils are wide-ranging but predominantly glacial, with a high mineral content, and the various microclimates share a common theme of hot days, cold nights and low rainfall. These conditions have proved excellent for aromatics, particularly Riesling and Pinot Gris, but the hero is Pinot Noir, which accounts for more than 75% of the region's plantings. Indeed, this is lauded as one of the best places outside Burgundy for cultivating this notoriously fickle grape.

It would take a good two days' touring to get a comprehensive taste of the *terroir*, with around 30 wineries regularly open to visitors, and many more by appointment. Visitors short on time could focus on the Gibbston Valley (with cycle touring a possibility), but a much broader picture is revealed beyond the gates of the dramatic Kawarau Gorge. Here you'll find the Cromwell Basin, where two thirds of Central Otago's grapes are grown.

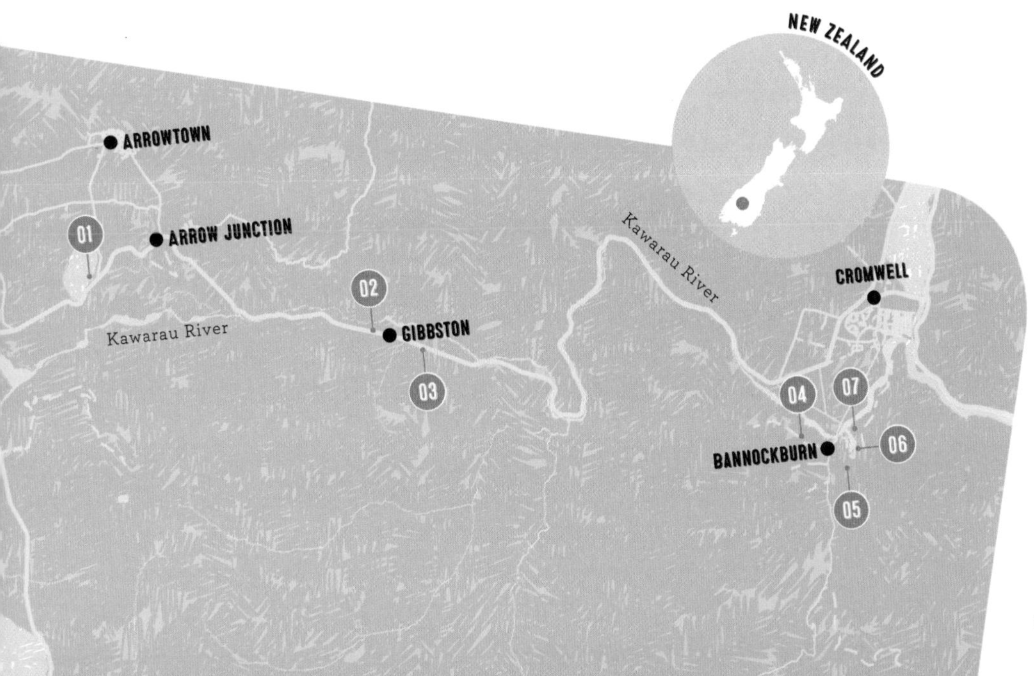

Courtesy of Mt Difficulty

Courtesy of Peregrine

01 AMISFIELD

Since it opened in 2005, Amisfield's cellar door restaurant has been an essential stop for gourmands and vinophiles visiting Central Otago. Indeed, its blend of fine wine, exciting cuisine, enviable architecture and stupendous views make it arguably the region's ultimate winery experience.

Capitalising on its proximity to the tourist hubs of Queenstown and Arrowtown, Amisfield Bistro lies within the mountain-lined Wakatipu Basin, overlooking Lake Hayes. The muscular building – fashioned from local schist and recycled timbers – is a fabulous setting for an alfresco lunch.

The Trust the Chef shared menu is the way to go, where wines are matched to local ingredients. In season, Bluff oysters may arrive with a glass of bright, Amisfield Brut, or Catlins paua (abalone) alongside a flinty, dry Riesling. Local venison is heavenly paired with Amisfield's plummy Pinot Noir.

The bistro and tasting room are the public face of the winery, located at Pisa, north of Cromwell. On a former merino sheep station, it's one of Central Otago's largest single vineyard estates, still relatively modest at around 80 hectares (200 acres).

www.amisfield.co.nz; tel +64 3-442 0556; 10 Lake Hayes Rd, Queenstown; 10am-6pm

02 PEREGRINE

Inspired by a falcon in flight, Peregrine's wing-like roofline is unmistakable along the Gibbston Highway. The cavernous tasting room squirreled beneath is moodily lit with a glass wall offering views through to a darkened hall filled with barrels. It's all perfectly poised for a lifestyle magazine shoot – flowers arranged, merchandise artfully positioned behind the altar-like tasting bar, attended by immaculately turned-out hosts.

The unhurried and informative tastings at Peregrine are a real class act, with the wines following suit. Silken Pinot Noir rates amongst the country's finest, but there's also luscious Riesling, Pinot Gris and Chardonnay, bursting with local character.

The 50 hectares (125 acres) of vineyards are certified organic, underpinned by their Bendigo farming operation. Cattle assist with the production of compost while goats and sheep control weeds, and roving chickens deal with a range of bugs. According to co-owner Lindsay McLachlan, 'Improving the environment is very important to the spectrum of Peregrine's operations.'

The feel-good factor doesn't stop there, with the winery working closely with two local conservation trusts to preserve endangered native birds,

such as the karearea (New Zealand falcon), saddleback and mohua. *www.peregrinewines.co.nz; tel +64 3-442 4000; 2127 Kawarau Gorge Rd, Gibbston Valley; 10am-5pm*

03 VALLI

With a heaving trophy cabinet and CV stretching to more than 40 vintages in the USA and at legendary Central Otago wineries, the name Grant Taylor is synonymous with world-class Pinot Noir. Since 2006, Taylor has focused on his own label, Valli, with an ethos of making wines that accentuate the various qualities of Central Otago's sub-regions. 'When you drink a Valli wine, you are enjoying more than just a wine, you are experiencing a place,' he says.

Encouraging a vertical tasting, Valli produces a range of distinct Pinot Noirs – Bannockburn (powerful and plummy), Gibbston Valley (lighter, perfumed and savoury) and Bendigo (dark and rich). A fourth – floral with a slug of herbs and spice – hails from the Waitaki Valley in North Otago, Taylor's birthplace and fledgling New Zealand wine region.

Over in Alexandra, hot days and cold nights concentrate the characteristics of Valli's Riesling vines, now more than 30 years old. Low cropping and judicious winemaking create some of the country's finest examples – dry, complex, and vibrantly acidic with stone-fruit characters, these wines are delicious now, but develop beautifully with age should you possess the necessary self-control.

Valli's cellar door is open for appointment only, but it's well worth a phone call to try your luck. Taylor is regarded as one of New Zealand wine's great characters, so an opportunity to meet him and sample his wines shouldn't be missed.

www.valliwine.com; tel +64 21-703 886; 2330 Gibbston Hwy, Gibbston Valley; by appointment

04 MT DIFFICULTY

The Gibbston Valley Highway funnels through the rocky narrows of Kawarau Gorge before emerging into the Cromwell Basin where the undulating brow of the Carrick Range casts a rain-shadow across Bannockburn's famous vines. One of the forerunners here is Mt Difficulty, established in the early 1990s when five growers collaborated to produce wine from the promising but unproven Central Otago region.

Winemaker Matt Dicey joined in 1999 and, while still producing excellent Pinot Noir, he has developed a range of wines of enviable breadth and quality. We love their luscious lemon-and-lime Target Riesling, although some of the most captivating drops come

Courtesy of Mike Wilkinson

01 Mt Difficulty's views, best served with wine and cheese

02 Peregrine winery's distinctive roof

03 Mt Difficulty, Cromwell

04 Vines in Central Otago's winter frost

05 Harvest time at Akarua

from the Grower's Range, bursting with concentrated, nuanced flavours expressive of the local *terroir*.

But wait, there's more. Perched on a hill with vast views over Cromwell Basin, Mt Difficulty's alluring restaurant encourages lingering over lunch. Sharp and modern with scrumptious fare and spectacular alfresco tables on the terrace, it will pay to book a table and sort out well in advance who's responsible for driving home.
www.mtdifficulty.co.nz; tel +64 3-445 3445; 73 Felton Rd, Cromwell; 10.30am-4.30pm

05 CERES

With a penchant for loud shirts and a passion for the local *terroir*, the Dicey menfolk epitomise the individuality and drive that put Bannockburn on the map. Adopting the lofty standards of Mt Difficulty, where father Robin was a founding *vigneron* and Matt and James are winemaker and viticulturist respectively, Ceres is the family collaboration focused on small-scale, handcrafted wines. The first vintage was released in 2005; the 2010 claimed the coveted International Wine & Spirit Competition Bouchard Finlayson trophy for best Pinot Noir.

Pulling up to Ceres' tiny cellar door makes this feat seem all the more remarkable. This is not a high-capacity, high-falutin' visitor experience. Perched on a bar stool, your personal tasting (which may also include the excellent Pinot Gris, Riesling and Gewürztraminer) may well be guided by a family member, one of whom is Odelle Morshuis, whose fine art graces the walls. Sister-in-law Alison Dicey is responsible for 'bean-to-bar' single-origin White Rabbit chocolate that begs to hop into your wine box.

With advanced notice, James Dicey will take you for a wander around their Inlet or Black Rabbit vineyards, overlooking the Kawarau River, where grapes for the Ceres Composition Pinot Noir are sourced.
www.cereswines.co.nz; tel +64 27-445 0602; 128 Cairnmuir Rd, Cromwell; 9.30am-4.30pm Mon-Fri, Sat & Sun by appointment

06 AKARUA

Like most great Central Otago wineries, Akarua is the architect of delectable Pinot Noir, but it's their rosé and crisp bubbles that really pop our corks.

For this we have winemaker Matt Connell to thank. Joining this Bannockburn winery in 2008, he quickly focused on adding a bit of fizz to Akarua's range. Their first *methode traditionelle* was launched in 2012, and within three years they claimed four major trophies, including top New Zealand bubbles at the 2014 Sparkling Wine World Championships for their 2010 vintage brut.

A victory lap, however, should be reserved for Akarua's 100% Pinot Noir rosé: a bouquet of strawberries and cream and pretty hard to top on a classic Central Otago summer's day. An aperitif of champions!

A recent vineyard purchase is sure to add punch to Akarua's heavyweight reputation, as grapes grown along the prestigious Felton Rd are set to be shown off in new top-tier wines. Watch this space.

The wines speak for themselves, so there's no need for bells and whistles at the cellar door. Accordingly, Akarua keeps it simple but smart, focusing on the warm welcomes and informative tastings that have been a hallmark of our repeated visits.
www.akarua.com; tel +64 3-445 0897; 210 Cairnmuir Rd, Bannockburn; 10.30am-4pm, closed Sat & Sun Jun & Jul

07 CARRICK

The beauty of Central Otago's cellar doors is that they offer a classy wine experience low on snoot-factor, with Carrick a case in point. This slick outfit may host plenty of jetsetting types, but it treats visitors with equal fervour regardless of their knowledge.

Like Mt Difficulty, Carrick is a spectacular spot for an indulgent lunch. The airy, art-filled atrium dining room opens on to a shady terrace and lush lawn. Framed by willows and vines is a view over Lake Dunstan's Bannockburn inlet to the Carrick Range, its foothills sculpted by old gold-mining sluices.

Starring their own olive oil and other local ingredients, Carrick's platters are a great complement to its wine range, which includes an intense, spicy Pinot Noir – their flagship drop – as well as a rich, toasty Chardonnay and citrusy aromatic varietals. Between the wine, food and wonderful setting, Carrick rises to the occasion. To take things totally over the top, take a helicopter trip from the winery around the super-scenic Cromwell Basin with a landing atop the Pisa Range.
www.carrick.co.nz; tel +64 3-445 3480; 247 Cairnmuir Rd, Bannockburn; 11am-5pm daily

ESSENTIAL INFORMATION

WHERE TO STAY

VILLA DEL LARGO
With unobstructed lake views and a scenic 25-minute walk to downtown, these fully self-contained suites and villas make an ideal Queenstown base.
www.villadellago.co.nz; tel +64 3-442 5727; 249 Frankton Rd, Queenstown

MILLBROOK RESORT
Set in 200 hectares (500 acres) of parkland with epic mountain views, this luxurious but unstuffy golf resort piles up the plaudits for its recreational facilities, day spa, 175 rooms and restaurants.
www.millbrook.co.nz; tel +64 3-441 7000; Malaghans Rd, Arrowtown

WHERE TO EAT

CROMWELL FARMERS MARKET
Held in the Old Town heritage precinct on the lake edge, this sweet little summertime market (Sunday morning November–February) has lots of local produce, with the bonus of live music and the chance to have a yarn with the locals.
Old Cromwell Town, cnr Melmore Tce & Mckinlay Lane, Cromwell

PROVISIONS
Just one of many cafes housed in Central Otago's charming historic buildings, Provisions serves excellent espresso alongside irresistible home baking. Make a beeline for the sticky bun.
www.provisions.co.nz; tel +64 3-445 4048; 65 Buckingham St, Arrowtown

WHAT TO DO

QUEENSTOWN TRAIL
This extensive, mostly easy, trail network is a memorable way to reach wine-tour highlights. Bike hire and regular shuttles make for enjoyable loops or tours around Lake Hayes and Gibbston Valley wineries, taking in AJ Hackett's bungy jump base at historic Kawarau Bridge.
www.queenstowntrail.co.nz

CELEBRATIONS

With its endearing old schist buildings, the bonny town of Clyde is an ambient setting for its annual Wine and Food Harvest Festival, held on Easter Sunday. It features 20-odd wine stalls and a raft of food producers, alongside live music, local art, and children's entertainment.

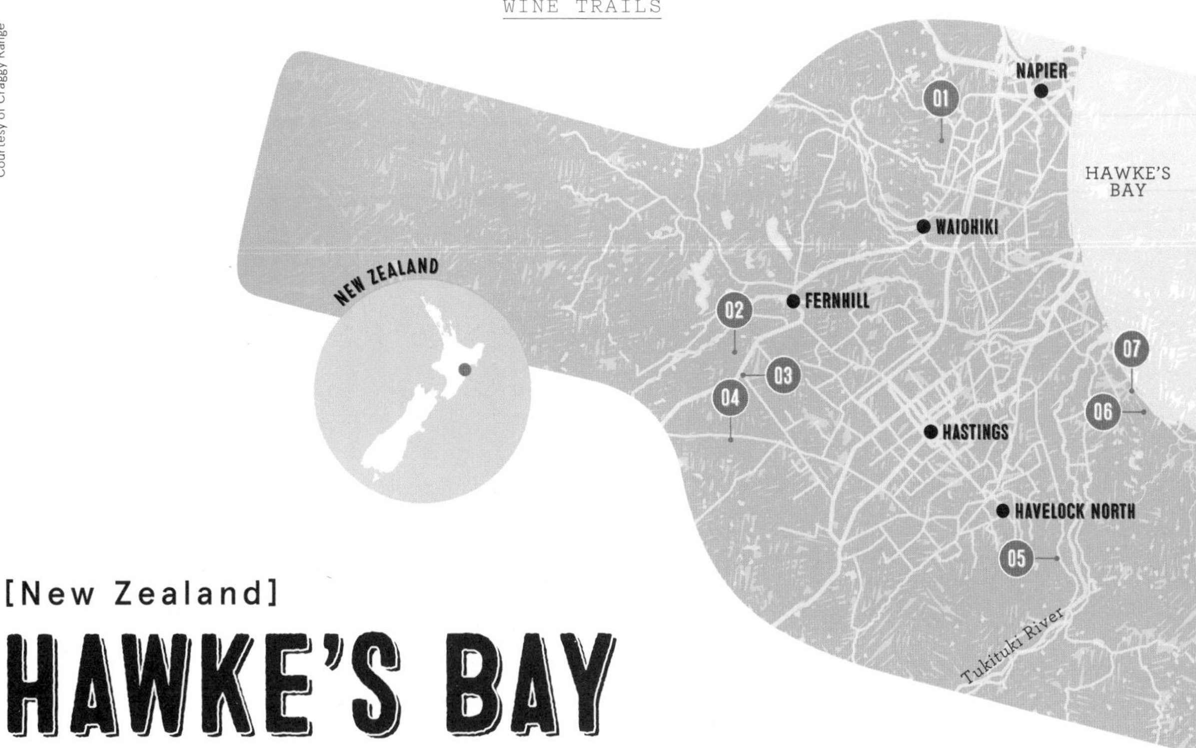

[New Zealand]

HAWKE'S BAY

In-the-know wine-lovers head to this North Island bay not only for wines of enviable quality but also breathtaking scenery and a town full of art deco gems.

Known as the 'fruit bowl of New Zealand', Hawke's Bay is a patchwork of orchards, vegetable gardens and vineyards, with pasture spliced in between. Alongside such delectable largesse is a raft of attractions, ranging from art-deco architecture farmers' markets and a sophisticated dining scene to surf beaches and cycle trails. It's no wonder this region is one of New Zealand's most popular holiday destinations. Happily, it's also the country's second-largest wine region. It's also the oldest, dating back to 1851 when Marist missionaries planted the first vines between Napier and Hastings.

While Hawke's Bay lacks a signature varietal such as Marlborough's Sauvignon Blanc or Central Otago's Pinot Noir, the Bay grows lots of grapes very well. Warm, sunny conditions swiftly ripen fruit from highly varied soils throughout diverse sub-regions such as the Bridge Pa Triangle on the Heretaunga Plains, to the cooler Esk Valley and coastal Te Awanga.

The most famous sub-region is the Gimblett Gravels, laid down by Ngaruroro River as it changed course over the ages. It was once considered a barren wasteland – the first vines were planted here in 1981 – but it wasn't until the early 1990s, when plans for a quarry were quashed, that winemaking in the gravels really gathered momentum.

Full-bodied reds rule the roost across the Bay, particularly the vast plantings of Merlot and Cabernet Sauvignon that lend the region the moniker of 'Bordeaux of New Zealand'. Syrah is also produced in significant volume. The dense, peppery profile of this cooler-climate, Rhône-style red accounts for the locals' tactical move to eschew the name 'Shiraz', thus distinguishing it from the vibrant, jammy Aussie versions. Chardonnay is another leader, nosing its way through a respectable field of contenders – Pinot Gris, Gewürztraminer and Pinot Noir are just a few. Like in most other New Zealand wine-growing areas, however, experimentation is rife.

The abundance, quality and diversity of the Bay's wines make for enjoyable touring, amplified by the volume of restaurants, cafes, and artisan food producers, all sandwiched together with splendid scenery and the option of cruising around by bike.

GET THERE
Auckland is the nearest major airport, 410km from Taradale. Flights go from Auckland to Hawke's Bay, 10km from Taradale. Car hire is available.

02

01 MISSION ESTATE

At the end of a tree-lined avenue, Mission Estate's centrepiece is the beautifully preserved seminary – La Grande Maison – built in 1880. Daily tours illuminate Mission's story and key chapters in the region's history (including a devastating 1931 earthquake), and foreground the wines available for tasting. Visitors can also partake in a refined luncheon in the seminary's formal front rooms, or out on the sun-drenched terrace.

Made to 'gladden the human heart', Mission's wines have been tended by Paul Mooney for the last 30 years. The range stretches across six tiers, from the great-value Mission Estate wines through to the classy Jewelstone and Huchet drops, crafted from Mission's most blessed grapes.

Hallmark Hawke's Bay exemplars include toasty Chardonnays from vines grown on-site, and Bordeaux-style reds and Syrah borne from the coveted Gimblett Gravels. A tasting at Mission, however, may also include aromatic Riesling, Pinot Gris and Gewürztraminer, an intense Marlborough Sauvignon Blanc or savoury Martinborough Pinot Noir.
www.missionestate.co.nz; tel +64 6-845 9353; 198 Church Rd, Taradale; 9am-5pm Mon-Sat, 10am-4.30pm Sun

02 TRINITY HILL

John Hancock, winemaker and co-owner of Trinity Hill, was an early pioneer and co-founder of the Gimblett Gravels Winegrowers Association. His impressive output has helped elevate the Gravels' reputation as the Bay's premier winegrowing district, particularly well suited to full-bodied reds.

Indeed, Trinity Hill produces a Rhône-rivalling Syrah, the Homage, made only in superlative years and ranked among New Zealand's greatest reds. Other varietals include exemplary Chardonnay and Merlot, as well as unusual and experimental varieties including a delicate Arneis and richly textured Marsanne/Viognier blend, both excellent with food. Iberian influences surface in a grunty fruit-driven Tempranillo, and Touriga Nacional port-style wine.

Located in the thick of cellar door territory in the countryside west of Hastings, Trinity Hill is not to be missed. Its high-ceilinged, concrete-slab tasting room is spacious and accommodating, with platters served in the garden in summertime.
www.trinityhill.com; tel +64 6-879 7778; 2396 State Hwy 50, Hastings; 10am-5pm summer, 11am-4pm Wed-Sat winter

03 TE AWA

Just a stone's throw from Trinity Hill and making wines from the same Gimblett Gravels *terroir*, Te Awa is also home to a restaurant boasting some of the best food in Hawke's Bay.

Courtesy of Trinity Hill

Douglas Pearson © Getty Images

01 Craggy Range, at the foot of Te Mata peak

02 Trinity Hill winery in Hastings

03 Sunset in Hawke's Bay

04 Napier is famous for its art deco buildings

John Hay © Getty Images

'Hawke's Bay is an exciting place to make wine, but also to live. We travelled the world, but were lucky enough to return to the land we came from, to settle and raise our family.'

–Tim Turvey, Clearview Estate

But let's not get ahead of ourselves, for this place is serious about its wines, produced under three labels. The flagship is Te Awa, a suite of single-estate wines – Bordeaux blends, Syrah and Chardonnay – that highlight the unique characteristics of the gravels' *terroir*. The best drops work their way up to the Kidnapper Cliffs premium range, accordingly priced and suited to cellaring, while the Left Field label is appended to Te Awa's 'weird and wonderful', more affordable wines.

Te Awa's timber-built tasting room and restaurant blends rural charm with a debonair air, with advance booking of an alfresco table essential. The menu presents shared plates of novel, exciting fare – lamb and green olive cigars with cumin salsa, fish crudo with ouzo mayo. With wine list in hand and warm sunrays playing through the trees, you could count yourself in for a very long lunch.
www.teawacollection.com; tel +64 6-879 7602; 2375 State Hwy 50, Hastings; 10am-4pm

04 SILENI

When a winery is named after Silenus, the most debauched, drunken and yet wisest of the Greek wine god Dionysus' followers, you get an inkling that there's fun to be had, here at one of the Bay's largest wineries.

Sileni lives up to the name by offering one of the region's most enjoyable wine tastings, often hosted by ebullient cellar-door manager, Anne Boustead. The pomp-free flight through their wines is injected with fascinating facts and a measure of good humour.

There's plenty to talk about. From its dramatic (and somewhat sci-fi) HQ secreted in the foothills of the Bridge Pa Triangle, Sileni produces consummate examples of Syrah and Chardonnay. Other varieties to shine include a fruity Pinot Gris, something winemaker Grant Edmonds thinks 'Hawke's Bay does a bloody good job of', and distinct Pinot Noirs from their cooler Plateau and Parkhill vineyards. Keep an eye out for the EV wines that flow from the best vintages.

Courtesy of Sileni

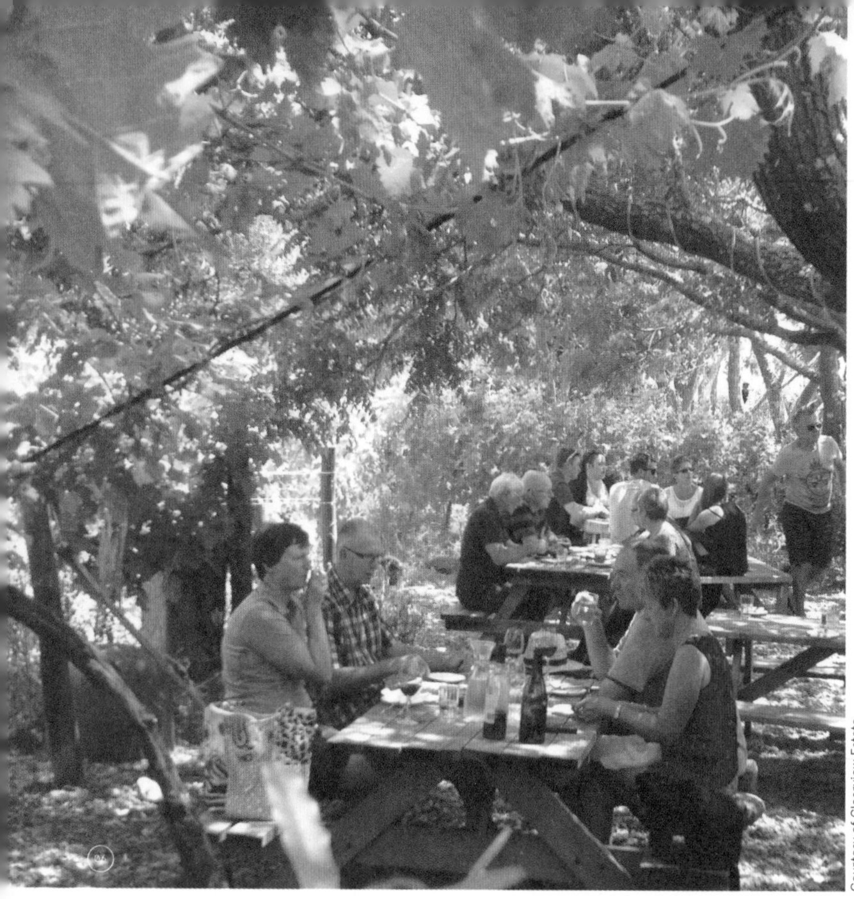
Courtesy of Clearview Estate

Visitors can enhance their Sileni experience with a winery tour, run twice daily in summer, or an alfresco wine-and-cheese tasting (by appointment). The cellar store also stocks goodies such as local chocolates and preserves.
www.sileni.co.nz; tel +64 6-879 4830; 2016 Maraekakaho Rd, Hastings; 10am-5pm daily Oct-Apr, to 4pm Mon-Fri May-Sep

05 CRAGGY RANGE

In a sublime setting alongside the Tukituki River, at the foot of Te Mata Peak, Craggy Range is worth visiting for the journey alone. Add in a modernistic collection of buildings housing the cellar door, restaurant and upscale accommodation, and pour in some of New Zealand's finest drops, and you've got yourself a wine-tour stop that's hard to top.

After a serendipitous meeting between Craggy Range founder Terry Peabody and Master of Wine Steve Smith in 1997, the pair set out to create 'single-vineyard New World classics' from various New Zealand wine regions including Martinborough, Marlborough and Central Otago, where they own their own vines. Peabody believes they produce 'some of the New World's most inspiring fine wines that are a true reflection of the place and the people'.

Quality is certainly high across the board, but it's Craggy's top-flight range where memories are made. Well-heeled wine-lovers may wish to indulge in a bottle of Le Sol Syrah, a dense and luscious drop from the Gimblett Gravels, best savoured with something gamey in the excellent Terrôir restaurant. A treasure trove of other Craggy Range vintages can be found in its formidable wine list.
www.craggyrange.com; tel +64 6-873 0141; 253 Waimarama Rd, Havelock North; 10am-6pm daily Nov-Mar, Wed-Sun Apr-Oct

06 CLEARVIEW ESTATE

Four wineries cluster together on the shingles of Te Awanga, near Cape Kidnappers. Not so long ago the naysayers said that wine grapes just wouldn't grow here on this cooler, sea-breezy coast. Clearview's Tim Turvey and Helma van den Berg have proven them wrong.

Determination and hard graft is the order of the day here, with the pair hands-on in all aspects of the enterprise, from viticulture to building the legendary cellar door and restaurant. Clearview's wines are all handcrafted, as they have been since the first vintage in 1989.

Wines are made predominantly from 20 hectares (50 acres) of Te Awanga vineyards, sporting 11 grape varieties in all. The star of the show is the Reserve Chardonnay, a golden fruit-and-honey specimen fermented in new French oak. Lauded as a classic, the wine has deservedly snaffled awards every year since its first vintage in 1992.

There are other high flyers, though, with Clearview's range amassing more than 100 gold medals and five-star ratings in 25 years. Great reds include a punchy Reserve Cabernet Franc and the sumptuous Merlot-dominant Enigma. The sticky Sea Red is a dryish fortified dessert wine pioneered by Turvey.

Fashioned from upcycled materials, the rustic 'red shed' restaurant is casual and family-friendly, with a

colourful interior and leafy courtyard. It champions regional, seasonal ingredients including produce from the onsite garden. 'Friendly Friday' pizza and music nights are popular on summer evenings.
www.clearviewestate.co.nz; tel +64 6-875 0150; 194 Clifton Rd, Te Awanga; 10am-5pm daily summer, Thu-Mon winter

07 ELEPHANT HILL

Contrasting starkly with the rustic charm of Clearview up the road, Elephant Hill is a striking, monolithic form clad in patinated copper and fronted with epic windows offering unobstructed views of Cape Kidnappers and the Pacific Ocean. It's very chic.

Elephant Hill's German owners fell for Te Awanga while on holiday. With the goal of creating a state-of-the-art winery marrying traditional and contemporary styles and techniques, they planted their first grapes in 2003 and set to it. The results are impressive, their Reserve Chardonnay displays a lovely fruit purity and depth typical of Te Awanga terroir, and their reds blend local and Gimblett Gravels' characters.

The circular tasting bar is an enticing introduction to the restaurant space, a classy affair complete with sunken lounge dressed in white leather and a sundeck perching above an infinity pool. It's rather distracting from the artful and sophisticated cuisine that competes for its attention.
www.elephanthill.co.nz; tel +64 6-872 6073; 86 Clifton Rd, Te Awanga; 11am-5pm Dec-Mar, to 4pm Apr-Nov

05 Matariki Balloon Fiesta, Hawke's Bay

06 Clearview winery's restaurant courtyard

ESSENTIAL INFORMATION

WHERE TO STAY

CLIVE COLONIAL COTTAGES
These courtyard cottages sit prettily amid gardens in a serene spot near the beach. Pick up the cycle trail alongside to ride around the vines.
www.clivecolonialcottages.co.nz; tel +64 6-870 1018; 198 School Rd, Clive

BLACK BARN RETREATS
This collection of cottages and lodges offers upmarket stays in locations around the Havelock North countryside. It's affiliated with Black Barn winery, and home to a lovely bistro, concerts and summer growers' market.
www.blackbarn.com; tel +64 6-877 7985; Black Barn Rd, Havelock North

WHERE TO EAT

HAWKE'S BAY FARMERS' MARKET
If you're around on a Sunday morning, don't miss one of New Zealand's best markets, a lively affair set in showgrounds and bursting with produce and gourmet picnic supplies.
www.hawkesbayfarmersmarket.co.nz; A&P Showgrounds, Kenilworth Rd, Hastings

MISTER D
With something for everyone, morning, noon and night, Napier's hottest dining spot offers bites from cinnamon doughnuts to bone-marrow ravioli.
www.misterd.co.nz; tel +64 6-835 5022; 47 Tennyson St, Napier

WHAT TO DO

Don your walking shoes or hop on a bike to admire Napier's collection of art-deco buildings. This fascinating chapter in the Bay's history is well told at the Art Deco Trust visitor centre, a good place to start your tour.
www.artdeconapier.com; tel +64 6-835 0022; 7 Tennyson St, Napier

CELEBRATIONS

The bay's major festival is the annual Art Deco Weekend in February, an extravaganza of art, architecture, music and Gatsby-esque costumes. Epicures might like to time their visit to coincide with the Hawke's Bay's Food and Wine Classic (FAWC), held twice yearly in June and November.
www.artdeconapier.com; www.fawc.co.nz

01

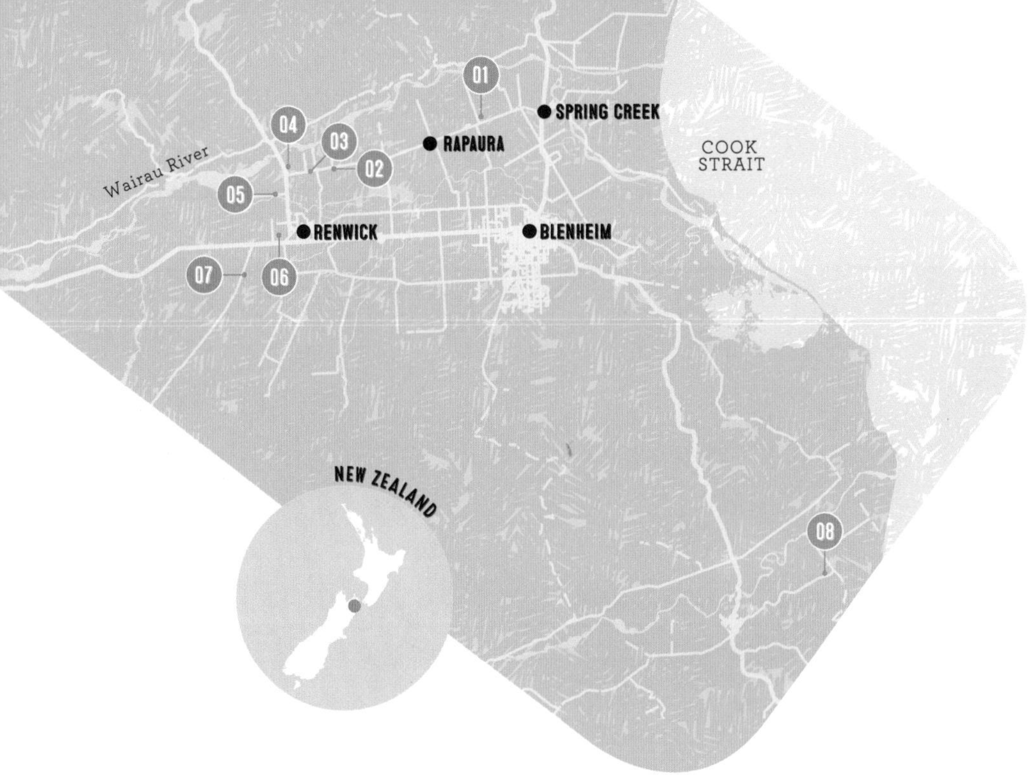

David Wall © Getty Images

[New Zealand]

MARLBOROUGH

Zingy Sauvignon Blanc is just the start of the story in a famous wine region bursting with variety, New World attitude – and coastal scenery to die for.

Marlborough is a vinous colossus, accounting for around three-quarters of New Zealand's wine. At last count there were nearly 600 growers tending 23,000 hectares (56,835 acres) of grapes, working their way into the wines of 151 producers. Remarkably, it has taken just 40-odd years for the Marlborough region to grow from first vines into the billion-dollar industry it is today.

So that's why you've probably heard of Marlborough Sauvignon Blanc; this New World classic is pungently aromatic, fruity and herbaceous, a dominant varietal that has stormed the global wine scene. Indeed, the ubiquity of big brands flooding supermarkets worldwide has led to accusations that Marlborough 'sav' has become predictable – even one-dimensional – but the region produces plenty that is exciting and distinct.

The majority of vineyards line up around Renwick in the Wairau Valley, although side valleys and coastal fringes have been colonised in response to the demand for land. While growing conditions throughout are generally sunny and dry, the soil is a veritable kaleidoscope of glacial stone, shingle, sand and silt, shifted and settled by river flows. The result is a highly varied *terroir*.

To home in on memorable Sauvignon Blanc, set your sights on smaller, independent wineries. They are more likely to offer tastings of single-estate wines, not just of Sauvignon Blanc but also of Marlborough's other notable varietals such as Pinot Noir and Riesling.

With plenty of accommodation in its rural surrounds, just 10km (6 miles) from Blenheim, Renwick makes a good base for wine touring. More than 20 of the region's 35 cellar doors can be found around here, along with bicycle hire, guided tours and shuttle services.

GET THERE

Auckland is the nearest major airport. Flights go from Auckland to Marlborough airport, 7km from Rapaura. Car hire is available.

01 SAINT CLAIR

Where better to start your Marlborough wine tour than with one of the region's oldest grape-growing families, the Ibbotsons, who set out on their own in 1994 after supplying fruit to the big boys since 1978?

Saint Clair has gone from strength to strength and now crafts some of Marlborough's – if not New Zealand's – most interesting and well-regarded wines. Consultant winemaker Matt Thomson credits this to the company's 'love of wine, not money'. Investment in small presses and tanks keeps vineyard batches separate, allowing the winemakers to scrutinise them individually. The enthralling Pioneer Block range presents distinct versions of numerous varieties. 'Everyone knows what a Marlborough Sauvignon Blanc tastes like,' remarks Thomson, 'but more emphasis needs to be made on the sub-regions and their different characters'.

Courtesy of Saint Clair

A broad selection of wines, including superlative Pinot Noir, can be tasted at their stylish cellar door and Vineyard Kitchen restaurant. Saint Clair's knowledgeable, friendly hosts are typical of Marlborough's wine-tour experience – this region may produce the bulk of New Zealand wine, but there's still plenty of personality and passion in the mix.

www.saintclair.co.nz; tel +64 3-570 5280; 13 Selmes Rd, Rapaura; 9am-5pm, 10am-4pm winter

02 WAIRAU RIVER

Marlborough dishes up plenty of mouth-watering fare, including crayfish, salmon and green-lipped mussels that surface from local waters. Wairau River winery is a pleasant spot to get a taste of it.

A family business dating back to the pioneering days, this is one of Marlborough's largest independent producers with a strong export business. It has, however, stayed true to its roots, offering honest wines and genuine hospitality at its cellar door and restaurant.

Located at a prominent junction, the stone-and-timber building has charming, rustic ambience sharpened with modern interior design. The capacious restaurant spills onto a patio and lawn, relaxing surrounds that will be welcome to weary wine-tourers and those with children in tow.

Wairau River's wines are well matched with refined, cafe-style fare, such as delicious mussel chowder with a glass of the zesty Sauvignon Blanc, or wood-smoked salmon salad with the honeyed Reserve Viognier. Wairau River's cheery cellar door staff will guide you proficiently and warmly through the range, before or after your meal.

www.wairauriverwines.co.nz; tel +64 3-572 9800; 264 Rapaura Rd, Blenheim; 10am-5pm

03 NO 1 FAMILY ESTATE

The man who brought a taste of France to Marlborough is Daniel Le Brun, scion of a winemaking family

stretching back 12 generations to 1780s Champagne. After emigrating to New Zealand in the 1970s, he married Adele with whom he established Cellier Le Brun, complete with caves burrowed into a Renwick hillside.

By 1996 Cellier Le Brun was in the hands of others, but its founder's dream of making wines to rival Champagne remained. So was born No 1 Family Estate in 1997, the only specialist *méthode traditionelle* maker in Australasia.

Still as hands-on as ever and growing all his own fruit, Le Brun crafts seven different styles of *traditionelle*. Non-vintage bubbles include the original Cuvée No 1, a complex, toasty Blanc de Blancs, and the elegant salmon-hued 100% Pinot Noir No 1 Rosé.

Sitting pretty at the top of the family tree is the vintage cuvée Adele, an opulent 80% Chardonnay, 20% Pinot Noir mix. You may well meet matriarch Adele at the cellar door, an intimate affair with a gilt-edged mirror and rows of bottles with bling.

www.no1familyestate.co.nz; tel +64 3-572 9876; 169 Rapaura Rd, Blenheim; 11am-4.30pm

04 HUIA

Huia was established in 1989 by Clare and Mike Allan, who named it after a beautiful native bird long since vanished through deforestation and a fashion for hat feathers.

As founding members of Marlborough's Natural Winegrowers group, their 32 hectares (80 acres) of grapes are managed under organic and biodynamic principles. 'It's all in the earth – that's what allows us to make such great wines,' say the Allans.

And they certainly do. Luscious, dry Gewürztraminer, grippy yet beautifully balanced Pinot Noir and intense Sauvignon Blanc are Huia highlights. The savoury 'non-rosé-drinker's rosé' is also a delight, as is their inexpensive Hunky Dory Tangle, a harmonious blend of Pinot Gris, Gewürztraminer and Riesling.

Tucked away off busy Rapaura Rd, the cellar door is simple and stylish; a proud presentation of wines is guaranteed. Our last tasting was hosted by Tui Allan – Claire and Mike's daughter – whose wine knowledge is extensive after a lifetime among the vines.

www.huia.net.nz; tel +64 3-572 8326; 22 Boyces Rd, Blenheim; 10am-5pm Oct-May

05 FRAMINGHAM

Framingham has earned a reputation as one of the world's leading producers of Riesling, built on a foundation of 33-year-old vines. A visit offers an illuminating lesson on this noble varietal.

Framingham's winemaker since 2002, Englishman Andrew Hedley is a firm Riesling fan. 'It can be interpreted in myriad styles, all compelling. It ages beautifully on the whole and is probably the best-value wine out in the marketplace.'

The range is diverse, with the selection varying according to vintage. The off-dry Classic and Germanic Spätlese styles are delectable standards, as are the stickies. And it's when the botrytis sets in that the real alchemy occurs. Created in tiny quantities bursting with flavour, these decadent nobles rival some of Europe's finest. The pinnacle is the sublime F-Series Trochenbeerenauslese.

Hedley and assistant Andrew Brown are no one-trick ponies, though. A passionfruit-laden Sauvignon Blanc makes up most of Framingham's output, with a cherry-like Pinot Noir and a zippy Viognier also rating highly.

David Wall © Getty Images

Wines can be sampled at the cellar door, set within a pretty walled garden. The guitar hanging on the wall hints at another of Hedley's passions, also evident in the strains of the Clash or Ramones that may drift in from the winery next door.
www.framingham.co.nz; tel +64 3-572 8884; 19 Conders Bend Rd, Renwick; 10.30am-4.30pm

06 TE WHARE RA

Great oaks from little acorns grow, so the saying goes. With roots in the 1970s, Te Whare Ra can count itself among Marlborough's mighty, producing some of its finest wines while staying grounded in the boutique league.

Established in 1979 and owned by winemakers Anna and Jason Flowerday since 2003, Te Whare Ra makes wines from seven varietals sourced from just 11 hectares (27 acres) of vines. Small scale keeps things high quality and hands-on at every stage of the process, starting with organic and biodynamic soil management that accounts for the excellent fruit.

Following in the footsteps of founder, Allen Hogan, the Flowerdays produce ambrosial, aromatic wines including a Gewürztraminer, two Rieslings and an Alsatian-style Pinot Gris. Ever keen to experiment, Te Whare Ra also produces Toru ('three' in Maori), an admirably proportioned blend of the three aromatic grapes. A plush Pinot Noir and peppery Syrah represent the red corner.

On the outskirts of Renwick, Te Whare Ra's modest cellar door shows that you don't have to be flash to be fabulous.
www.twrwines.co.nz; tel +64 3-572 8581; 56 Anglesea St, Renwick; 11am-4.30pm Mon-Fri, noon-4pm Sat & Sun Nov-Mar, by appointment Apr-Oct

07 SPY VALLEY

Squirrelled up the Waihopai Valley are two giant golf balls, known to the locals as the 'spy base' for the cloak-and-dagger 'communications monitoring' that takes place there. It is this intrigue that inspired Spy Valley in everything from its name, branding and cheeky merchandise.

Spy Valley also pushes the style boundaries of the New World winery through its architecture. The award-winning building is a striking statement in the picturesque valley, its edgy lines softened by lush, sculptural landscaping. The tasting room inside is airy, suffused with natural light.

There's no smoke and mirrors when it comes to Spy Valley's wines. The family-owned enterprise produces consistent, affordable wines from sustainably grown fruit. High points include a vibrant, barrel-aged, single-vineyard Sauvignon Blanc, an intense, spicy Gewürztraminer, and a couple

of food-friendly reds. In the upper echelons are the Envoy wines, made from select grapes.
www.spyvalleywine.co.nz; tel +64 3-572 6088; 37 Lake Timara Rd West, RD6 Blenheim; 10.30am-4.30pm daily, Mon-Fri winter

08 YEALANDS ESTATE

Yealands lies on the edge of the wine region, 31km (19 miles) south-east of Blenheim, but it's an easy side trip for those driving to or from Kaikoura. Blanketing 1000 hilly hectares (2500 acres) in the Awatere Valley, it's the largest privately owned vineyard in the country.

Yet despite its size, Yealands keeps its eyes on the prize – environmentally sustainable winemaking, a carbon-zero footprint, and total self-sufficiency. These efforts are evident on the enjoyable self-drive tour that loops through Seaview vineyard, passing picnic spots and lookouts, windmills, wetlands and compost piles along the way. There's also the odd peacock, sheep, chicken or duck. (The pigs were banished after they piggybacked one another to chomp the grapes.)

The corporate but casual cellar door experience is best started with the short film relaying the colourful Yealands backstory. As for tasting, while the winery is known for an abundance of super-value drops, there are plenty of delightful single-vineyard wines and reserves. Their S1 Block Sauvignon Blanc is a winner, while relative newcomers Grüner Veltliner and aromatic blend PGR are making waves.
www.yealands.co.nz; tel +64 3-575 7618; cnr Seaview & Reserve Rds, Seddon; 10am-4.30pm

01 Queen Charlotte Drive in Marlborough

02 Vineyard Kitchen, Saint Clair

03 Drink beside the vines at Saint Clair

04 The domes of Waihopai Spy Base

ESSENTIAL INFORMATION

WHERE TO STAY

OLDE MILLE HOUSE
These dyed-in-the-wool locals win over guests with their heritage home and homemade goodies for breakfast. Lovely gardens, spa and free bikes make this a tip-top base for exploring wine country.
www.oldemillhouse.co.nz; tel +64 3-572 8458; 9 Wilson St, Renwick

MARLBOROUGH VINTNERS HOTEL
These smart suites make the most of panoramic, vine-lined Wairau Valley views. Opt for the Outdoor Bath suite to survey Marlborough's night skies while having a soak.
www.mvh.co.nz; tel +64 3-572 5094; 190 Rapaura Rd, Renwick

WHERE TO EAT

GIBB'S ON GODFREY
Located in the thick of Renwick wine country, this elegant restaurant offers 'a taste of Marlborough' by focusing on local produce fashioned into contemporary yet crowd-pleasing dishes. Mesmerising wine list.
www.gibbs-restaurant.co.nz; tel +64 3-572 7989; 36 Godfrey Rd, Renwick

ROCK FERRY
This stylish cafe is a popular lunchtime spot for seasonal fare and stupendous sweet treats matched with Rock Ferry's own organic wines.
www.rockferry.co.nz; tel +64 3-579 6431; 80 Hammerichs Rd, Blenheim

WHAT TO DO

OMAKA AVIATION HERITAGE CENTRE
Original and replica WWI aircraft are brought to life at this museum abetted by Peter Jackson's Wingnut Films and Weta Workshop. Vintage biplane flights are a great way to survey the Wairau Valley.
www.omaka.org.nz, 79 Aerodrome Rd, Blenheim

CELEBRATIONS

MARLBOROUGH WINE & FOOD FESTIVAL
New Zealand's largest and longest-running wine and food festival is held at the big kahuna, Brancott Estate in February. Watch a cooking demo, boogie down to the band, or just chill out on the grass, savouring the bliss of a Marlborough summer.
www.marlboroughwinefestival.co.nz

01

[Portugal]

THE DOURO

Take a slow boat (or train) along the beautiful Douro Valley in northern Portugal, to experience historic estates, riverside vineyards and some of the world's best reds.

The river's surface is so still that it reflects the slowly shifting clouds overhead. This is the Douro, which flows westwards more than 850km (530 miles) from central Spain to the Portuguese coast. Just before it reaches the Atlantic, it passes through the magnificent valley that bears its name. As the water meanders through the landscape, steep hills rise up on either side, carved into neat dry-stone terraces seemingly waving with bright vine leaves. From the water, the valley is an ever-shifting diorama of gently rounded hills ribbed with lines of green.

The sun drifts down to cast a soft light over the vineyards and the landscape takes on a glow. A glance up from the riverbank reveals dozens of whitewashed manor houses dotted among the terraced hills; these are the wine estates known as *quintas*, ranging from the grandly traditional 18th-century farmhouse of Quinta de la Pacheca to the sleek, angular architecture of the Quinta do Seixo, further east. On these estates, world-famous port wines, boosted by a touch of *aguardente* (distilled grape spirits similar to brandy) have been produced since the 17th century. More recently, they're the source of some superb dry red wines.

Winegrowing in the Douro Valley stretches back to Roman times, when the arduous process of hand-carving the terraces began. The valiant effort of generations past in hand-pruning and picking the grapes and maintaining the terraces without the aid of machinery is continued across the valley today. This is partly for the sake of tradition but also because it's necessary, due to the vertiginous slopes. And although the grapes can be crushed by machines, many *quintas* in the Douro maintain the old ways. Come harvest time in mid-September, when golden light bathes the valley, the hills ring with the sound of chanting and laughter as workers crush the grapes with their bare feet, accompanied by accordion music and, of course, wine. It's a beautiful time to tour the Douro.

GET THERE
Porto, 127km from the Douro, is the nearest airport, with international flights also arriving at Lisbon.

02

Matt Munro © Lonely Planet Images

01 QUINTA DO CRASTO

Brothers Tomas and Miguel Roquette run this 400-year-old estate, one of the most interesting in the Douro. The *quinta* was one of the first to produce table wines in addition to fortified port wines and the extra experience reveals itself in their phenomenal reds. Old vines – a mix of varieties, including Touriga Nacional; a local variety of Tempranillo known as Tinto Roriz; and Bastardo (yes, really, known as Trousseau elsewhere) – and the schist-rich soil produce mature red wines with rich fruitiness (look for raspberry, cherry and blackberry) tempered by a mineral edge. Tomas and Miguel are also members of the Douro Boys, a fun-loving alliance of five winemaking families in the Douro that promotes the Douro's dry wines. *www.quintadocrasto.pt and www.douroboys.com; by appointment (contact andreia.freitas@quintadocrasto.pt)*

02 QUINTA NOVA

At Quinta Nova, sprawling over a bend in the river Douro, wine producer Duarte Costa guides visitors through the art of blending a red wine. With lots of different microclimates in the Douro, thanks to the variation in altitudes of the vineyards, the result is a uniquely diverse range of wines – and knowing how to balance their flavours is something that takes years to master.

The hillside winery is surrounded by rows of vines above and below. 'What we produce in this region,' explains Duarte, 'is special because it didn't just appear like this. All of this was created by the work of men over centuries, with their bare hands. You can see all that effort in the final product – it makes for a unique taste that can only come from here.' *www.quintanova.com; tel +351 254 730 430; Quinta Nova, Covas do Douro; you can be a winemaker for a day, see website for details*

03 QUINTA DE LA ROSA

This small estate, just outside Pinhão, has been in the Bergqvist family since it was gifted to Tim Bergqvist's mother as a Christening present. It's a rarity among Douro properties, being a 'single *quinta*' in which they own vines growing from the top of the hill all the way down to the river. Winemaker Jorge Moreira's wines exhibit the classic Douro characteristics of a floral scent and a dark, fruity depth. Rooms are available at Quinta de la Rosa and your hosts can organise picnics, followed by a dip in the Douro. *www.quintadelarosa.com; tel +351 254 732 254; 5085-215 Pinhão; tour daily 11am (book in advance)*

04 WINE & SOUL

The careers of Douro's younger generation often start by making garage wines. Sandra Tavares da Silva and Jorge Borges Serôdio had larger ambitions and bought a warehouse in the sought-after Pinhão Valley. The warehouse came with granite *lagares* (basins) in which their first batch of grapes, from a tiny plot of 70-year-old vines, was crushed by foot. This wine became the award-winning Pintas, which has now been joined by a white wine and a port. These are natural wines, made without pesticides; Sandra and Jorge explain their philosophy on a tour of the winery.

Pinhão itself is also worth exploring. Its blue *azulejo*-tiled station is a stop on the Linha do Douro, one of the world's great (and best value) train routes: take a train out of Porto for Régua, then change to the line that runs along the Douro for a memorable way of seeing the terraces. On summer weekends a steam train plies the route.
Tel +351 254 731 948; 5085-101 Pinhão; by appointment

05 TAYLOR'S PORT LODGE

That Porto is famous for port wine is not news. But the fortified wine goes back further than many suppose; as a protected wine region the Douro predates Bordeaux by a century. Its popularity began in 18th-century London, thanks in part to a war with France that prevented the import of French wines but also because importers knew that the smooth but powerful wine would survive the sea journey. British wine importers set up shop and their names live on: Graham, Cockburn, Croft, Taylor – all offer tours.

At Taylor's Port Lodge on the south side of the river, try three of the company's port wines, including a 10-year-old Tawny Port (which might prompt you to buy the more voluptuous 20-year-old Tawny).
www.taylor.pt; tel +351 223 772 956; Rua do Choupelo 250, Vila Nova de Gaia; 10am-6pm Mon-Fri, 10am-5pm Sat & Sun (fees apply to tours)

01 Tasting port wines

02 Terraces along the Douro River

03 Quinta Nova

ESSENTIAL INFORMATION

WHERE TO STAY

QUINTA NOVA DE NOSSA SENHORA DO CARMO

Located on the Quinta Nova winery estate, this 19th-century manor house has luxurious rooms with a mix of traditional furniture and modern fittings. The restaurant is exceptional, serving up contemporary takes on classic Douro dishes, paired with wines from the estate.
www.quintanova.com; tel +351 254 730 430; Quinta Nova, Covas do Douro

WHERE TO EAT

DOC

The destination restaurant in this part of Portugal is chef Rui Paula's DOC, famed for its superb wine list (with lots available by the glass) and its waterfront setting deep in the Douro Valley. A sister restaurant, DOP, opened in Porto's city-centre Palace of Arts in 2010, offering contemporary cuisine in a minimalist dining room.
Cais da Folgosa, Estrada Nacional 222, Folgosa, 18 5110-204

WHAT TO DO

Take a cruise along the river. You can travel all the way from Porto, or catch a boat from Porto to Régua and pick up a hire car. A short distance north of the Douro Valley is the Parque Nacional da Peneda-Gerês, a spectacular region of mountains and forests where wild horses, boar and wolves still roam. The park is created by the folds of four mountain ranges and is the perfect place for a couple of days of hiking, punctuated by cooling dips in the clear rivers and pools.

CELEBRATIONS

Midsummer sees one of Europe's most enthusiastic street festivals take over Porto: Festa de São João do Porto, celebrating St John the Baptist. The party starts on the afternoon of 23 June and features live music and dancing, barbecues, fireworks and a lot of wine.

Arcangelo Pia © 4Corners

[Slovenia]

BRDA

Taste thrilling experimental and historic wines in this multicultural frontier zone, defined by gentle hills and unforgettable hospitality.

In western Slovenia, home to the beautifully contoured wine region of Brda, the Italian border is fluid; it's possible to cross between the two countries several times a day without noticing. Understanding this frontier status through an encounter with the wines on both sides of the border is critical to an appreciation of the Brda's wines. Brda literally means 'hills', and defines the Slovene extension of the wider Gorizia Hills, once an ancient seabed, which continue into Italy under the name Collio. Although deeply influenced by both countries, there is a special culture here that one could call 'Gorizian', and which predates the European nation-state. Extraordinary wines are made on both sides of the border from the same grape varietals, mostly white, and with very similar techniques. Often, the fermentation vessel is clay, and the wine rests on its skins to become honey-coloured, layered and captivating.

Some of the most violent and drawn out battles of both world wars happened here, resulting in massive depopulations in the early part of the 20th century. Conflict has left deep scars, some of which are still visible, yet Gorizians remain warm and generous, and fiercely loyal to their land, which in many cases they fought and paid dearly to keep. That pride of place is illustrated by one of the local realities of winegrowing: above solid rock there is a lack of topsoil; often, in order to plant a viable vineyard, earth must be brought from elsewhere and layered directly on the stone. Take a walk with a family grower – the meaning of 'family' here carries special weight – and they'll make sure to explain the historical significance of their surrounding landmarks, before taking a moment to admire the many vistas the landscape affords.

GET THERE

Trieste-Friuli Venezia Giulia is the nearest major airport, 30km from Dobrovo. Car hire is available.

01 MOVIA

There's no denying that Movia's restless, charismatic winemaker Ales Kristancic has almost single-handedly brought Slovenian wine to the world stage. Movia currently stands as a true 'border wine': half of the vineyards lie in the Italian Collio, and a full 80% of production is exported. When he's not in the vines or cellar, Ales travels the world, a relentless apostle for his region and his wines.

And what wines! There's little that hasn't been tried here: biodynamic viticulture attuned to lunar cycles, deeply extended skin macerations, and undisgorged sparkling wines, to name but a few. These techniques were all put in place to achieve, as Ales would put it in his inimitable language, an ultimate goal of purity and soul, a transparent connection to the earth. Don't miss his entirely additive-free 'Lunar' bottling, from Ribolla, and the 'Puro' sparkling rosé.

The back balcony of Movia's large, rambling house offers a stunning outlook over these lands – and much of the region as a whole, in fact. Linger and savour the view.

www.movia.si; tel +386 53 95 95 10; Ceglo 18, Dobrovo, Slovenia; by appointment

Courtesy of Marjan Simcic

02 SIMCIC MARJAN

You could leave your car at Movia and walk across the street to visit fifth-generation winemaker Marjan Simcic at his impressive modern-style winery. As with Movia, Marjan's vines straddle the Italo-Slovene border, yet the wines are less idiosyncratic and enjoy a wider appeal. Marjan bottles his wines in three distinct tiers: entry-level 'Brda Classic', specially selected 'Complex Wines', and the 'Opoka Cru', released in exceptional years and matured in oak. Together, they provide an easy-to-understand portrait of the varietals the region is best known for, including Ribolla, Sauvignon and Merlot.

www.simcic.si; tel +386 53 95 92 00; Ceglo 3b, Dobrovo, Slovenia; by appointment

03 RADIKON

Stanko Radikon's estate is home to some of the most radically appealing, complex wines in the world. His terraced vines form an amphitheatre around his family's home and winemaking facility, where he and his son Sasa craft wines that hew closely to those of his grandfather's time, with as little intervention as possible. Ask to taste in the family dining room/kitchen, which faces onto the entrance to the home and the vineyards – it gives one of the warmest and most intimate tasting experiences in the region.

Their white wines, largely based on Tokaj and Ribolla, are perhaps better understood as 'amber', or 'orange'; they see several months of extended skin contact in Slavonian oak (and sometimes several years of bottle age), before release, and convey richly layered, honeyed textures alongside powerful acidity.

www.radikon.it; tel +39 48 13 28 04; località Tre Buchi 4, Oslavia, Gorizia, Italy; by appointment

04 ČOTAR

Branko Čotar (pronounced 'Chó-tar') began making wine for his own restaurant (see opposite) in 1974, and eventually became drawn into winemaking full-time, bottling his first commercial vintage in 1990. Today, he's joined by his son Vasja. They're a hardworking pair; ancestral methods are the rule here, from vineyard to winery.

The Čotars are amazing hosts. They provide not only an intimate, detailed view of their cellar and vineyards, but also a short tour of significant sites in

the region. If there's time, make sure to pair their selection of dried hams with their wines. They primarily work with local varietals to produce a small range of still and sparkling wines. Each of their bottlings are delicious, but pay special mind to the dry, sparkling red Teran, labelled 'Crna Penina', and the still, cidery, white Vitovska.
www.cotar.si; tel +386 57 66 82 28; Gorjansko 4a, Komen, Slovenia; by appointment

05 EDI KANTE

Edi Kante is regularly referenced as a pioneer of Carso winemaking. By carving a three-storey cellar and winemaking facility into the thick karst rock beneath his home, he has been able to achieve a control of the temperature for elaboration and maturation. The resulting wines are taut and lean, clearly reflecting the ruggedness of their source. The unique 'KK' spumante stands as one of the region's finest sparkling wines.
www.kante.it; tel +39 40 20 02 55; Prepotto 1/A, Trieste, Italy; by appointment

06 VODOPIVEC

The famous estate of Paolo Vodopivec lies 35 minutes south-east of the Gorizia/Oslavje zone, yet it's very much worth the trip. Paolo works with one varietal, the Vitovska grape, which is currently elaborated in three separate bottlings, aged in Georgian clay amphora and Slavonian oak. Dark-hued and fragrant, often recalling qualities of rooibos tea and fine sake, they stand as a benchmark for the region and varietal.
www.vodopivec.it; tel +39 40 22 91 81; Località Colludrozza 4, Sgonico, Italy; by appointment

01 The hilly landscape of Brda

02 Simcic Marjan winery in Dobrovo

ESSENTIAL INFORMATION

WHERE TO STAY

HOMESTEAD BELICA
Perched high atop the village of Medana, this eight-room homestead offers lovely views, along with an outdoor pool and delectable local prosciutto.
www.belica.si; tel +386 53 04 21 04; Medana 32, Dobrovo, Slovenia

GRAND HOTEL ENTOURAGE
The historic city of Gorizia is a gorgeous place to call home during your stay in the region, and few hotels in the city can match the Entourage's elegance and charm.
www.entouragegorizia.com; tel +394 81 55 02 35; Piazza San Antonio 2, Gorizia, Italy

WHERE TO EAT

OSTERIA LA SUBIDA
Started in 1960 by Slovenian Josko Sirk, this family-run restaurant has become famous for its uncompromising devotion to local traditions. Beyond the seasonal menu, an exploration of the cellar of rare local wines is a must.
www.lasubida.it; tel +39 48 16 05 31; Via Subida 52, Cormons, Italy

ČOTAR RESTAURANT
This terrific restaurant is run by one of the region's finest winemakers, but only opens at weekends – make sure to call ahead! The menu celebrates regional specialities, honed to perfection over generations.
Tel +386 57 66 81 94; Komen, Slovenia

WHAT TO DO

Near the famous Gorizia Castle, in the centre of town along the Via Roma, the Palazzo Attems Petzenstein stands as one of the region's finest examples of architecture, combining baroque, rococo, and neoclassical details, and housing an impressive art gallery.

CELEBRATIONS

In late April, the Brda and Wine Festival is held in the tiny Slovenian border town of Smartno. A few weeks later, the nearby village of Visnjevik hosts a Rebula (wine grape) and Olive Oil festival. On the second Sunday in September, the Italian town of Cormons celebrates the new grape harvest.

[South Africa]

FRANSCHHOEK & STELLENBOSCH

Wine lovers are spoiled for choice in buzzy Stellenbosch and French-flavoured Franschhoek, with excellent wines and gourmet restaurants.

Tasting the exceptional wines that South Africa's Cape region is now producing while in the actual vineyards themselves is a unique experience. Just half an hour's drive from Cape Town and the iconic Table Mountain are the immense open landscapes of Africa, where vast estates with hundreds of hectares of vines blend in with towering mountain ranges, lakes and wild vegetation.

The heart of the Cape winelands is the buzzing town of Stellenbosch, a wine lover's paradise of bars and bistros, the perfect place to be based for a few days of serious vineyard visiting. Grapes have been cultivated around Stellenbosch for more than 350 years, and wine tourism is a highly developed business: every winery seems to offer everything from guesthouses and restaurants to wine-paired picnics, and kids' playgrounds so parents can enjoy a serious tasting.

For many years, Stellenbosch has dominated wine awards, especially for South Africa's signature Pinotage, a hybrid of the Pinot Noir and Cinsaut grapes that was bred in the local university back in 1925. But more recently, attention is turning to nearby Franschhoek, which draws on the French heritage of its original Huguenot settlers, who brought vine seedlings with them on their perilous voyage from France. You could almost be in a Provencal village, with names such as 'Le Bon Vivant' and 'Quartier Francais', though in reality no one here actually speaks French any more. The restaurant scene in Franschhoek is definitely gourmet, the resort hotels luxurious and young *vignerons* are making sensational wines – not just classic Chenin Blanc and Pinotage, but intense Syrah, complex Pinot Noir and Sauvignon. And most importantly, estates are finally, though slowly, implementing inclusive ownership programmes for their black workforces.

GET THERE
Cape Town is the nearest major airport, 35km from Stellenbosch. Car hire is available.

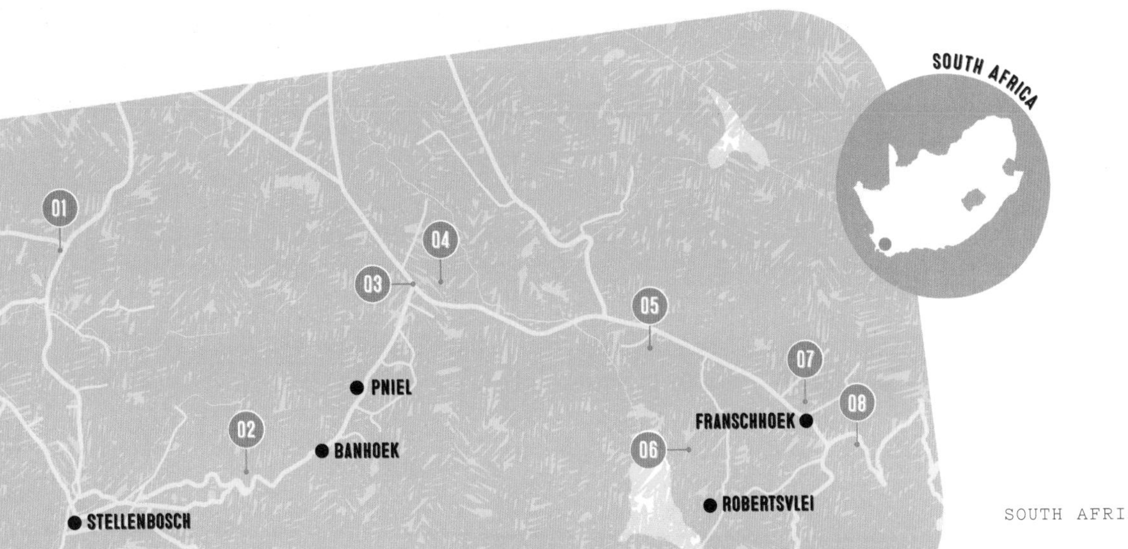

Walter Bibikow © Getty Images

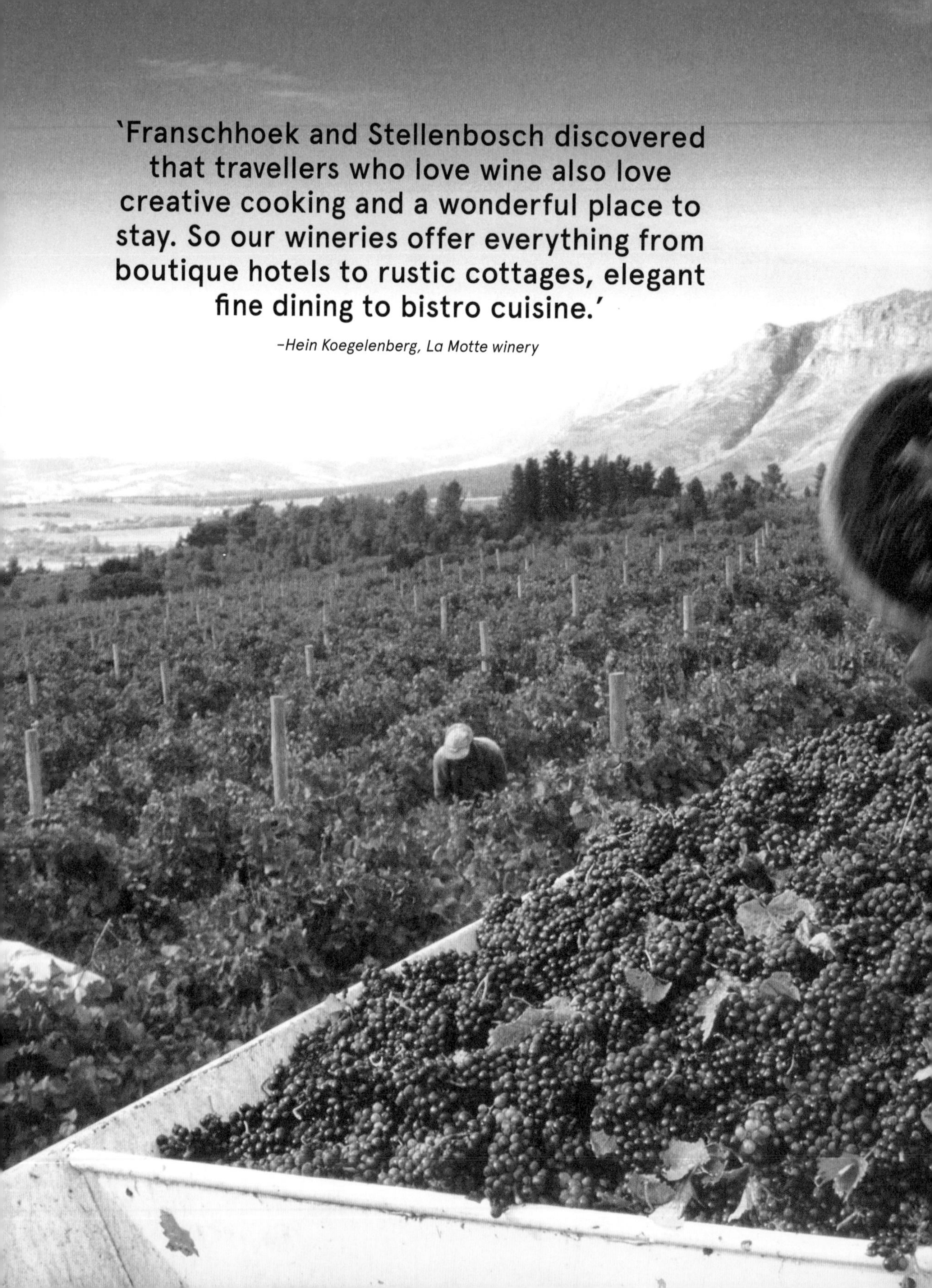
'Franschhoek and Stellenbosch discovered that travellers who love wine also love creative cooking and a wonderful place to stay. So our wineries offer everything from boutique hotels to rustic cottages, elegant fine dining to bistro cuisine.'
–Hein Koegelenberg, La Motte winery

02

Christer Fredriksson © Getty Images

01 In the shadow of Table Mountain

02 Harvesting Pinot Noir grapes

03-05 Haute Cabrière boasts gourmet food and stunning views

06 The restaurant of Pierneef a la Motte

01 KANONKOP

The historic estate of Kanonkop is a 30-minute drive outside Cape Town, at the outskirts of Stellenbosch, South Africa's unofficial capital of wine tourism. The entrance is marked, rather ominously, by a black cannon, and the surprise as you drive towards the huge cellars through the vineyards that line the slopes of the Simonsberg Mountain is that there are as many traditional free-standing bush vines here as the more modern Guyot. In fact, Kanonkop oozes tradition. The estate tour takes you into a hall of open shallow concrete vats used for hand-punching and fermenting after harvest, which the winemaker, Abrie Beeslar, claims is the secret of the high quality of Kanonkop's wine. The Pinotage range is intense and tannic, taken from minimum 50-year-old bush vines and aged in French oak – certainly not to be drunk young.

www.kanonkop.co.za; tel +27 21 884 4656; R44, Stellenbosch, 9am-5pm Mon-Fri, 9am-2pm Sat

02 TOKARA

Under the guidance of master oenologist Miles Mossop, Tokara is the modern face of Stellenbosch winemaking. The winery is a stunning example of futuristic architecture, filled with daring contemporary art and sculpture. Mossop creates distinctive wines from three different vineyards, reflecting personality and characteristics of not just Stellenbosch, but the emerging regions of Elgin and Hermanus. Sadly, Tokara's signature Pinotage will not be available for some time, as the majority of their ancient vines were destroyed in a fire. Still, don't miss the straw-coloured Director's Reserve White, a vibrant blend of Sauvignon and Semillon, while the Syrah, hand-picked on the slopes of the Simonsberg Mountain, is incredibly intense in flavour and colour. The tastings here are free, a rarity in Stellenbosch, and afterwards, be sure to try the fruity olive oil made on their 60-hectare (148-acre) olive farm. There is also a casual deli and gourmet restaurant with spectacular panoramic views as far as Cape Town's mythic Table Mountain.

www.tokara.co.za; tel +27 21 808 5900; Helshoogte Rd, Stellenbosch; contact for tastings

03 ALLÉE BLEUE

Like many large Cape wine estates, Allée Bleue is owned by foreign investors who have transformed a fruit farm by replacing some of the orchards with 25 hectares (61 acres) of vines. And their *vigneron*, Vanzyl Dutoit, a beefy rugby-playing enthusiast, could not look happier, as he has been given carte blanche to create a state-of-the-art cellar. Allée Bleue is the place to taste Pinotage, South Africa's most famous grape – a cross of Burgundy's Pinot Noir with Chateauneuf-du-Pape's Cinsault, or Hermitage – created in 1925 in Stellenbosch. The vines at Allée Bleue are young, aged in steel vats to produce what Vanzyl calls 'our quaffing wine'. But their flagship, full-bodied and tannic Pinotages are made from grapes that come by lorry from 50-year-old vines three hours away, a method Vanzyl mischievously describes as '*terroir* by truck'. He pinpoints three key characteristics for Pinotage: 'colour – a very deep, ruby red; a very intense nose, plums and cherry; and then there is the tannin, which the old-school winemakers prefer supple, aged in large old wood barrels, while the newer generation like me prefer to emphasise by using small new barriques.'

www.alleebleue.co.za; tel +27 21 874 1021; Intersection R45 & R310, Groot Drakenstein; 9am-5pm Mon-Fri, 10am-5pm Sat & Sun

04 SOLMS DELTA

Winemaker Hagen Viljoen is only 32, but has strong ideas about the wines he wants to produce, and this is certainly a winery with a vision, making a concrete attempt to empower the cooperative black workforce, which has been given one-third ownership. 'The owners are trying to address the post-apartheid heritage,' explains Hagen. 'The history of this farm goes back four centuries and we have a museum, housed in the original 1740 wine cellar, illustrating life here when all farms and wineries were originally worked with slave labour. The idea is to come to terms with the issue of slavery rather than brush it under the carpet.' The choice of wines to taste are daring blends of highly concentrated Rhone varietals such as Syrah, Grenache, Carignan and

Courtesy of Haute Cabrière

05

Mourvèdre, made essentially from desiccated grapes. And the estate's restaurant, Fyndraai, is perfect for a wine-pairing lunch, with dishes such as smoked ostrich and fynbos greens or bobotie stew with fresh mango. Chef Shaun Schoeman uses herbs from his native African heritage and Cape Malay spices.
www.solms-delta.co.za; tel +27 021 874 3937; Delta Rd, Groot Drakenstein; tours by appointment

05 MORESON

Moreson is the boutique vineyard of Franschhoek mover-and-shaker Richard Friedman, who also owns the luxury Quartier Francais resort in town. But a visit to Moreson revolves around two men, the dapper Clayton Reabow, who became winemaker here aged 23, and grizzled Brit Neil Jewell, the mad master butcher and charcutier of the funky Bread&Wine bistro. It is a marriage made in heaven for wine pairings, with organic meats such as lamb prosciutto or the lethal Devil salami (25% chilli). You can begin with an aged blend of Pinot Noir and Chardonnay, then light Pink Brut Rosé, and finish with Solitaire, blended from four different vintages. And Clayton has strong views on his barrel-aged Chardonnay: 'We want to bring people back to a subtly oak-aged wine after the backlash of the ABC trend of Anything But Chardonnay'.
www.moreson.co.za; tel +27 21 876 3055; Happy Valley Rd, Franschhoek; book wine-tasting tours online

06 GLENWOOD

Glenwood is Franschhoek's hidden secret, tucked away in a remote valley at the end of a dusty 7km dirt track. The domaine resembles the Big Country ranch, with vines dramatically enclosed by steep mountain slopes, a vast expanse once inhabited by herds of elephants. The genial cellar master, DB Burger, has been making award-winning wines here for 23 years, and suggests that 'visitors give a call first, because our tasting is more personalised than most places, I hope. I try to be available, and there is not the feeling you are being told what to think by some student taster who is repeating comments that he has learnt by heart.' He is most proud of his elegant Chardonnays, both the oaky Vigneron Selection and the crisper Chardonnay Unwooded, but the spicy Syrah is also excellent. Burger explains, 'Franschhoek has metamorphosed into perhaps the leading Cape wine region. In my early days, grapes were just grown to be sold to the cooperative. Then winemakers started replanting vines that are only now growing into maturity, explaining the recent radical improvement in quality.'
www.glenwoodvineyards.co.za; tel +27 21 876 2044; Robertsvlei Rd, Franschhoek; 11am-4pm Mon-Fri, 11am-3pm Sat & Sun

07 CHAMONIX

Chamonix is a vast domaine encompassing a vineyard, farmland, and a sprawling game reserve with guest lodges surrounded by wildebeest, zebra and springboks. But the wines stand out, masterminded by dynamic young oenologist Gottfried Mocke, who is experimenting in the cellar, ageing in a mix of concrete tanks, steel vats, barriques, large casks and the latest trend, high-tech 'concrete eggs'. The stars here are the Chenin Blanc and Sauvignon, Pinot Noir and a supple Pinotage, made 'passito' style similar to Amarone. Gottfried feels that 'Chenin was planted here in vast amounts 50 to 60 years ago, primarily to make brandy, but I think over the years the vine has mutated to our climatic conditions to become virtually an autochthonous South African grape.' He is also trying to shift attitudes, promoting a luscious 2009 Sauvignon: 'I'm holding back a small part of our production rather than sell everything quickly, so people can see how the wine develops rather than always drinking young.'
www.chamonix.co.za; tel +27 21 876 8426; Uitkyk St, Franschhoek; 9.30am-5pm daily

08 HAUTE CABRIÈRE

It is worth driving out from the edge of Franschhoek and up the mountainside just for the views over the valley from the sunny wine-tasting terrace of Haute Cabrière. The estate was named in 1694 by one of the founding French Huguenot settlers, Pierre Jourdain, after his home town, when this area was still known as Olifantshoek – Elephant's, rather than French, Corner. The present owners, Achim von Arnim and his son Takuan, are on a mission to produce high-quality Champagne-standard sparkling wines, and have planted Chardonnay on the sandstone soil on one side of the vineyard, and Pinot Noir on the stony clay terroir on the west-facing slopes. Yes, these are officially South African Methode Cap Classique, but it is difficult to tell them apart from a French Champagne in a blind tasting, especially over a meal in their restaurant, which overlooks the cathedral-like cellar.
www.cabriere.co.za; tel +27 21 876 8500; Lambrechts Rd, Franschhoek; 9am-5pm Mon-Fri, 10am-4pm Sat, 11am-4pm Sun

ESSENTIAL INFORMATION

WHERE TO STAY

HOLDEN MANZ
Just outside Franschhoek, the modern boutique winery and restaurant contrasts with the irresistible old-world charm of this property, housed in a romantic 17th-century Cape Dutch thatched manor. *www.holdenmanz.com; tel +27 21 876 2738; Green Valley Rd, Franschhoek*

RICKETY BRIDGE COUNTRY HOUSE
Dating back to 1792 when it was part of La Provence, one of Franschhoek's original Huguenot estates, Rickety Bridge, is a boutique winery with three sumptuously furnished guest rooms. *www.ricketybridgewinery.com; tel +27 21 876 2994; R45, Franschhoek*

MIDDEDORP MANOR
Perfectly located in the downtown heart of bustling Stellenbosch, this stately Victorian guesthouse is decorated with a mix of contemporary and Cape Dutch styles. *www.middedorp.com; tel +27 21 883 9560; 16 Van Riebeeck St, Stellenbosch*

WHERE TO EAT

CAFE DES ARTS
Favourite hangout for local winemakers, serving simple comfort cooking, such as lamb's liver with chilli-roasted potatoes, onion and bacon, and the freshest yellow-tail tuna delivered straight from the Indian Ocean. *www.cafedesarts.co.za; 7 Reservoir St West, Franschhoek; tel +27 21 876 2952*

PIERNEEF A LA MOTTE
La Motte is one of the oldest and still most important Franschhoek wineries, and in its flagship gastronomic restaurant, chef Michelle Theron creates tantalising dishes. *www.la-motte.com; tel +27 21 876 8000; R45, Franschhoek*

DUTCH EAST RESTAURANT
Pasch Duploy is a gregarious butcher/chef, smoking and ageing his own meats, and his buzzing bistro is the place to feast on wild game such as springbok, eland and ostrich. *www.dutcheast.co.za; tel +27 21 876 3547; 42 Huguenot St, Franschhoek*

WHAT TO DO

A favourite activity in Cape Town is learning to cook like a Cape Malay mama. Gamidah Jacobs of Lekka Kombuis will show you how to make perfect samoosas, dhaltjies (chilli bites), rootis (flat breads) and chicken curry at the classes she runs in her historic turquoise-painted Bo-Kaap home.

CELEBRATIONS

Franschhoek goes back to its French roots with a huge 14 July party to celebrate Bastille Day.

06

Courtesy of Pierneef a la Motte

01

[South Africa]

WELLINGTON, SWARTLAND & TULBAGH

Small vineyards with enthusiastic, independent owners offer the visitor a special insight into the future of winemaking in this fertile region.

Cape winemaking has long been symbolised by the grand old established estates in Stellenbosch, Franschhoek and Constantia, where the first vines were planted on the African continent as far back as 1659. But today there is a host of regions further afield in the Cape that are developing their own *terroir* characteristics, and are not limiting themselves to the classic Chenin Blanc and Pinotage for which South Africa is famous. With its maritime climate, Walker's Bay is well known for Chardonnay, a flinty Sauvignon and Pinot Noir, while the higher-altitude vineyards in Elgin favour Sauvignon Blanc and Bordeaux blends. And for sheer variety, and for smaller family-run wineries who offer a friendly, genuine welcome rather than organised wine tourism, the adjoining regions of Wellington, Swartland and Tulbagh offer a refreshing alternative. Winery tastings are more likely to be free here, and instead of hearing a tour guide reciting a set speech, you may well have a face-to-face encounter with the winemaker. It quickly becomes clear that in these emerging regions estate owners are happier to take risks, and experiment and plant new types of grape.

Swartland is known as the bread bowl of the Cape, farming wheat and breeding cattle and horses. Here immense vineyards were owned by anonymous cooperatives producing bulk wine and brandy. But the co-ops have all but disappeared, replaced by a band of cutting-edge vintners with small, manageable estates, many of whom are experimenting with biodynamic production. Wellington used to be dominated by fruit production, and wandering through one of the rural towns of a Friday when labourers get paid is like stepping back into South Africa's unequal past. Yet vineyard owners here are some of the most progressive in the Cape, with the black workforce genuinely having a voice in the running of an estate. In the remote valley of Tulbagh, visitors discover farms producing certified organic wines and taking important steps to preserve the fragile ecosystem surrounding the vineyards.

GET THERE
Cape Town is the nearest major airport, 70km from Wellington. Car hire is available.

Courtesy of Badenhorst

⓪① RIJK'S PRIVATE CELLAR

Tulbagh is one of the under-the-radar wine regions of the Cape, a fertile valley ringed by a bowl of three tall mountain ranges. The cellar at Rijk's is the personal fief of one of South Africa's most renowned winemakers, Pierre Wahl, who modestly declares, 'With the top-quality grapes that are harvested here, I am simply entrusted with gently guiding the wine into the bottle with the least interference possible.' This is something of an experimental winery, where a vineyard was planted from scratch with many different cultivars in this largely *schist* soil, and three years later, after the first harvest, plants producing Merlot, Cabernet Sauvignon and Franc were dug up, with production now concentrated on Chenin Blanc, Pinotage and Shiraz. While Rijk's presents a range of younger wines, with slight oak influences, what's really interesting is the Private Cellar selection, kept in oak barrels for two years, then bottle-aged for three years. Attached to the winery is a traditional whitewashed country house, transformed into an elegant hotel. The perfect place to sample Rijk's intriguing wines is the sunny terrace of the restaurant, which offers idyllic views over a lake, with the vineyard and the imposing mountains in the background.
www.rijks.co.za; tel +27 23 230 1622; Van der Stel St,Tulbagh; 10am-4pm Mon-Fri, 10am-2pm Sat

⓪② WAVERLEY HILLS

While Rijk's is just at the edge of bustling Tulbagh town, Waverley Hills sits alone in the middle of a wild landscape in the foothills of Witzenberg Mountains, right at the other end the valley. The vineyard was founded in 2000 and has very different objectives to most other wineries. To begin with, this is one of the few Cape vineyards to produce genuine organic wines, with a biodiversity programme that ranges from a flock of ducks to combat snails, to a huge parcel of virgin land set aside to conserve endangered veld and keep out alien vegetation.

Johan Delport is Waverley's vintner, supervising not only the vineyard and olive groves, but also a plant nursery and an educational eco-centre. Generally, the wines are light, mineral and not strong in tannin, as much ageing is done in steel vats rather than wooden barrels, while screw tops have replaced cork. The real surprise comes when Johan opens his Cabernet Sauvignon, a 'natural'

Wil Punt/Peartree Photography

wine made without sulphites.

After a tour of the modern cellar, with its huge steel vats, visitors arrive in the minimalist tasting room, which doubles as a deli for the farm's organic olive-oil production. And for the whole healthy, sustainable experience, the restaurant serves a five-course food-and-wine pairing. *www.waverleyhills.co.za; tel +27 23 231 0002; R46, Tulbagh; 10am-4pm Mon-Sat, 11am-3pm Sun*

03 DOOLHOF

You have to drive well out of Wellington right to the remote end of the snaking Bovlei valley to get to Dennis Kerrison's splendid Doolhof estate. The whole farm is enormous, with 40 hectares (98 acres) planted in the 1990s with vines, although grapes for wine and brandy have been grown here since the early 1700s. It is a complex vineyard made up of a labyrinth of parcels of vines planted on different *terroirs* with different microclimates, meaning a lot of careful blending is required in the cellar. Only two whites are produced, Sauvignon and Chardonnay, while the red blends are dominated by Merlot, Pinotage, Shiraz and Petit Verdot.

For those who want to splash out, you can stay in the totally luxurious Grand Dédale Country House, where guests are pampered by a private chef. Alternatively, there is a casual restaurant and tasting room or, even better, forego the indoors entirely, order a picnic with chilled wine and follow a leisurely river trail through the estate.
www.doolhof.com; tel +27 21 873 6911; Bovlei, Wellington; 10am-5pm Mon-Sat, 10am-4pm Sun

04 NABYGELEGEN

James McKenzie bought this idyllic property in the shadow of the looming Snow Mountains 15 years ago, but the estate dates back to 1748. He lives in the original manor house and rents out a beautifully preserved 18th-century cottage as a B&B, while the vines run down to a romantic lake, perfect for a chilled glass of his distinctive mineral Chenin Blanc at sunset. James works the small farm and 17-hectare (42-acre) vineyard on his own, saying: 'It is a lot of hard work, but for me this is like living in paradise. This used to be a farm supplying the local wine cooperative, so I inherited fabulous 40- to 70-year-old bush vines. Most winemakers around here would just dig them up and replant, but I couldn't be happier, as the quality they yield is exceptional.' After a tasting in the old forge, visitors are given a vineyard tour by this gentle giant of a man, accompanied by a horde of his eight dogs. His latest project is a small plot of vines high up on the mountains where he has planted Pinot Noir.
www.nabygelegen.co.za; tel +27 21 873 7534; Bovlei Division Rd, Wellington; tours by appointment

05 VAL DU CHARRON

Arriving at the entrance to this 1920s estate is more Sunset Boulevard than South Africa, with tall palm trees lining the monumental driveway against a backdrop of neatly spaced vines and the gaunt rocky cliffs of Groenberg Mountain. When Catherine and Stewart Entwhistle decided to change lifestyle and become *vignerons*, they embarked on a huge project. This was essentially a fruit farm with no vines, and in 2002 they planted 22 hectares

'Rather than forever planting and replanting high-yield vines, winemakers in Swartland and Wellington are rediscovering the potential of the ancient bush vines, free-standing beauties that produce a fantastic quality, thick-skinned grape.'

–Adi Badenhorst, winemaker

Courtesy of Badenhorst

Courtesy of Val du Charron

(54 acres) from scratch with quite a startling variety of 18 different grapes 'because we didn't want to say 20 years later, "Oh, why didn't we plant this?"' says the spirited Catherine with a smile. Fortunately, they are advised by one of the Cape's top cellar masters, Bertus Fourie, and he uses the varietals in blends, waiting till the vines are older to concentrate on a reserve selection with single grapes such as Chardonnay, Cabernet Sauvignon and Shiraz. A visit here is like stepping into a party, with tastings around the poolside, art exhibitions and theatre performances in the cellar.
www.vdcwines.com; tel +27 21 873 1256; Bovlei, Wellington

06 BOSMAN FAMILY VINEYARDS

Eight generations of the Bosmans have been producing handcrafted wine in Wellington. Jannie Bosman, his children and their families still live together in the estate's grand mansions, and though the flagship domaine covers 150 hectares, there are two other sizeable vineyards in nearby Swartland and the emerging Walker's Bay. After tasting the Chenin and Pinotage in the historic 260-year-old cellar, visitors will gain a sense of the family's winemaking heritage. But the Bosmans look to the future too, setting up a Vine Nursery supplying baby vines of over 50 different varietals to winemakers all over South Africa.
www.bosmanwines.com; tel +27 21 873 3170; Hexberg Rd, Wellington; 8am-5pm Mon-Fri, by appointment Sat only

07 DIEMERSFONTEIN

Diemersfontein is another South African winery brimming with new ideas. It offers travellers plush accommodation in a lavish Cape Dutch mansion, a healthy restaurant, and a performing-arts centre that promotes local musicians and actors. The latter is run by the workers association, who also control one third of the estate and produce their own line of wines, Thokozani. The wines are a surprise too, from For the Birds, where a percentage goes to help save the penguin population, to Coffee Pinotage, invented by Diemersfontein's cellar master, and a huge commercial success. Toasted barrel staves are dropped into steel vats to give the rich red Pinotage wine a Mocha aroma and flavour. Experts consider it heresy, but people love it. The owner, David Sonnenberg, is often to be found reminiscing during tastings: 'During apartheid I was disillusioned and left to live in London for 20 years working as clinical psychologist, but it was Nelson Mandela and the changes here that inspired me to come back to the winery, and I have never regretted it'. *www.diemersfontein.co.za; tel +27 21 864 5050; Jan van Riebeck Dr, Wellington; 10am-5pm daily*

08 ADI BADENHORST

Swartland is all about rock-and-roll winemaking. Just finding the windswept farm of Adi Badenhorst is challenging, though the welcome of this friendly bear of a man quickly makes up for it. He works in his cellar like an anarchic alchemist, using everything from huge old oak casks to 500L French barrels, cement and steel vats, and a couple of Noblot cement eggs. His tasting room is a barrel next to a battered fridge, but this doesn't matter once you start tasting such stellar bottles as Secateur Chenin Blanc; Secateur Red, an explosive blend of Grenache, Carignan and Cinsault; and Funky White, which one year might be a Vin Jaune, the next a Muscat de Frontignan. This whole area was historically dominated by the Swartland Cooperative, but when farmers couldn't afford to replant their old vines in favour of high-yield young ones, many were forced to sell. This allowed maverick vintners like Adi to inherit low-yield bush vines that can date back over 100 years. *www.aabadenhorst.com; tel +27 82 373 5038; Kalmoesfontein, Jakkalsfontein Rd, Malmesbury; by appointment*

01 Adi Badenhorst

02 A festival at the Bosman family estate

03 Val du Charron's old cellar

04 Adi Badenhorst inspects the vines

05 Val du Charron's Wellington estate

06 An angel in Val du Charron's vineyard

ESSENTIAL INFORMATION

WHERE TO STAY

TULBAGH HOTEL
Smack in the middle of Tulbagh's high street, this imposing 1850s hotel mixes contemporary design with nostalgic colonial touches. Cosy restaurant, pool and sunny terrace bar. *www.tulbaghhotel.co.za; tel +27 23 230 0071; 22 Van der Stel St, Tulbagh*

OUDE WELLINGTON WINE ESTATE
This wine and brandy estate welcomes guests in enchanting traditional Cape Dutch thatched cottages; a little rustic since they date back to the early 18th century. Try the traditional braai barbecue in the poolside garden. *www.wellington.co.za; tel +27 21 873 2262; Bainskloof Rd, Wellington*

WHERE TO EAT

READERS RESTAURANT
The oldest house in Tulbagh dates back to 1754 and hosts the cosy Readers restaurant, where Carol Collins creates inventive recipes that reinterpret traditional dishes. Great homemade ice-cream with balsamic vinegar or olive oil, and irresistible Cape Brandy Pudding. Outstanding list of local wines, many by the glass. *www.readersrestaurant.co.za; tel +27 23 230 0087; 12 Church St, Tulbagh*

BAR BAR BLACKSHEEP
Funky bar and bistro where Swartland winemakers hang out over long, lazy Sunday lunches. The kitchen uses organic, locally sourced products, preparing slow-cooked country fare such as cabrito goat stew, and tender rum pork. Big selection of independent garage wines and great cocktails too. *www.bbbs.co.za; tel +27 22 448 1031; Short St, Riebeek Kasteel*

WHAT TO DO

The Cape is a nature paradise, so take a day off to explore a wildlife reserve or head to the coast for whale-watching.

CELEBRATIONS

Inspirational winemakers come from far and wide to celebrate the Swartland Revolution each November in Riebeek Kasteel, a nonstop weekend wine and food party. *www.theswartland-revolution.com*

01

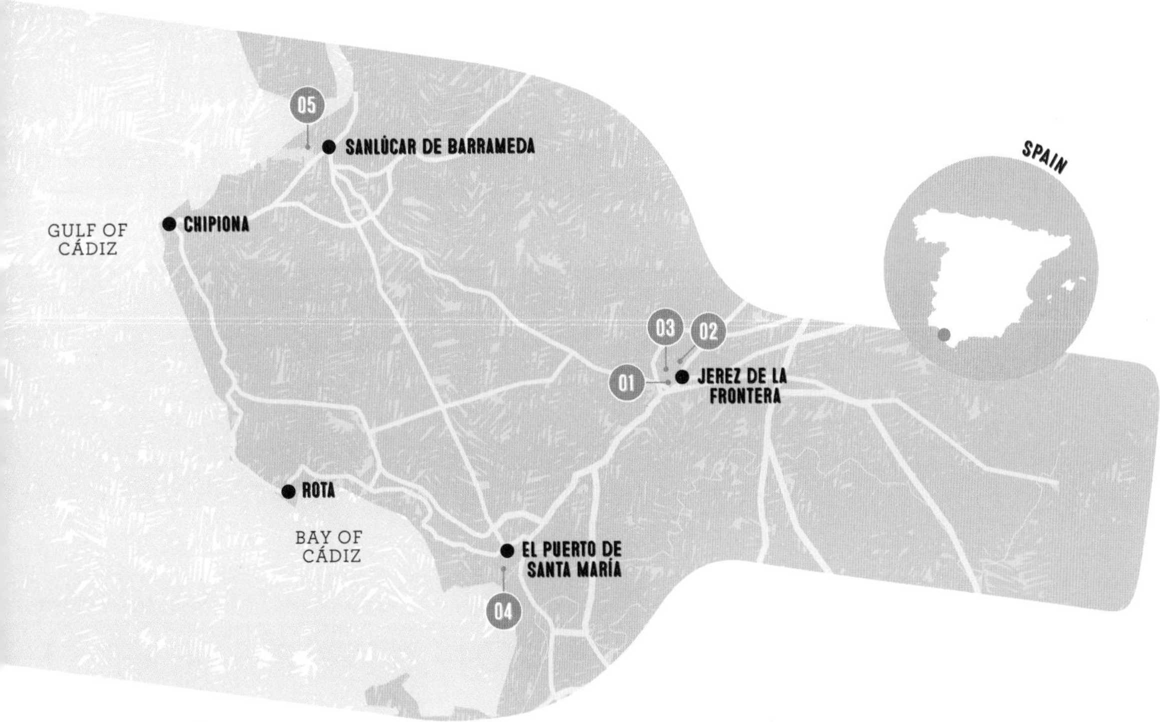

05 SANLÚCAR DE BARRAMEDA
GULF OF CÁDIZ
CHIPIONA
SPAIN
03 02
01 JEREZ DE LA FRONTERA
ROTA
BAY OF CÁDIZ
EL PUERTO DE SANTA MARÍA
04

Yadid Levy © Lonely Planet

[Spain]

JEREZ

Sherry is stylish again. Head to the source of the ultimate tapas companion in this handsome Andalucian city for the low-down on Fino.

Beware: you could get lost for days, maybe weeks in the Sherry Triangle. Formed by the three towns of Jerez de la Frontera (known as Sheris in medieval times), Sanlucar de Barrameda to the west and El Puerto de Santa Mariá , this corner of Spain's southern region of Andalucia is the only source of sherry, the fortified wine that is regaining well-deserved favour among food-lovers.

Every evening in bars across Andalucia a pre-dinner ritual is repeated. You take a seat and the bartender pours a small glass of pale gold liquid, the colour of an eagle's eye, then slides across the counter a plate of slivers of *jamón ibérico*, the air-dried local ham, or some cubes of cheese. This is Fino, the palest and driest of sherries, alive with a mouth-puckeringly savoury tang and, as legions of hip bar-hoppers are discovering, it's the perfect companion to sociable snacking.

The world of sherry is small but it can be bafflingly complex – it's not one drink but about five or six and it's not immediately obvious how a refined Fino relates to the sickly, orange sherry from your great-aunt's drinks cabinet. This Wine Trail reveals everything.

Sherry's journey back to the bar-top began in the mid-1990s when inland Jerez and El Puerto de Santa María and Sanlucar de Barrameda on the Spanish coast gained recognition and protection from the European Union as Protected Designation of Origin (PDO).

Your journey starts in Jerez, where all the big producers have a bodega that is open to the public. It can be quite a commercial experience – González Byass even has a model train to ferry visitors around – but it's a good introduction. Afterwards, take to Jerez's paved streets to get a flavour of flamenco, an Andalucian invention. If dancing horses are more your thing, Jerez can do that too. Next, hit the bars to put your new-found know-how to the test.

The Wine Trail continues out of the city to the coast; make sure you find time to stop in fabulous, dissolute Cádiz along the way.

GET THERE
Malaga, Seville and Cadíz are the closest regional airports.

Yadid Levy © Lonely Planet

01 Cellar master José Blandino Carrasco at Bodegas Tradición

02 Moscatel grapes

03 Sampling sherry at Bodegas Tradición

04 The Royal Andalusian School of Equestrian Art

01 GONZÁLEZ BYASS

Close to the cathedral, González Byass' bodega is the most vistor-oriented of all Jerez's bodegas. Fittingly, its Tio Pepe Fino is the world's biggest-selling sherry. It's a good place to get a grip on the basics of sherry production. There are several different types of sherry, from dry to sweet. At the driest end of the spectrum (and these have led sherry's revival) are Fino and Manzanilla. The tangy flavours of Fino are caused by a yeast known as *flor* that forms a film on the surface of sherries as they rest in the barrel for a minimum of three years (often much longer for the high-end vintages). This layer protects the sherry from the air (keeping it pale in the process).

After Fino, the next step for a sherry is the bone-dry Amontillado, which is a Fino that has continued ageing in contact with the air. As a result, it's darker and richer; expect to get pleasantly woody and dry citrus flavours. The González Byass Amontillado is an attention-grabbing treat, as are most of the bodega's older sherries.

Next on the sherry sweetness scale is Oloroso, which is fortified after fermentation to stop the *flor* forming. As it ages in the barrel, in contact with air, it grows darker, richer and fruitier. Pedro Ximénez is a dessert wine made from the grape of the same name; the more mature the better. Any extra-sweetened sherries beyond this point tend to be for export only...

www.bodegastiopepe.com; tel +34 956 357 016; C/Manuel María González, 12; tours hourly, book online

02 SANDEMAN

Harvey, Osborne and Sandeman: it's the names that reveal sherry's genesis. Sherry's character might be Spanish but the business is British. Blame Sir Francis Drake for Britain's sherry obsession: the Elizabethan privateer sacked Cádiz in 1587 and made off with 3000 barrels of the local vino. Before long the Brits back home had developed a taste for Spain's fortified wine and a new industry was born. Entrepreneurs such as George Sandeman from Perth, Scotland set up businesses in Jerez and the rest, as they say, is history.

The Sandeman bodega was established in 1790, close to the Royal Andalusian School of Equestrian Art in the heart of the city. With guided tours in multiple languages and a museum, it's a good place to get the background of sherry's story (trivia: Sandeman's logo, the dashing, caped figure, was designed by the Scottish artist George Massiot Brown). *www.sandeman.com; tel +34 675 647 177; C/Pizarro 10, Jerez de la Frontera; see website for tour details*

03 BODEGAS TRADICIÓN

In the cellar of Bodegas Tradición, boutique producer of rare, aged sherries, amid the gloom of 625L casks of American oak, the smell of sherry is overwhelming. In the tasting room, among artworks by Goya and Velasquez and ceramic tiles painted by an eight-year-old Picasso, visitors seek out the unusual Palo Cortado, a nutty, smoky style lying between an Amontillado and Oloroso. The bodega's own full-bodied Oloroso combines vanilla, ginger, and the smell of Christmas cake.

Sherry, more than any other wine, requires human intervention at every step, and José Blandino, the cellar master at Bodegas Tradición, who has worked in the industry for almost five decades, treats his sherries like his own offspring. 'When we start out, the wines are like little children. We have to teach them how to grow, to help them through the varying stages of getting older. It takes a lot of time and hard work, so that they can become adults we can be proud of.'

But even José admits that each person's response to the final product is as important, and as personal as his own role in the process. 'We can show people what to look for. But the only standard that really matters is whether or not you like it.' *www .bodegastradicion.es; tel +34 956 16 86 28; C/de los Cordobeses, 3, Jerez de la Frontera; tours by appointment*

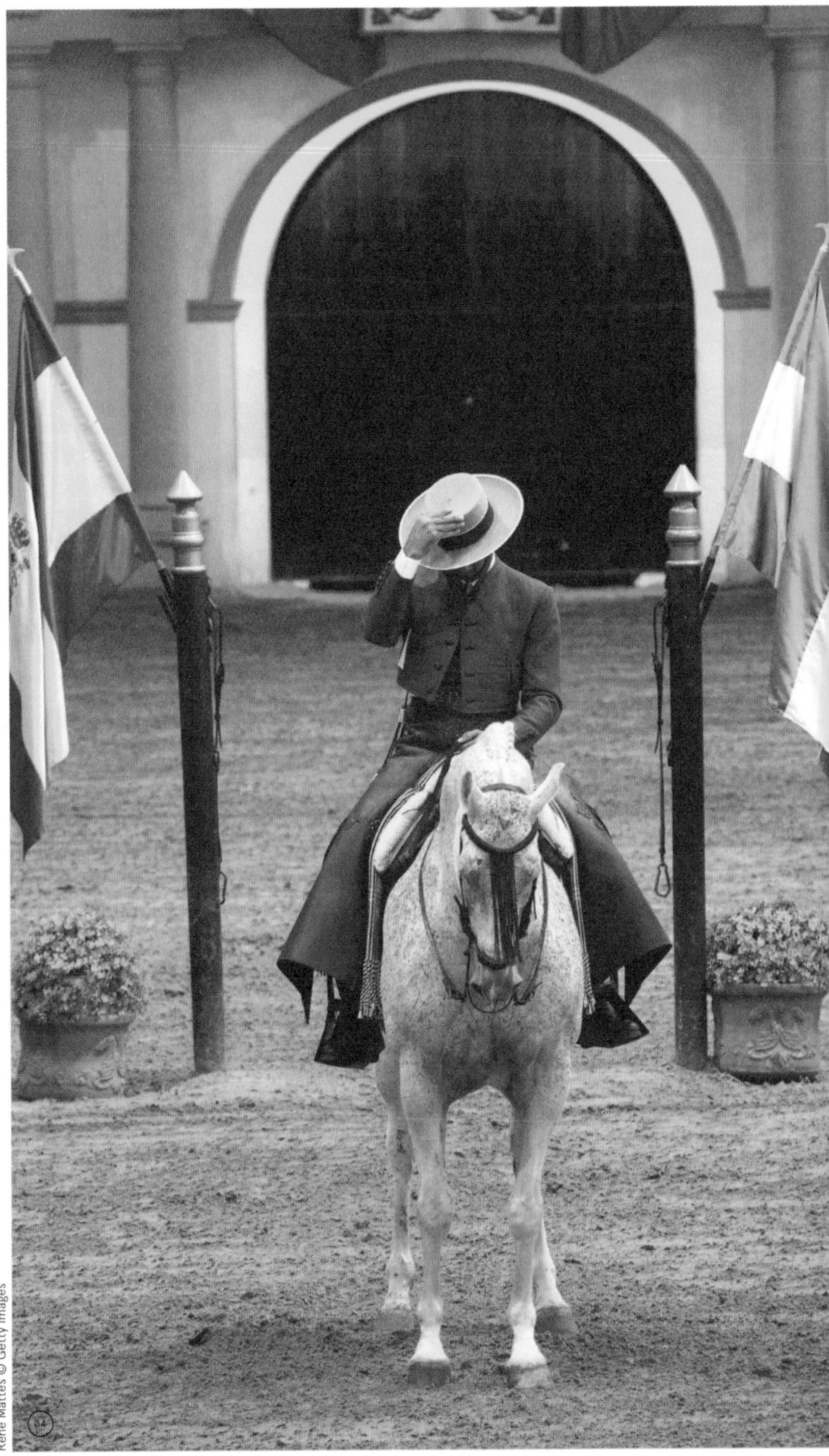
04

VIÑA POMAL
RIOJA
GAMBAS ... 18
LANGOSTINOS .. 18
ALMEJAS ... 12
CHOCOS 10
PRESA Ib ... 12
Solomillo Ib ... 11
Boquerones 6
05

04 OSBORNE MORA

This handsome bodega is in the most southern point of the Sherry Triangle and specialises in the light Fino Quinta. It's a mouthwatering place to learn about food-matching with sherry – the company has a division dedicated to producing jamón ibérico from free-ranging, acorn-fed black Iberian pigs.

Visitors can also learn about the *solera* system for blending sherries, in which wine of varying ages is decanted from one barrel to another, keeping barrels filled with younger wine that feeds the *flor* – this is what the stack of barrels in the cellar is all about. It means that sherry ageing is only an average; a sherry from a *solera* started ten years ago will have ten-year-old wine in it but also younger wine. Some *soleras* can be very old; a glass of Osborne's superb Solera India Olorosa helps you figure it out. *www.osborne.es; tel +34 956 869 100; C/los Moros, El Puerto de Santa Maria; email visitas.bodegas@osborne.es*

05 DELGADO ZULETA

It's a tough gig being a sherry grape. The three varieties permitted in the production of sherry are Palomino, Moscatel and Pedro Ximénez; all have to cope with summer temperatures touching 40°C (104°F), their metres of roots driving deep down into the *albariza* soil – limestone – in the search for water. At Delgado Zuleta, those grapes are turned into Manzanilla, a speciality of Sanlúcar de Barrameda, where the *flor* grows thickest and the saline tang is enhanced by the cool seaside climate. *www.delgadozuleta.com; tel +34 956 360 543; Av de Rocío Jurado, Sanlúcar de Barrameda; visits by appointment*

Yadid Levy © Lonely Planet

05 Tapas time

ESSENTIAL INFORMATION

WHERE TO STAY

HOTEL CASA GRANDE

This hotel occupies a carefully restored 1920s mansion, with rooms spread over three floors and set around a patio or beside the roof terrace, which has views of Jerez's roofline. Manager Monika Schroeder is a mine of information about Jerez. *www.hotelcasagrande.eu; tel 956 34 50 70; Plaza de las Angustias, 3, Jerez*

WHERE TO EAT

LA CARBONA

Dishes at this family-friendly restaurant in Jerez are paired with different sherries. Inventive dishes use the best of Spanish ingredients, from spicy chistorra sausage from Navarra to langoustines from Sanlúcar de Barrameda. It's a trick that works well for both partners; sherry cooking classes with chef Javier Munoz are available if you want to learn more. *www.lacarbona.com; tel +34 956 34 74 75; C/San Francisco de Paula, 2*

WHAT TO DO

In Jerez, the Royal Andalusian School of Equestrian Art has daily performances of prancing horses. But a free day is best spent in shabby-chic Cádiz, one of Europe's oldest continuously inhabited settlements. Romantic, mysterious, much-contested over the ages, Cádiz intoxicates with its edgy aura. *www.realescuela.org; www.cadizturismo.com*

CELEBRATIONS

In most wine-growing regions of Spain, the annual grape harvest is celebrated with a Fiesta de la Vendimia. In Jerez it kicks off on 8 September, the feast of the Nativity of Our Lady. Expect processions of vine-bedecked carts, some flamenco and fireworks. No other Spanish city celebrates Carnaval with as much fervour as Cádiz, where it becomes a 10-day singing, dancing and drinking fancy-dress party spanning two weeks in February.

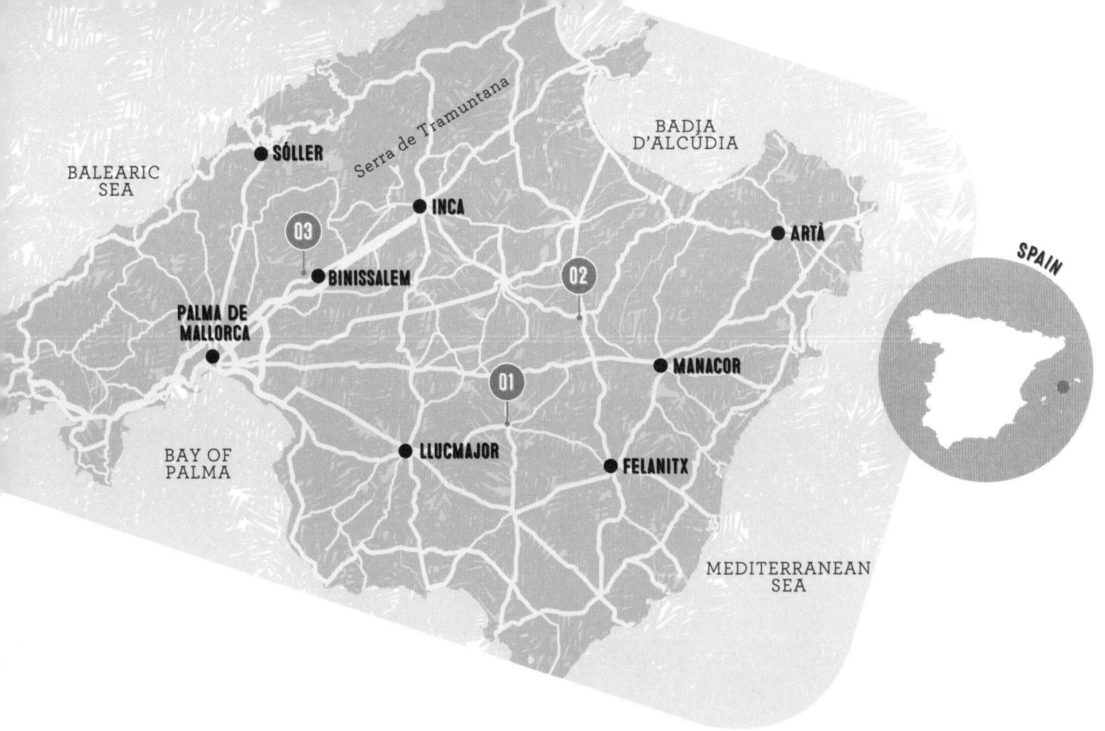

BALEARIC SEA
SÓLLER
Serra de Tramuntana
BADIA D'ALCÚDIA
INCA
ARTÀ
03
BINISSALEM
02
PALMA DE MALLORCA
MANACOR
01
LLUCMAJOR
FELANITX
BAY OF PALMA
MEDITERRANEAN SEA
SPAIN

Gonzalo Azumendi © Getty Images

[Spain]

MALLORCA

Sun, sea, sand and surprisingly good wines: head inland and discover this holiday isle's wines, made in the shadow of the Serra de Tramuntana and on the central plains.

Mallorca, the largest of Spain's Balearic islands, has been a wildly popular holiday destination for millions of northern Europeans for almost a century – but it has survived this invasion and prospered. A group of earlier invaders – the Romans – were evicted from the Mediterranean island in AD425, leaving behind two things: vines and olive trees. A fair price, perhaps.

Since wine has been part of the landscape of this enchanting island for more than 2500 years you can expect some old vines; grapes are routinely harvested from 60-year old plants in Mallorca's two *Denominació d'Origen* (DO) zones, Binissalem and Plà i Llevant (the central plain). Most Mallorcan bodegas (anything from a warehouse to a stone cellar) concentrate on the island's traditional grape varieties: Callet, Manto Negra and Prensal Blanc. These are typically pepped up with dashes of Cabernet, Merlot or Shiraz. Malvasia, an ancient grape, is making a comeback on the terraced vineyards of the Serra de Tramuntana mountain range, which runs along the west edge of the island and is the first land to meet incoming weather fronts.

Wine touring on Mallorca has two great joys: firstly, most of the bodegas are within a short drive of one another. Mallorca is a small island and you're never more than a half an hour from a good restaurant, a beach or a sensational view. And, secondly, the vast majority of the island's bodegas are family-run businesses, often located in old sandstone buildings in the centre of towns. If you meet the families who make the wine you'll catch some of their passion for this island and its food, wine, traditions and landscapes. The island has long produced rough-and-ready wines – dark and unfiltered from sun-baked vineyards – but with the combination of decades of tradition and the ambition of younger generations, Mallorcan wine is becoming more sophisticated. Only minuscule quantities are exported, which is all the more reason to investigate them in person.

GET THERE
The island capital, Palma, receives flights from all over Europe. There's also a slow ferry from mainland Spain

01 JAUME MESQUIDA

'My job is my passion,' says Bárbara Mesquida, the diminutive winemaker who runs this pioneering winery in the dusty backstreets of Porreres, a market town on the island's central plain. 'My great-grandfather planted the first vines, so they're quite old now. We were the first winery to grow Cabernet, Merlot and Shiraz on the island.' You can see Señor Mesquida's vines on the east edge of town, their roots digging down into the rust-red soil. History is important to Jaume Mesquida; the winery was founded in 1945 and the original cellars can be visited on a tour that also shows off the shiny new steel vats.

Since 2004 the brother-and-sister team of Jaume and Bárbara have invigorated Mallorca's wine industry. 'This is a good time for wine in Mallorca,' she says. 'You cannot compare us to mainland Spain – we have a very special location. Our wines express Mallorca's thin soil and maritime weather.' The thin soil, hot sun and cooling breezes intensify flavours in the indigenous grape varieties.

Jaume Mesquida blends tradition and innovation. 'Results are more important than pedantry,' says Bárbara. 'We have the means to study things that our grandparents couldn't, to see how it is done abroad.' Visiting the bodega is to see ambition bottled. But this doesn't mean losing touch with the endeavours of previous generations; you just have to follow Bárbara down into the cellars to see the winery's heritage, where dusty bottles lie protected by thick stone walls. Above ground, there's a packed calendar of lunches, art shows, concerts and tours of the vineyard and cellar. Bárbara's enthusiasm for her wine and her work is infectious. 'I never know if it is Monday or Friday,' she smiles. And which of Mallorca's many other winemakers does she rate? 'Miquel Oliver in Petra. I like the project.'

www.jaumemesquida.com; tel +34 971 647 106; Carrer Vileta 7, Porreres; 8am–7.30pm Mon–Fri, 9am–1pm Sat

02 MIQUEL OLIVER

Wiping grape juice from her hands, the short, dark-haired figure of Pilar Oliver emerges from the back of her bodega – which looks like an open-fronted garage – to greet her visitors. It's September and harvest time but this family-run winery in central Petra is keen to show off its most successful wines so far: Ses Ferritges, a Callet, Shiraz, Merlot and Cabernet blend; and Aia, an award-winning merlot. This is a hard-working, no-frills bodega. There are no art galleries or gift shops, just serious but enthusiastic winemakers Pilar

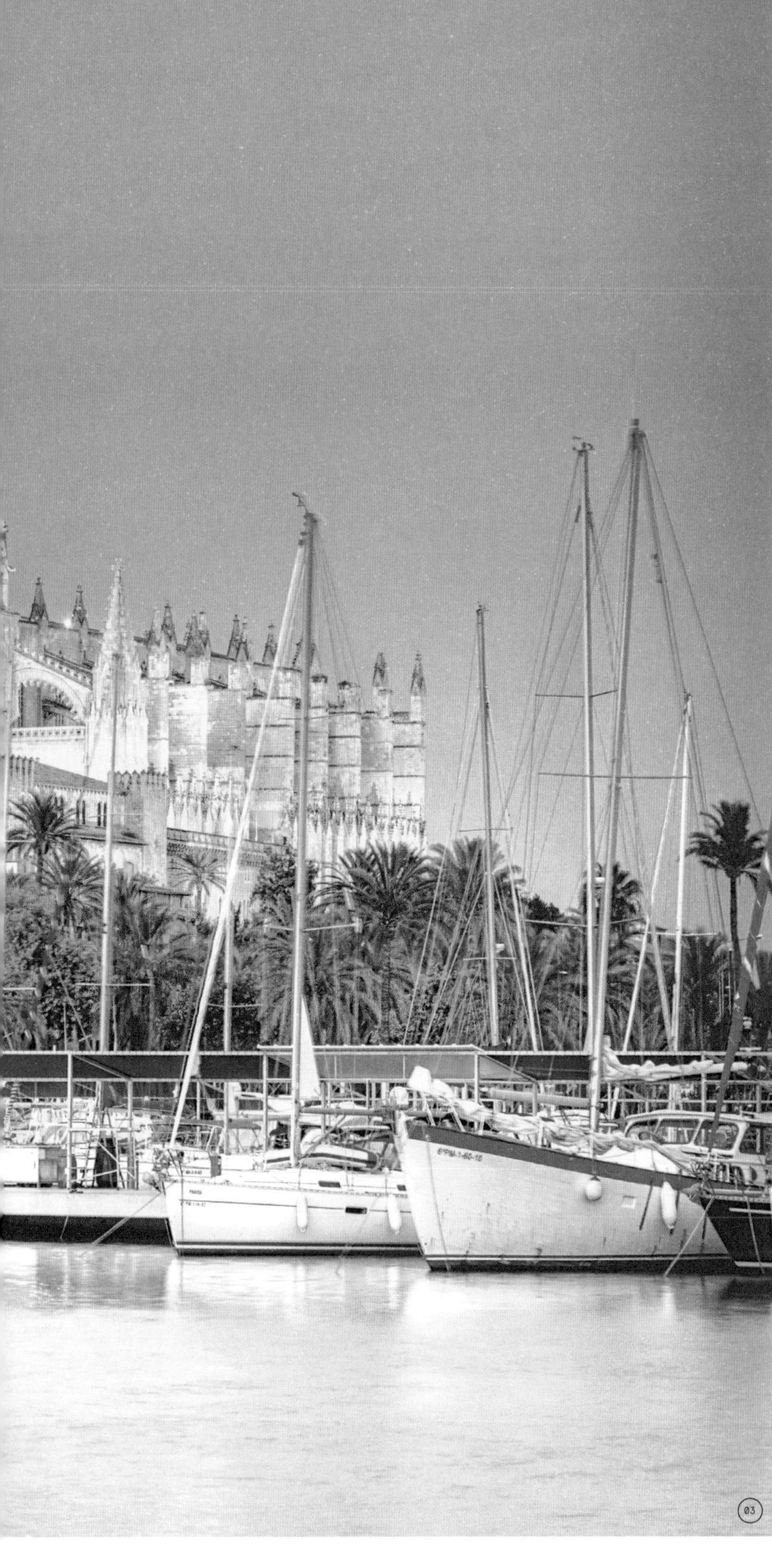

Michele Falzone © Getty Images

01 Vines growing in Binissalem

02 The grape battle of Binissalem

03 Palma's harbour and cathedral

Oliver and Jaume Olivella and their magnificent creations.

Miquel Oliver falls within one of Mallorca's two Protected Designations of Origin (PDO): Vins des Pla i Llevant. This designation covers the plains of central Mallorca, where Miquel Oliver grow their Callet, Manto Negra and Prensal Blanc vines, divided by dry stone walls from fields of almond trees (the trees blossom in February, making the month a spectacular time to visit inland Mallorca).

Petra's claim to fame is that it is the birthplace of Father Junípero Serra, the priest who not only founded the Mexican and Californian missions that became San Diego, Santa Barbara and San Francisco but also introduced vines to California. It is strange to think that Napa Valley's (p294) origins lie in a sleepy Mallorcan town that has changed little since Serra started his walkabout in 1749. Whatever you do, catch the sunset views from his hilltop hermitage, 4km out of town, preferably with a glass of something from Miquel Oliver in your hand. The bodega itself dates from 1868. With Pilar and Jaume raising the next generation of Olivers, the future of one of Mallorca's top wineries is in good, if slightly sticky, hands.
www.miqueloliver.com; tel +34 971 561 117; Carrer Font 26, Petra; 10am–2pm, 3.30am–6.30pm Mon–Fri

03 MACIÀ BATLE

'People thought we were crazy investing in wine rather than a golf

04

course or hotel,' says Ramón Servalls i Batle, director of Macià Batle. 'But they're realising that there's so much more to Mallorca than sun and sand.' As one of the largest and most diversified wineries on the island – its shop stocks olive oils, chocolates and appetisers – Macià Batle stands at the opposite end of the winemaking spectrum to Miquel Oliver. Here wines are blended in a high-tech laboratory (you can watch from behind a glass partition) and bottled by a €500,000 machine.

But for all the trappings of big business, Macià Batle remains a family-owned winery with a friendly welcome for all and a firm attachment to tradition. All Ramón's wines are based on indigenous grape varieties, such as Callet and Manto Negra, hand-picked from vines that can be more than 40 years old. Some vines are so old that they produce just one bunch of grapes. The bodega has been on this site, in the foothills of the Serra de Tramuntana range just south of the wine-producing hub of Binissalem, since 1856 and the vines are managed with local know-how. 'Days are so warm that the grapes need a cooling breeze, so we take away leaves, letting the wind get to the grapes,' says Ramón. After pressing, some of the juice is matured in the crimson-painted cellars under the courtyard, where there's space for 850 barrels. A wide range of wines emerge, including a raspberry-scented rosada, a blanc de blancs and a spicy crianza.
www.maciabatle.com; tel +34 971 140 014; Camí de Coanegra, Santa Maria del Camí; 9am-7pm Mon-Fri mid-Jun-mid-Oct; 9am-6.30pm Mon-Fri, 9.30am-1pm Sat mid-Oct-mid-Jun

04 Cap de Formentor, the tip of the Tramuntana

ESSENTIAL INFORMATION

WHERE TO STAY

HOTEL ES RECÓ DE RANDA
At the foot of the Puig de Randa, Hotel Es Recó de Randa is the best hotel in the Pla i Llevant region, close to Felanitx, Porreres and Petra. The kitchen prides itself on traditional Mallorcan cuisine.
www.esrecoderanda.com; tel +34 971 660 997; Carrer Font, 21, Randa

READ'S HOTEL AND RESTAURANT
This luxurious hotel is in the Binissalem *Protected Designation of Origin*.
www.readshotel.com; tel +34 971 140 261; Carretera Santa Maria del Camí–Alaró

WHERE TO EAT

SIMPLY FOSH
One of Mallorca's top chefs, Marc Fosh's restaurant in Palma's Hotel Convent de la Missio has earned a Michelin star. He has a brasserie, Misa, on C/Can Maçanet.
www.simplyfosh.com; tel +34 971 720 114; Carrer Missió, 7, Palma

ES VERGER
Grab a pew in this rustic restaurant halfway up Àlaro mountain. The shoulder of local lamb – perfect with one of the island's earthy reds – is one of Mallorca's essential dining experiences.
Tel +34 971 182 126; Camí des Castell, Alaró

WHAT TO DO

WALK THE TRAMUNTANA
Walk off the food and wine on the Dry Stone Route, a 170km path along the Tramuntana mountain range, around sandy coves and through aromatic patches of wild herbs and pine forest. It can be broken into eight stages so you can do as much or as little as you like. The project includes several refuges where you can spend the night. Maps and reservations are available from the Consell de Mallorca.
www.conselldemallorca.net; tel +34 971 173 700; Ruta de Pedra Sec

CELEBRATIONS

The best time of year to visit is just after the annual harvest in September when Binissalem's wine festival concludes with the Battle of the Grapes: not a wine tasting but a full-on food fight, so don't wear your best clothes.

Parc Natural de la Serra de Montsant
03 ESCALADEI
SIURANA
POBOLEDA
LA VILELLA BAIXA
LA VILELLA ALTA
02
GRATALLOPS
01
PORERRA
04
05
FALSET
PRADELL DE LA TEIZETA
SPAIN

Courtesy of Clos Mogador

[Spain]

PRIORAT

Meet the pioneers of Spain's most adventurous viticultural region, and experience some of the wildest wines and landscapes in the country.

Less than two hours' drive south of Barcelona lies the Wild West of Spanish wine-making. Bordered by the great escarpment of the Parc Natural de la Serra de Montsant to the north, the compact and rugged region of Priorat was once the sort of place where undrinkable wine was sold by the litre. It was an impoverished corner of Catalonia: the older generation eked out a living and and the young yearned to escape to Barcelona.

Then, in the late 1970s, a band of five long-haired pioneers, including René Barbier of Clos Mogador and Alvaro Palacios, realised the potential of Priorat. For on dry, sun-drenched slopes so steep that mules are still used at harvest time instead of tractors, vines of Carignan and Grenache 70 or 80 years old grew, delving deep into the rock. The gradients are so steep – up to 60° – that the vines struggle to find water; the result is that yields are extremely low and it can take seven to ten plants to make just one bottle of Priorat. These visionary winemakers knew that hard-working vines meant complex, potent wines were waiting to be unleashed. But first they had to tame the alcohol content, which could hit 18%, and tame the land. They succeeded at the first challenge but Priorat's land remains as wild and rugged as ever, a densely beautiful landscape dotted with old villages and tiny parcels of vineyards, most at an altitude of 350-400m but some at 900, even 1000m.

Thirty years after those pioneers turned Priorat's fortunes around, the region now boasts one of Spain's most expensive wines, Alvaro Palacios's L'Ermita. And it's one of world's most interesting wine regions to tour. 'It was a wine region about to disappear,' says René Barbier, 'but now young people are coming back and they're proud to be part of it.'

GET THERE
The closest airport is in Barcelona; it's an easy 2hr drive south to Priorat via Tarragona.

Courtesy of Clos Mogador

01 CLOS MOGADOR

'Welcome to Machu Picchu', says Katja Simon, the winery guide at Clos Mogador, arguably Priorat's most characterful winery. And 'guide' is the right word, for this is more a wine safari than a wine tour. If Priorat is like a bowl then Clos Mogador clings to its rim, just outside the hilltop village of Gratallops. A tour (book in advance) starts in a battered 4WD and the first stop is a geology lesson. The ground high up here consists of shards of schist, a rock known locally as llicorella. Gnarled old Carignan and Grenache vines emerge from this poor soil, which lends Priorat wines their unique mineral edge.

The next lesson is botany, for René Barbier, Clos Mogador's shaggy-bearded founder is obsessed with biodiveristy. He wants wine to be part of the natural environment, which is why 30 types of flowers and wild herbs such as fennel, rosemary and thyme flourish in his vineyards. Almond, olive, fig, cherry and walnut trees punctuate the vines. 'We want nature to be free,' he says (up to a point: wild boar from the forest are kept away from the grapes by electric fences).

Born in Tarragona, Barbier would go hiking in Priorat: 'It was pure, untouched and wild.' Inspired by the hippie movement of the late 1960s and 1970s he returned, as he says, 'to plant the seeds of a better world.' His self-professed hippie philosophy extends to his wine-making. He uses only rainwater for irrigation and plants wheat around the wines, which, when cut, reduces evaporation. Grapes are picked and sorted by hand in September, then pressed using a small cast-iron press, allowing the winemaker to keep tasting the must; just 50,000 bottles are produced in an average year. And although he's one of the forefathers of Priorat, and has studied its vineyards and villages for dozens of years, he's still experimenting.

So, how best to enjoy Priorat's big personality? It's a wine that benefits from being decanted; these are not light wines and, once allowed to breathe, a classic Priorat blend of Grenache, Carignan with a dash of Shiraz and Cabernet Sauvignon, such as Clos Mogador's eponymous wine, will reveal a smoky swirl of cherries, cedar and herbs. 'Wine is all about passion and patience,' says René, 'what I want is for what you have in your glass to be what you see outside.'

www.closmogador.com; tel +34 977 839 171; Camí Manyetes, Gratallops; book online for winery tours

02 BUIL & GINÉ

This hilltop complex on the road north out of Gratallops is one of the most modern wineries in Priorat, founded by local Xavi Buil in 1998. Although it's set close to Alvaro Palacios' famous L'Ermita vineyard, source of Priorat's most exclusive single-estate wine, the approach at Buil & Giné is far more varied, with a dozen different types of wine produced including rosé and dry whites. Above the tasting room is a restaurant with views towards the picturesque village of la Vilella Baixa.

www.builgine.com; tel +34 977 839 810; Carretera Gratallops-la Vilella Baixa, km11.5; tours by appointment

03 CELLERS DE SCALA DEI

Continuing northeast from la Vilella Baixa to the quiet town of Escaladei, you'll reach one of the oldest wineries in Priorat. Monks introduced vines to the region in the 12th century and at this monastery, founded in 1194, you can tour the cellars in which wines are still aged. The monks seem to have taken the responsibility of wine-making very seriously and by 1263 they had produced a manual

noting the varieties that grew best (Grenache and Mataró, also known as Mourvèdre). Places to eat here include El Rebast de la Cortoixa.
www.cellersdescaladei.com; tel 977 827 027; Rambla Cartoix, Escaladei, 12pm-5 (Apr-Oct), to 4pm (Nov-Mar) Mon-Fri; 10am-12pm, 1.30pm-5 (Apr-Oct); 1.30pm-4.30 (Nov-Mar) Sat-Sun

04 CLOS DOMENIC

The drive to Porrera is spectacular, crossing a high plateau from where you can watch the weather rolling across Priorat. Porrera is home to a few smaller wineries, including the family-run Clos Domenic, which produces only 13,000 bottles with their own grapes. Its vineyards and wines are divided into Vinyes Baixes (low) and Vinyes Altes (high), each using differing proportions of Carignan and Grenache, but the results are often impressive.
Tel +34 977 828 215; Carrer Prat de la Riba, Porrera, call for tastings

05 EL CELLER COOPERATIVA DE FALSET

Back in Falset, stop by the town's wine cooperative, built in 1919 by architect Cèsar Martinell, a disciple of Gaudì, though eschewing his flourishes for a cathedral-inspired Modernism. A guided tour at midday on Wednesday and Sunday (March to December) uses an actor to usher visitors through a history of winemaking in the region. In November and December there is also an interesting series of tastings from the vats and the barrels to introduce your senses to the different stages of the process.
Tel +34 977 830 105; Carrer Miquel Barceló, 31, Falset; closed Mon & Jan-Mar. Reservations required for tours

01 Priorat from Clos Mogador

02 Vines at Clos Mogador

ESSENTIAL INFORMATION

WHERE TO STAY

There's not a huge choice of accommodation in the region but many of the larger country houses have been converted to boutique hotels, such as Cal Porrerà in Porrera and Cal Llop in Gratallops.

CAL PORRERÀ

This country house is close to Plaça de l'Església in the centre of Porrera, on the east side of the region.
www.calporrera.com; tel +34 977 828 310

CAL LLOP

Cosy Cal Llop in the hilltop village of Gratallops has balconies overlooking Priorat's vine terraces.
www.cal-llop.com; tel +34 977 83 95 02;

WHERE TO EAT

Several good restaurants are found in Gratallops, including Restaurant Cellers de Gratallops on Career del Piró.

CELLER DE L'ASPIC

Chef Toni Bru cooks updated Catalan classics at this Falset fixture. The wine list is notably good.
www.cellerdelaspic.com; tel +34 977 831 246; Miquel Barceló 31, Falset

WHAT TO DO

Pack your hiking boots because Priorat is laced with outstanding trails, especially to the north, along the edge of the Parc Natural de la Serra de Montsant. From an eyrie at the top of this wall of rock you look out over the whole of Priorat's amphitheatre. A network of *via ferrata* cables aids novice climbers. Book guides and pick up maps from the visitor centre in La Morrera de Montsant.

It's not just climbers who head to the cliffs in the northeast of the region around Siurana, for this lost-in-time clifftop village is a fabulous place to explore and enjoy the views from the restaurant.

CELEBRATIONS

In early May the annual wine fair takes over Falset for a week, with more than 60 producers showcasing their wines, including Clos Mogador and Alvaro Palacios. It's a hugely sociable event, with a program of events plus organised activities for children. A Bus de Vi (wine bus) runs from Tarragona and Reus to Falset.
www.firadelvi.org

SPAIN
VILANOVA DE AROUSA
ATLANTIC OCEAN
Umia River
02
CASAL DO RÍO
PONTE ARNELAS
03
01
CAMBADOS
Umia River
Courtesy of Martín Códax

[Spain]

RÍAS BAIXAS

For sea, shellfish and a very special wine, make a pilgrimage to this rugged nugget of Galicia.

Perched just above Portugal, on the Iberian peninsula's northwest coast, Galicia is a corner of Spain with a rich sea-faring tradition and sought-after seafood. All year round its granite headlands are blasted by the Atlantic's wind and waves, but in between those rock bulwarks lie sheltered inlets – or rías. It is these that lend their name to Galicia's Rías Baixas wine region, the most interesting of the five *Denominacion de Origen* (DO) regions in Galicia.

They do things differently in Galicia. Here, vines are suspended 2m above the ground from granite pillars, all the better to gain extra ventilation in this humid region and prevent mould. And the grapes that hang from these canopies are also a little bit special. Stony yet fruity, the Albariño grape that grows in Rías Baixas produces a white wine that is a mesmerising alternative to Chablis (Chardonnay) and Sauvignon Blanc – and this is its heartland.

This grape is the key to how Rías Baixas' white wines manage to meld the savoury, saline flavours of their surroundings with a Viognier-like fruitiness to mouthwatering effect. On a sunny afternoon, there is no better companion to a plate of seafood – oysters and octopus are the obvious options but don't fear the local speciality of *percebes* (lobster-flavoured goose barnacles, harvested from cliffs in between crashing waves). Outside Galicia, spicy Asian food is another great partner for Albariño.

Many visitors to Galicia arrive on foot, having made the pilgrimage to Santiago de Compostela on the Way of St James. Rías Baixas is a couple of hours' drive south of the Galician capital, and the revitalising coastal setting, with its wide and sheltered beaches, backed by aromatic pine and eucalypt forests in the interior, appeals to footsore pilgrims and wine-seeking sybarites alike.

GET THERE
The closest international airport is at Santiago de Compostela. It's an hour's drive south to Cambados.

Courtesy of Pazo de Señorans

01 MARTÍN CÓDAX

From the tasting terrace at Martín Códax, high on a hilltop behind Cambados, visitors enjoy views of the ocean, including the mussel and oyster beds in the bay that produce the ideal accompaniment to its white wines.

It's all about Albariño at this co-operative, where 280 members pool harvests every September and October from their small plots. A great way to understand the grape is to book a tasting. Four wines are produced: Organistrum (the label is of the cathedral in Santiago de Compostela) is the only Albariño aged in French oak and is bottled in small batches. You should get fresh citrus and apples from this one. Burgans has the same acidity but more sugar, so more nectarines, melon and soft fruit come through in the flavour. Lias is more rounded and softer. Finally, Gallecia is made when it has been a hot and dry season. Grapes are picked late, after botrytis has set in, creating a golden colour with raisin and fig jam flavours but retaining a fresh edge. These wines are all made from the same grape but are deliciously different.

www.martincodax.com; tel +34 986 526 040; Burgáns 91; tours 11am, 12pm, 1pm Mon-Sat; 5pm, 6pm, 7pm Mon-Fri

02 PAZO DE SEÑORANS

You can tell the importance of a property by the size of the *horreo* - and the *horreo* at Pazo de Señorans has 10 pillars per side. It's a big one. A *horreo* is the outdoor food store for a house, raised above the ground to stop vermin getting in. The *horreo* at Pazo de Señorans indicates that this was a wealthy estate, yet in the 1970s the building was a ruin. It was restored by Marisol Bueno and Javier Mareque and, now at the heart of the Rías Baixas DO, it celebrated its 25th anniversary in 2015. Before you try the wine, the *pazo* (country house) itself is a fascinating place to explore: pagan and Christian symbols above the gate show typically pragmatic loyalties; a small chapel is decorated with palm trees, a symbol of travelling the world. And there's also a panic room where Edward, the last king of Portugal, is thought to have hidden.

In Galicia, explains Javier Izurieta Romero, land was more important than money. 'Family inheritances split each parcel of land so none could be sold without the agreement of all. Each family had its own vines, its own pig and a cow. They optimised the land, growing potatoes beneath the vines.' The result is that Pazo de

'The best way to see a place is through its wine.'

–Javier Izurieta Romero, Pazo de Señorans

Senorans is supplied with grapes by 163 growers from 500 parcels of land. The sugar and acidity of the grapes is measured at each. 'If you do a good job in the vineyard you can leave the wine alone,' says Javier.

The winemaking is similarly simple, with no oak used. Just two wines are made by winemaker Anna Quintella, but the difference between the years is striking. 'Albariño is not just a wine to drink young and cold,' explains Javier. As it ages, the flavours mellow from citrus and green apple (and, some years, rose petals) to nectarines and apricots, becoming more buttery. After pressing, the skins of the grapes are used to make aguardiente, a punchy aperitif, in a distillery on the property. Nothing goes to waste in Galicia. *www.pazodesenorans.com; tel +34 986 715 373; Lugar Vilanoviña, Meis, tours and tastings by appointment*

03 BODEGAS DEL PALACIO DE FEFIÑANES

Hidden in the granite cloisters of this vast, austere palace in the heart of Cambados, this winery was one of the earliest producers of wine in Rías Baixas. The surrounding stone is a clue to Albariño's savoury edge: the mineral-rich, granitic soil. As owner Juan Gil de Araújo puts it: 'a wine must be loyal to its origins.' *www.fefinanes.com; tel +34 986 542 204; Plaza de Fefiñanes, tours by appointment*

01 Martín Códax

02 Pazo de Senorans

ESSENTIAL INFORMATION

WHERE TO STAY

The coastal town of Cambados is the best base for exploring the Salnes sub-region. Tip: if you stay in the local city of Pontevedra ensure that your hotel has allocated parking.

PARADOR DE CAMBADOS

Set in an ancestral country house in the old quarter of Cambados, this parador has grand bedrooms (some with air-conditioning), a restaurant serving Galician specialities, and sea views from the promenade. *www.parador.es; tel +34 986 542 250; Paseo Calzada, Cambados*

WHERE TO EAT

There are several restaurants on Rua Albergue, Rua Real and Rua Principe in Cambados. In Pontevedra, many of the restaurants are concentrated in the streets of the old town.

EIRADO DA LEÑA

Enjoy a deliciously creative culinary experience in an intimate little stone-walled restaurant, set with white linen and fresh flowers. The set menu at lunch and dinner features four beautifully present courses, served with a smile. *www.eiradoeventos.com; tel +34 986 860 225; Praza da Leña, Pontevedra*

WHAT TO DO

If you're not ready for the Way of St James, a pilgrimage/hiking route across the Pyrenees that winds up in Santiago de Compostela, the Ruta de la Camelia is a gentler, more floral, alternative. This route follows the southern coast of Galicia, taking in 11 ornamental gardens. Two that are close to Pontevedra are Pazo de Quinteiro da Cruz, which has no fewer than 1500 varieties of camellia, and the grand estate of Pazo de Rubiáns. *www.pazoquinteiro-dacruz.es*

CELEBRATIONS

On the first Sunday of August, Cambados hosts its annual wine festival, which is Albariño's day in the sun. The fiesta was born out of a contest between local winemakers but is much more than that today, with parades, live music at night and the naming of the year's winning wines.

01

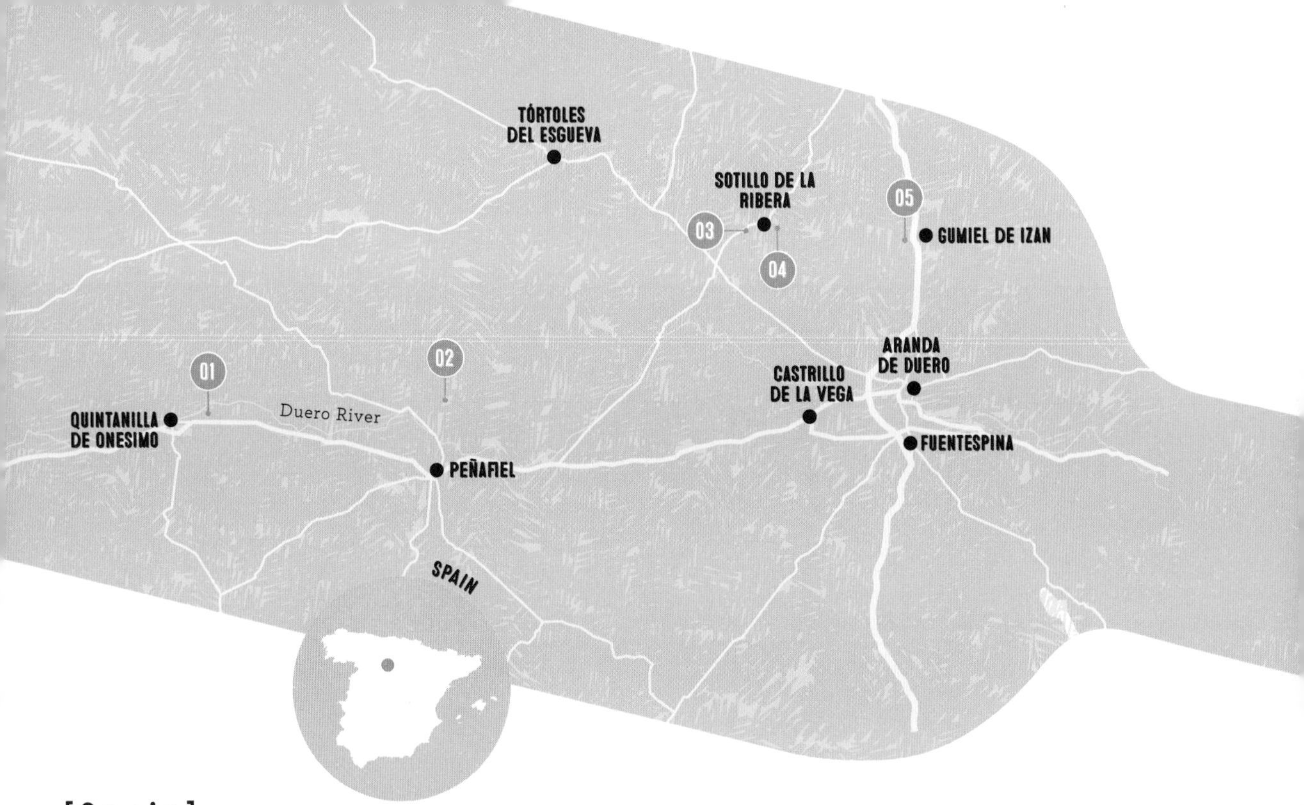

[Spain]

RIBERA DEL DUERO

Enjoy tasty Tempranillo and slow-cooked lamb in the rustic, riverside region that threatens to usurp Rioja as the source of Spain's most sophisticated red wines.

In a country where traditions are slow to change, some of the wineries in Ribera del Duero (as they are in Priorat too) are at the frontier of winemaking. Just two hours' drive north of Madrid, what Ribera del Duero lacks in scenic majesty – these are Spain's high plains, lacking the sea views of Rias Baixas, the mountains of Rioja and the rugged valleys of Priorat – it makes up for with its wonderful wines. Violet when young, the Tempranillo – the grape attraction here – is seemingly inkier than Rioja, with a flavour that is less dependent on oak, more open to the winemaker's influence. It was only in 1982 that Ribera del Duero gained a *Denominación de Origen*: 'This is a young DO,' says winemaker Raphael Cherda, 'we can try new things, we're more flexible than Rioja.'

Thanks to its altitude – this is one of the highest wine-growing places in the world – the growing season in Ribera del Duero is short and it can be very hot during the day and very cold at night. But it's this variation, of up to 25°C (77°F) that creates the special growing conditions for incredible wines from vineyards along the Duero river (known as the Douro in Portugal, see p208). Those vineyards include Vega Sicilia, source of Spain's most famous wine, from plots developed by Eloy Lecanda y Chaves in 1864.

Younger Riberas taste fresh with ham and fish. The crianzas, aged for 12 months, are perfect with the local speciality of *lechal al horno* (slow-cooked lamb).

Make no mistake: aside from the wine, this is an undeveloped expanse of Castile and León. The landscape of bare plateaus, sometimes topped with a gimlet-eyed castle, is bleak; the towns and villages functional. But the wines? The wines are wonderful.

GET THERE
Madrid is the closest city to Aranda del Duero, which makes the best base for a weekend.

TÓRTOLES DEL ESGUEVA
SOTILLO DE LA RIBERA
GUMIEL DE IZAN
01 02 03 04 05
QUINTANILLA DE ONESIMO
Duero River
PEÑAFIEL
CASTRILLO DE LA VEGA
ARANDA DE DUERO
FUENTESPINA
SPAIN

⓿① VIÑA MAYOR

Depending on where you're staying, it makes sense to start at the far end of Ribera's 'Golden Mile', a strip of wineries strung along the very fast and straight N-122 (be warned!) before venturing off the beaten path. Vinya Mayor near Peñafiel offers an excellent introduction to the region, with a guided tour of the winery explaining such nuances as the difference between American and French oak barrels (American barrels impart a coffee-like flavour; French barrels have more delicate vanilla notes – it's all about the pores in the wood), before concluding in a glass-fronted tasting room overlooking the orange, iron-rich earth and vines stretching down to the road. Wines are produced in both a classic style and, under the Secreto label, a modern style; a three-hour tasting course with Gema García Muñoz highlights the differences.
www.vina-mayor.com; Carretera Valladolid-Soria km325, Quintanilla de Onésimo; visits by appointment

⓿② COMENGE

'This is nature, but controlled,' says Comenge's winemaker Raphael Cherda. The winery earned its reputation as one of Ribera del Duero's best, thanks to an approach that blends technology with ecology. An example: Comenge uses its own natural yeast – but that yeast was selected as the best for the wine at the University of Madrid (where Raphael studied) from 300 samples taken from its vineyards.

Comenge is a small, young winery, with 32 hectares (79 acres) of Tempranillo vines, half of them surrounding the modern building, which was built by the Comenge family in 1999. At 700-800m, the tasting room and terrace overlooks the valley of the river Duero (the Douro in Portuguese), and in turn is overlooked by Curiel's hilltop castle, now a boutique hotel and no longer an 11th-century defence against the Moors. The ecological approach means that pesticides and herbicides are not used. Instead they let the grass grow (the competition for water is good for the vines) then cut it to insulate the vines later in summer. They're looking for fewer clusters and smaller grapes. 'We don't try to make the same wine every year,' says Raphael. 'It's important to express what happened in the vineyard that year and every year is different. The most important thing is the grape.'

Grapes are picked by hand in autumn; the local Tempranillo is quick to ripen in the warm, sunny days but the cold nights help the wine retain its distinctive colour. Raphael's skill and the winery's attention to detail ensures that the Don Miguel, made from grapes grown in the highest plots, strikes a great balance between fruit and toasty oak flavours; at €25 it's half the price of comparable wines.
www.comenge.com; tel +34 983 880 363; Camino del Castillo, Cuniel de Duero; visits by appointment

01 Ribera del Duero's landscape

02 Horse and cart tours at Comenge

03 Bodegas Ismael Arroyo

Courtesy of Comenge

© Robin Barton

'When I travel, I want to try different things, especially the wines.'

–Alvaro Comenge

03 FÉLIX CALLEJO

It's a family affair at Félix Callejo: father Félix is from Sotillo and returned to the village in 1989 to start his winery, which now employs both his daughters (Beatrice is on the business side, Noelia is a winemaker) and his son José, who studied winemaking at the University of Madrid with Raphael Cherda from Comenge. His mission was not only to make better wine (isn't that the goal of every winemaker?) but to revive an old-fashioned local white grape called Albillo. Previously in this part of Spain, families made their own wines and had their own cellar (see Arroyo, p258). They would plant a small plot with eight or nine vines of white, for eating, around a walnut tree. But the white grapes they didn't eat were mixed with red wine to make 'clarette' - named for its clear colour - which they pressed with their feet. 'Our grandparents' generation,' explains Beatrice, 'drank a lot of wine so it had to be lighter.' Callejo has a 3-hectares (7 acres) ha plot of these white grapes and in 2014 made their second season of this white.

But Félix's main focus is on Tempranillo, which is grown on limestone across 23 plots within 3km of the winery at a height of 860-930m. This altitude means that it's cold at night, so the local variety of Tempranillo has developed a thicker skin, allowing more flavour to be extracted at pressing. It's not the only advantage this part of Ribera del

Duero enjoys over Rioja: the weather is warmer and drier. Callejo uses only its own grapes; some of the vines are now 25 years old, which go into a gran reserva that is aged for 24 months. 'We do everything by hand,' says Beatrice,' so you get to know the land, to know which plots from which to make which wine.'
www.bodegasfelixcallejo.com; tel +34 947 532 312; Avda. del Cid, km16, Sotillo de la Ribera; tours noon Mon-Sat, book by email

04 BODEGAS ISMAEL ARROYO

To understand even more of Ribera del Duero's history, continue to Arroyo on the other side of Sotillo. As was usual in many of the region's villages, every building in Sotillo had a *lagar*, a cave for storing wine, tunnelled into the hills in the village. Owner Miguel Arroyo explains: 'Villagers would carry wine in goat skins, which were just the right size to lift when full, to the *lagars* after the grapes had been pressed.'

These cellars were built between the 16th century and the 1960s and Arroyo is one of very few wineries still using their family cellar, which is in the hill behind the winery and still used for tastings. 'You can understand how important wine was culturally,' says Miguel, 'because the stones inside were expensive and only otherwise used for palaces and churches.' Inside the narrow cellar it's cool - always 11°C (52°F), winter or summer - and when lit by flickering wall lights, slightly eerie. The family started making its own wine in 1979, breaking away from the local cooperative. They still do things the old-fashioned way: no pesticides and only a natural yeast are used.
tel +34 947 532 309; Los Lagares 71, Sotillo de la Ribera; tours by appointment

05 BODEGAS PORTIA

Wine meets architecture on the road into Aranda de Duero from the north. Here stands Portia, a vast, squat, high-tech winery designed by British architect Norman Foster. It's a stark contrast to wineries such as Arroyo, and one of two star-architect-designed projects in Ribera del Duero; the other is Richard Rogers' Bodegas Protos in Peñafiel. But where Protos resembles a provincial airport, Portia has more of a space-port look to it – which is why we prefer it.
www.bodegasportia.com; tel +34 947 102 700; Antigua Carretera N-1, Gumiel de Izán; Tours: 10am, 12pm & 4pm Mon-Sat, 11am, 1pm Sun. Check in advance in August

© Robin Barton

04 Aranda de Duero

05 Bodegas Portia

06 Wines at Bodegas Ismael Arroyo

ESSENTIAL INFORMATION

WHERE TO STAY

For a city stay, Aranda de Duero makes a good base, with the widest selection of accommodation. Some the bodegas have also started to offer accommodation. Options are limited in the countryside.

HOTEL TORREMILANOS

West of Aranda de Duero, this hotel is based in the Bodegas Peñalba Lopez. Rooms are spacious, the location is good and you can tour the bodega. *www.torremilanos.es; tel +34 947 512 852; Finca Torremilanos, Aranda de Duero*

WHERE TO EAT

EL LAGAR DE ISILLA

In central Aranda de Duero, El Lagar de Isilla is the go-to place for traditional, rib-sticking Ribera cooking – slow-cooked lamb, not many vegetables – that is the perfect companion to the region's wines. The restaurant is part of a winery business that also owns ancient cellars beneath Aranda de Duero that are open to visitors. *www.lagarisilla.es; tel +34 947 510 683; C/Isilla, 18, Aranda de Duero*

MOLINO DE PALACIOS

If it's autumn, fans of fungi should head for this converted water mill in the west of the region. Wild mushrooms are a seasonal obsession in northern Spain and this place does them best. *www.molinodepalacios.com; tel +34 983 880 505; Av de la Constitucion, 16, Peñafiel*

WHAT TO DO

For entertainment – there being little else happening on the *meseta* (plateau) – most locals go to Burgos, which might seem like a typically sombre northern-central Spanish city but has plenty of good restaurants and nightlife along C/de San Juan, C/de la Puebla and C/del Huerto del Rey, northeast of the city's stand-out Gothic cathedral.

CELEBRATIONS

Sonorama is an annual music festival hosted in Aranda de Duero, which must be one of the few pop, rock and dance music festivals in the world to also feature wine-tasting courses and events in the city's underground wine cellers. *sonorama-aranda.com*

01

[Spain]

RIOJA

Hemmed by mountains, provisioned by adventurous Basque cuisine, and home to spectacular wineries, Rioja is arguably the world's most rewarding wine region.

Rioja is Spain's rockstar region, the Jagger to Ribera's Richards. It's moneyed, flamboyant, and fantastic fun for a wild weekend away.

Firstly, it was blessed with natural good looks: the region sits at the foothills of the Cantabrian mountains, beyond which lies the Basque country and such delights as foodie hotspot San Sebastián. The mountains are a barrier to clouds from the north, creating a sunny microclimate. Next, it had perfect timing, hitting the big-time as French wine faltered, and attracting wealthy investors who splashed out on star architects (more on this later), state-of-the-art wineries and winemaking talent. The result is that there are now 540 wineries in Rioja. Not all are open for tastings, but those that do offer some of the most fascinating visitor experiences in the wine world.

GET THERE
Bilbao's international airport is 1½hr north of Logroño by car.

The River Ebro flows eastward through the region, on its way to the Mediterranean, passing through Logroño. This university city is the fulcrum for Rioja's three sub-regions. To the south is Rioja Baja, north of the river is Rioja Alavesa, which includes the fortified hilltop town of Laguardia, and to the west of Logroño is Rioja Alta; the focus of this Wine Trail falls on the latter two regions.

Laguardia, just north of Logroño, makes a good base for exploration. From here it's easy to reach Haro, where Rioja's original winemakers set up shop in the 1800s. Tradition is still at the heart of Rioja's wine but the old-fashioned leathery Tempranillo is fading away in the face of fresh competition from Ribera del Duero. Its wineries range from fascinating timewarps to engineering marvels and contemporary curios.

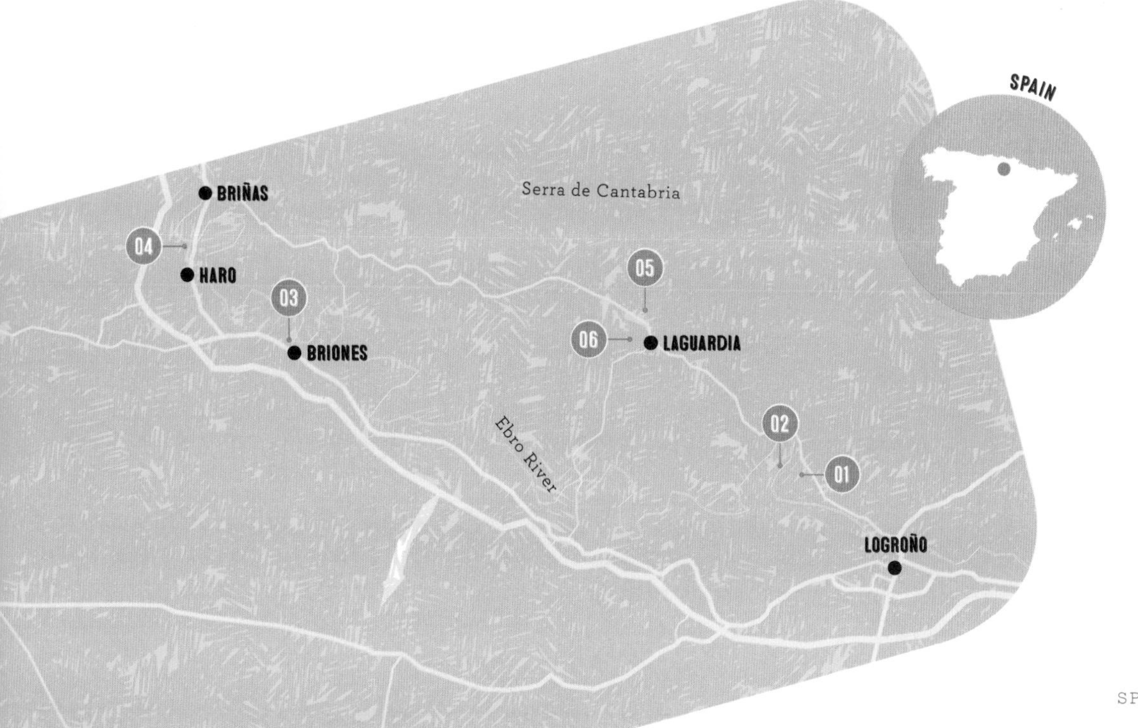

Nassima Rothacker © Lonely Planet

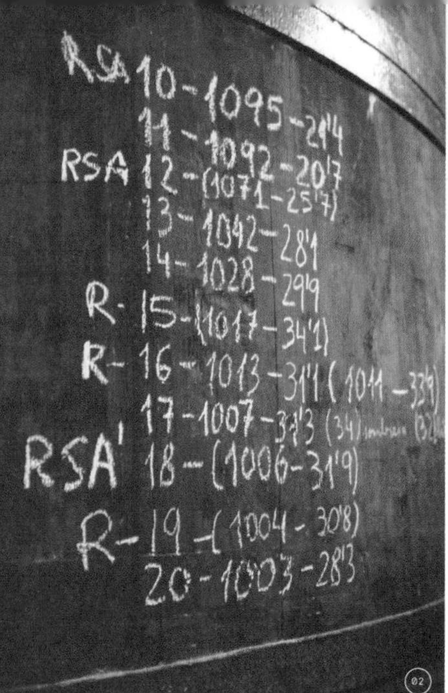

Nassima Rothacker © Lonely Planet Images

© Robin Barton

01 VIÑA REAL

When Viña Real was completed in 2004, after seven years in the making, it was one of Rioja's first modern wineries. And it's an engineering marvel on a grand scale, courtesy of Bordeaux architect Philippe Mazières, whose father was a winemaker. First, a corner was cut out of a table-top mountain between Laguardia and Logroño. Two tunnels were bored 120m deep into the remaining mountain using the machines that excavated the tunnels of Bilbao's metro system. Then a 56m-wide barrel-shaped building was sunk into the levelled-off corner. In the centre of this twin-storey circular room is a revolving crane arm that moves huge vats around, using gravity to pour grape juice from one to another. Head winemaker Maria Larrea monitors everything from a laboratory reached by a walkway. Think winery-meets-Bond-villain-lair.

Beneath the production area is a raw concrete bunker where 2000 barrels of the reserva are stored. In the cave there are 20,000 barrels of the crianza, which is aged for at least two years, one of which must be in a barrel. Viña Real is part of the CVNE group, which started in 1879 when French winemakers relocated to Rioja, bringing with them barrel-ageing techniques. While the group is the largest in Rioja, producing 2.5 million bottles, the winery hasn't lost the personal touch - the Reserva is made from grapes hand-picked from 90-year-old vines.

www.cvne.com; tel +34 941 304 809, Carretera Logroño-Laguardia, km4.8; book visits online

02 CONTINO

Cradled in a loop of the River Ebro, Contino is a chateau-style, single-estate vineyard, part of the CVNE (Compañía Vinícola Norte Espana – the Cune on the bottle is a misprint) empire. But it's a very different experience to Viña Real up on the hill nearby. The stone property, just outside Laserna, is very sheltered – ideal for sitting outside in the shade on old mill stones, listening to the birdsong with a glass of the white Rioja to catch your breath. Contino's vineyards reach all the way down

01 Bodegas Ysios, the water-damaged winery

02 Giant vats at López-Heredia

03 Spanish snacks

04 Harvest at López-Heredia

05 Table wine at López-Heredia

Nassima Rothacker © Lonely Planet Images

to the river Ebro, past ancient olive trees (one is 800 years old).

Seven grape varieties are permitted in Rioja wine, four red and three white: Tempranillo, Grenache (or Garnacha), which adds a bit of weight, Carignan (or Mazuelo) and Graciano are the red grapes. Contino is notable for having developed the rare and delicate Graciano grape and produces a 100% Graciano wine, which is worth comparing with a typical Tempranillo-driven Rioja.
www.visitascvne.com; San Rafael Bidea, Laserna; 9.30am-1.30pm, 3pm-6.30 Mon-Sat

03 VIVANCO

Not satisfied with just building a modern winery on the outskirts of Briones, in the west of Rioja Alta, the Vivanco family added a restaurant and a museum (full name: Vivanco Museum of the Culture of Wine). And it's not a half-hearted effort: with 4000 sq m of space and items from the family's personal collection spanning 8000 years of winemaking, from amphorae to art by Joan Miró, you're guaranteed to learn something about human ingenuity (though you might want to skip a few of the 3000 corkscrews). At weekends there are also tasting courses to explore Vicanco's wine. The winery itself is next to the museum and underground. 'I've always felt that our wines had to tell a story,' says winemaker Rafael Vivanco, but the museum also does a great job of telling it.
www.vivancowineculture.com; tel +34 941 322 323; Carretera Nacional N-232, km442, Briones; see website for opening times & tours

04 LÓPEZ-HEREDIA VILLA TONDONIA

The story of López-Heredia Villa Tondonia is the story of Rioja wine. Founder Rafael López-Heredia was a Basque who lived in Chile but returned to fight for the Spanish king, lost, and was exiled to France. There he started to work for a Bayonne wine merchant. Here he absorbed tips and techniques from French winemakers, who would, for example, de-stem grapes. The disaster of phylloxera, a vine disease that destroyed the French industry, was a blessing for Rioja. People like Raphael returned to Spain bringing new ideas and French winemakers. Recognising the region's similarities with Bordeaux, he settled in Haro in 1877, close to the train station, invested all his money in five vats and began making table wine, selling it fast and cheaply.

Fast forward four generations and one thing has changed at López-Heredia - the wine is outstanding (but not as cheap). Other things haven't changed: they still use a bunch of dried viura vine stalks as a filter, as was traditional; they don't use steel vats, only 100-year old oak vats; and they still make (some) of their own barrels. Everything is still picked by hand and carried in baskets then lightweight poplar barrels.

A tour begins in a modern annex designed by Zaha Hadid to resemble a wine decanter. But the real interest lies in the old winery next door. Here, the hand-excavated wine gallery dates from 1890 and extends all the way back to the river – workers were given 4L of wine a day, two of which they could drink in the winery. In its darker corners the cave is coated with penicillium, a white furry mould, which helps keep the temperature constant by absorbing humidity. Back out in the light of the cooperage and the barrel builder is repairing the winery's collection of 225L American oak barrels – he makes them a bit thicker so they last up to 25 years.

The last stop is in the tasting room to sample López-Heredia's Viña Bosconia, a five-year-old Burgundy style wine, and Viña Tondonia, a six year-old Bordeaux style wine. Both are a blend of mostly Tempranillo with some Grenache and a little Graciano. As you'd expect, after more than a century of practice, both are sublime.
www.lopezdeheredia.com; tel +34 941 310 244; Avenida de Vizcaya, 3, Haro; book visits Mon-Sat in advance

Courtesy of Cune

06 The barrel cellar at Viña Real

07 San Vicente de la Sonsierra, La Rioja

08 Cooper at work, López-Heredia

09 Hotel Marques de Riscal

Nassima Rothacker © Lonely Planet Images

05 BODEGAS RUIZ DE VIÑASPRE

This family owned winery is set in the foothills between Laguardia and the Cantabrian mountains to the north (you can see it from Laguardia's walls).

You'll also notice its neighbour, Bodegas Ysios, one of Rioja's most iconic wineries, thanks to its spectacular wave-like roof, designed by Spanish architect Santiago Calatrava to reflect the mountain backdrop. Sadly, the roof proved to be less waterproof than desired, which has disrupted Ysios' work and kept its lawyers busy. Ruiz de Viñaspre is a smaller operation, with all the grapes (100% Tempranillo) coming from the winery's own vineyards.
www.bodegaruizdevinaspre.com; tel +34 945 600 626; Camino de la Hoya, Laguardia; 9am-1pm Mon-Sat (by appointment)

06 CASA PRIMICIA

According to legend, King Sancho Abarca of Navarra once climbed a hill at the foot of the Cantabrian mountains, which overlooked the River Ebro and what is now Rioja. Recognising the hill's strategic importance, a few months later he founded La Guardia de Navarra on its top. The date was 908. More than a thousand years later, and Laguardia offers a (very popular) glimpse into the past. The hill is riddled with unexplored tunnels and blessed with some beautiful architecture, including the church of Santa Maria de los Reyes.

But for wine lovers, the Casa Primicia is just as interesting. The 'first house' is the oldest property in the medieval hamlet, dating from the 15th century. It was here that grapes taxed from the local area were stored. From the 16th century, wine was made on the site and the restoration of the building, which owner Julián Madrid began in 2006, has revealed how it was done. And the tunnels that form a sort of subterranean twin town turn out to be perfect cellars for storing Bodegas Casa Primicia's own wines. Tours include tastings, and tours of the building and the vineyards.
www.casaprimicia.com; tel +34 945 600 256; C/Páganos 78, Laguardia; tours Mon-Thu

ESSENTIAL INFORMATION

WHERE TO STAY

If you're based in the walled hilltop town of Laguardia you'll be able to reach all the featured wineries easily. The town is popular with tourists but it's easy to escape to Logroño for better value meals. There are several hotels inside Laguardia, depending on your budget.

09

Nassima Rothacker © Lonely Planet Images

CASA RURAL ERLETXE
This guesthouse, in the thick walls of the town, is hosted by María Arrate Aguirre, who makes delicious homemade breakfasts including honey from her bees stationed up in the Cantabrian hills.
www.erletxe.com; tel +34 945 621 015, Rua Mayor de Peralta 24-26, Laguardia

MARQUES DE RISCAL
For a less understated stay, try the Marques de Riscal hotel. The Frank Gehry-designed property, a cascade of ribbons of steel, lies between Logroño and Haro.
www.hotel-marquesderiscal.com

WHERE TO EAT

LA TAVINA
This hip wine club in Logroño serves 60 wines by the glass (at shop prices) and modern tapas plates. In winter it hosts group tastings and courses.
www.latavina.com; tel +34 941 102 300; C/Laurel 2, Logroño

RESTAURANTE GARIMOTXEA
Further afield, explore the National Park Izki and lunch at this eatery in Urturi, where the locally sourced menu features dishes such as aubergines stuffed with wild mushrooms, duck leg confit in orange, and homemade yoghurt with wild berries.
Tel +34 945 37 81 21

WHAT TO DO

An extended food and wine pilgrimage has to take in San Sebastián, one of Europe's most delightful coastal cities and the epicentre of cutting-edge gastronomy in Spain. The city has hundreds of bars serving pinxtos, the Basque equivalent of tapas, and also a constellation of garlanded restaurants such as Arzak.

With the mountains so close, pack a pair of hiking boots (or cycling shoes) and head into the hills on one of the many signposted hikes.

CELEBRATIONS

If you're in the area in October, the annual mushroom festival at Ezcaray is a treat for fungi fans, with autumn's bounty on display, expert talks, guided mushroom-picking walks in the Cantabrian mountains and lots of tastings in village square. More famous is the annual Batalla del Vino (wine fight – really) in Haro at the end of June. The fiesta begins on the night of 28 June with a street party then the battle commences the following morning.
www.batalladelvino.com

01

[Turkey]

THRACE

Follow this new wine route from Edirne to the shore of the Dardanelles to sample some of Turkey's most exciting vintages.

Vines have been cultivated in Thrace (Trakya) since ancient times. Homer wrote about the honey-sweet black wine produced here in his *Iliad*, and generations of local farmers have capitalised on the mineral-laden soil, relatively flat geography and benign climate of the area to grow grapes for wine and spirit (particularly *rakı*) production. In recent years, a number of local boutique wineries have built reputations for their refined vintages featuring French and Turkish varietals.

Chief among these are the 12 vineyards that together form the Thracian Wine Route (*Trakya Bağ Rotası*), which starts near the former Ottoman capital of Edirne, 240km north-west of İstanbul, and meanders through four lush regions – Kırklareli, Tekirdağ, Şarköy and Gelibolu – for approximately 400km (250 miles), ending in the town of Eceabat on the shore of the Dardanelles. The route passes through dense forest, past ancient ruins and alongside three major waterways – the Sea of Marmara, the Gulf of Saros and the Dardanelles Strait – providing plenty of scenery to admire and historic sights to visit. A number of the vineyards have restaurants and at least one offers accommodation – more are likely to follow suit in the near future. All charge a modest fee for tastings.

White grapes thrive here, and wineries such as Arcadia and Suvla are producing examples with balanced acidity and rich, fruity aromas that have the international wine community sitting up and taking notice. The smaller operations tend to concentrate on red varietals, particularly Cabernet Sauvignon, and the quality of these is improving as each year goes by. The best time to visit is from late April, when the buds 'break', to the end of October, when the harvest is completed. As well as the wineries mentioned here, Vino Dessera, Barel, Barbare, Melen and Gülor welcome visitors. See www.thracewineroute.com for details.

GET THERE
Istanbul Atatürk is the nearest major airport, 160km from Lüleburgaz. Car hire is available.

Courtesy of Kalpak

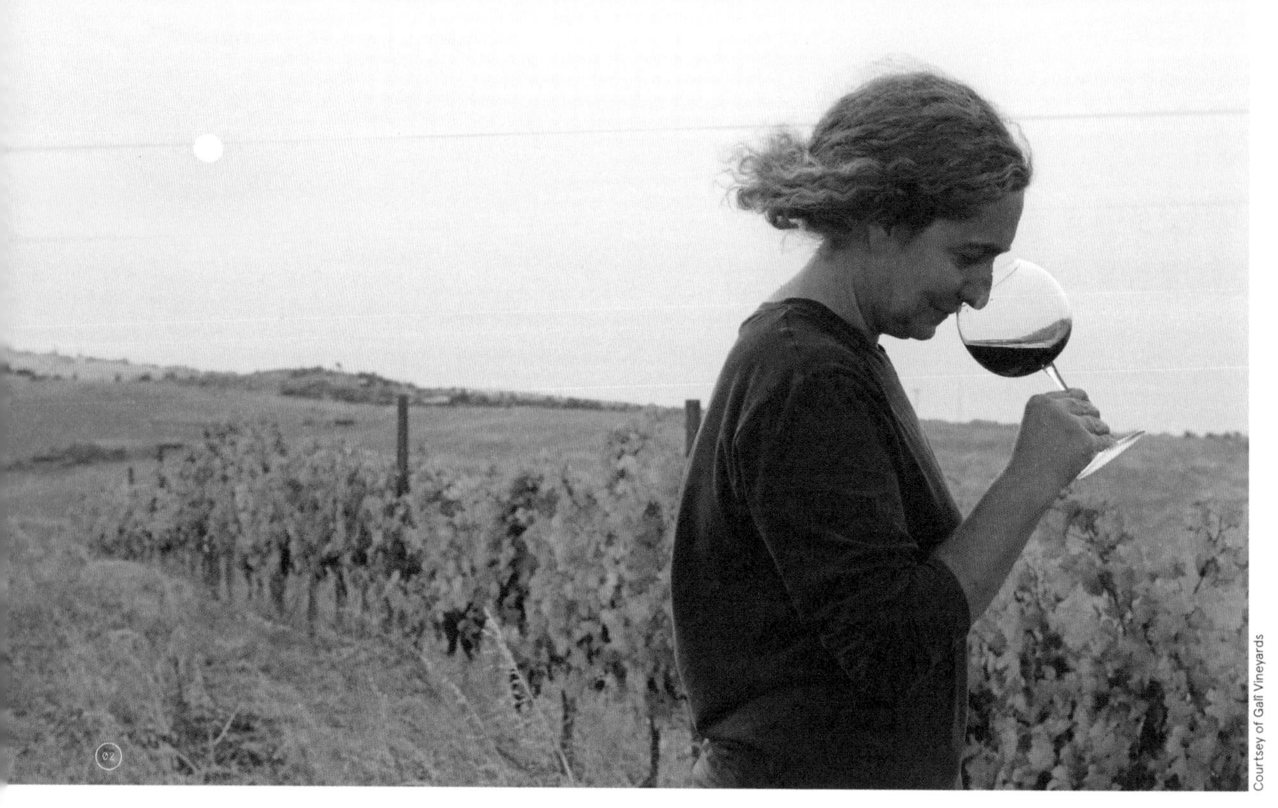
Courtsey of Gali Vineyards

01 ARCADIA VINEYARDS

Taking its name from the nearby town of Lüleburgaz, known as Arcadiopolis in ancient times, this decade-old operation is a labour of love by business entrepreneur, art collector and filmmaker Özcan Arca and his film-producing daughter Zeynep. They work hard to realise what Zeynep calls 'the forgotten potential of Northern Thrace for world-class *terroir* wines'.

Consulting oenologist Michel Salgues trained in France and worked at the Roederer estate in California for many years, and under his influence Arcadia is producing refined hand-harvested wines including a Sauvignon Gris, a Cabernet Franc and two blends: the GRI (Sauvignon Gris and Pinot Gris) and A Blend (Cabernet Sauvignon and Cabernet Franc). These can be tasted in the winery building or over lunch in the estate restaurant (May to November only). There's even a boutique hotel on site for those keen to overnight in this idyllic corner of Kırklareli.

www.arcadiavineyards.com; tel +90 533-514 1490; Lüleburgaz; 9am-5.30pm daily Dec-Apr, Sat & Sun May-Nov by appointment

02 CHAMLIJA WINES

Mustafa Çamlıca's family has been farming in Büyükkarıştıran since emigrating from Bulgaria in 1936. His large land holding, with its rich red soil and spectacular backdrop of the Istranca Mountains, is scattered over eight local villages and densely planted. The restaurant is open daily, closed Monday lunch.

Chamlija wines are known for their colourful labels, which are the work of Mustafa's artist daughter İrem, and he is fond of saying that he hopes that people 'are attracted by the wine labels, and just as impressed by the wine's quality'.

www.chamlija-wine.com; tel +90 288-436 1349; Büyükkarıştıran; 8.30am-5.30pm by appointment

03 CHATEAU NUZUN

After spending years in California, Nazan and Necdet Uzun made a big call: the rich agricultural land of Thrace was just as good as the Napa Valley for viniculture and they would head back to their homeland to establish their dream business, a boutique vineyard and winery. This 14.5-hectare (36-acre) estate in the poetically named village of Çeşmeli (Water Fountain) is the result, and the Uzuns now produce vintages of Cabernet Sauvignon, Merlot, Syrah and Pinot Noir made using the estate's organically certified fruit.

www.chateaunuzun.com; tel +90 0530-871 4250; Çeşmelı; May-mid-Nov, mid-Nov-Apr by appointment, tours 2pm & 4pm Sat & Sun May-mid-Nov

'Thrace preceded Greece in producing famous wines in antiquity. I'm proud to participate in the project to resuscitate the lost wines of Kırklareli.'

– Dr Michel Salgues, winemaker Arcadia Vineyards

04 GALÎ VINEYARDS

Located on a windswept plain where the Gallipoli Peninsula meets the Thracian mainland, Galî's 24-hectare (60-acre) vineyard is planted with Cabernet Merlot, Cabernet Franc and Cabernet Sauvignon and commands magnificent views of the Aegean and Marmara Seas, the Gulf of Saros and the Dardanelles.

www.gali.com.tr; tel +90 212-671 1991; Evreşe; by appointment

05 SUVLA

Since launching its first vintages in 2012, Suvla can well and truly be said to have taken the country's wine scene by storm. Local wine menus are now as likely to list its vintages as those made by well-known outfits, such as Doluca and Kavaklıdere, and its Grand Reserve Cabernet Sauvignon and Roussane Marsanne are winning awards both in Turkey and internationally.

Suvla's organically certified vineyards are in Bozokbağ on the Gallipoli Peninsula and its winery, restaurant and wine-tasting room are in the nearby town of Eceabat, on the shore of the Dardanelles.

www.suvla.com.tr; tel +90 286-814 1000; Çınarlıdere 11, Eceabat; open 8.30am-5.30pm

01 Château Kalpak in Şarköy

02 Galî Vineyards

ESSENTIAL INFORMATION

WHERE TO STAY

GALLIPOLI HOUSES

Located 11km (7 miles) from Eceabat in the Gallipoli National Park, this boutique hotel offers a restaurant, 10 comfortable rooms and a tranquil, rural atmosphere. Owner Eric Goossens is a mine of information about local battlefields and wineries.

www.thegallipolihouses.com; tel +90 286-814 2650; Kocadere

WHERE TO EAT

UMURBEY WINEHOUSE

Located opposite the Tekirdağ waterfront, this convivial place is operated by the Umurbey Vineyard located in nearby Yazır Köyü. Sample the estate's Cabernet Sauvignon or Sauvignon/Merlot blend accompanied by Modern Turkish dishes including tapas, bruschetta, pasta and grills.

tel +90 282-260 1379; Atatürk Bulvarı, Tekirdağ

CHÂTEAU KALPAK

The purpose-designed building at this boutique winery in Şarköy sits atop a hill and commands majestic views of both the Greek island of Samothrace and the islands of the Sea of Marmara, to be enjoyed over lunch on the terrace of the vineyard's cafe.

tel +90 532-277 1137; Gelibolu Yolu, Şarköy

WHAT TO DO

No trip to this part of Turkey is complete without a visit to the ancient city of Edirne, one-time capital of the Ottoman Empire, with its World Heritage-listed Selimiye Mosque and Sultan Beyazıt Mosque Complex.

To be reminded of a more recent history, head to the pine-scented battlefields of the Gallipoli Historical National Park. In 1915, Turkish and Allied troops fought bloody battles here that still resonate in national psyches. It's a fascinating, beautiful and emotionally charged place to explore on foot or by car.

www.nationalparks-ofturkey.com

CELEBRATIONS

The testosterone-charged Kırkpınar Oil-Wrestling Festival, held in Edirne in early July, coincides with the main visiting season in the wineries.

[USA]

CENTRAL COAST

Big Sur is the big deal for road-trippers here, but some of the oldest and newest vines in California give you an equally thrilling taste of the state.

The Central Coast is where the state changes from southern into northern California, with some of the state's best wineries to be found on either side of the divide. Some of those in the rugged Santa Cruz Mountains to the north are among the oldest and most well known in California, while many of the newest and most exciting can be found in hot and dusty Paso Robles in the south.

Travelling the length of California's Central Coast means covering a lot of ground. Once you head north from Santa Barbara you can follow it all the way to San Francisco, and there is much more than just wineries and vineyards on this stretch of the western seaboard. Surfing enthusiasts will feel right at home in Santa Cruz, music fans can take a pilgrimage to Monterey (where Jimi Hendrix torched his guitar) and lovers of a good drive will marvel at the 150km (90-mile) coastal road known as Big Sur.

This famous highway hugs the rugged coastline, boxed in by the Pacific Ocean on one side and the towering, densely forested mountains on the other, providing the visitor with some of the most stunning views in all of California and the opportunity to spot elephant seals sunbathing on the beach from one of the viewpoints along the road. While it is possible to drive Big Sur in a few hours, why not slow down and make a weekend of it? Anyone with a fondness for the great outdoors will find hiking trails and abundent wildlife to rival anywhere in the state, not to mention plenty of restaurants and lodges for rest and refuelling along the way.

GET THERE
San Francisco is the nearest major airport, 310km from Paso Robles. Car hire is available.

01 J. LOHR

Jerry Lohr was one of the early pioneers of Paso Robles viticulture, planting vineyards in the mid-1980s, but he already had an enviable track record of producing quality wines further north on the Central Coast from his winery in San Jose. Today, J. Lohr is one of the most important wineries in the region, and not just because it makes great wines. They have the largest solar-energy tracking system of any winery in North America, which generates enough power to offset 75% of their energy usage.

There is no appointment required or fee charged to taste at J. Lohr (except for the flights of their limited-edition wines). Enjoy your wine while admiring the view over the adjacent Seven Oaks vineyard.
www.jlohr.com; tel +1 805-239-8900; 6169 Airport Rd, Paso Robles; open 10am-5pm

02 L'AVENTURE

The name refers to the adventure undertaken by owners Stephan and Beatrice Asseo when they left their native Bordeaux in 1997 to set up a winery in California. Having spent years toeing the administrative line making wine in Bordeaux, Stephan grew tired of playing by the rules – what he really wanted to do was marry the structure and elegance of the Bordeaux varieties with the rich and ripe flavours of Syrah, Grenache and Mourvedre. L'Aventure's full-bodied blended wines have since helped to establish Paso Robles as a region associated with top-class vino.

Tastings cost $15; the wines are made in such small quantities that a visit to the tasting room is the best way to get acquainted with them.
www.aventurewine.com; tel +1 805-227-1588; 2815 Live Oak Rd, Paso Robles; 11am-3.30pm by appointment

03 TURLEY

While the wines at Turley could well be described as 'big', they could never be accused of lacking balance or complexity, and time spent with them is often a thought-provoking experience. It's no coincidence then, that all of the above could be used to describe winemaker Teagan Passalacqua, a man who is widely considered to be one of the most talented young people in Californian wine. Since his boss Larry Turley founded the winery in 1993, the Turley name has become synonymous with single-vineyard Zinfandel and Petite Syrah from some of the oldest and most revered vineyards in the state.

The standard tasting costs $10 (refunded with a two-bottle purchase) and reserve wines cost an additional $5 each. For those that want to go into even more detail, an in-depth private tutored tasting is

Courtesy of L'Aventure / Chandler Smiley, Marissa Winchester

01 The Central Coast's rugged landscape

02 L'Aventure's vineyards

03 L'Aventure's Stephan Asseo and his daughter Chloe

04-05 Tablas Creek

available ($40; reservation required) and comes highly recommended. *www.turleywinecellars.com; tel +1 805-434-1030; 2900 Vineyard Dr, Templeton; 9am-5pm daily*

04 JUSTIN

When Justin Baldwin established his vineyards and winery in Paso Robles back in 1981, it was a bold move. Back then, the world was only just getting its head around the idea of high-quality wine being made in the Napa Valley, let alone anywhere else in California.

But by the late 1980s Justin was an estate to be reckoned with and nowadays it is considered one of the must-visit wineries of the Central Coast. While the Rhône varieties tend to dominate the conversation in Paso, Justin has always preferred the Bordeaux grapes (Cabernet Sauvignon and Merlot) and in their 'Isosceles' blend they have a wine that has had more than its fair share of plaudits.

Aside from the comfortable hotel and impressive restaurant at Justin, there is also one of the best managed tasting rooms in the region. Nestled in the picturesque estate vineyards, it offers a $15 tasting of five wines (no appointment required) and a range of tours and tutored seminars. *www.justinwine.com; tel +1 805-238-6932; 11680 Chimney Rock Rd, Paso Robles; 10am-4.30pm daily*

05 TABLAS CREEK

Château de Beaucastel is one of the most revered names in France's Rhône Valley (where the winemakers produce exceptional wines in Châteauneuf-du-Pape), so when they decided to join forces with the Haas family and establish a vineyard in California, it came as no surprise that they chose Paso Robles. The grape varietals grown in this part of the Central Coast bear more than a passing resemblance to those of Beaucastel's homeland – Syrah, Grenache, Mourvèdre, Marsanne and Roussanne – and the wines match a certain European finesse with the richness and charm of the Californian sun.

The experience in the tasting room at Tablas Creek follows two formats. The regular 'estate' tasting costs $10 and includes six to eight wines, while the seated 'reserve' tasting costs $40 (reservation required), but includes older vintages and samples of its flagship wines. In addition to the tastings, free tours of the organic vineyards take place every day (though reservations are required), while the diary of regular events and seminars should not be missed. *www.tablascreek.com; tel +1 805-237-1231; 9339 Adelaida Rd, Paso Robles; 10am-5pm, tours 10.30am & 2pm daily*

06

'California's Central Coast is a land of transition between the cool, piney north and the sunny, palm-lined south. Its winemakers shape the influences of sun and fog, ocean and mountains into wines as diverse, memorable and dramatic as the landscape.'

–Jason Haas, Partner and General Manager, Tablas Creek

Courtesy of Post Ranch Inn / Kodiak Greenwood

06 Spectacular views from Post Ranch Inn

07 Randall Grahm of Bonny Doon

08 SLOWINE's annual Roll out the Barrels festival

Courtesy of Bonny Doon

06 BONNY DOON

Named after the small hamlet in the Santa Cruz Mountains where the winery is based, Bonny Doon is a renowned producer of Californian wine, as much for the pioneering spirit and idiosyncratic thinking of winemaker Randall Grahm as for the high quality of its bottles. One of the original 'Rhône Rangers', a term used to describe Californians that choose to focus on the grapes of France's Rhône Valley rather than Bordeaux or Burgundy, Randall is a true one-off (as evidenced in his brilliant book *Been Doon So Long*) and the individuality of his superb range of wines is testament to this.

To take a peek into the world of Doon, head to the winery's tasting room in Davenport – no appointments are necessary (unless you're a group of eight or more). One of Bonny Doon's most famous bottlings is Le Cigare Volant, an homage to Châteauneuf-du-Pape with an iconic label – be sure to have the tasting room staff explain it to you.

www.bonnydoonvineyard.com; tel +1 831-471-8031; 450 Hwy 1, Davenport; 11am-5pm Sun-Thu, to 6pm Fri & Sat

07 RIDGE VINEYARDS

For lovers of Californian wine, Ridge Vineyards' sumptuous, silky reds and rich, elegant whites from the Santa Cruz Mountains are hard to beat. Its winery up in Sonoma produces some of the best Zinfandels in the state, but it is the Monte Bello vineyard just outside Cupertino that, under the watchful eye of chief winemaker Paul Draper since the 1960s, has given birth to a seemingly endless list of genuinely compelling bottles.

This really is Californian wine royalty, but don't think that means the guys at Ridge take themselves too seriously – the team are wholly committed to putting smiles on people's faces, whether that be through the delicious wines they produce or delivering the incredible experience that awaits visitors to the estate.

There are three tasting options available, costing $5, $10 and $20 respectively, depending on the quality level of the wines. The $20 option includes a taste of the legendary (and simply delicious) Monte Bello Cabernet Sauvignon, which is not to be missed. It is also possible to organise five-wine historic tastings for an extra fee, which might be the best money you spend all holiday.

www.ridgewine.com; tel +1 408-867-3233; 7100 Montebello Rd, Cupertino; open 11am-5pm Sat & Sun, Mon-Fri by appointment

ESSENTIAL INFORMATION

WHERE TO STAY

POST RANCH INN

This luxurious hotel in Big Sur might have the best view in all of America, looking out across the Pacific Ocean while surrounded by rugged mountains and lush forests. It boasts wonderful rooms and a restaurant well worth visiting. If you're here for a special occasion, then the Post Ranch Inn will make it a memorable celebration. *www.postranchinn.com; tel +1 831-667-2200; 47900 Hwy 1, Big Sur*

JUST INN

Aside from being a lovely hotel with well-appointed rooms, the Just Inn just happens to be in the middle of Justin vineyards. If you can wrap your tongue around that, then your overnight stay will include breakfast and a tour of the winery. *www.justinwine.com; tel +1 805-591-3224; 11680 Chimney Rock Rd; Paso Robles*

WHERE TO EAT

PICNIC BASKET

If you find yourself in Santa Cruz, wandering around near the boardwalk looking for a quick bite, head to the Picnic Basket for one of its excellent sandwiches. *www.thepicnicbasketsc.com; tel +1 831-427-9946; 125 Beach St, Santa Cruz*

BANTAM

If you are in need of a Mediterranean fix, don't miss Bantam. The delicious pizzas are cooked in a wood-fired oven and the ingredients are top notch. *www.bantam1010.com; tel +1 831-420-0101; 1010 Fair Ave, Santa Cruz*

ARTISAN

The best restaurant in Paso Robles is Artisan, a farm-to-table eaterie that focuses on local produce and Central Coast wines. Chef Chris Kobayashi's inventive take on seasonal food makes for some mouth-watering dishes. *www.artisanpasorobles.com; tel +1 805-237-8084; 843 12th St, Paso Robles*

08

Courtesy of SLO Wine Country

WHAT TO DO

The wildlife around Big Sur is incredible and well worth stopping for – mountain lions, condors, bald eagles and elephant seals can all be spotted in the area. Visitors to Paso Robles should pay a visit to Tin City, a rejuvenated industrial park now home to some boutique wineries with tasting rooms (Field Recordings and Giornata are two of the best). *fieldrecordingswine.com; giornatawines.com*

CELEBRATIONS

The annual Santa Cruz Clam Chowder Cook-Off takes place on the boardwalk in late February, and California Roots in Monterey is one of the state's best music festivals in late May. Further south, the whole month of April is given over to the 'Roll Out the Barrels' wine festival in San Luis Obispo. *californiarootsfestival.com; slowine.com*

MT TH

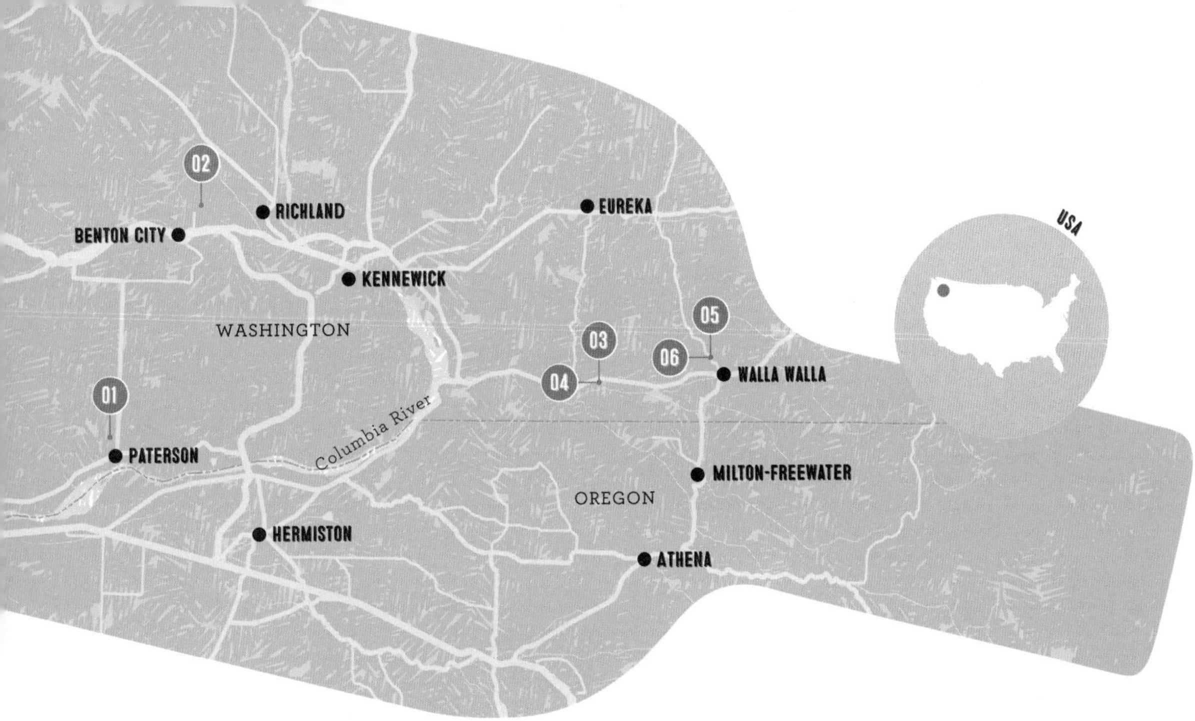

Danita Delimont © Alamy

[USA]

COLUMBIA VALLEY

Over the mountains from foggy Seattle lies the Wild West of American winemaking, complete with cowboys, rodeos and some world-class labels.

Driving out of the weather-beaten city of Seattle, first time visitors to Washington State will have no idea what awaits them on the other side of the imposing Cascade Mountains. Within a couple of hours, the verdant green forests and persistent rain give way to the stark desert terrain of the Columbia Valley. It's a barren and unforgiving place that just happens to be one of the USA's most exciting wine regions, and the growing community of winemaking estates here are rightfully proud of the wines that result from their fascinating landscape.

There is a frontier spirit about Columbia Valley's best wineries that is impossible not to admire. The last thing that was in the mind of the original settlers in the region was viticulture, but once they had figured out how to survive they pretty quickly got to thinking about how to thrive. By the 1980s it was clear that the grape-growing pioneers of the 1970s had been on to something, and since then the number of top-quality American Viticultural Areas (AVAs) in Washington State has increased rapidly. It might still be considered cowboy country out here (and there are plenty of cattle ranches and rodeos to prove it), but there's no doubting its credentials as wine country too. It's something that has attracted outsiders and persuaded locals to pursue the life of a Washingtonian winemaker.

Down in the bottom-right corner of the state is the charming town of Walla Walla, which is full to bursting with winery tasting rooms and places to eat, making it the ideal base when visiting the Columbia Valley. The surrounding vineyards, such as those of the Walla Walla Valley, Red Mountain or the Horse Heaven Hills, are home to world-class wines from some extremely talented producers.

GET THERE

Seattle-Tacoma is the nearest major airport, 360km from Paterson. Car hire is available.

Courtesy of Charles Smith Winery

01 COLUMBIA CREST

When Columbia Crest released its inaugural vintage in 1984, it was a one-wine brand (an off-dry white wine). Nowadays Columbia Crest is easily the largest winery in the state, producing solid varietal wines that are considered to be as consistent as they are great value.

In tandem with its sister property, Chateau Ste Michelle (an excellent place to visit if you are near Seattle), Columbia Crest has spread the message about Washington's wines far and wide from its base in the Horse Heaven Hills AVA, so it's well worth building them into your itinerary.

The experience for visitors to the winery and tasting room is second to none and the setting, overlooking the Columbia River and surrounded by vineyards, is stunning. On weekends there is a guided tour and tasting (free, but a reservation is required) but visitors on any day can walk themselves around on a self-guided tour before tasting a complimentary wine flight. Every other weekend they organise a wine and food pairing experience ($25, reservations required) – call ahead for dates. *www.columbiacrest.com; tel +1 509-875-4227; 178810 Hwy 221, Columbia Crest Dr, Paterson; open 10am-4pm*

02 HEDGES FAMILY ESTATE

The imposing château building at Hedges Family Vineyards is not the only thing here that harks back to the old world. The family's French heritage also shines through in their elegant, restrained wines and commitment to the land – they are one of the few estates to practise biodynamic farming in the region.

The land in question is Red Mountain, a 1400ft (425m) elevation that was carved out of the landscape a few million years ago by glacial floods. The result was soil that is a blend of clay, loess and granite; ideal conditions for the cultivation of red wine grapes and, thanks to the pioneering work of a select band of true believers, Red Mountain has become one of the most talked about appellations for high-quality wine in the Columbia Valley. Unfortunately, this has led to the spectre of commercial development in the area, so you should visit now before the inevitable Disney-fication starts to take place!

Anyone can show up on weekends for $5 tastings, but visits at other times can also be arranged and there are plenty of options for private tours by appointment. The family are incredibly knowledgeable about the local area, so you are sure to learn all there is to know about Red Mountain. *www.hedgesfamilyestate.com; tel +1 509-588-3155; 53511 North Sunset Rd, Benton City; open 11am-5pm Sat & Sun Apr-Nov, or by appointment*

The northern latitude and glacial soils create a beautiful balance of new-world fruit and old-world structure.'

–Marty Clubb, Owner/Winemaker, L'Ecole No.41

01 Harvest time in Walla Walla

02 The bold bottle labels of the Charles Smith winery

03 Woodward Canyon

04 The Inn at Abeja

05 The inimitable Charles Smith

Steven Morris @ Getty Images

Courtesy of The Inn at Abeja

03 L'ECOLE NO. 41

Founded in 1983, L'Ecole No. 41 is the third-oldest winery in Walla Walla and still considered to be one of its very best. The wines never fail to impress; managing to tread the fine line between power and elegance while showcasing Walla Walla's hallmark vibrant, succulent, dark-berry fruit. Their estate wines from (Ferguson, Perigee and Pepper Bridge) can be spectacular in the best vintages.

The name L'Ecole No. 41, refers to the location of the winery – a schoolhouse in district number 41 that was built back in 1915 – and the tasting room occupies one of the two classrooms. How appropriate, then, that a visit to L'Ecole No. 41 is one of the best ways to learn about the Walla Walla Valley's *terroir*. You can even go on a field trip to the adjacent estate vineyard.

No reservation is required to enjoy a flight of six or seven wines (the $5 fee can be refunded against a wine purchase). If you want to taste the seriously good stuff, then the 'Reserve tasting' (3pm Fridays April to November, $30, reservation required) includes a private tour of the winery and a chance to taste older vintages and limited releases.

www.lecole.com; tel +1 509-525-0940; 41 Lowden School Rd, Lowden; 10am-5pm

04 WOODWARD CANYON

If you enquire about other good wineries to visit at L'Ecole No. 41, you'll likely be sent next door to Woodward Canyon, a winery with an even longer track record in Walla Walla (albeit only by a couple of years). The guys here pride themselves on following the

'Wine is for everyone. And everyone should have easy access to it, whether you have a pocket full of coins or a wallet full of C-notes.'
–Charles Smith, founder K Vintners
Courtesy of Charles Smith Winery

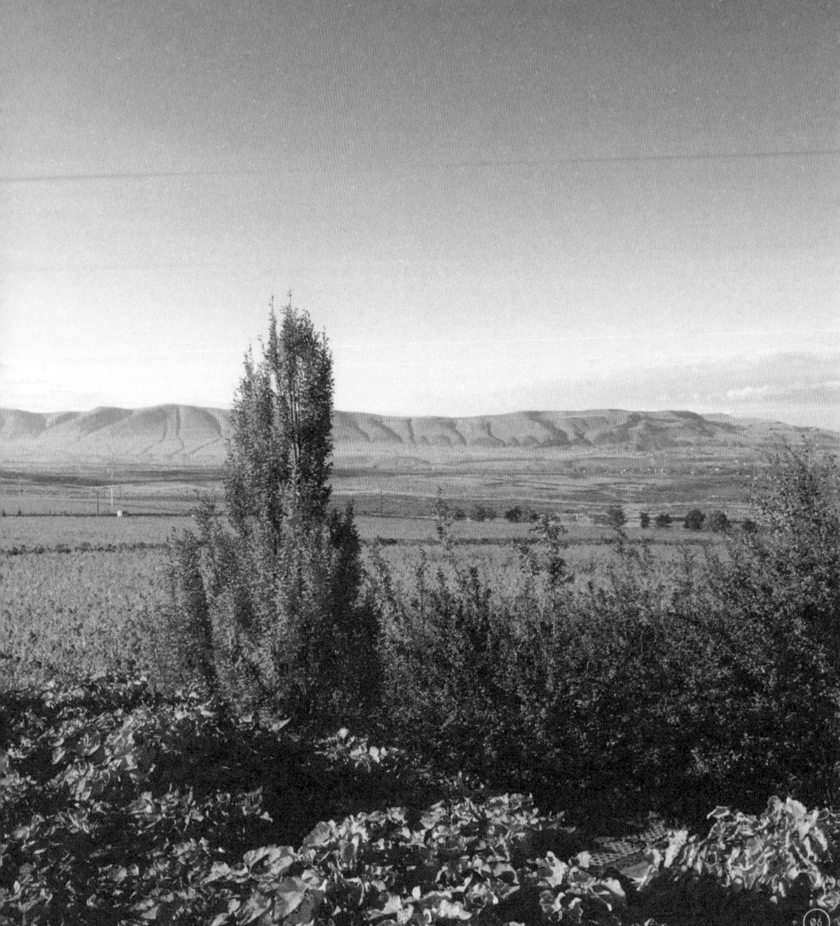

Courtesy of Hedges Family Vineyard

06 Hedges Family Estate

07 The Inn at Abeja

'Woody Way': working hard in the vineyard, never cutting corners or compromising, making balanced wines that age well, and always working sustainably. Clearly, there is something to it, as the wines are as elegant as they are delicious.

In the beautiful tasting room at Woodward Canyon you will sample a range of offerings for $5 (refundable against a purchase), or for $25 you can enjoy a private tasting that includes some really interesting bottles. The on-site farm-to-table restaurant, the Reserve House, is a great place to stop for lunch, with delicious food made from local ingredients.

www.woodwardcanyon.com; tel +1 509-525-4129; 11920 West Hwy 12, Lowden; open 10am-5pm

05 GRAMERCY CELLARS

Not so long ago, Gramercy Cellars was little more than an insider's tip (with production at just a few thousand cases per year, that's hardly a surprise), but now it is one of the hottest wineries in the USA. Greg Harrington's wines are light on their feet but packed full of flavour and reflect what is getting people so excited about the wines in this northwestern corner of America.

This is not a winery looking to draw attention to itself, so you won't see any big signage out front. The tasting is free and you are assured a warm and knowledgeable welcome.

www.gramercycellars.com; tel +1 509-876-2427; 635 North 13th Ave, Walla Walla; open 11am-5pm Sat, Wed-Fri by appointment

06 CHARLES SMITH & K VINTNERS

All wine regions have their rebellious characters, and Charles Smith certainly fits the bill for Walla Walla – he looks like a rock star, which is no surprise considering he spent years managing rock bands touring across Europe. He returned from the old world having been bitten by the wine bug and, after a stint as a merchant, decided to teach himself how to make the stuff. Nowadays he makes full-throttle wines with personalities as big as his own, and names like Kung-Fu Girl Riesling or Boom Boom Syrah. Under his K Vintners label, Smith has created some of the highest-rated (and most expensive) wines in Washington State history, helping to establish the Columbia Valley's reputation for serious wine and engaging a younger crowd in the process.

A visit to the Charles Smith tasting room in downtown Walla Walla is not for the fuddy-duddy wine geek (though they are welcome to give it a try too). The rock music and converted warehouse setting make for a fun environment in which to taste one of two six-wine selections, the Modernist Project flight ($5) or the K Vintners flight ($10). The wines and the man ensure that this is a must-visit on the Walla Walla tasting circuit, so be warned – it can get busy.

www.charlessmithwines.com; tel +1 509-526-5230; 35 South Spokane St, Walla Walla; open from 10am

ESSENTIAL INFORMATION

WHERE TO STAY

VINE & ROSES

This restored Victorian house in downtown Walla Walla is now a comfortable B&B overlooking lovely Pioneer Park. The proprietors also own Sinclair Estate Vineyards and will happily arrange for guests to visit the nearby tasting room. *www.vineandroses.com; tel +1 509-876-2113; 516 South Division St, Walla Walla*

INN AT ABEJA

If your idea of staying in wine country is bunking down in a converted farmstead, surrounded by woodland and vineyards, then the Inn at Abeja is for you. The assorted cottages on this charming property don't come cheap (from $295 per night), but it is an idyllic base from which to explore the surrounding area. *www.abeja.net; tel +1 509-522-1234; 2014 Mill Creek Rd, Walla Walla*

WHERE TO EAT

SAFFRON MEDITERRANEAN KITCHEN

It may be tiny, but Saffron is building a big reputation as one of the best restaurants in Washington State. Located in Walla Walla, it is a regular haunt for many of the top names in the local winemaking community. *www.saffron-mediterraneankitchen.com; tel +1 509-525-2112; 124 West Alder St, Walla Walla*

WHITEHOUSE-CRAWFORD

Dining at Whitehouse-Crawford is considered an essential part of the Washington food and drink experience, with the seasonal food and first-class wine list at this Walla Walla institution earning a well-deserved reputation for excellence. *www.whitehousecrawford.com; tel +1 509-525-2222; 55 West Cherry St, Walla Walla*

WHAT TO DO

Visitors arriving in Seattle stop off in the adjacent town of Woodinville, full of tasting rooms and home to Chateau Ste Michelle (the oldest winery in the state). The Reach, in Richland, is a national monument and wildlife refuge where regular events bring the region to life. The town of Toppenish, in the Yakima Indian Reservation, has three museums and 75 murals dotted around the town to illuminate the fascinating local history. *www.visitthereach.org; www.visittoppenish.com*

CELEBRATIONS

The Gorge Blues & Brews Festival in late June is not to be missed. The 4 July parade and Rodeo in Toppenish will give visitors a taste of the Wild West, while vegetable lovers should check out Walla Walla's Sweet Onion Festival in June, or Pullman's National Lentil Festival in August. *www.gorgebluesandbrews.com; www.sweetonions.org; www.lentilfest.com*

07

Courtesy of The Inn at Abeja

01

Courtesy of Hearts and Hands wines

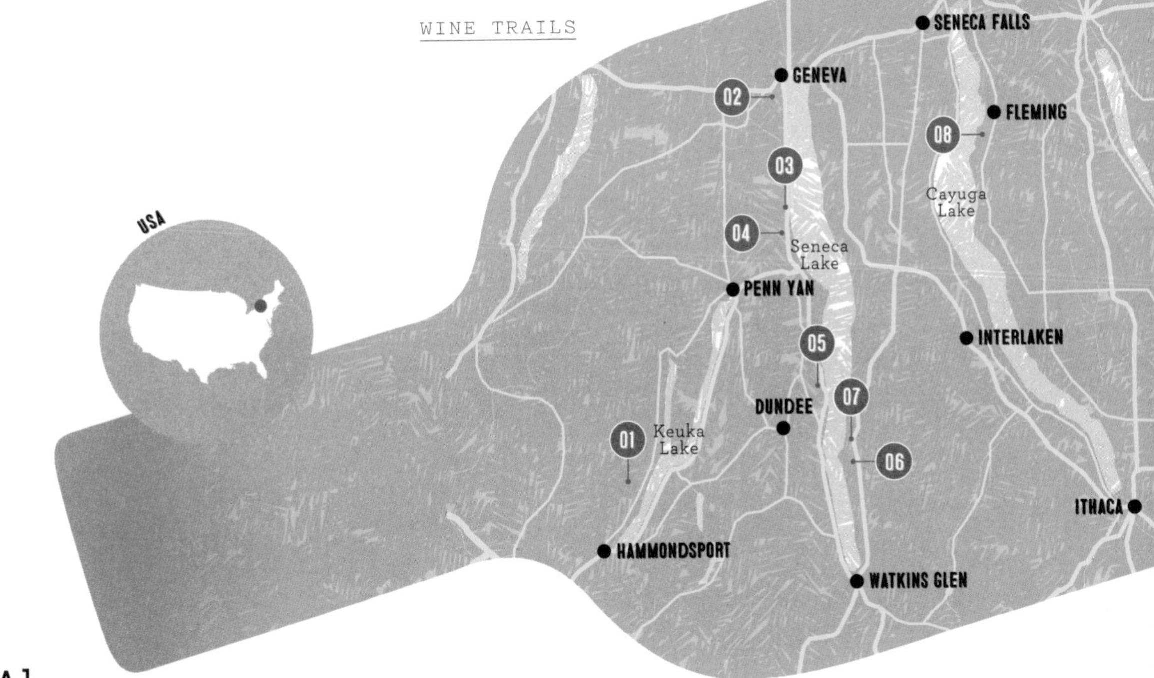

[USA]

FINGER LAKES

An infectious sense of freedom – and gorgeous lakeside views – await you here, where European vines grow at the northern limit of the New World.

The Finger Lakes of New York represent one of the furthest limits of winemaking in North America. The winters can be very harsh; for most of its history only native American and hybrid grapes were planted here, with the belief that the higher-quality European *vinifera* vines wouldn't survive. While wine has been made here since the mid-1800s, with a boom in sparkling and sweet wine in the last half of that century, only in the 1960s, after the twin plagues of phylloxera and Prohibition, did *vinifera* grapes begin to be taken seriously. Their ability to thrive in the Finger Lakes, the state's largest wine region, is no longer in doubt. Today's pressing question is: which *vinifera* grapes, and where? How will the Finger Lakes identify itself?

The shores of four of the area's eleven lakes (Seneca, Cayuga, Keuka, and Skaneateles) are home to the great majority of its wines, and these, in turn, are defined by a wide variety of soil types and exposures. In dealing with that variety, every Finger Lakes winery has had to decide what to champion: a grape, its site, or the region at large. A number of winemakers believe that Riesling and Pinot Noir are the finest vehicles to discover and convey the Finger Lakes' *terroirs*. Others embrace a host of grapes, and consider questions of method most important: such as native or laboratory yeast, machine or hand-harvesting, oak or steel. There are a host of opinions in between. It's an exciting time to taste and explore the reality on the ground.

The beautiful, glacier-carved lakes are incredibly deep; their moderating influence is the chief factor that allows winemaking to happen here. They are also very long, as much as 40 miles north to south; as you travel up and down them, by car or bicycle, you'll want to plan your time carefully. To that end, it can be most convenient to centre yourself at one of the region's two city hubs, Watkins Glen or Ithaca, at the respective southern tips of Seneca and Cayuga Lakes.

GET THERE

JFK or Toronto are the nearest major airports. Flights go from JFK to Ithaca, 85km from Hammondsport. Car hire is available.

Courtesy of Frank wines

01 DR KONSTANTIN FRANK

Along with Hermann J Wiemer's, this pioneering estate, home to the first *vinifera* plantings in the region, was founded in 1962 by Ukrainian immigrant Dr Konstantin Frank, and has been instrumental in changing the game for the Finger Lakes. Currently transitioning into a fourth-generation of family ownership, Dr Frank is now home to three tiers of wine: the old-vine, estate-driven Dr Konstantin Frank, value-oriented Salmon Run, and sparkling-exclusive Chateau Frank. Starring wines are Rkatsiteli, Grüner Veltliner, Riesling Semi-Dry and Chateau Frank Vintage Brut.
www.drfrankwines.com; tel +1 800-320-0735; 9749 Middle Rd, Hammondsport; 9am-5pm Mon-Sat, noon-5pm Sun

02 RAVINES WINE CELLARS ON SENECA LAKE

Ravines Cellars' Morten Hallgren grew up in Provence, France, and learned winemaking at his family estate, Domaine de Castel Roubine. After further training in Bordeaux and various locations in America (including six years at Dr Konstantin Frank), Morten and his wife Lisa secured a set of vineyards between two large ravines on the eastern shores of Keuka Lake in 2000.

Since then, they've gone from strength to strength, and today, with wide distribution and a popular wine club, 'Ravinous', are one of the most representative Finger Lakes wineries nationwide. Ravines' wines have an uncomplicated appeal, and while proud of his Riesling and Pinot Noir, Morten also bottles other grapes such as Cabernet Franc and Gewürztraminer, staking the Finger Lakes' fame on quality. The 'Argetsinger Vineyard' Dry Riesling and 'Keuka Red' are two of their finest bottlings to date.

The tasting-room experience here, located in a converted old barn, is especially warm. The building itself oozes memories of generations past, and the kind, knowledgeable staff are eager to please. After your visit, take a short drive to the nearby city of Geneva. Some of the Finger Lakes' most significant history happened here, and it's easy to soak up via a stroll through the tree-lined streets.
www.ravineswine.com; tel +1 315-781-7007; 400 Barracks Rd, Geneva; 10am-5pm

03 FOX RUN VINEYARDS

Canadian-born senior winemaker Peter Bell helms the ambitious wine programme at Fox Run with thoughtful skill. His facilities, in a converted century-old dairy barn overlooking Seneca Lake, include a market and a cafe where top artisanal Finger Lakes cheeses are paired with Fox Run wines. Here, it's possible to taste through one of the widest stylistic arrays from a single estate in the Finger Lakes, from red and white to sparkling, from rosé to port styles. The most exciting tier of wines, however, is called the Geology series, which started in 2010. Its objective: to learn about the expression of single vineyard sites through separate Riesling bottlings,

is of clear relevance to the Finger Lakes as a whole. While here, make sure to put your feet up with a glass of rosé on the back patio – it provides one of the area's very best views of Seneca Lake.
www.foxrunvineyards.com; tel +1 315-536-4616; 670 Rte 14, Penn Yan; 10am-6pm Mon-Sat, 11am-6pm Sun

04 ANTHONY ROAD WINE COMPANY

Anthony Road's story is something of a mirror to the Finger Lakes' as a whole. Ann and John Martini planted the vineyard's first vines – all hybrids – in 1973, and have since replanted nearly all the vines to *vinifera* varietals such as Chardonnay, Riesling, Pinot Gris, Cabernet Franc and Merlot. Today, the great majority of their delicious bottlings are strictly *vinifera*, but they also offer a semi-sweet hybrid wine (of Vignoles), giving a window to the recent past.

Anthony Road is super to visit to enhance your wine education (especially after Hermann Wiemer), and it's also great fun. Very close to Seneca Lake, the bring-your-own-picnic-friendly open-lawn patio (which also serves local cheese) offers spectacular views, and provides an ideal spot to mingle with other travellers. Inside, a frequently changing gallery features the work of local artists. Don't miss the Art Series Riesling and the Devonian Slate Red.
www.anthonyroadwine.com; tel +1 315-536-2182; 1020 Anthony Rd, Penn Yan; 10am-5pm Mon-Sat, noon-5pm Sun

05 HERMANN J WIEMER

In 1979 German-born Hermann Wiemer founded his eponymous estate. Since then he has – through his relentless insistence on *vinifera*'s (specifically Riesling's) success here – done more than any other person to change the Finger Lakes' image. Hermann retired in 2007, and the current winemaker, his former assistant, Fred Merwarth, is taking the estate to new heights. His current experiments in *terroir* – matching varietal and style to site, and carefully mapping the results – are absolutely critical to the Lakes' winemaking future.

Oskar Bynke is Fred's partner in this project, and serves as the public face for the estate – his wine presentations are keenly insightful. All the wines here are made with an eye for detail, but don't miss the Magdalena Vineyard Riesling, the Limited Release Vintage Blanc de Noir, and the Cabernet Franc.
www.wiemer.com; tel +1 607-243-7971; 3962 Rte 14, Dundee; 10am-5pm Mon-Sat, 11am-5pm Sun

06 BLOOMER CREEK

The Bloomer Creek tasting room is a short walk from the Stonecat Cafe, and if you visit on a weekend afternoon, you're likely to be served by a tall, affable gentleman named Kim Engle. Along with his wife, artist Debra Bermingham, Kim started Bloomer Creek nearly 30 years ago, and continues to make the wine with the help of only one employee. In a region where many growers focus on Riesling, and most harvest by machine, these wines stand out: here, the red wines of Loire, France, are the model, and natural methods, including hand-harvest and native yeast ferments, are the goal. Kim makes terrific wines from Gewürztraminer, Pinot Noir, Riesling, and other grapes, but it is his Cabernet Francs that most clearly give an original profile of Finger Lakes *terroir*. Be on the lookout for the lip-smacking Bloomer Creek rosé and the elegant, ageworthy White Horse Meritage Red.
www.bloomercreek.com; tel +1 607-546-5027; 5301 Rte 414, Hector; noon-5pm Sat & Sun

07 FORGE CELLARS AT THE HECTOR WINE COMPANY

Forge Cellars is an exciting artisan micro-project housed (for now) inside Hector Wine Company's modern wooden barn, immediately off Rte 414. Entering HWC's new, spacious tasting room/gift shop – where you can find 'all things Finger Lakes', including oil, salts, crafts, even T-shirts. You would hardly think they were here, but some of the Finger Lakes' most pristine wines are just through the back door, resting in the street-level cellar.

Courtesy of Hearts & Hands Winery

Forge is the joint venture of three partners: Justin Boyette of HWC, NY-based Rick Rainey, and Louis Barruol from Gigondas in the Rhône. Like a handful of others in the region, they work strictly with Pinot Noir and Riesling, believing that these are the best grapes for Finger Lakes' *terroir*. This narrow focus allows Forge a meticulous approach to quality – the grapes are hand-picked and elaborated without manipulation. The results are gorgeous and, even at this early stage, speak for a great ageing potential.
www.forgecellars.wordpress.com; tel +1 607-387-1045; 5610 Rte 414, Hector; 11am-6pm Sun-Thu, to 7pm Fri & Sat

08 HEART & HANDS WINERY

If you're heading to or from Skaneateles from Ithaca, treat yourself to a lovely drive along the east side of Cayuga Lake on Rte 90. This winding road takes you right along the lake, past a wildlife refuge, beside open fields and through cute historical towns, until you reach the town of Union Springs. Here is where Tom and Susan Higgins (and their Swiss Mountain dog Caliza) have set up their artisan winery, Heart & Hands. Consummate hosts, the Higgins' are passionate about three things: limestone soil, Pinot Noir and Riesling. At their young and developing winery, started in 2006, they're quietly making a convincing case for vineyard-specific Pinot and Riesling as the Finger Lakes' signature varietals, and also craft an extraordinary vintage sparkling Brut.
www.heartandhandswine.com; tel +1 315-889-8500; 4162 Rte 90, Union Springs; noon-5pm Fri-Sun, or by appointment

ESSENTIAL INFORMATION

01 The view from the tasting room of Heart & Hands Winery

02 Dr Frank wines

03 Tom and Susan Higgins (and Caliza) of Heart & Hands Winery

04 The ever-popular Stonecat Cafe

WHERE TO STAY

HUMBLE HILL LODGE AND FARM STAY

A short drive south of Ithaca, down Hwy 96B, this homey lodge is located on a small chemical-free family farm, and offers affordable stays, both short- and long-term, for individuals or groups. The breakfasts are particularly delicious. *www.humblehill.com; tel +1 607-738-6626; 467 Tallow Hill Rd, Spencer*

THE WILLOWS ON KEUKA LAKE

Located directly on Keuka Lake, with a beautiful waterfront deck and available pontoon boat. Host Kathy Yonge goes out of her way to give her guests the most comfortable stay possible. *tel +1 315-536-5653; 6893 East Bluff Dr, Penn Yan*

WHERE TO EAT

DANO'S HEURIGER ON SENECA

Make sure you arrive here early in the evening; this traditional Austrian *heuriger* (wine tavern) offers stunning views of the sun setting over Seneca Lake. The food is deliciously classic – *schnitzel*, *currywurst*, *spätzle* and *Sacher Torte* are among the staples – and the exciting wine list offers a selection of Austrian and German wines alongside a wide range of the best from the Finger Lakes. *www.danosonseneca.com; tel +1 607-582-7555 9564 Rte 414, Lodi*

STONECAT CAFÉ

All the locals swing through the Stonecat at some point; it's like a *Cheers* bar for wine lovers and winemakers. The atmosphere is relaxed and casual – it's easy to hang out here all day, thanks in part to the excellent selection of Finger Lakes wines and beers. The open-air back dining room gives onto a sloping garden where most of the food on the menu is sourced – it doesn't get more 'farm-to-table' than that! A perfect spot to recharge at the end of a long tasting day. *www.stonecatcafe.com; tel +1 607-546-5000; 5315 Rte 414, Hector*

WHAT TO DO

Enjoy a morning hike through otherworldly cliffs of **Watkins Glen State Park**, where 19 waterfalls crash along a 3km (2-mile) course, and learn about the Finger Lakes' unique geology. (Don't forget to take a quiet moment to admire the Central Cavern Cascade.)

CELEBRATIONS

In the middle of July, Watkins Glen hosts the terrific Finger Lakes Wine Festival, where more than 80 wineries pour their new releases in a cheerful Woodstock-like scene of campers, wine lovers, and live music. Ravines Cellars hosts a crowded Fall Harvest Festival at its Seneca Lake tasting room in late September. Over every weekend in December, Skaneateles is transformed into a Dickensian Christmas celebration, with costumed characters roaming the snowy streets.

04

Courtesy of Stonecat Café

01

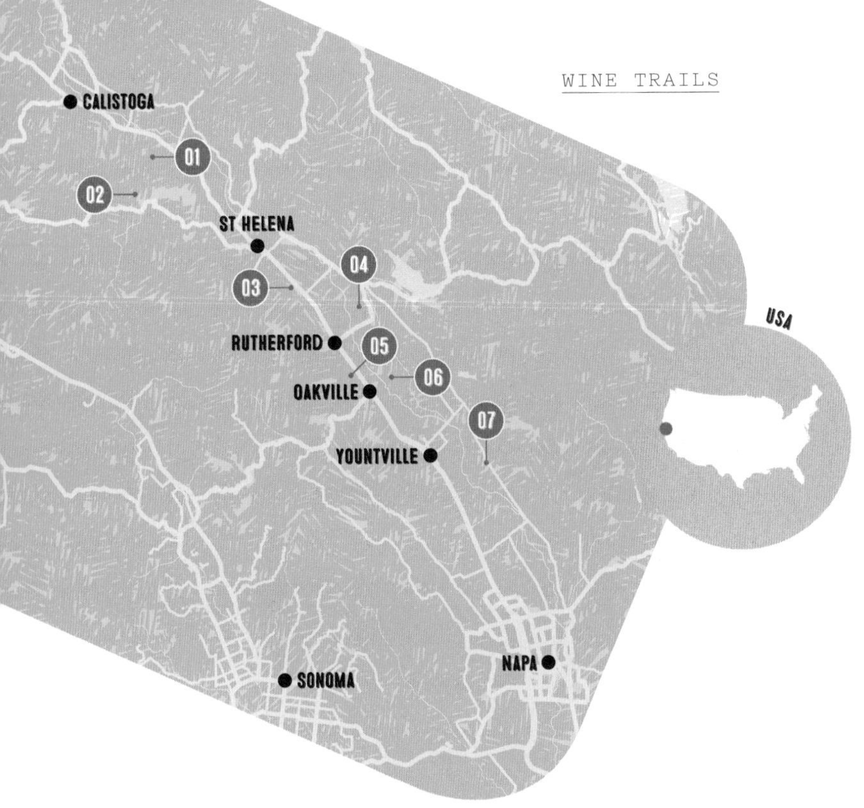

[USA]

NAPA VALLEY

A road trip north of San Francisco to this famous valley will reveal plenty of fascinating smaller wineries with the feel of old California.

Today's Napa Valley is unquestionably California's most glamorous wine region. Home to some of the world's most famous and critically acclaimed wineries, it is as moneyed and manicured as it gets – a far cry from the rural backwater that visitors would've discovered up until the mid-1970s. While some vestiges of the old Napa remain, things have never been the same since the 'Judgement of Paris' tasting took place in 1976, when a handful of plucky upstarts from California pitched their wines in a blind tasting against the mightiest estates of Bordeaux and Burgundy in France. The winners in both the red (Cabernet Sauvignon) and white (Chardonnay) were revealed to be from the Napa Valley – a result that shook the wine world to its foundations and triggered a surge of interest in the wines of California.

Ever since this marketing coup (the customary bestselling book and a Hollywood movie called *Bottleshock* have already been released), full-bodied reds made from Cabernet Sauvignon and whites from Chardonnay have continued to be the main draw, though there are some excellent sparkling wines and a wide range of other grape varieties to be found if you know where to look.

While the glitz and polish of the Napa Valley may mean it lacks the down-home authenticity of some other regions, it is welcoming, easy to navigate and an excellent place to explore the history of Californian wine, especially if you are prepared to look beyond the 'open-all-hours' wineries trying to grab the tourist dollar, and head instead to the more interesting cellar doors, of which there are many.

GET THERE
San Francisco is the nearest major airport, 142km from Calistoga. Car hire is available.

02

Courtesy of Gott's Roadside

01 SCHRAMSBERG VINEYARDS

Located high up on Diamond Mountain is Napa Valley's second-oldest commercial winery. Founded by Jacob Schram way back in the 1860s, it fell into disrepair during the years of prohibition. But since 1965, when it was purchased by current owners the Davies family, Schramsberg has built a reputation as the leading producer of sparkling wines in the USA (being served at White House state dinners by every president since Richard Nixon). They make a wide range of wines, some of which – such as the Blanc de Blancs and the J. Schram – can give Champagne a run for its money.

While visits are by appointment only, they are well worth the effort. The fee of $60 gets you a tour of the 125-year-old cellars, an introduction to the production method for high-quality bubbly and a tasting of various wines from their collection.

www.schramsberg.com; tel +1 707-942-4558; 1400 Schramsberg Rd, Calistoga; by appointment

02 SMITH-MADRONE

Fans of Napa Cabernet Sauvignon will often be heard debating the respective merits of 'mountain' Cabernet vs those from the valley floor. Those curious enough to taste the difference for themselves should head up Spring Mountain to the rustic but welcoming winery of Smith-Madrone, where brothers Stu and Charlie Smith have been making some of the valley's most underrated Cabernet (not to mention Riesling and Chardonnay) since 1971. These are wines that not only taste great when they are young, but also age superbly if you have the patience to stick them away for a few years.

A visit to Smith-Madrone not only gives you the chance to spend time talking and tasting with some of the friendliest and most genuine winemakers in the business, it also offers up some of the most spectacular vistas in the entire Napa Valley. The old barn is full of charm and the fact that there is no fee just leaves more cash to spend on buying a few bottles to take away!

www.smithmadrone.com; tel +1 707-963-2283; 4022 Spring Mountain Rd, St Helena; 10am-4pm Mon, Wed, Fri & Sat by appointment

03 CORISON

Cathy Corison is one of the most revered winemakers in the Napa Valley. Her reputation grows from her role as a pioneer for women in the industry (she was among the first females to enter the trade, back in the 1970s) and her unflinching belief in an elegant, refined style of Cabernet Sauvignon that has never fit the 'blockbuster' stereotype preferred by

'Napa Valley will remind any experienced vinous traveller of the great Cabernet vineyards of Bordeaux's Médoc.'

–John Williams, owner/winemaker, Frog's Leap

03

04

Courtesy of Napa Valley Wine Train

major critics. Today, a new generation of Californian winemakers consider Cathy to be a role model, and after tasting her spectacular wines it is not difficult to see why. Her winery is in a beautiful barn situated on the St Helena highway, nestled amongst the vines of her beloved 'Kronos' vineyard, from which she makes one of California's finest and most age-worthy Cabernets.

Corison offers visitors a tour of the vineyards, barrel room and winery, followed by a tasting of current releases ($35) or the full Library Experience ($55). Either fee is waived when wine is purchased to the value of $120 or $250 respectively. These world-class wines are a must-try for anyone looking to discover what the vineyards of Napa Valley are capable of in the right hands.

www.corison.com; tel +1 707-963-0826; 987 St Helena Hwy, St Helena; 10am-5pm by appointment

04 FROG'S LEAP

John Williams arrived in the Napa Valley during the 1970s just before the 'Judgement of Paris' changed everything and, after working at some of the best wineries in the region, he founded Frog's Leap in 1981. Nowadays John is not only known for making some of the most delicious wines in the valley – the Estate Cabernet, Sauvignon Blanc, Merlot and Zinfandel are all excellent – but also as a pioneer of organic and sustainable viticulture (the winery has been certified since 1989).

There is a sense of fun and genuine passion for what they do at Frog's Leap. Visitors to the bucolic winery will be given a warm reception, but should book early to avoid disappointment. The Guided Tour and Tasting or the Signature Seated Tasting ($25 each) are the most popular experiences, and both are as enjoyable as they are informative.

www.frogsleap.com; tel +1 707-963-4704; 8815 Conn Creek Rd, Rutherford; 10am-4pm by appointment

05 MONDAVI

Robert Mondavi looms large in the Napa Valley as perhaps the most influential figure in its modern wine industry – the winery that bears his name was founded in 1966 and set new standards for excellence in an era dominated by low-grade commercial booze. It's no overstatement to say that Californian wine was transformed by Mondavi's commitment to quality and tireless efforts to spread the gospel around the world during his lifetime. The list of wines produced at Mondavi is long but there are numerous highlights, including the rich but refreshing Fumé Blanc (an oaked version of Sauvignon Blanc) and silky-smooth Oakville or Reserve Cabernet Sauvignons.

01 Napa vines

02 Fill up at Gott's Roadside

03 Castello di Amorosa – get there aboard the Napa Valley Wine Train

04 The Napa Valley Wine Train

05 Stag's Leap vineyard

06 Pedal around the wineries with Napa Valley Bike Tours

Visitors are spoiled for choice on a visit to the iconic winery (one of the architectural wonders of the valley), which has a comprehensive program of tours and tastings that are among the most informative in the region. Experiences last from 20 minutes to 1½ hours and cost between $20 and $55, depending on how much you want to learn and taste. The Signature Tour & Tasting is recommended for first-time visitors (available in English or Mandarin), giving guests a comprehensive introduction to the wine-making process and a tutored tasting of three wines ($35). Appointments are not mandatory, but recommended, as it can get very busy. *www.robertmondaviwinery.com; tel +1 707-226-1395; 7801 St Helena Hwy, St Helena; 10am-5pm*

06 SILVER OAK

Named after the winery's position between the Silverado Trail and the town of Oakville, Silver Oak is one of a handful of Napa estates that can genuinely claim to have attained cult status. Since being established in 1972, their sumptuous, silky and full-blooded red wines have gone on to grace the cellars of many collectors and restaurants. In 2012 the Duncan family purchased a second winery in the neighbouring Alexander Valley, but the original home in Oakville is the place to visit if you want to understand what it takes to make great valley floor Cabernet Sauvignon.

Guests that arrive at the attractive tasting room without an appointment will be able to enjoy the current release tasting ($25). Those with the opportunity to call or email in advance can enjoy a range of other options (full details available online), such as the Napa Valley Cabernet Vertical Tasting ($60), a six-wine tasting stretching back to 2005 that demonstrates the class and longevity of Silver Oak.
tel +1 707-942-7022; silveroak.com; 915 Oakville Cross Rd, Oakville; 9am-5pm Mon-Sat, from 11am Sun

07 STAG'S LEAP WINE CELLARS

When Warren Winiarski founded Stag's Leap Wine Cellars in the early 1970s, he could never have foreseen the effect that he would have on the world of wine, but after his Cabernet triumphed at the 'Judgement of Paris' tasting in 1976, Winiarski, his winery and the Napa Valley became overnight sensations. This place in history makes Stag's Leap a must-visit stop on any wine-tasting itinerary to Northern California, and those that do visit will be thrilled by a portfolio of wines that are among the best in the state.

Back in 1976 the winery was a little more basic than it is now, and visitors today have the chance to wander through the iconic Stag's Leap Vineyard as well as enjoy flights of wine in the modern tasting room. For groups fewer than five, no appointment is necessary to taste their Napa Valley Collection ($25) or Estate Collection ($40); the latter is highly recommended, as it includes the best wines. Those that plan ahead and want the full 90-minute Fire & Water tour and tasting ($95) will get a comprehensive insight into this renowned estate and its wines. *www.cask23.com; tel +1 707-944-2020; 5766 Silverado Trail, Napa; 10am-4.30pm daily*

Courtesy of Stag's Leap Wine Cellars

ESSENTIAL INFORMATION

WHERE TO STAY

ELM HOUSE INN

There is a wide range of hotels in Napa City, from the plush to the basic. Sitting roughly in the middle of the spectrum and just a stone's throw from downtown is the Elm House Inn; a home-away-from-home style place with comfortable rooms and a great breakfast. *www.bestwesterncalifornia.com; tel +1 707-255-1831; 800 California Blvd, Napa*

NAPA VALLEY RAILWAY INN

Slap-bang in the middle of the valley is Yountville, home to world-famous restaurant the French Laundry and a host of other fine eateries. Travellers looking for characterful accommodation that won't break the bank should check in to the Railway Inn, a collection of spacious converted rail carriages that is full of charm and represents great value for money. *www.napavalleyrailwayinn.com; tel +1 707-944-2000; 6523 Washington St, Yountville*

WHERE TO EAT

OENOTRI

There is a long history of Italian influence in the Napa Valley, and the Southern Italian fare at this wonderful Napa restaurant reflects this heritage in superb home-made *salumi*, delicious pizza and pasta, and an exceptional wine list. *www.oenotri.com; tel +1 707-252-1022; 1425 1st St, Napa*

GOTT'S ROADSIDE

Fast-food for grown-ups, Gott's serves delicious burgers (try the house-special ahi tuna burger), salads and shakes on the main highway, with outdoor seating for those that like a side order of sunshine. *www.gotts.com; tel +1 707-963-3486; 933 Main St, St Helena*

WHAT TO DO

Hiring a bicycle is a great way to get to know this beautiful part of California, whether you join an organised group like Napa Valley Bike Tours or decide to soak up the scenery on your own. If you prefer locomotive to pedal power, the Napa Valley Wine Train offers a variety of 'experiences' over lunch or dinner, with stops at some of the region's leading wineries. The Napa Valley Wine Trolley is tourism at its most kitsch, but offers a 'fun' guided tour of the valley in a converted San Franciscan cable car. *www.napavalleybiketours.com; www.winetrain.com; www.napavalley-winetrolley.com*

CELEBRATIONS

There is always something going on in the Napa Valley, from the Yountville Live music festival in March, to Arts in April (which includes film screenings, art exhibitions and demonstrations) or the annual charity auction and associated parties in June. *For full listings visit events.visitnapavalley.com. auctionnapavalley.org*

06

Courtesy of Napa Valley Bike Tours

01

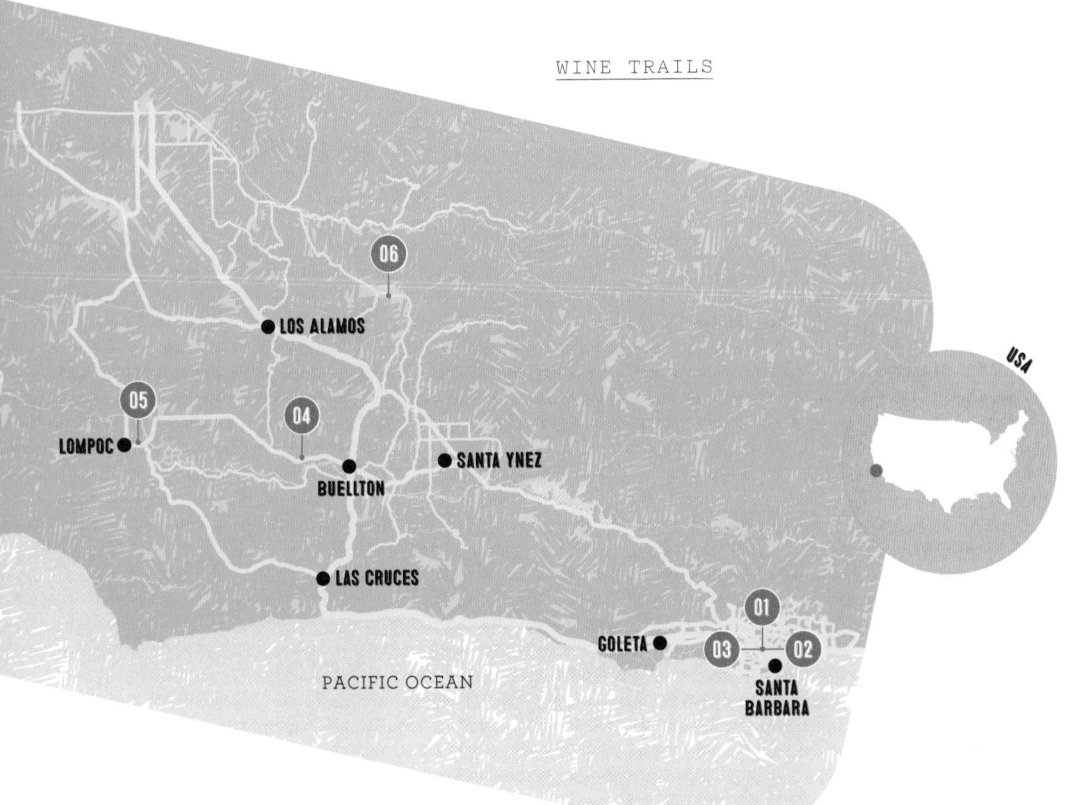

Courtesy of The Lark

[USA]

SANTA BARBARA

Hollywood might have paid tribute to its Pinot Noir, but that's just one of the sensational wines coming out of this dynamic region near Los Angeles.

Despite not having the history of Sonoma or the Napa Valley, Santa Barbara still has an excellent reputation in wine circles, thanks to the high quality of its Chardonnays and Pinot Noirs. Of course, it helps to have an Oscar-winning movie made about wine tasting in the region. The 2004 release of *Sideways* catapulted Santa Barbara to fame and ensured that one of Pinot's rival grapes would be banished into ignominy, thanks to an immortal line on the merits of drinking Merlot.

While it is possible to follow in Miles' and Jack's footsteps and taste where they tasted, that would ignore the fact that a whole host of great wineries have emerged in the decade since the film was made. The fact that Santa Barbara itself is a wonderful place to live has certainly helped to attract talent to the area, but the truth is that the surrounding valleys are ideal places to grow grapes. Added to this, a long list of gifted young winemakers are making a name for themselves in a burgeoning winemaking community called the Lompoc Wine Ghetto, which has transformed an industrial estate in a nondescript town into a hotbed of world-class wine production.

There's a can-do attitude and a love of life in the air in Santa Barbara, allied to a deep attachment to food and wine that is manifest in a vibrant gastronomic and tasting-room scene in the city and surrounding towns. Being just a couple of hours' drive north of Los Angeles (and five or six south of San Francisco) it is difficult to beat for a weekend's wine touring.

GET THERE
Los Angeles is the nearest major airport, 153km from Santa Barbara. Car hire is available.

Courtesy of Domaine de la Côte

01 THE VALLEY PROJECT

Seth Kunin makes wine under his Rhône-influenced Kunin brand, producing some of the best small-batch Syrah, Grenache and Viognier on the Central Coast. He has now added a new label, called the Valley Project, which has given him licence to explore the *terroir* of the region's five American Viticultural Areas (AVAs) and bottle each of them separately. Best of all, his tasting room (called AVA Santa Barbara) in the 'Funk Zone', gives visitors the chance to taste for themselves, using an enormous chalkboard map to help them get bearings.

First things first, the wines are great; but a visit to The Valley Project is about much more than that. The range of varieties and appellations to taste, the knowledge of the staff and the visual aids make this a seriously informative experience. Santa Barbara's geography is complex, with each of its valleys having distinct microclimates and soil types, so starting your wine tour of the region here will give you so much more understanding of the wines you taste subsequently. Rarely has studying been this much fun! A tasting flight of five wines costs $12.

www.avasantabarbara.com; tel +1 805-453-6768; 116 East Yanonali St, Santa Barbara; noon-7pm

02 SANTA BARBARA WINE COLLECTIVE

Picture this: you're in downtown Santa Barbara, in the heart of the Funk Zone. You've swotted up on your wine geography at AVA Santa Barbara, had lunch at the Lark and the funkiness is

01 Dining at the Lark, Santa Barbara

02 The tasting room of Domaine de la Côte

03 Decor at the Lark

'Santa Barbara's valleys funnel the cool marine air and create something we call "refrigerated sunlight" – a climate ideal for premium wine production.'

–Sashi Moorman, Owner/Winemaker, Domaine de la Côte

off the scale. Where do you go next? Simple – you head next door to the Santa Barbara Wine Collective.

This tasting room does not belong to a single winery, but rather a collective of six top producers all under one (very funky) roof. Babcock, Fess Parker, Ca' del Grevino and the Paring all make very good wines from a wide range of varieties, but it is the Rhône-styled wines of Qupé and the Chardonnay and Pinot Noirs from Sandhi that steal the show.

The location and atmosphere at the Collective make it ideal for late-afternoon/early-evening drinks before going out in Santa Barbara. Flights are $15 and can feature wines from across the range of producers. *www.santabarbarawinecollective.com; tel +1 805-456-2700; 131 Anacapa St, Santa Barbara; noon-6pm Tue-Thu, to 7pm Fri & Sat, 11am-6pm Sun*

03 AU BON CLIMAT

One of Jim Clendenen's wines is a Chardonnay called Wild Boy, with a label that features his head, replete with long flowing blond locks, set on a psychedelic background. That's a pretty good introduction to the man who has been making some of Santa Barbara's best wines for the past three decades, though it is far from the whole story. A wild boy he may be, but Jim Clendenen is also a winemaker at the top of his game.

03

Courtesy of The Lark

Having trained for years in Burgundy, Jim Clendenen brought back a love of balanced, elegant wines that pair well with food (he's something of a legendary chef on the side) and set about crafting wines from some of Santa Barbara's best vineyards. Names such as Sanford & Benedict and Bien Nacido are to be found on some of the best Au Bon Climat bottles, but there is a wide range of Pinot Noir and Chardonnay wines and all of them deserve your attention.

The winery is up in the Santa Maria Valley, but the tasting is done in downtown Santa Barbara in the heart of the city's Urban Wine Trail. There are two tasting options – $10 for the Classic tasting and $15 for the Pinot Reserve experience. *www.aubonclimat.com; tel +1 805-963-7999; 813 Anacapa St 5b, Santa Barbara; noon-6pm*

04 PENCE

If you're looking for a piece of archetypal Southern California, then Pence Ranch is the place for you. This beautiful property is a working ranch, with cattle, horses and a range of crops being raised on its 80 hectares (200 acres). Thirty-seven of these are given over to Pinot Noir, Chardonnay, Syrah and Gamay, all of which are farmed organically and planted on an elevated plateau, ensuring that they are well exposed to the cool winds coming in from the Pacific Ocean and resulting in wines of purity and elegance.

Blair Pence is a man committed to getting the most out of his estate's potential for great wine, and there is plenty to see and do for visitors to

Courtesy of Qupé

04 Looking north from the Santa Barbara Wine Collective

05 The Wayfarer is an ideal bolthole

06 The Lark's patio

the ranch, including a vineyard tour followed by a tasting by the pond or various other picturesque spots on the property. Prices range from $15 to $75 per person, depending on whether food is involved. There is also a calendar of events running through the year.
www.penceranch.com; tel +1 805-735-7000; 1909 West Hwy 246, Buellton; by appointment

05 PIEDRASASSI & DOMAINE DE LA CÔTE

To the untrained eye, the town of Lompoc doesn't have much going for it. Most of the vehicles that trundle down its dusty main road are on their way somewhere else, which is unsurprising – there isn't much reason to stop. But look a little closer and you will spot the signposts for the Lompoc Wine Ghetto, a set of industrial buildings that is home to some of the USA's most exciting wineries and their tasting rooms.

Among the names to look out for in the ghetto are Gavin Chanin, Tyler and Longoria Wines, but the tasting room for Piedrasassi and Domaine de la Côte ($15 tasting fee) is the one that you cannot miss – they even bake and sell their own delicious bread. Winemaker Sashi Moorman is behind some of the best wines being made in California at the moment, and these two projects demonstrate his skill with two of the region's most important varieties. Piedrasassi is focused on a range of Syrah wines (there are limited amounts of some other varietals too) that are so good they give the Northern Rhône Valley a run for its money. Domaine de la Côte is an estate vineyard that Sashi runs with his friend and world-renowned sommelier Rajat Parr, producing lacy, elegant and incredibly complex Pinot Noirs.

Some wineries you visit for the glitzy tasting room, some for the beautiful vineyards and picturesque views. This is a tasting room to visit if you want to know just how exciting California's wine scene is right now and what the vineyards of Santa Barbara are capable of.
www.piedrasassi.com, www.domainedelacote.com; tel +1 805-736-6784; 1501 East Chestnut Ave, Lompoc; 11am-4pm Fri-Sun, or by appointment

06 ZACA MESA

As one of the very first wineries in Santa Barbara (the vineyards were planted in 1973), Zaca Mesa is an essential stop for anyone looking to get their head around the wine region's history. It has also proved to be a launch pad for some of Santa Barbara's most influential winemakers – Jim Clendenen (Au Bon Climat), Adam Tolmach (Ojai) and Bob Lindquist (Qupé) all apprenticed at Zaca Mesa.

There is a wide range of wines made from their 80 hectares (200 acres) of sustainably farmed vineyards, all of which are renowned for being great value. Their speciality is the Rhône varieties, so be sure to sample the Black Bear Block Syrah.

There is real warmth about the service in the Zaca Mesa tasting room, which is also a great spot for a picnic (or a game of life-size chess, if that's your thing). The tasting flight of seven wines costs $10 per person and winery tours can be arranged for large groups that call ahead.
www.zacamesa.com; tel +1 805-688-9339; 6905 Foxen Canyon Rd, Los Olivos; 10am-4pm daily

ESSENTIAL INFORMATION

WHERE TO STAY

THE WAYFARER

This great-value crash pad is in a perfect downtown location, in and among Santa Barbara's Urban Wine Trail. An ideal place to stay if you want clean, comfortable accommodation in the heart of the action. *www.pacificahotels.com/thewayfarer; tel +1 805-845-1000; 12 East Montecito St, Santa Barbara*

BALLARD INN

A lovely B&B in the middle of Santa Barbara wine country. The excellent staff are well versed in helping visitors with their wine-tasting itineraries. *www.ballardinn.com; tel +1 800-638-2466; 2436 Baseline Ave, Solvang*

WHERE TO EAT

THE LARK

A vibrant and fun place to eat inventive Californian food that draws on European, Mexican and Asian influences and applies them to top-quality local produce (the chance to eat and drink al fresco is also a major draw). Before or after dining at the Lark, be sure to stop in for a drink at Les Marchands, the excellent wine bar next-door. *www.thelarksb.com; tel +1 805-284-0370; 131 Anacapa St, Santa Barbara*

05

Courtesy of The Wayfarer

06

Courtesy of The Lark

MATTEI'S TAVERN

This former stagecoach stop dates back to 1886 but was restored in 2013 and now houses a top-drawer restaurant. The region's best winemakers dine and drink here, thanks to a wine list that has won acclaim from far and wide. Those with their hearts set on reliving the *Sideways* experience should head over to the Hitching Post II in nearby Buellton. *www.matteistavern.com; tel +1 805-688-3550; 2350 Railway Ave, Los Olivos*

WHAT TO DO

The city of Santa Barbara is perfectly set up for wine lovers, and the Urban Wine Trail takes in many of the tasting rooms and wine experiences located in downtown. Those staying in Los Olivos could hike the Figueroa Mountain trail, or pay a visit to Solvang – the 'Authentic Danish Village' – where you can visit the Hans Christian Andersen Park or museum. *urbanwinetrailsb.com*

CELEBRATIONS

Every August the Old Spanish Days Fiesta, a five-day version of Mardi Gras, brings throngs of people to the city, as does the Santa Barbara County Vintners' Festival, celebrating the region's wines every April. *www.oldspanishdays-fiesta.org; www.sbvintnersweekend.com*

01

Courtesy of Paradise Ridge

[USA]

SONOMA

Next stop from Napa, Sonoma Valley's astonishingly varied geography and climate, plus its bold winemakers, create some of California's best wines.

Stunning Sonoma is a diverse patchwork of microclimates and *terroirs*, where many of the best estates treat their land with a reverence usually reserved for the vineyards of the old world. It is also home to many of California's most skilled and forward-thinking winemakers. Pinot Noir and Chardonnay are the star grape varieties (though Zinfandel and Syrah are also very successful), and the region's best wines are becoming increasingly collectable. You could say that if the Napa Valley is California's answer to Bordeaux, then Sonoma shares many similarities with Burgundy (although the locals are fiercely proud of the many things that make their region unique).

While today's Sonoma is certainly at the cutting edge of the state's wine scene, it is also where the first commercial winery was established back in the 1850s. This long history is evidenced in many gnarled old vineyards, some of which are over 100 years old. It is a land of incredible diversity – baking hot inland, but downright cold out on the wet and windy 'Extreme' Sonoma Coast (where some of the state's most awe-inspiring vistas are to be found). In between, there is a variety of geographies and microclimates that are suited to a wide range of different grape varieties, and this results in a wide variety of wine styles.

Wine and food is embedded in the culture of the people in this part of Northern California, something which is evident in the first-rate tasting rooms and restaurants in the town of Healdsburg, the ideal place to base yourself during a visit to this exciting and beautiful wine region.

GET THERE

San Francisco is the nearest major airport, 92km from Sonoma. Car hire is available.

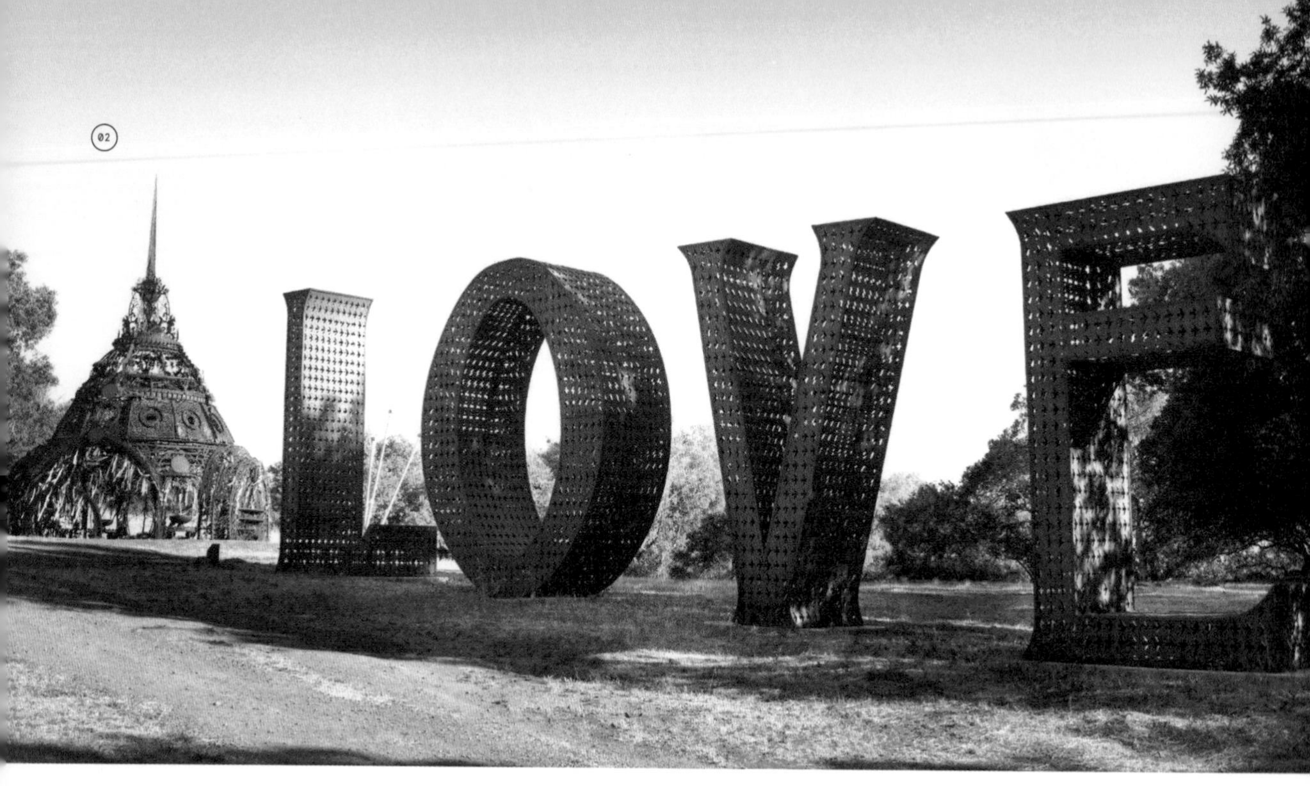

Courtesy of Paradise Ridge

01 CLINE CELLARS

Fred Cline grew up surrounded by a wealthy family. When his grandfather – a certain Mr Jacuzzi – wasn't welding water pumps to domestic bathtubs, he would spend time on the family farm in Oakley, instilling a love of the land into his grandson. These old vineyards, planted with Zinfandel, Mourvèdre and countless other red and white grape varieties, inspired Fred to learn winemaking and set up Cline Cellars. It moved from its original home to an incredible 140-hectare (350-acre) property in Carneros in 1993. Since then, Cline has focused on gutsy, full-bodied wines that fly the flag for some of the lesser-known varieties common in California, and therefore represent some of the best value in the state. A visit to Cline is a flexible affair. No appointment is required to participate in one of their free tours or tastings of five wines, and a flight of three 'reserve' wines is just $5.

www.clinecellars.com; tel +1 800-546-2070; 24737 Arnold Drive, Hwy 121, Sonoma, 10am-6pm daily

02 RAVENSWOOD

'No wimpy wines' was the slogan that made Ravenswood famous, and their robust Zinfandels are certainly not for the faint-hearted. While Sonoma can do 'elegance' with the best of them, it is also home to wines that pack a punch and the winery that Joel Peterson (the 'Godfather of Zin') founded is proud to produce reds that are 'no holds barred, full-throttle and full-flavoured'.

If that sounds like your sort of vino, then you're in for a treat when visiting the winery, as they have a whole host of interesting experiences to offer. The tour and barrel tasting is a great way to get to know Ravenswood and costs $25, but there is always a program of daily tastings (prices vary) and private tutored events ($40) that include the more interesting wines in the portfolio. Best of all, why not blend your own Ravenswood wine? For $50 (reservations required) you can play winemaker and take your efforts home with you.

www.ravenswoodwinery.com; tel +1 888-669-4679; 18701 Gehricke Rd, Sonoma; 10am-4.30pm daily

03 LITTORAI

One of the Sonoma wine trade's deepest thinkers, not to mention most talented winemakers, Ted Lemon of Littorai is a man who takes farming very seriously. The fruit that he harvests from his biodynamic vineyards and the resulting Chardonnay and Pinot Noir wines are among the region's best, and a visit here is a must for anyone interested in what makes Sonoma so special.

Having inspired a new generation of young winemakers with his dedication to crafting artisanal wines, Ted hasn't forgotten about inspiring the public. In the tasting

Courtesy of Wind Gap Wines / Clay McClachlan

01 Wine and artisan cheese at Paradise Ridge

02 Paradise Ridge champions the arts

03 Dining at Wind Gap Wines

04 Wind Gap's wines are world class

room, two options are available to visitors. The Single Vineyard Tasting is a 45-minute exploration of Littorai's vineyard-designated releases ($25), while the Gold Ridge Estate Tour & Tasting will lead you through the vineyards and farming methods before the tasting gets started, lasting 1½ hours in all ($40). Reservations required.
www.littorai.com; tel +1 707-823-9586; 788 Gold Ridge Rd, Sebastopol; open Mon-Sat by appointment

04 WIND GAP WINES

Although Sonoma's wine industry has plenty of history, it is also the heartland of what wine writer Jon Bonné has dubbed the 'New California Wine'. This moniker relates to a new way of thinking in certain winemaking circles, with the emphasis on freshness, elegance and balance rather than power and ripeness (the style that has dominated for the past 25 years).

Leading this charge towards delicious restraint is Pax Mahle and his Wine Gap wines, a range of whites and reds that are among the most drinkable in the world. This winery is also a hotbed of talent, with assistant winemakers Scott Schultz (Jolie-Laide) and Ryan Glaab (Ryme Cellars) just the latest rising stars to have benefitted from Pax's tutelage.

The tasting room at Wind Gap also happens to double as one of the coolest places in the area to spend an afternoon or early evening having a drink. There are always multiple tasting flight options available (prices vary), including library wines and some seriously limited production releases.
www.windgapwines.com; tel +1 707-331-1393; suite 170, 6780 McKinley St, Sebastopol; open noon-8pm Thu-Sun

05 PARADISE RIDGE

The Russian River Valley is one of Sonoma's most famous American Viticultural Areas (AVAs) and is full of excellent wineries worth visiting. What sets Paradise Ridge apart, in addition to its well-made Pinot Noir, Chardonnay and Sauvignon Blanc wines, is their love of the arts. There is an annually changing exhibit in the winery grounds (at the time of writing, the show, 20@20, celebrated the past two decades of art at Paradise Ridge), and an indoor historical exhibit that is viewable during tasting room opening hours.

No appointment is necessary for the classic tasting flight ($15, waived with a two-bottle purchase), but the Wine & Artisan Cheese Tasting requires a reservation 24 hours in advance.
www.prwinery.com; tel +1 707-528-9463; 4545 Thomas Lake Harris Dr, Santa Rosa; open 11am-5pm

06 COPAIN

The beautiful surroundings at Copain are enough to make you want to pack it all in and move to California

05

George Rose © Getty Images

05 Dine at Rustic, the restaurant at Francis Ford Coppola Winery

06 The spa retreat at Fairmont Sonoma Mission Inn

to make wine. Of course, the reality is a bit more complicated than that, and Wells Guthrie spent many a year apprenticing with some of France and California's most respected winemakers before setting up on his own in 1999. Since then the wines have become progressively more silky and elegant in style, to the point that Copain's reputation for quality is now as impressive as the view from its tasting room.

It's not just about the view though – the tasting experiences are also top notch. The 'Appellation Tasting' ($25) is a great introduction to the wines of Copain, using five samples to tell the story of the surrounding region. Things get a bit more detailed with the 'Single Vineyard tasting' ($40), which includes vineyard-designated wines made from Chardonnay, Pinot Noir and Syrah. The 'Reserve Flight' ($50) is a rare chance to taste six top-of-the-range releases from older vintages. All three options are accompanied by small bites and cheeses, and visitors are advised to call ahead to make a reservation.
www.copainwines.com; tel +1 707-836-8822; 7800 Eastside Rd, Healdsburg; 10am-4pm by appointment

07 BANSHEE

The town of Healdsburg is a great place to base yourself for a wine-tasting trip, as not only do you have the region's vineyards and wineries on your doorstep, but also the town's numerous tasting rooms! Banshee, just a stone's throw from the main plaza, is the best of the bunch – great wines, friendly, knowledgeable staff and a lively but relaxed atmosphere. The winemaker, Ross Cobb, is among the most talented in Sonoma (he also has his own project, Cobb Wines, and is head winemaker at the widely respected Hirsch Vineyards), so you can be sure that whatever you choose to taste, it will be delicious.

With a comprehensive list of wine flights ranging from $15 to $30, this is a great place to come and learn more about Sonoma wine.
www.bansheewines.com; tel +1 707-395-0915; 325 Center St, Healdsburg; 11am–7pm daily

08 FRANCIS FORD COPPOLA

Not content with being one of the most influential people in Hollywood, Francis Ford Coppola has also played a leading role in the modern Californian wine industry. In 1975 he purchased one of the most historic estates in the Napa Valley (Inglenook – though he only recently managed to reunite the property with its brand name, which was sold separately) and ever since then he has expanded his wine operations each time he made a hit movie.

The Sonoma winery produces a wide range of wines and has set the standard for wine tourism – visitors can expect everything from the usual tasting flights (from free of charge up to $25, depending on what you taste) to a variety of wine experiences that include a winery tour and tasting ($20), learning the art of blind tasting ($25), tasting with music ($60) and tasting in the dark ($75)! There is also a restaurant, a swimming pool, a gallery of movie memorabilia and a calendar of events for the whole family.
www.francisfordcoppolawinery.com; tel +1 707-857-1471; 300 Via Archimedes, Geyserville; 11am-6pm.

ESSENTIAL INFORMATION

WHERE TO STAY

H2

H2 is a boutique hotel with beautifully attired rooms, a swimming pool and a perfect location just off the main plaza. It also has a great bar and restaurant (Spoon Bar) that is well worth a visit even if you're not staying here. *www.h2hotel.com; tel +1 707-431-2202; 219 Healdsburg Ave, Healdsburg*

VINTNERS INN

The town of Santa Rosa is well situated in the middle of Sonoma wine country. Surrounded by 37 hectares (92 acres) of beautiful vineyards and gardens, there is also an award-winning restaurant (John Ash & Co). *www.vintnersinn.com; tel +1 707-575-7350; 4350 Barnes Rd, Santa Rosa*

WHERE TO EAT

SCOPA

This tiny Italian restaurant combines delicious food with a first-rate wine list, and on a Wednesday evening you may be served your vino by the winemaker in person! Reservations can only be made by phone and competition is fierce, but fear not if you don't get in – the same owners run the equally excellent Campa Fina round the corner. *www.scopahealdsburg.com; tel +1 707-433-5282; 109a Plaza St, Healdsburg*

FREMONT DINER

A must-visit for foodies, The Fremont Diner is full of ramshackle charm and the menu is a collection of comfort-food classics. Breakfast, lunch and dinner are all fantastic, served with a great list of local wines and craft beer. *www.thefremontdiner.com; tel +1 707-938-7370; 2698 Fremont Dr, Sonoma*

WHAT TO DO

There is plenty of history in Sonoma, and much of it can be found in Sonoma State Historic Park, which is collection of historic attractions relating to the founding of the state of California. Hikers (and drinkers) will love the 5km (3 mile) countryside trek that begins at Bartholomew Park Winery, and the thermal hot springs at Fairmont Sonoma Mission Inn and Spa are the perfect place to relax when you're done. *www.parks.ca.gov; www.bartpark.com; www.fairmont.com*

CELEBRATIONS

The Sonoma County Harvest Fair in early October is a three-day celebration of the region's produce, with wine, beer and cider tastings, seminars and cookery demonstrations. Sebastopol's famous Gravenstein apples are honoured every August at its own fair, while the LGBT community come out in force for the Pride Parade and the 'Gay Wine Weekend' in June. *www.harvestfair.org; www.gravensteinapplefair.com; www.outinthevineyard.com*

06

Courtesy of Fairmont Sonoma Mission Inn and Spa

[USA]

WILLAMETTE VALLEY

Burgundian expats and Portland hipsters have helped turn the north-west of the USA into a food and wine powerhouse in just a few decades.

It is remarkable what has been achieved by Oregon's wine producers in the last 50 years. Before then, there was hardly a vineyard to be found in this densely forested state, but today its foremost wine region, the Willamette Valley, is renowned as one of the best places in the world to grow Pinot Noir. Anyone doubting this claim should talk to one of the numerous Burgundian expatriates who have enthusiastically established wineries here to produce delicate, elegant reds that bear more than a passing resemblance to the wines of their homeland. White-wine lovers need not worry, as Pinot Noir is not the only game in town – Pinot Gris and Chardonnay also perform well here, and aromatic whites from Riesling and Gewürztraminer are getting better with every vintage.

The 6070 hectares (15,000 acres) of vineyards in the Willamette Valley (the vast majority of which are Pinot Noir) stretch out to the south and south-west of the state's largest city, Portland, which serves as an ideal staging post for visits to the region. Portland has a reputation for eccentricity (you may well see signs and graffiti imploring residents to 'Keep Portland Weird') and is rumoured to be the birthplace of the hipster, but it is also a vibrant city that offers visitors a dazzling array of great restaurants and places to drink. An abundance of organic produce, artisanal coffee, craft beer and street food are evidence of a foodie culture in which wine plays a leading role, and over 250 wineries are just a short drive away, making a trip to Oregon the ideal combination between a city break and rural wine-tasting experience.

GET THERE
Seattle-Tacoma is the nearest major airport, 300km from Forest Grove. Car hire is available.

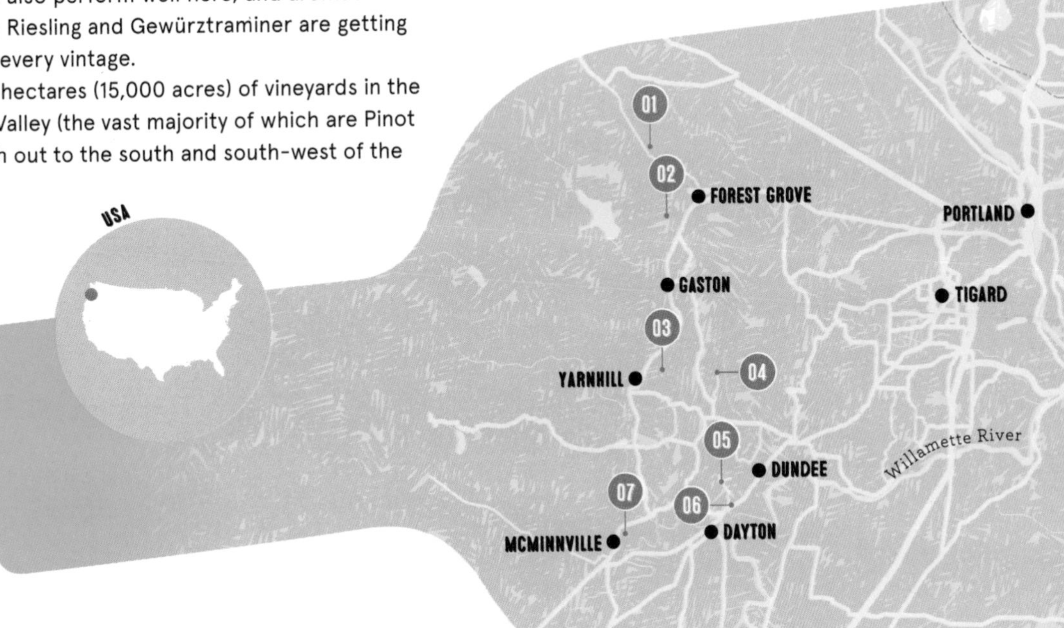

David H. Collier @ Getty Images

Courtesy of Jim Fischer

01 DAVID HILL

This beautiful estate has more history than most in the Willamette Valley – wine was being made here way back in the late 1800s, long before it was considered a sensible pursuit for an Oregonian. In 1919 Prohibition put paid to all that, though, and it wasn't until the mid-1960s that people started planting vineyards again. When that happened, the place originally known as 'Wine Hill' (the name was later changed to honour the local David family) was one of the first to see grapevines and it continues to thrive to this day, with many of the original vineyards still intact. Pinot Noir wines form the bulk of the line-up, but David Hill also produce wines from a range of other varieties and even has some fortified port-style wines.

Visiting the winery is a relaxed affair, worthwhile as much for the stunning views as the wines. A $10 tasting fee gets you a choice of seven pours from their range, and is refundable against purchases of $40 or more.

www.davidhillwinery.com; tel +1 503-992-8545; 46350 Northwest David Hill Rd, Forest Grove; 11am-5pm

02 MONTINORE

Established in 1982, Montinore is a great place to get to grips with what makes the Willamette Valley special. Pinot Noir is the most important variety here, as it is throughout the valley, but owner Rudy Marchesi is also very fond of aromatic white wines and their Riesling, Gewürztraminer and Pinot Gris are some of the region's best. The estate is Demeter-certified, so anyone interested in seeing the realities of biodynamic agriculture can learn more about this fascinating way of farming. The Willamette Valley has a remarkably high number of biodynamic practitioners.

The tasting room overlooks the estate's 85 hectares (210 acres) of vines and a $10 fee will get you a flight of six wines. If the weather is good, Montinore is also the perfect place to bring a picnic and spend some time wandering through the vineyards.

www.montinore.com; tel +1 503-359-5012; 3663 Southwest Dilley Rd, Forest Grove; open 11am-5pm

01 Portland, Oregon

02 President of Montinore, Rudy Marchesi

03 Bergström Winery

03 WILLAKENZIE ESTATE

Willakenzie is a splicing together of the names of the Willamette and McKenzie rivers, which between them are responsible for the distinctive soil type found in this part of the region. The Lacroute family that founded the estate back in 1991 have French roots (Burgundy, naturally) and their belief in the Willamette Valley's *terroir* (translated into the local parlance as 'dirt matters') prompted them to adopt the practice of making single-vineyard wines from their most interesting parcels of vines. Willakenzie Estate is considered to be one of the foremost players in the drive for quality in the Willamette Valley, but it is also one of the best set up to receive visitors.

Drop-ins are welcome in the tasting room and a $20 fee gets you one of two tasting flights. There is also a six-wine tasting with matching cheese ($40) that includes some of the estate's most coveted single-vineyard bottlings.
www.willakenzie.com; tel +1 503-662-1327; 19143 Northeast Loughlin Rd, Yamhill; 10am-5pm May-Oct, to 4pm Nov-Apr

04 BERGSTRÖM

When many Burgundians were coming over to Oregon to establish wineries, Josh Bergström (son of the founders of Bergström Wines) was heading in the opposite direction. After learning to make wine in Pinot Noir's spiritual home (and finding his lovely wife Caroline in the process), Josh returned to the Willamette Valley and has since established a reputation as one of the very best winemakers in the state. He will tell you that the secret is conscientious farming – the 15 hectares (36 acres) of vineyards are organically certified, but Josh also farms biodynamically to ensure the fruit is perfect.

If you want to get to grips with how good Oregon Pinot Noir can be, this is the place to do it, as everything from their Cumberland Reserve up to the Bergström Vineyard is superb. Josh is a dab hand with Chardonnay too, so be sure to taste the whites while you are there. No reservation is required to pop into the charming winery and tasting room for a flight of these benchmark wines ($20).
bergstromwines.com; tel +1 503-554-0468; 18215 Northeast Calkins Lane, Newberg; open 10am-4pm

'Here we believe in nurturing this majestic landscape, in the pursuit of hand-crafting America's greatest Pinot Noirs.' *–Josh Bergström, Owner/Winemaker, Bergström*

05 DOMAINE DROUHIN

The Drouhin family are a big name back in their native Burgundy, so their decision to plant vineyards in the Willamette Valley was critical in legitimising the idea that Oregon can grow world-class Pinot Noir. Since they arrived in 1988 many more have followed, but Véronique Drouhin's Pinot Noirs still set the standard and their Cuvée Laurène is a contender for the state's best wine.

Visitors can swing by the idyllic tasting room and terrace without an appointment to taste a flight of three wines ($10). Those with a bit more time (and some forward planning – a reservation is essential) can take part in the Drouhin Experience, a fascinating tour of the winery that culminates in a comparative tasting of Oregon and Burgundy wines (with cheese). For $30 this is something of a bargain, and a great way to fully understand the Oregon–Burgundy dynamic that is a crucial element of the region's wine identity.
www.domainedrouhin.com; tel +1 503-864-2700; 6750 Breyman Orchards Rd, Dayton; open 11am-4pm Wed-Sun

Courtesy of Montinore Estate

04 On the road in Willamette Valley

05 The Montinore Estate

06 Pok-Pok serves up authentic Thai cuisine

07 The Jupiter Hotel

Courtesy of Pok-Pok / David Reamer

06 SOKOL-BLOSSER

This family-run winery was established in 1971 by Bill Blosser and Susan Sokol-Blosser, and has always played a pioneering role in the Willamette Valley's wine scene. Sure, they were one of the first wineries in the region, but they were also the first to open a tasting room to welcome visitors back in 1978 and their innovative range of wines has always kept them at the forefront of the region's wine scene. The customary Pinot Noir forms the core of the Sokol-Blosser range, but there are other varieties available and their Evolution red and white blends are some of the best-value wines in Oregon.

Guests at the winery are not just in for a sensory treat with the wines – the visitors centre itself is an architectural gem. Beautifully designed, with incredible views of their vineyards and the Cascade Mountains, it has Standard or Reserve tasting flights on offer ($15 or $25 respectively); a full tour of the vineyards and winery with tasting and nibbles ($50); and a half-day educational hike through the estate with a catered lunch and (much needed) glass of wine ($75). If there's one winery that you must visit during your trip to Oregon, this is it.
www.sokolblosser.com; tel +1 503-864-2282; 5000 Northeast Sokol Blosser Lane, Dayton; open 10am-4pm

07 EYRIE VINEYARDS

A tour of the Willamette Valley is not complete without visiting Eyrie Vineyards, the estate where it all started. In 1965, David Lett planted the first Pinot Noir in Oregon against the advice of every 'expert' in the USA at the time, and followed this by planting the first commercial vineyards of Pinot Gris in the New World. People thought he was mad, but by the mid-1970s his wines were winning international acclaim and his bravery served as an inspiration for the entire Oregon wine industry. A recent tasting of old Eyrie Vineyards wines was greeted with widespread praise by the critics that were present, proving that this really is a special wine estate. Today Eyrie is run by David's gifted son, Jason Lett, and the wines are as good as ever.

The tasting room at the winery is in downtown McMinnville. A six-wine Exploration Flight costs $15 and the two-wine Library Tasting of older wines (highly recommended) is an additional $10. These are some of the most age-worthy wines in the New World, so be sure to get a couple of bottles and save them for a special occasion.
www.eyrievineyards.com; tel +1 503-472-6315; 935 Northeast 10th Ave, McMinnville; open noon-5pm

ESSENTIAL INFORMATION

WHERE TO STAY

KENNEDY SCHOOL

One of the McMenamins group of hotels, Kennedy School is a converted schoolhouse classed as an historic landmark. Nowadays this quirky venue is home to a brewery, numerous bars, a gym that doubles as a live-music venue and 57 well-appointed guest rooms. *www.mcmenamins.com; tel +1 503-249-3983; 5736 Northeast 33rd Ave, Portland*

JUPITER HOTEL

Those looking for a cool, comfortable crash pad in central Portland should consider the Jupiter Hotel. It has the feel of a deluxe motel, with spacious rooms and a lively bar – the Doug Fir Lounge – that is an attraction in itself. *www.jupiterhotel.com; tel +1 503-230-9200; 800 East Burnside St, Portland*

WHERE TO EAT

LE PIGEON

Although small in size, Le Pigeon is big in influence – Portland's food lovers will tell you that it was one of the restaurants that kick-started the city's contemporary dining scene, now one of the most exciting in the USA. *www.lepigeon.com; tel +1 503-546-8796; 738 East Burnside St, Portland*

POK-POK

From humble beginnings on a nondescript street, Andy Ricker's Pok-Pok has become something of a global sensation. He has since transported his authentic take on northern Thai food to New York and Los Angeles, but the original is still the best and visitors to Portland would be crazy to miss it. No reservations. *www.pokpokpdx.com; tel +1 503-232-1387; 3226 Southeast Division St, Portland*

WHAT TO DO

With more breweries than any other city on earth, Portland is a craft-beer lover's dream. Plan a DIY itinerary at www.portlandbeer.org, or take an organised tour with Brewvana. The city's street food scene is taken just as seriously, so check out Food Carts Portland for live information about what's cooking. *experiencebrewvana.com; foodcartsportland.com*

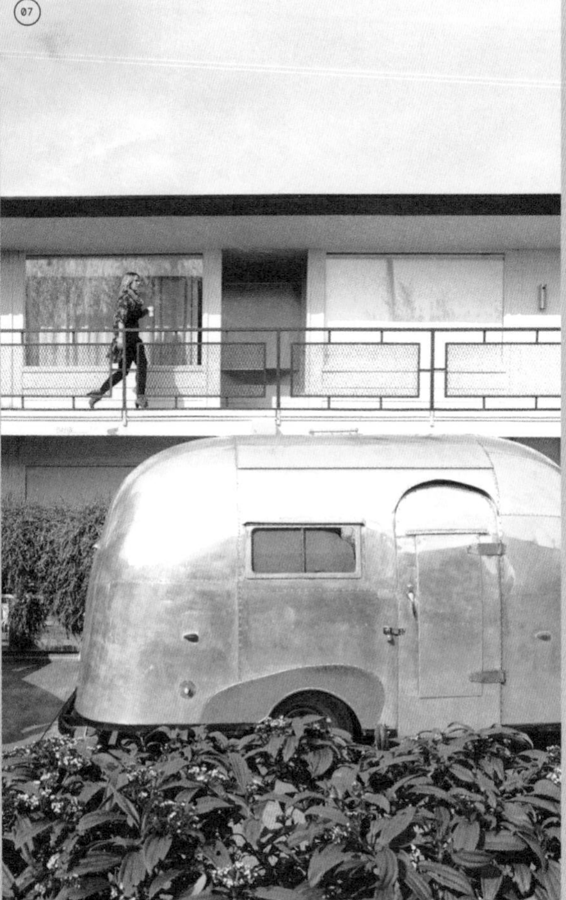
07

Courtesy of The Jupiter Hotel

CELEBRATIONS

A packed calendar of events includes the Portland Rose Festival (May/June), World Naked Bike Ride (June) and the Adult Soapbox Derby (August). Weekly markets are also important to Portlanders and the best are Portland Saturday Market and the Portland Farmers Market, which has a weekly programme of live music and cooking demonstrations by top chefs. *rosefestival.org; pdxwnbr.org; soapboxracer.com; portlandsaturdaymarket.com; portlandfarmers market.org*

First Edition
Published in August 2015 by Lonely Planet Global Limited
ABN 36 005 607 983
www.lonelyplanet.com
ISBN 978 1 7436 0750 3

Printed in China
10 9 8 7 6 5 4

Managing Director Piers Pickard
Associate Publisher and Commissioning Editor Robin Barton
Art Direction Daniel Di Paolo
Layout Johanna Lundberg
Editors Monique Perrin, Simon Williamson, Karyn Noble
Cartographer Wayne Murphy
Pre-press Production Robert Griffiths
Print Production Larissa Frost, Nigel Longuet

Thanks to Jessica Cole, Vanessa Harriss, Aisha Zia

Authors: Mark Andrew (USA except Finger Lakes), Robin Barton (Australia, England, Spain), Sarah Bennet & Lee Slater (New Zealand), John Brunton (France, Italy, South Africa), Bridget Gleeson (Argentina & Chile), Virginia Maxwell (Lebanon), Jeremy Quinn (Canada, Finger Lakes, Georgia, Germany, Greece, Slovenia), Helen Ranger (Morocco), Luke Waterson (Hungary/Slovakia)

Lonely Planet offices

AUSTRALIA The Malt Store, Level 3, 551 Swanston St, Carlton, Victoria 3053 T: 03 8379 8000

IRELAND Unit E, Digital Court, The Digital Hub, Rainsford St, Dublin 8

USA 124 Linden St, Oakland, CA 94607 T: 510 250 6400

UK 240 Blackfriars Rd, London SE1 8NW T: 020 3771 5100

STAY IN TOUCH lonelyplanet.com/contact